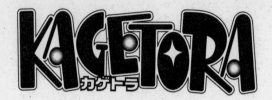

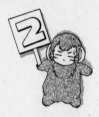

Akira Segami

TRANSLATED BY
Akira Tsubasa

ADAPTED BY
Nunzio DeFilippis & Christina Weir

LETTERED BY
Janice Chiang

BALLANTINE BOOKS · NEW YORK

Kagetora volume 2 is a work of fiction. Names, characters, places, and incidents are the products of the author's imagination or are used fictitiously. Any resemblance to actual events, locales, or persons, living or dead, is entirely coincidental.

A Del Rey Trade Paperback Original

Published in the United States by Del Rey Books, an imprint of The Random House Publishing Group, a division of Random House, Inc., New York.

Del Rey is a registered trademark and the Del Rey colophon is a trademark of Random House, Inc.

Publication rights arranged through Kodansha Ltd.

First published in Japan in 2003 by Kodansha Ltd., Tokyo.

SBN 0-345-49142-4

Printed in the United States of America

www.delreymanga.com

8 7 6 5 4 3 2 1

anslator—*Akira Tsubasa*
daptor—*Nunzio DeFilippis & Christina Weir*
ttering—*Janice Chiang*

A Note from the Author

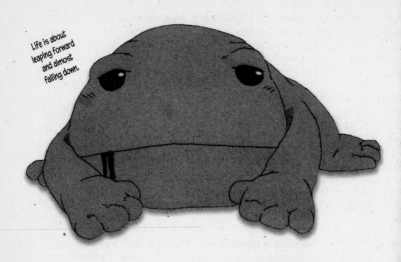

Life is about leaping forward and almost falling down.

Conversation with a doctor one day.

Author: Well, I've been pushing myself and my body is all messed up.
Dr.: No worries. You're pretty tough.
Author: ...I'm tough...?
Dr.: Yep. You're tough. (he said it with confidence)

So, I guess I can still keep on going.

Segami

Honorifics Explained

Throughout the Del Rey Manga books, you will find Japanese honorifics left intact in the translations. For those not familiar with how the Japanese use honorifics and, more important, how they differ from American honorifics, we present this brief overview.

Politeness has always been a critical facet of Japanese culture. Ever since the feudal era, when Japan was a highly stratified society, use of honorifics—which can be defined as polite speech that indicates relationship or status—has played an essential role in the Japanese language. When addressing someone in Japanese, an honorific usually takes the form of a suffix attached to one's name (example: "Asuna-san"), or as a title at the end of one's name or in place of the name itself (example: "Negi-sensei," or simply "Sensei!").

Honorifics can be expressions of respect or endearment. In the context of manga and anime, honorifics give insight into the nature of the relationship between characters. Many translations into English leave out these important honorifics, and therefore distort the "feel" of the original Japanese. Because Japanese honorifics contain nuances that English honorifics lack, it is our policy at Del Rey not to translate them. Here, instead, is a guide to some of the honorifics you may encounter in Del Rey Manga.

-san: This is the most common honorific and is equivalent to Mr., Miss, Ms., or Mrs. It is the all-purpose honorific and can be used in any situation where politeness is required.

-sama: This is one level higher than "-san" and is used to confer great respect.

-dono: This comes from the word "tono," which means "lord." It is an even higher level than "-sama" and confers utmost respect.

-kun: This suffix is used at the end of boys' names to express familiarity or endearment. It is also sometimes used by men among friends, or when addressing someone younger or of a lower station.

-chan: This is used to express endearment, mostly toward girls. It is also used for little boys, pets, and even among lovers. It gives a sense of childish cuteness.

Bozu: This is an informal way to refer to a boy, similar to the English term "kid" or "squirt."

Sempai/Senpai: This title suggests that the addressee is one's senior in a group or organization. It is most often used in a school setting, where underclassmen refer to their upperclassmen as "sempai." It can also be used in the workplace, such as when a newer employee addresses an employee who has seniority in the company.

Kohai: This is the opposite of "sempai" and is used toward underclassmen in school or newcomers in the workplace. It connotes that the addressee is of a lower station.

Sensei: Literally meaning "one who has come before," this title is used for teachers, doctors, or masters of any profession or art.

[blank]: Usually forgotten in these lists, but perhaps the most significant difference between Japanese and English. The lack of honorific means that the speaker has permission to address the person in a very intimate way. Usually, only family, spouses, or very close friends have this kind of permission. Known as *yobisute,* it can be gratifying when someone who has earned the intimacy starts to call one by one's name without an honorific. But when that intimacy hasn't been earned, it can also be very insulting.

KAGETORA
カゲトラ

瀬上（せがみ）あきら

②

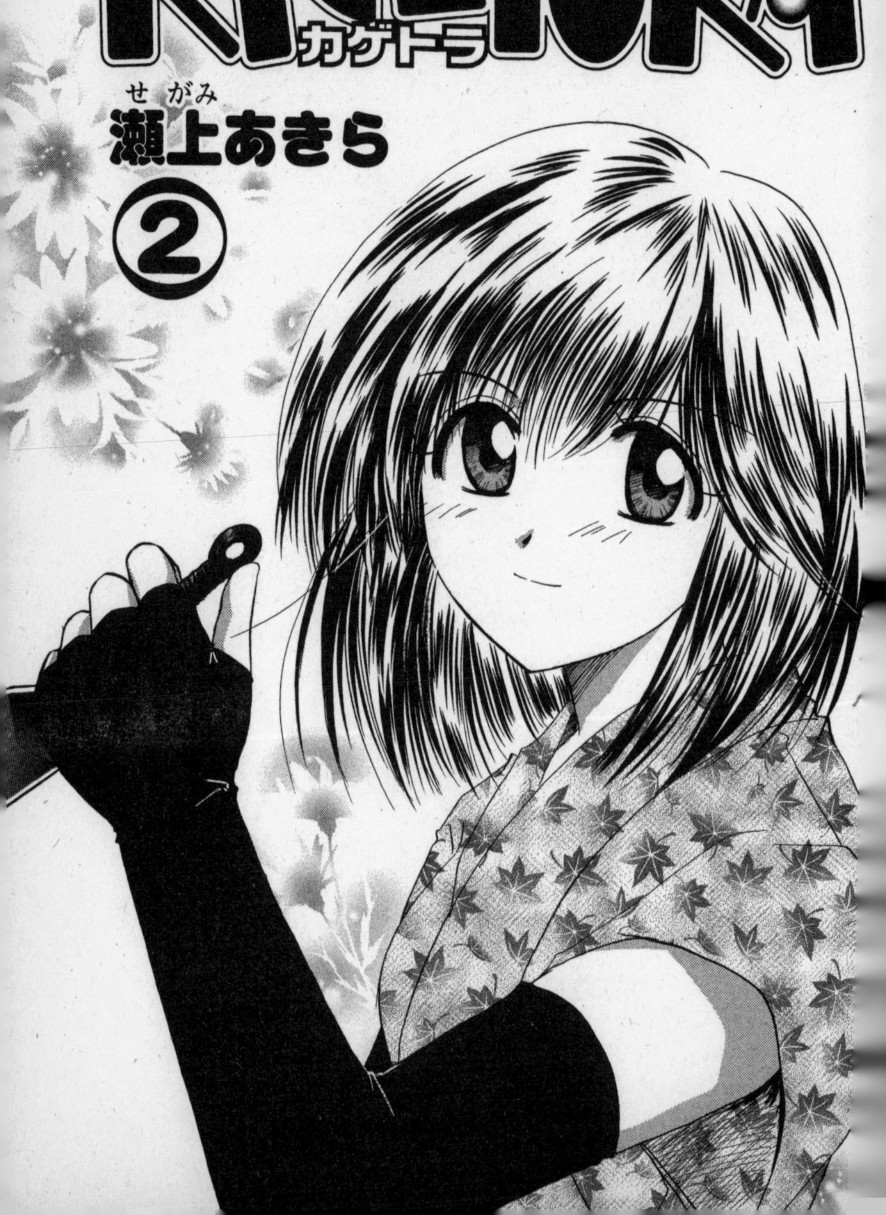

CONTENTS

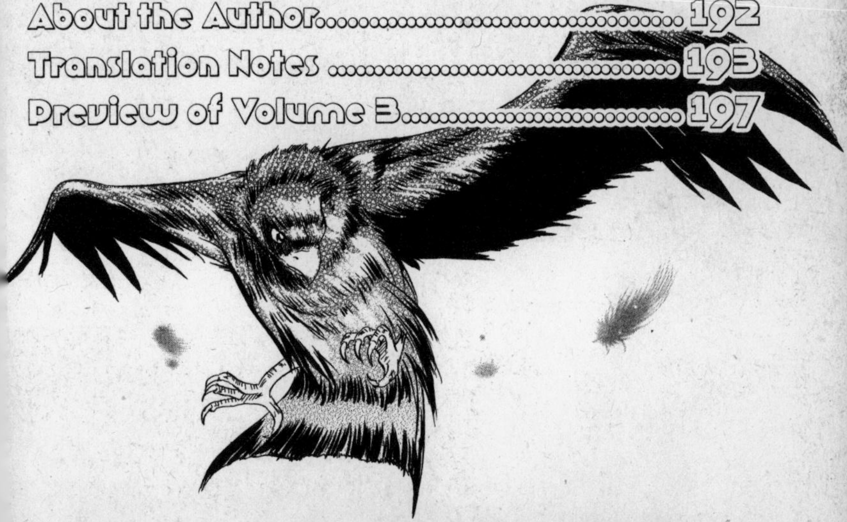

KAGETORA

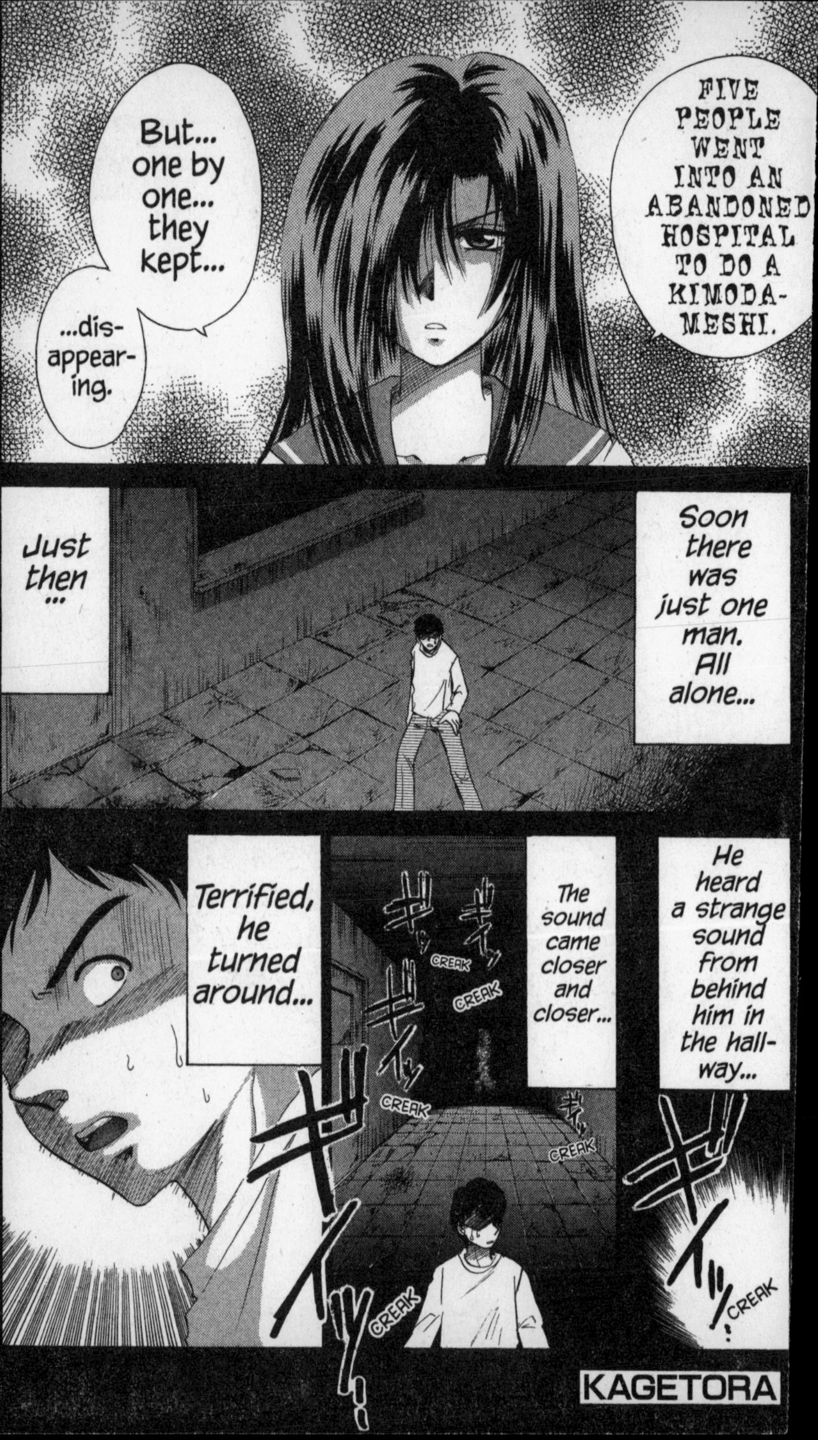
FIVE PEOPLE WENT INTO AN ABANDONED HOSPITAL TO DO A KIMODA-MESHI.
But... one by one... they kept...
...dis-appear-ing.
Soon there was just one man. All alone...
Just then...
He heard a strange sound from behind him in the hall-way...
CREAK
The sound came closer and closer...
CREAK
CREAK
CREAK
CREAK
Terrified, he turned around...
CREAK

KAGETORA

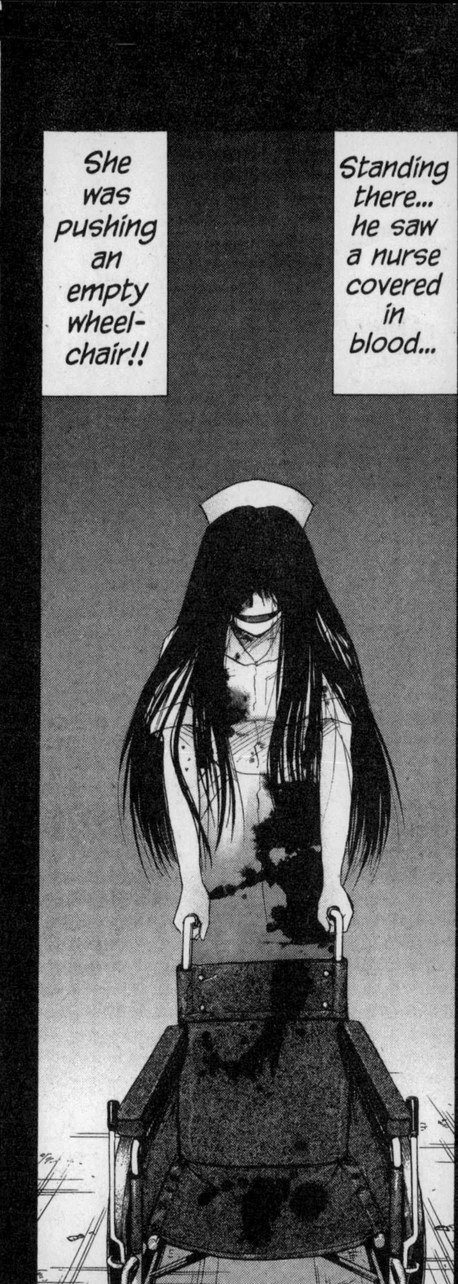
Standing there... he saw a nurse covered in blood...
She was pushing an empty wheel-chair!!

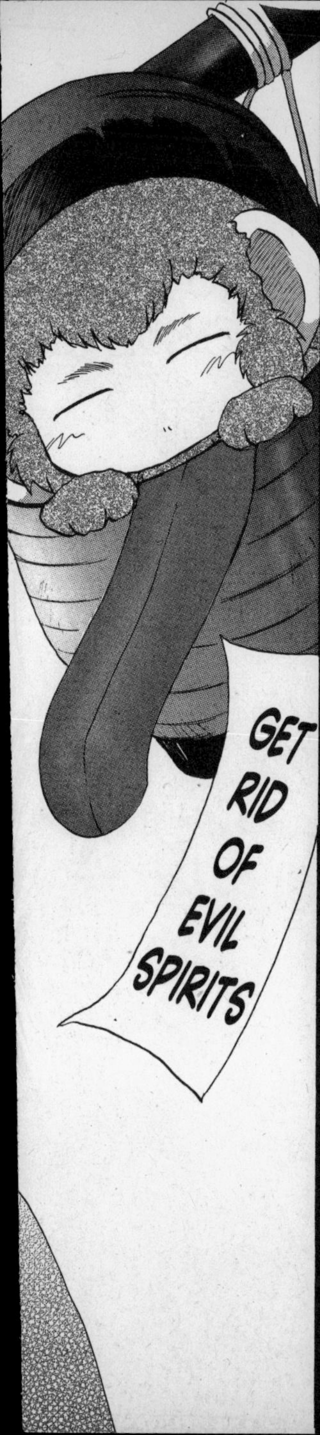
GET RID OF EVIL SPIRITS

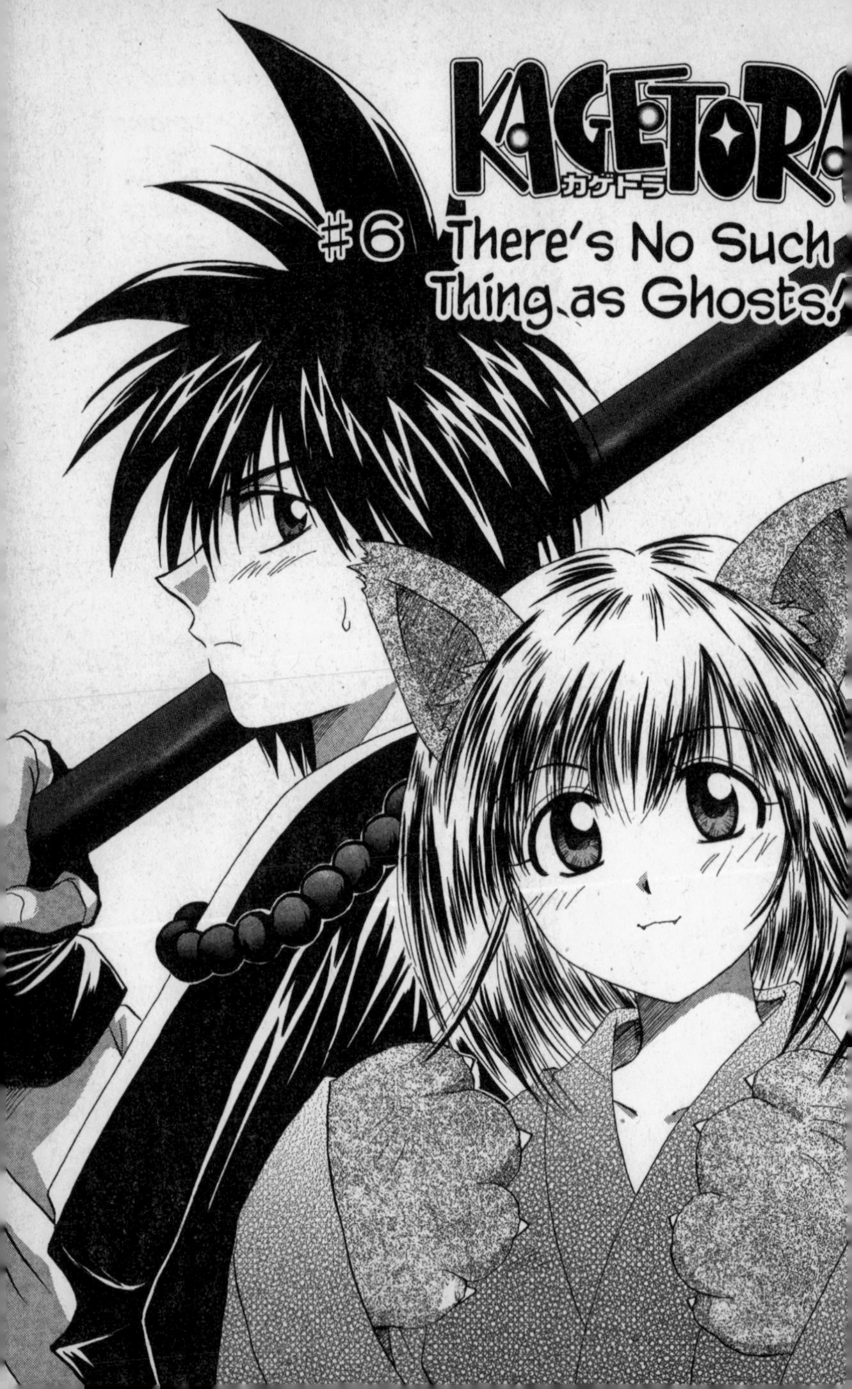
KAGETORA
カゲトラ
#6 There's No Such Thing as Ghosts!

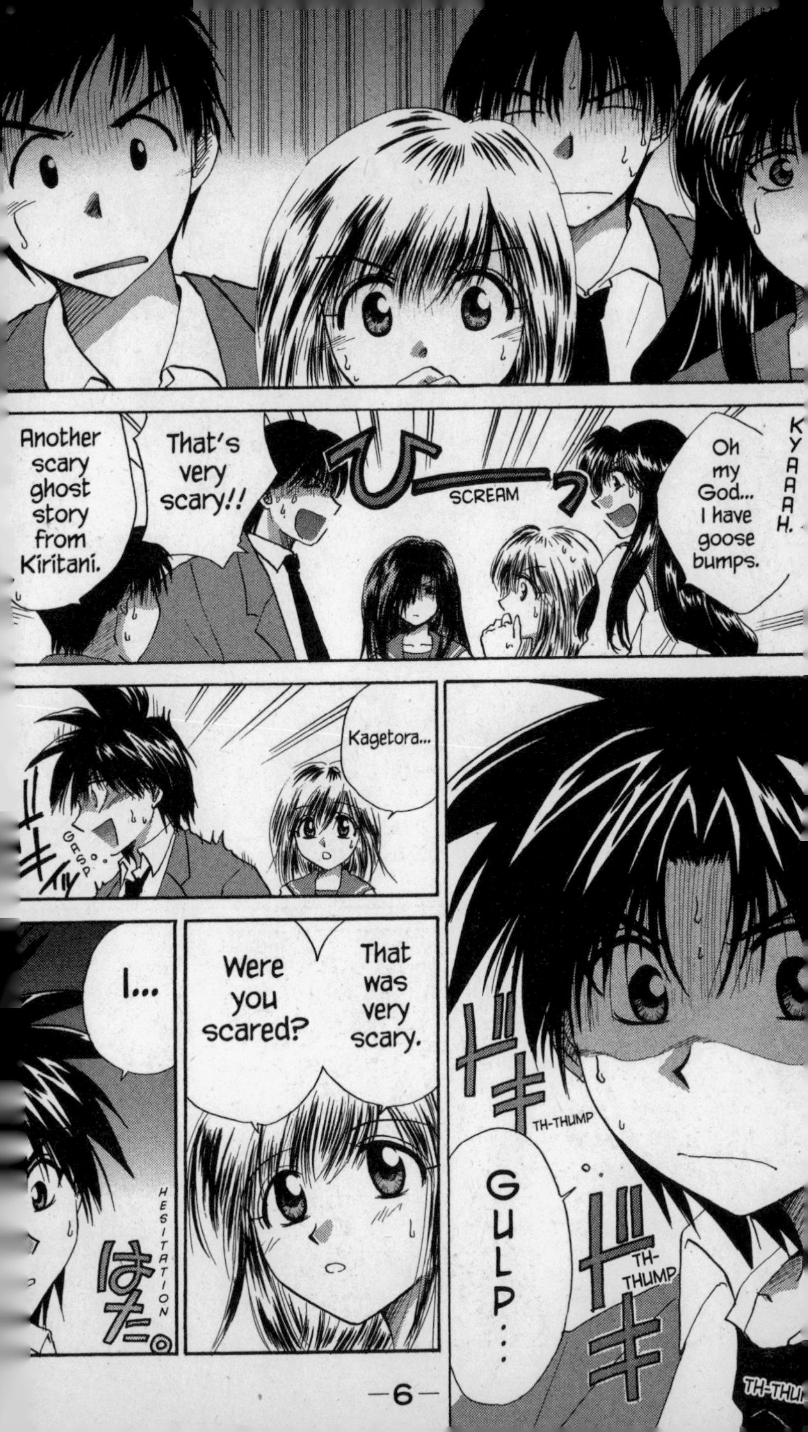
KYAAAH.
Oh my God... I have goose bumps.
SCREAM
That's very scary!!
Another scary ghost story from Kiritani.
TH-THUMP
GULP...
TH-THUMP
Kagetora...
GASP
That was very scary.
Were you scared?
I...
HESITATION

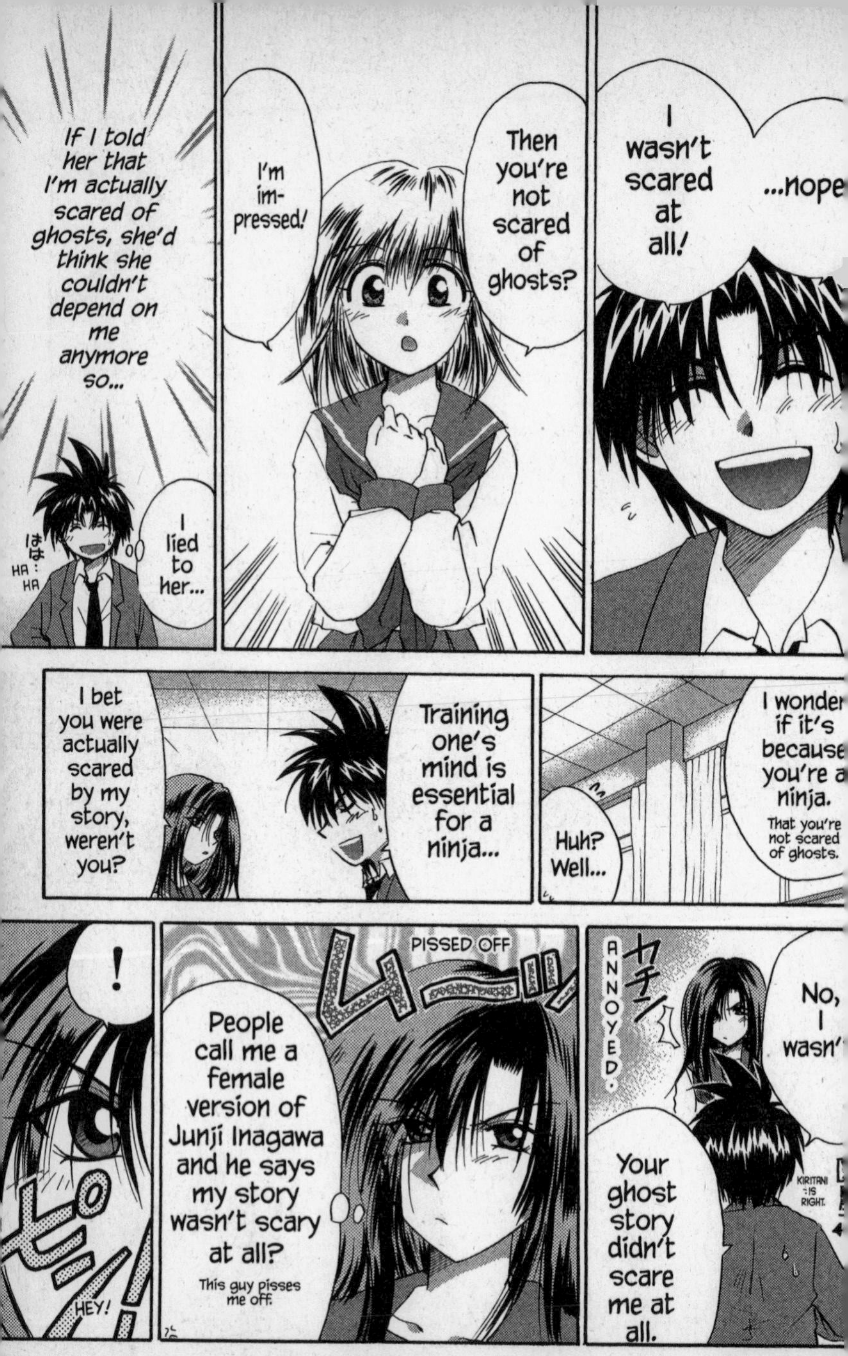
...nope
I wasn't scared at all!
Then you're not scared of ghosts?
I'm im-pressed!
If I told her that I'm actually scared of ghosts, she'd think she couldn't depend on me anymore so...
I lied to her...
はは
HA: HA
I wonder if it's because you're a ninja.
That you're not scared of ghosts.
Huh? Well...
Training one's mind is essential for a ninja...
I bet you were actually scared by my story, weren't you?
No, I wasn'
ANNOYED.
Your ghost story didn't scare me at all.
KIRITANI IS RIGHT.
PISSED OFF
People call me a female version of Junji Inagawa and he says my story wasn't scary at all?
This guy pisses me off.
!
HEY!

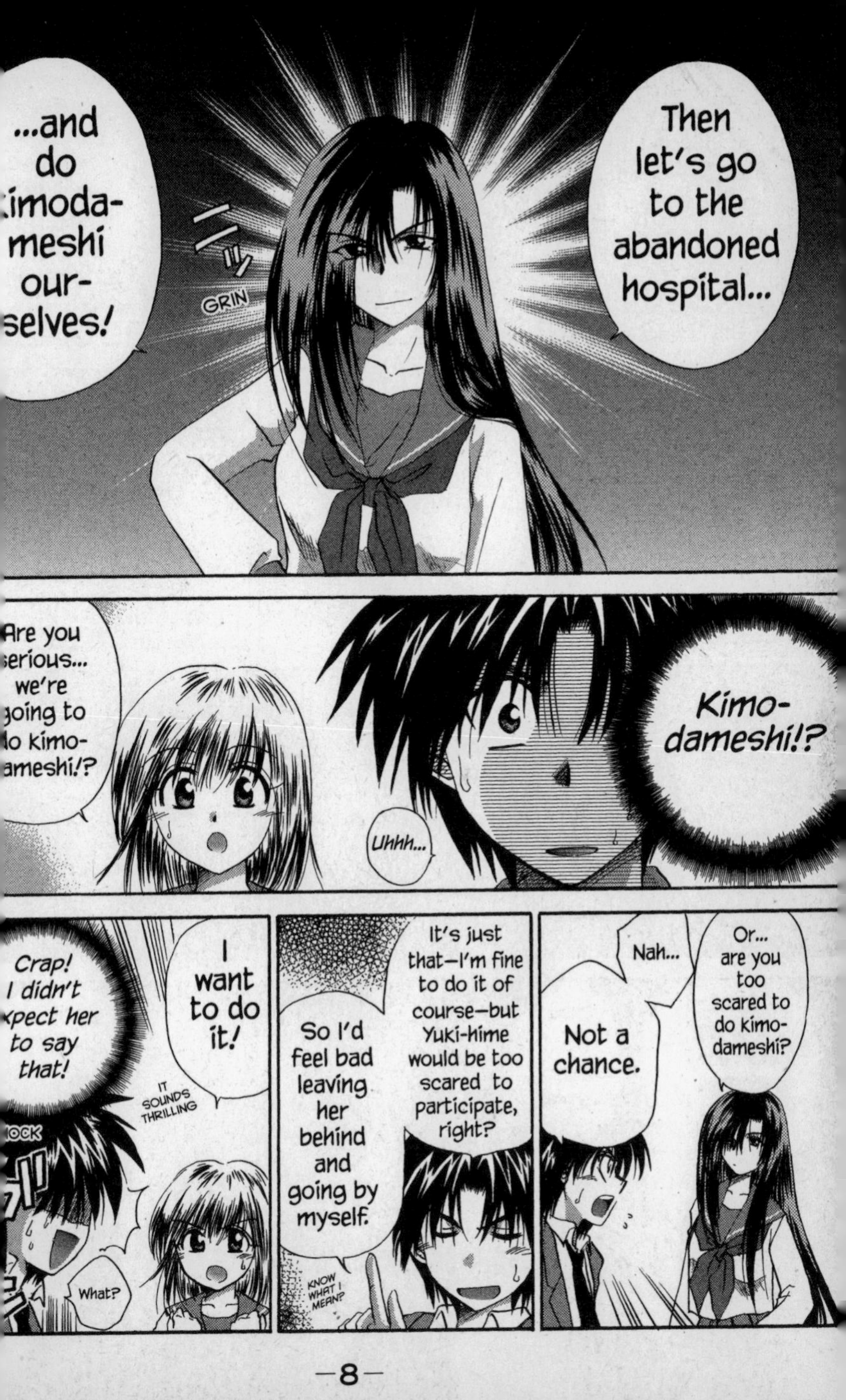

Then let's go to the abandoned hospital...
...and do imoda-meshi our-selves!
GRIN
Kimo-dameshi!?
Uhhh...
Are you erious... we're joing to lo kimo-ameshi!?
Or... are you too scared to do kimo-dameshi?
Nah...
Not a chance.
It's just that—I'm fine to do it of course—but Yuki-hime would be too scared to participate, right?
So I'd feel bad leaving her behind and going by myself.
KNOW WHAT I MEAN?
I want to do it!
IT SOUNDS THRILLING
Crap! I didn't xpect her to say that!
OCK
What?

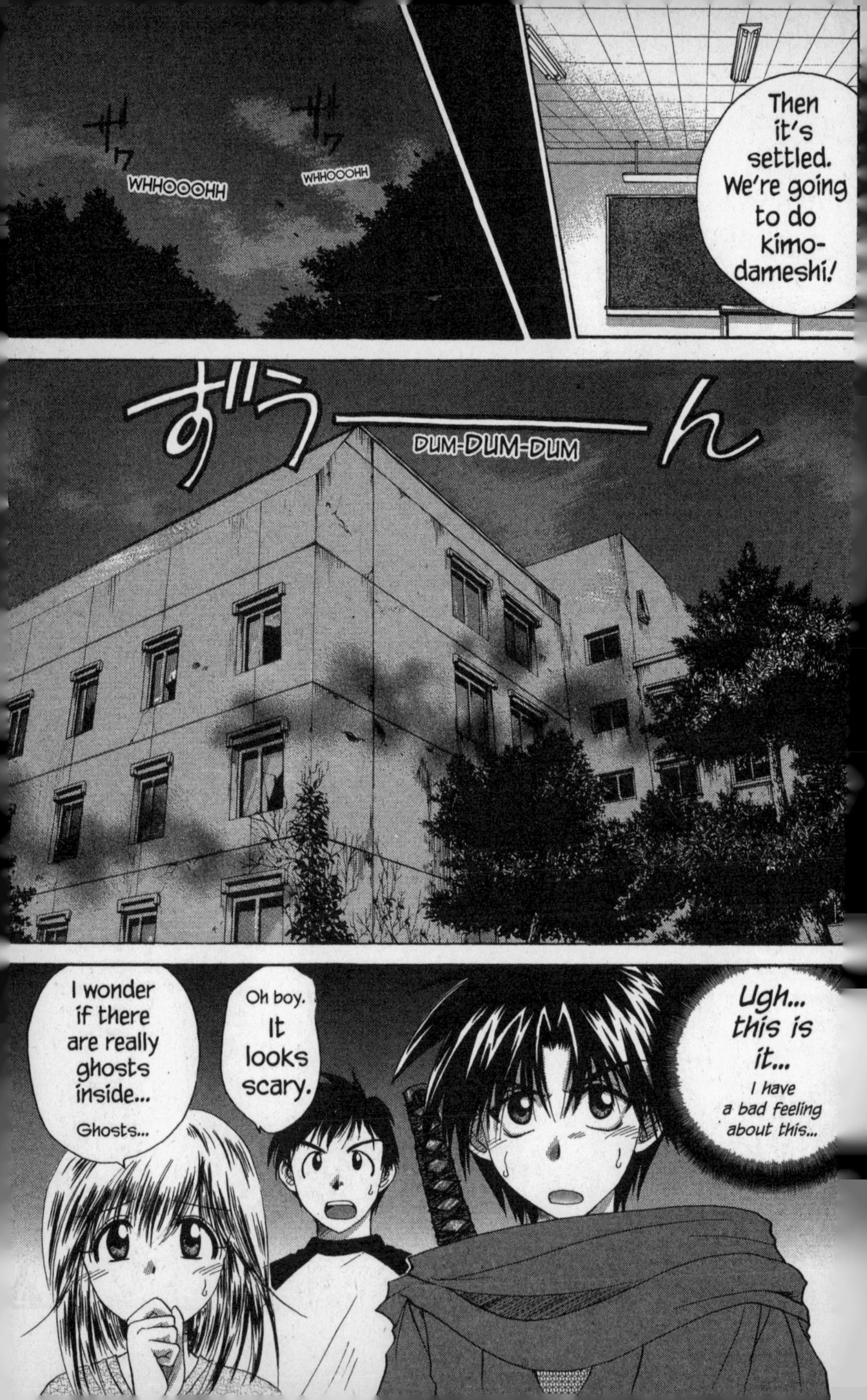
Then it's settled. We're going to do kimo-dameshi!
ザワ
WHHOOOHH
ザワ
WHHOOOHH
ずうーーーん
DUM-DUM-DUM
Ugh... this is it...
I have a bad feeling about this...
Oh boy.
It looks scary.
I wonder if there are really ghosts inside...
Ghosts...

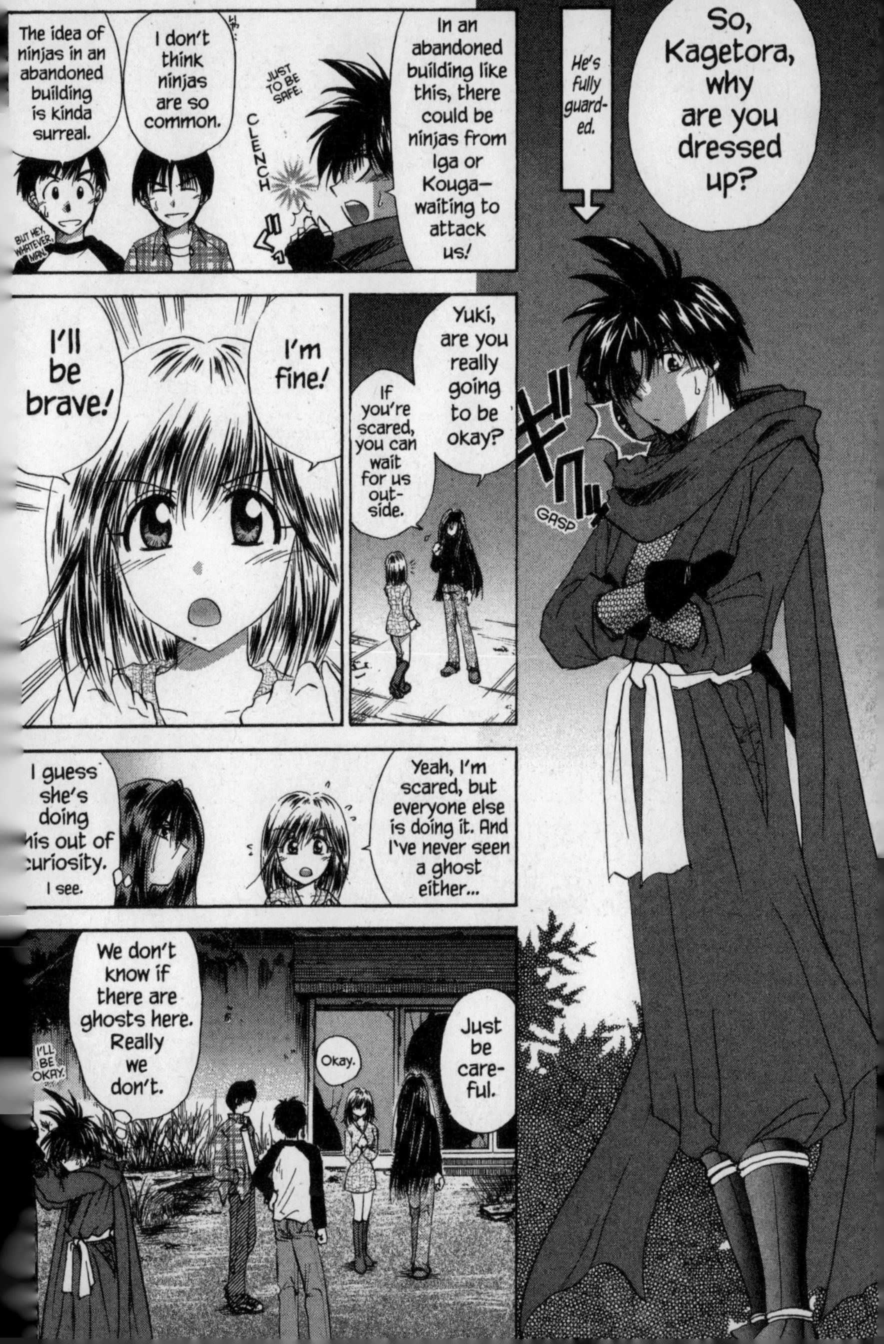
He's fully guard-ed.
So, Kagetora, why are you dressed up?
GASP
In an abandoned building like this, there could be ninjas from Iga or Kouga—waiting to attack us!
JUST TO BE SAFE.
CLENCH
I don't think ninjas are so common.
The idea of ninjas in an abandoned building is kinda surreal.
BUT HEY, WHATEVER, MAN.
Yuki, are you really going to be okay?
If you're scared, you can wait for us out-side.
I'm fine!
I'll be brave!
Yeah, I'm scared, but everyone else is doing it. And I've never seen a ghost either...
I guess she's doing his out of uriosity.
I see.
Just be care-ful.
Okay.
We don't know if there are ghosts here. Really we don't.
I'LL BE OKAY.

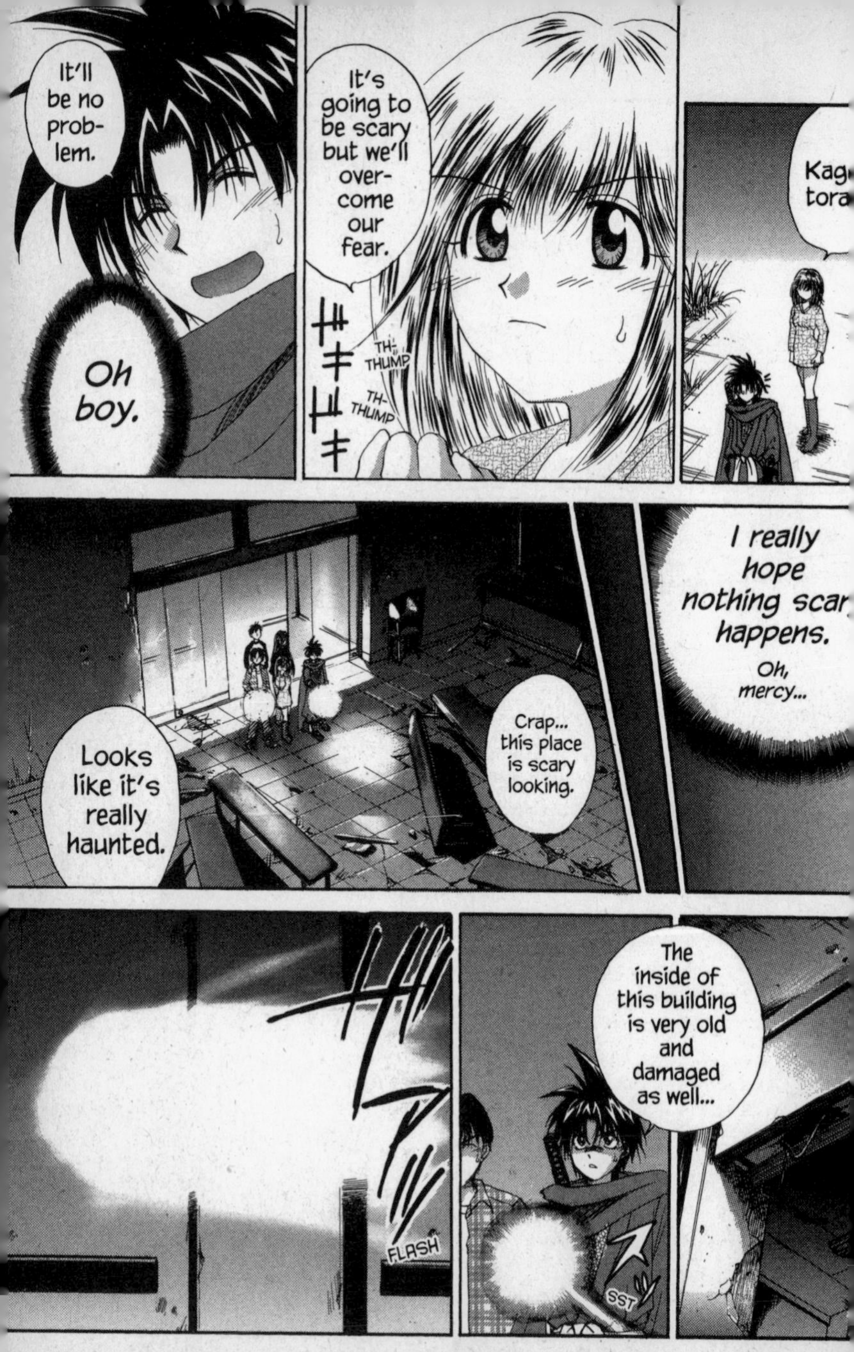
Kag tora
It's going to be scary but we'll over-come our fear.
TH-THUMP
TH-THUMP
It'll be no prob-lem.
Oh boy.
I really hope nothing scar happens.
Oh, mercy...
Crap... this place is scary looking.
Looks like it's really haunted.
The inside of this building is very old and damaged as well...
SST
FLASH

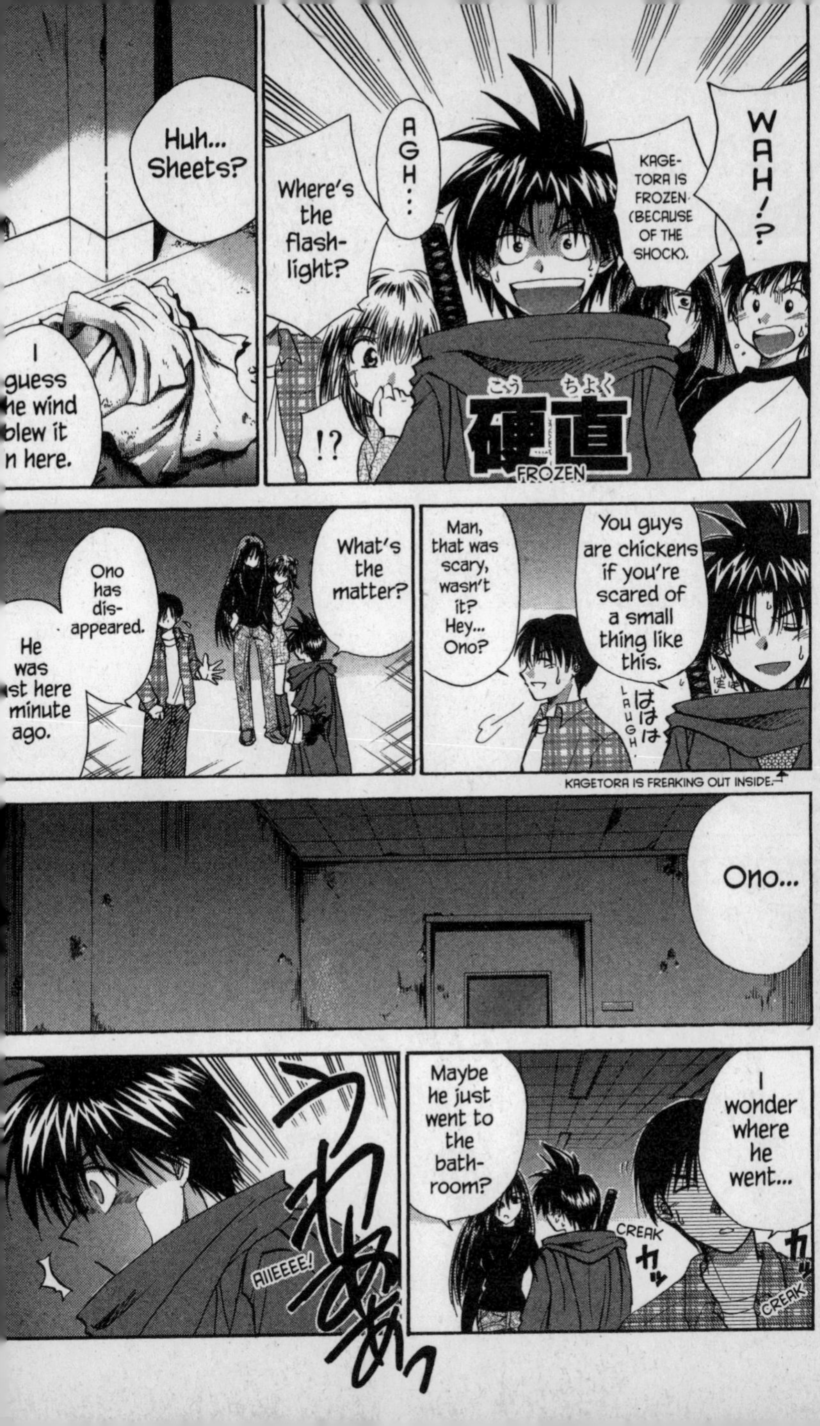
WAH!?
KAGE-TORA IS FROZEN (BECAUSE OF THE SHOCK).
AGH...
Where's the flash-light?
!?
こう ちょく
硬直
FROZEN
Huh... Sheets?
I guess he wind blew it n here.
You guys are chickens if you're scared of a small thing like this.
ははは
LAUGH
Man, that was scary, wasn't it? Hey... Ono?
What's the matter?
Ono has dis-appeared.
He was st here minute ago.
KAGETORA IS FREAKING OUT INSIDE.
Ono...
I wonder where he went...
カッ
CREAK
Maybe he just went to the bath-room?
カッ
CREAK
うわあっ
AIIEEEE!

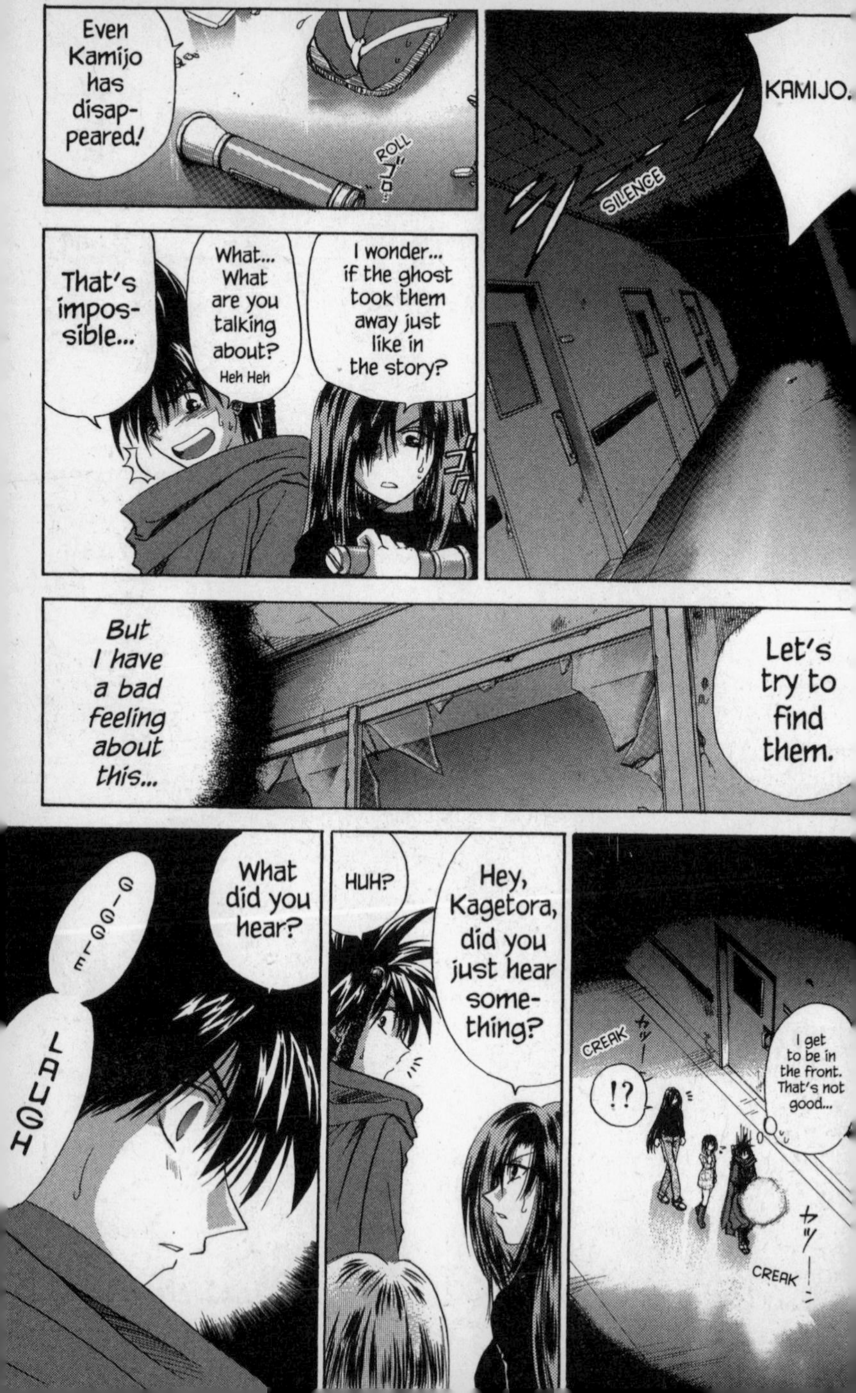
KAMIJO.
SILENCE
Even Kamijo has disappeared!
ROLL
I wonder... if the ghost took them away just like in the story?
What... What are you talking about?
Heh Heh
That's impossible...
Let's try to find them.
But I have a bad feeling about this...
CREAK
!?
I get to be in the front. That's not good...
CREAK
Hey, Kagetora, did you just hear something?
HUH?
What did you hear?
GIGGLE
LAUGH

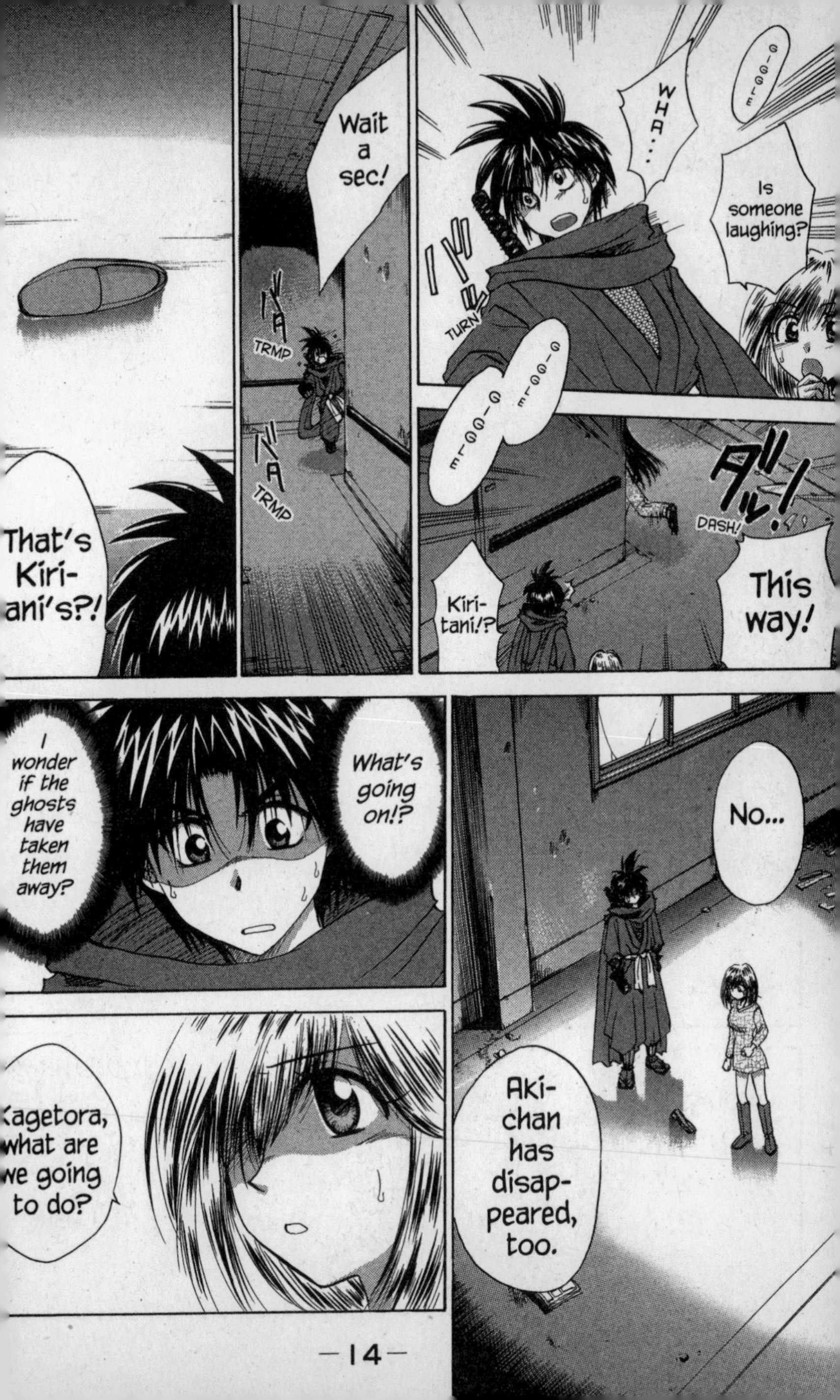
GIGGLE
WHA...
Is someone laughing?
TURN
GIGGLE
GIGGLE
DASH!
This way!
Kiri-tani!?
Wait a sec!
TRMP
TRMP
That's Kiri-ani's?!
No...
Aki-chan has disappeared, too.
What's going on!?
I wonder if the ghosts have taken them away?
Kagetora, what are we going to do?

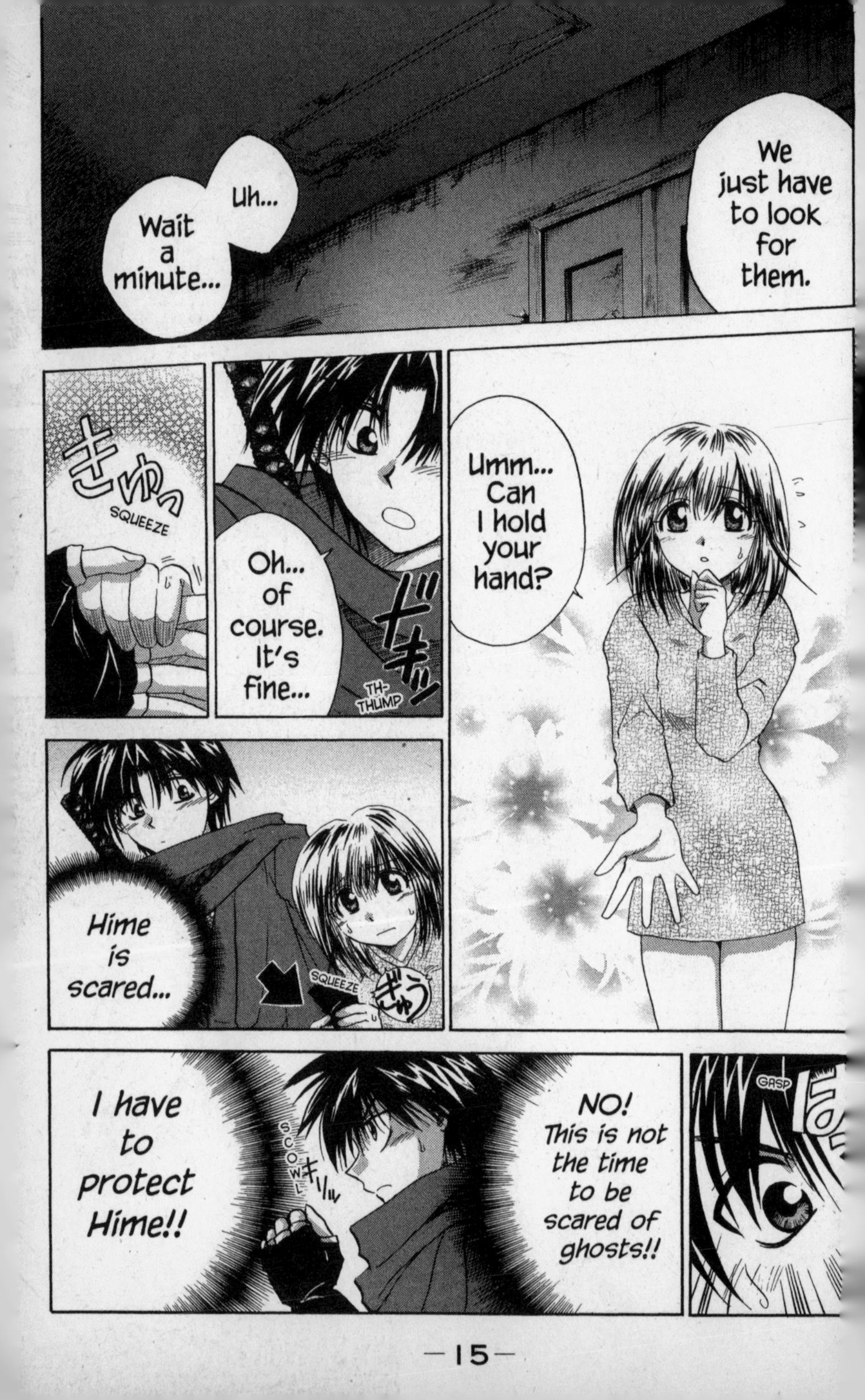
We just have to look for them.
Uh...
Wait a minute...
Umm... Can I hold your hand?
Oh... of course. It's fine...
TH-THUMP
きゅっ
SQUEEZE
Hime is scared...
SQUEEZE
ぎゅう
GASP
NO! This is not the time to be scared of ghosts!!
SCOWL
I have to protect Hime!!

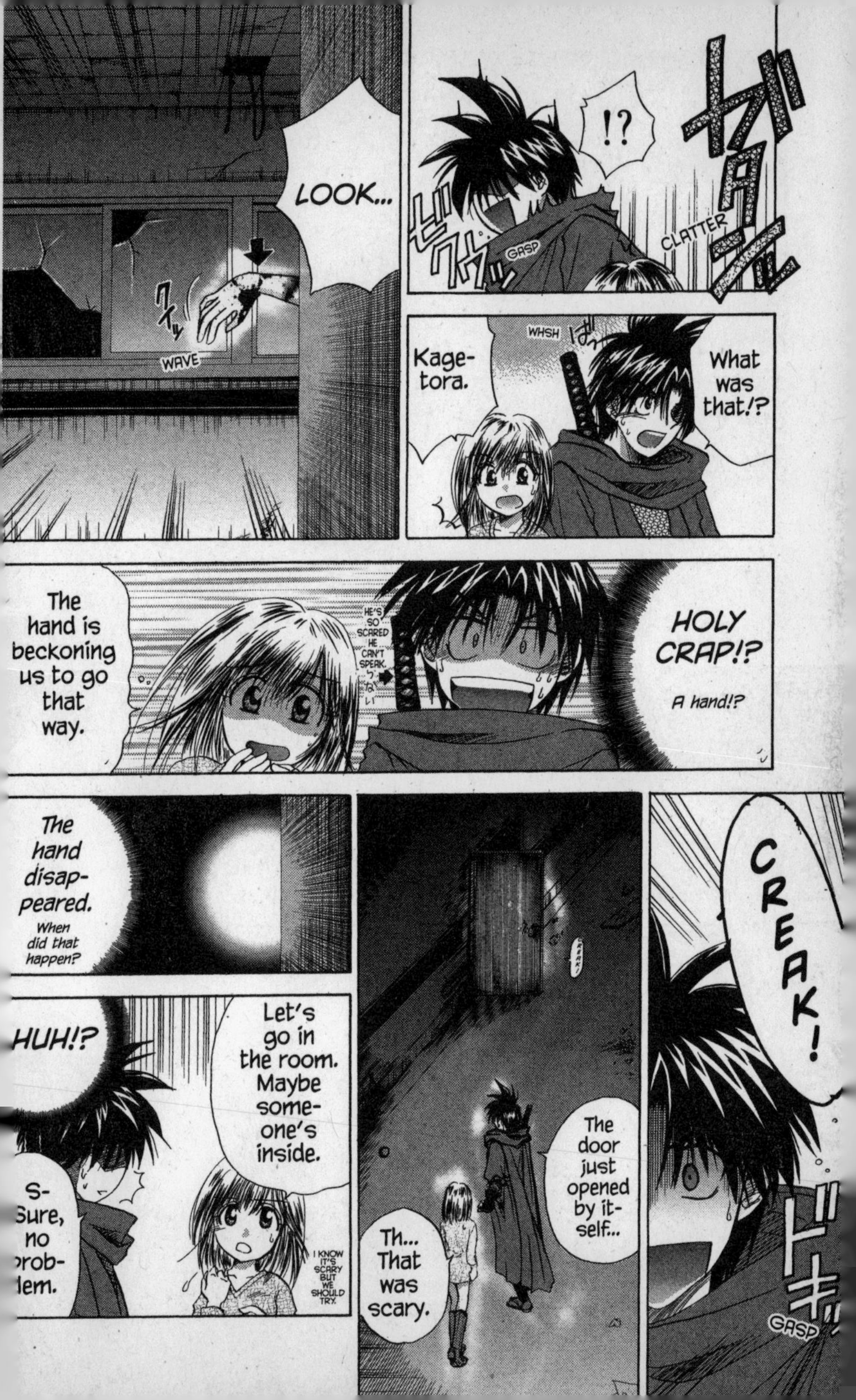

!?
CLATTER
GASP
What was that!?
Kage-tora.
WHSH
LOOK...
WAVE
HOLY CRAP!?
A hand!?
HE'S SO SCARED HE CAN'T SPEAK.
The hand is beckoning us to go that way.
CREAK!
GASP
The door just opened by it-self...
Th... That was scary.
The hand disap-peared.
When did that happen?
HUH!?
Let's go in the room. Maybe some-one's inside.
S-Sure, no prob-lem.
I KNOW IT'S SCARY BUT WE SHOULD TRY.

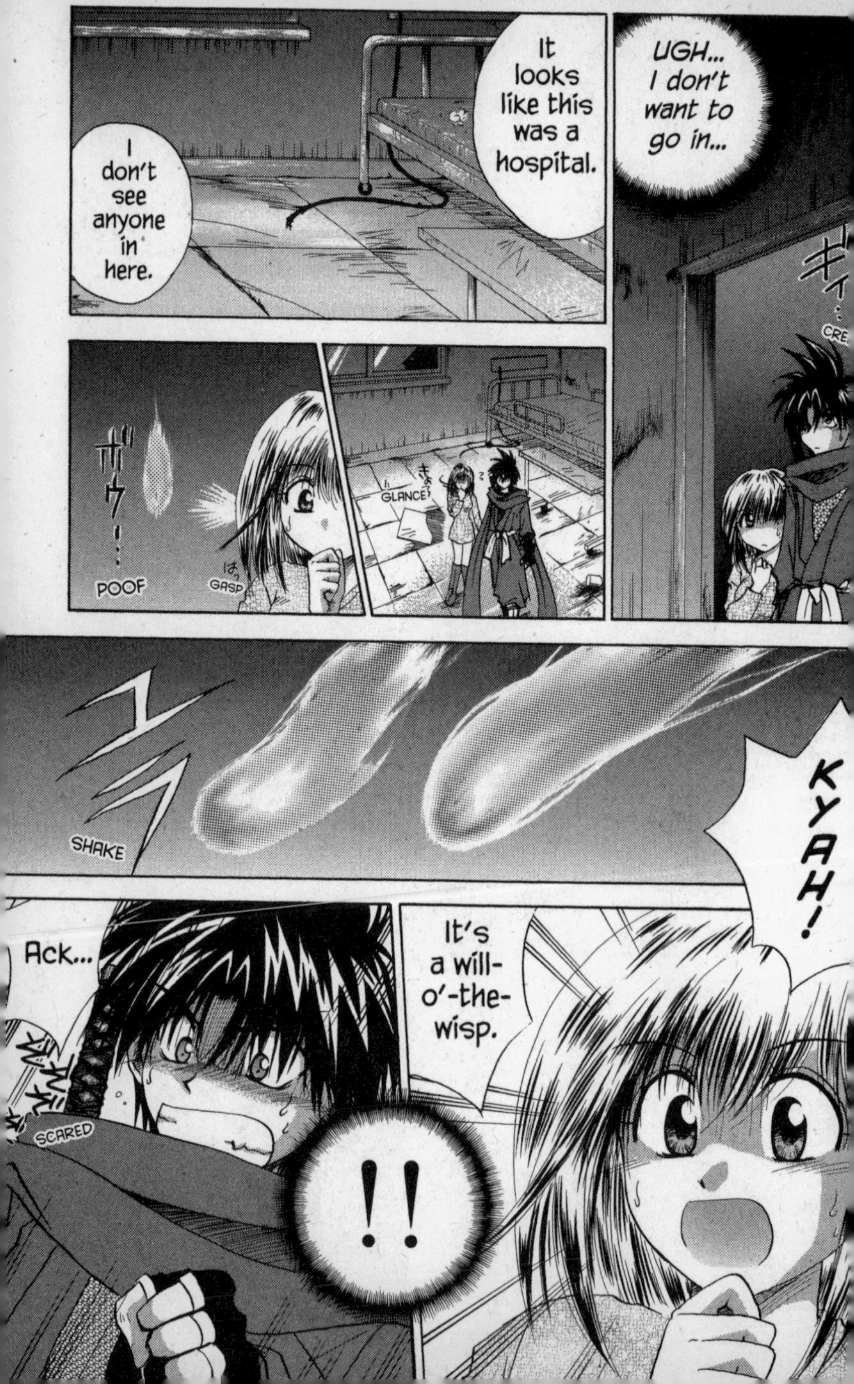
UGH... I don't want to go in...
CRE
It looks like this was a hospital.
I don't see anyone in here.
GLANCE
POOF
GASP
SHAKE
KYAH!
It's a will-o'-the-wisp.
!!
Ack...
SCARED

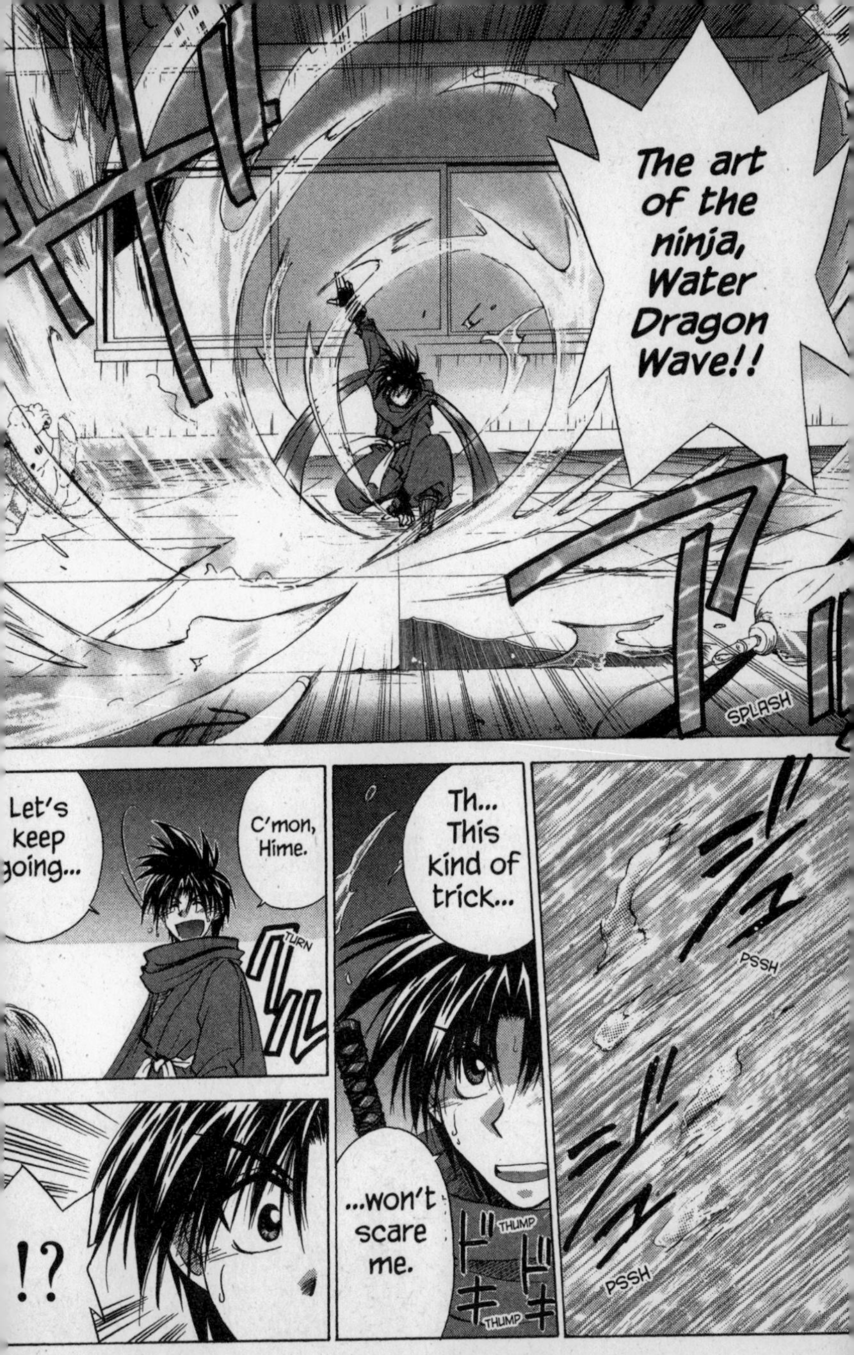
The art of the ninja, Water Dragon Wave!!
SPLASH
PSSH
PSSH
Th... This kind of trick...
...won't scare me.
THUMP
THUMP
C'mon, Hime.
Let's keep going...
TURN
!?

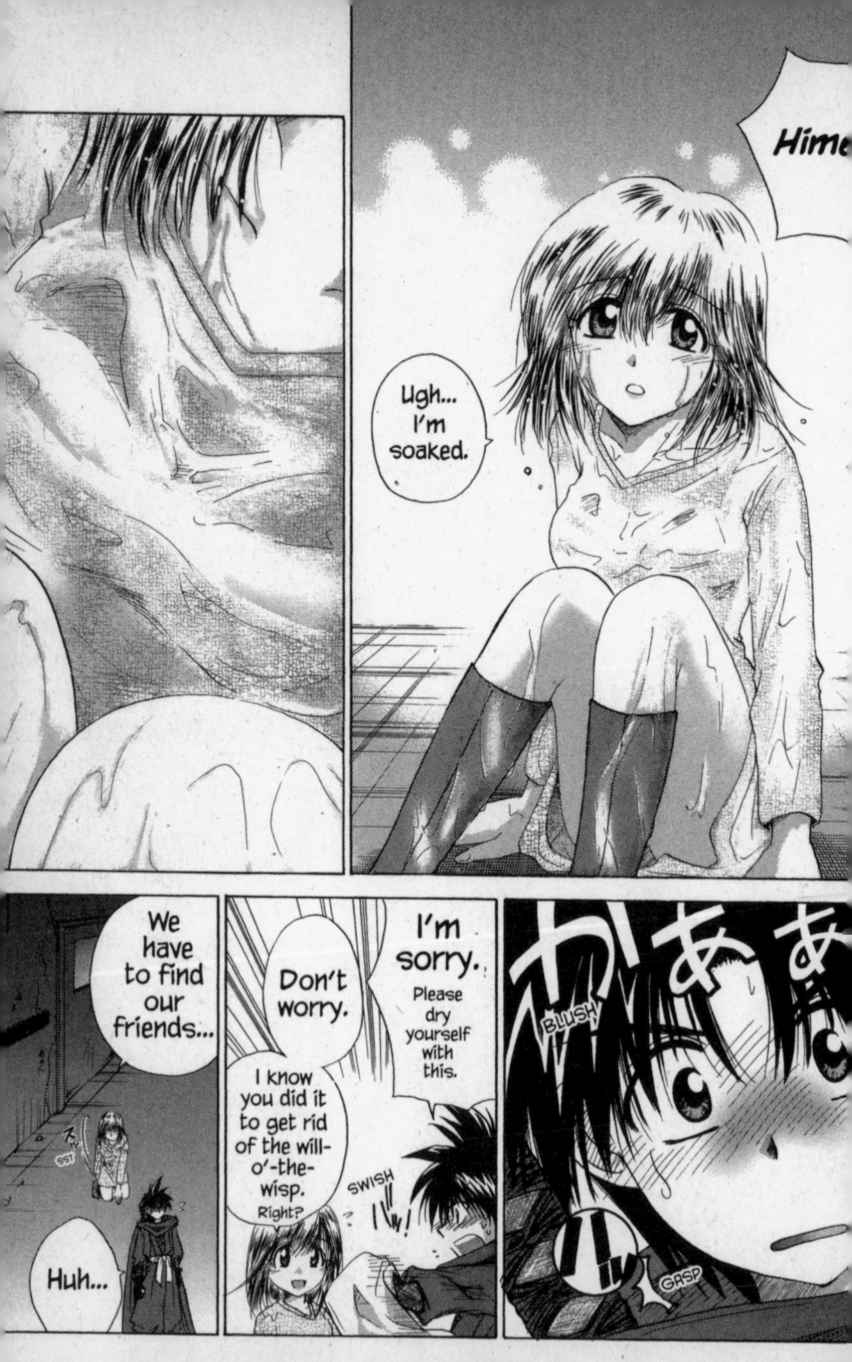
Hime
Ugh... I'm soaked.
わああ
BLUSH
GASP
I'm sorry.
Please dry yourself with this.
Don't worry.
I know you did it to get rid of the will-o'-the-wisp. Right?
SWISH
We have to find our friends...
SST
Huh...

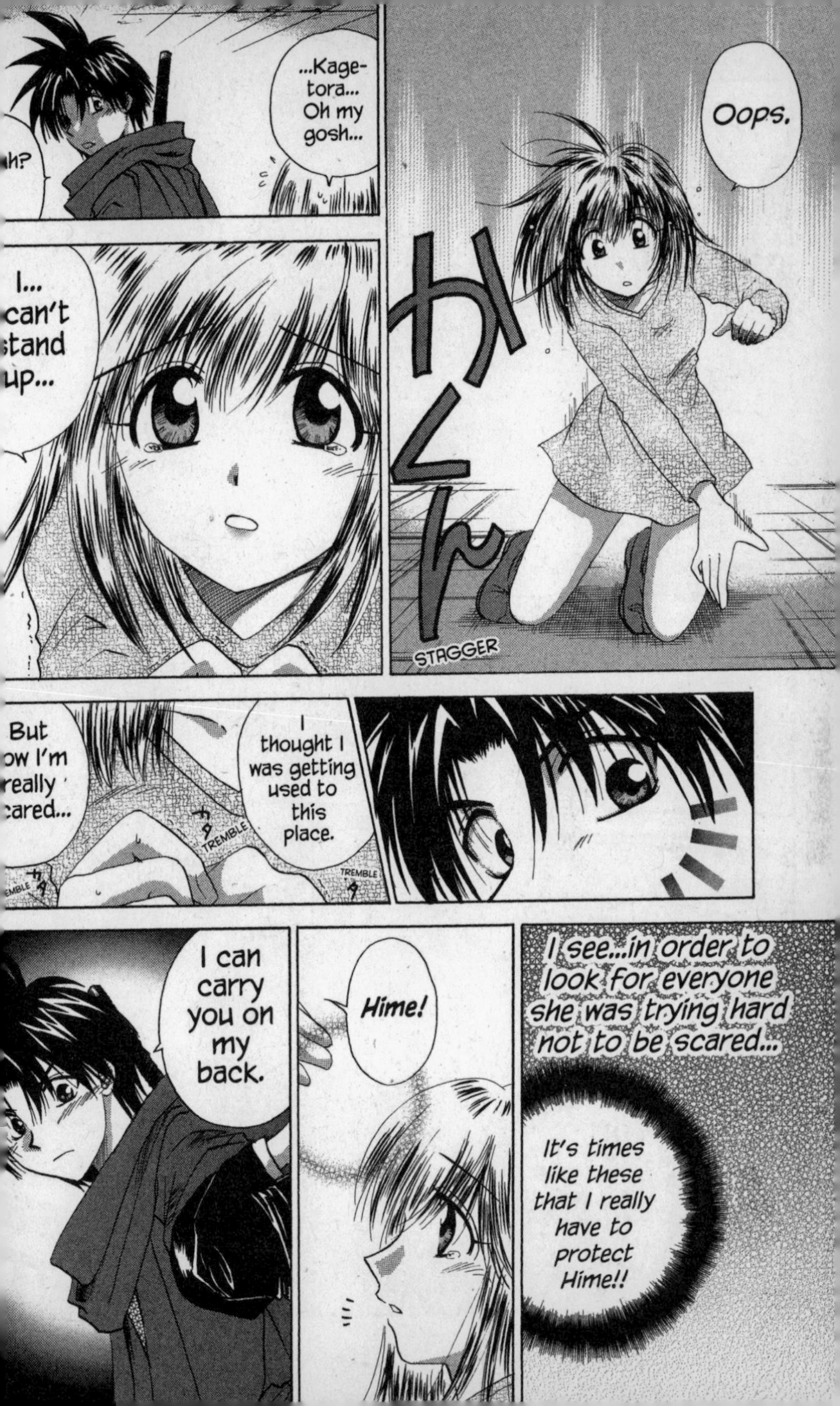

Oops.
STAGGER
...Kage-tora... Oh my gosh...
h?
I... can't tand up...
I thought I was getting used to this place.
But ow I'm eally cared...
TREMBLE
TREMBLE
EMBLE
I see...in order to look for everyone she was trying hard not to be scared...
It's times like these that I really have to protect Hime!!
Hime!
I can carry you on my back.

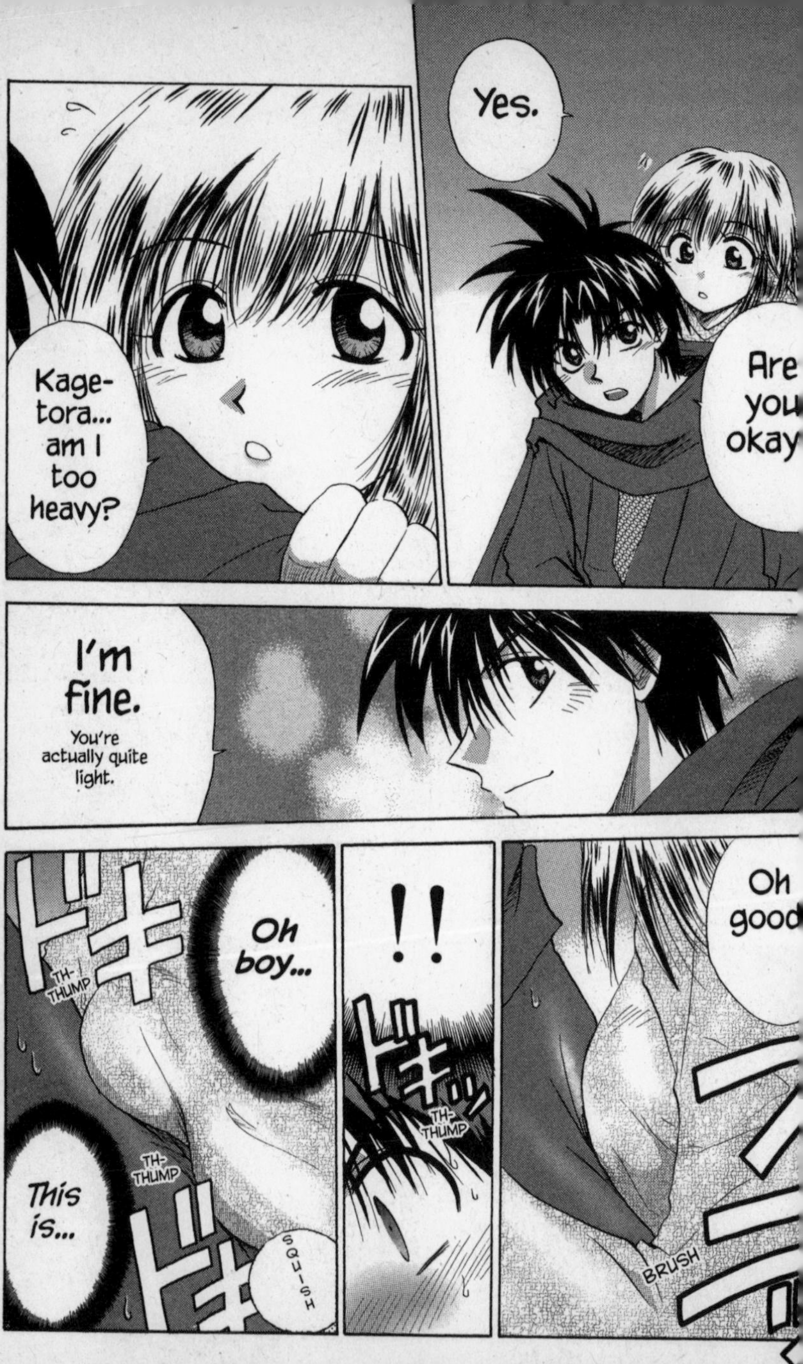
Yes.
Are you okay
Kage-tora... am I too heavy?
I'm fine.
You're actually quite light.
Oh good
BRUSH
!!
TH-THUMP
Oh boy...
TH-THUMP
This is...
TH-THUMP
SQUISH

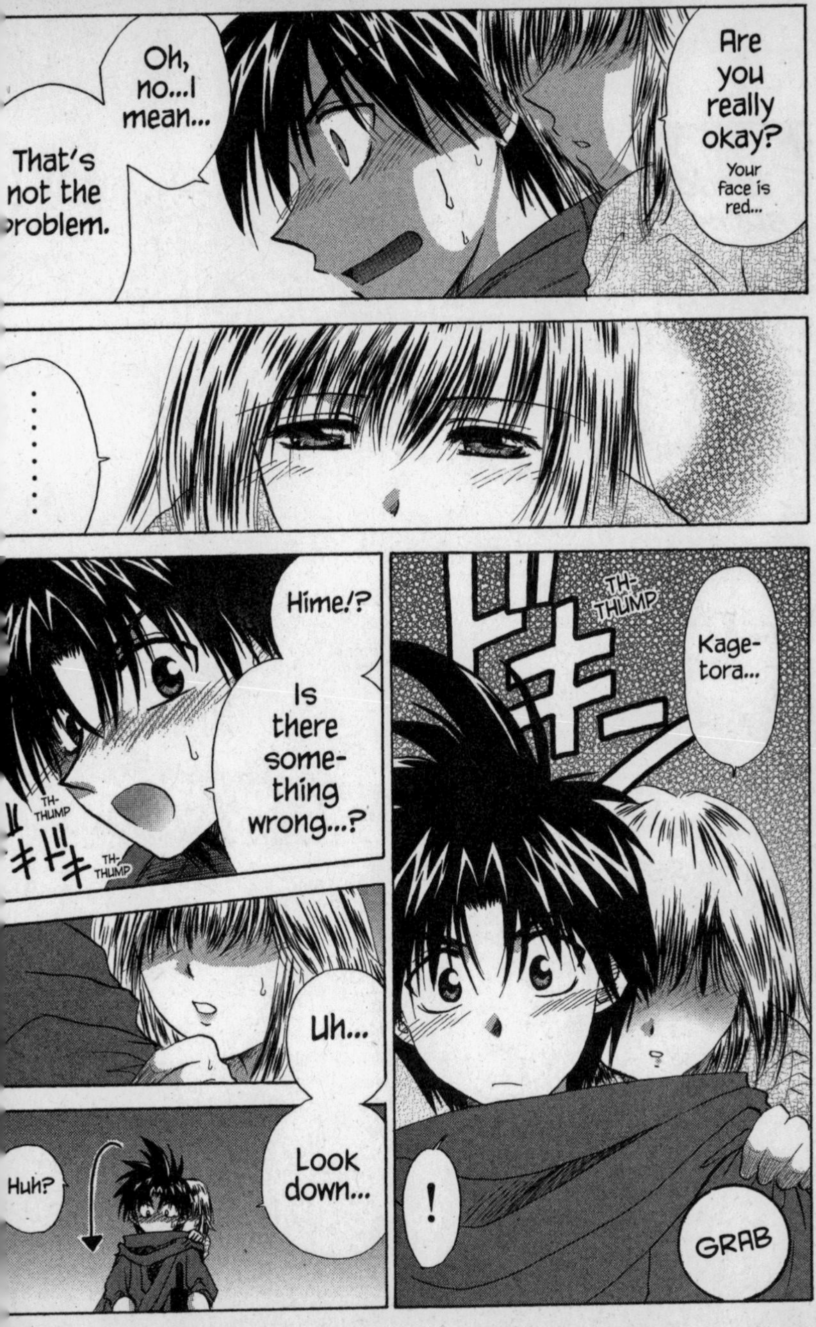
Are you really okay?
Your face is red...
Oh, no...I mean...
That's not the problem.
......
TH-THUMP
Kage-tora...
!
GRAB
Hime!?
Is there some-thing wrong...?
TH-THUMP
TH-THUMP
Uh...
Look down...
Huh?

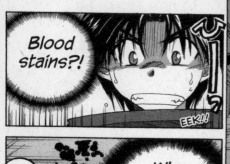

Blood stains?!

EEK?!!

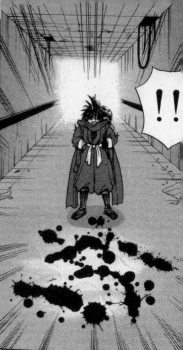

!!

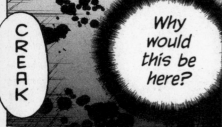

CREAK

Why would this be here?

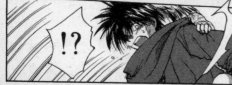

!?

WHIP

CREAK

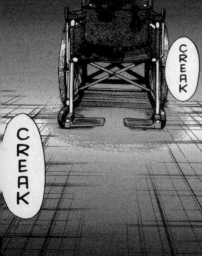

CREAK

CREAK

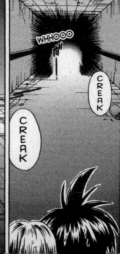

WHHOOO

CREAK

CREAK

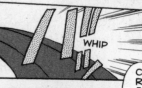

CREAK

CREAK

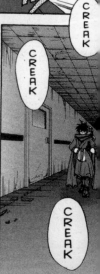

CREAK

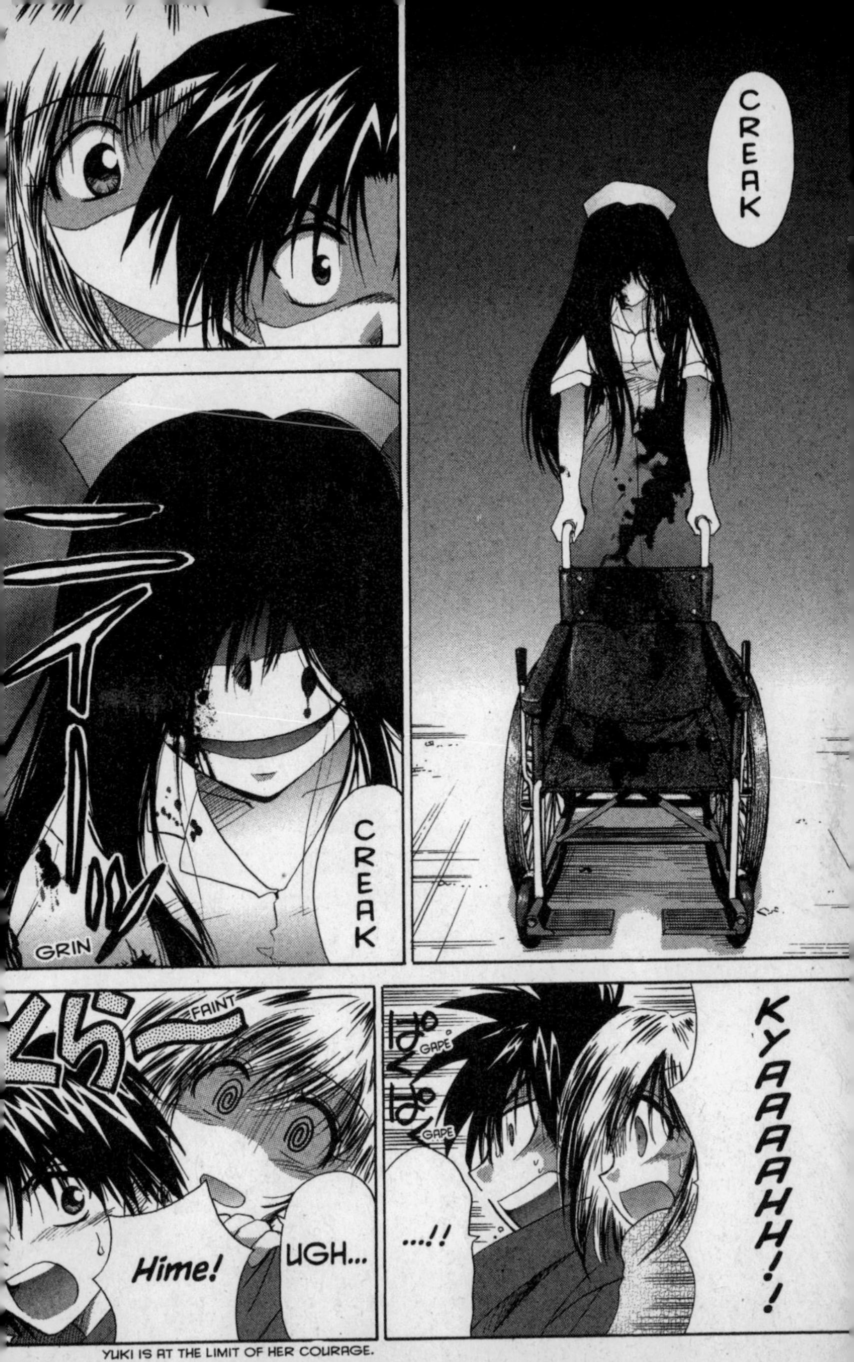
CREAK
GRIN
CREAK
KYAAAAAHH!!
GAPE
GAPE
...!!
FAINT
UGH...
Hime!

YUKI IS AT THE LIMIT OF HER COURAGE.

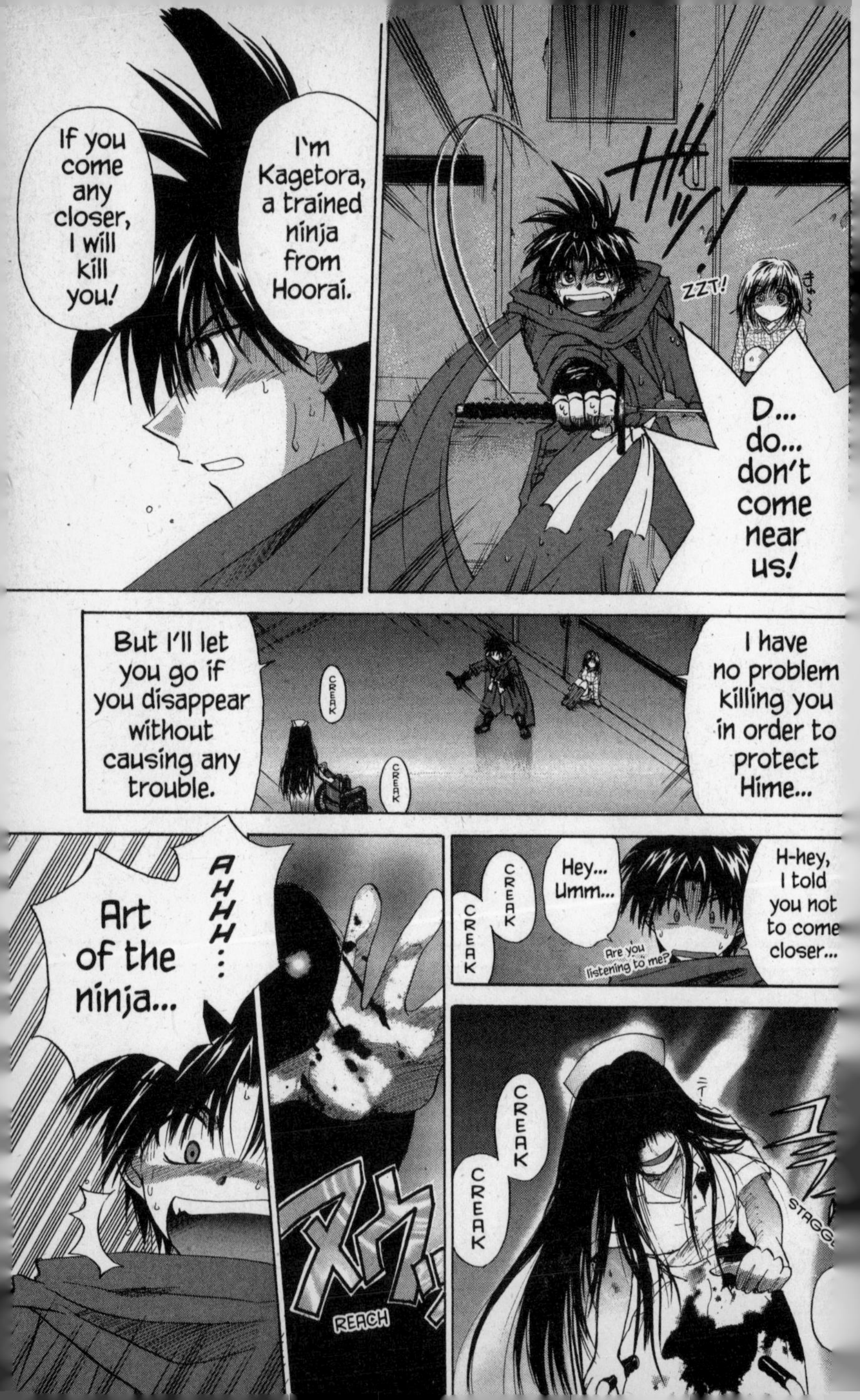
ZZT!
D... do... don't come near us!
I'm Kagetora, a trained ninja from Hoorai.
If you come any closer, I will kill you!
I have no problem killing you in order to protect Hime...
CREAK
CREAK
But I'll let you go if you disappear without causing any trouble.
H-hey, I told you not to come closer...
Hey... Umm...
Are you listening to me?
CREAK
CREAK
CREAK
CREAK
AHHH...
REACH
Art of the ninja...

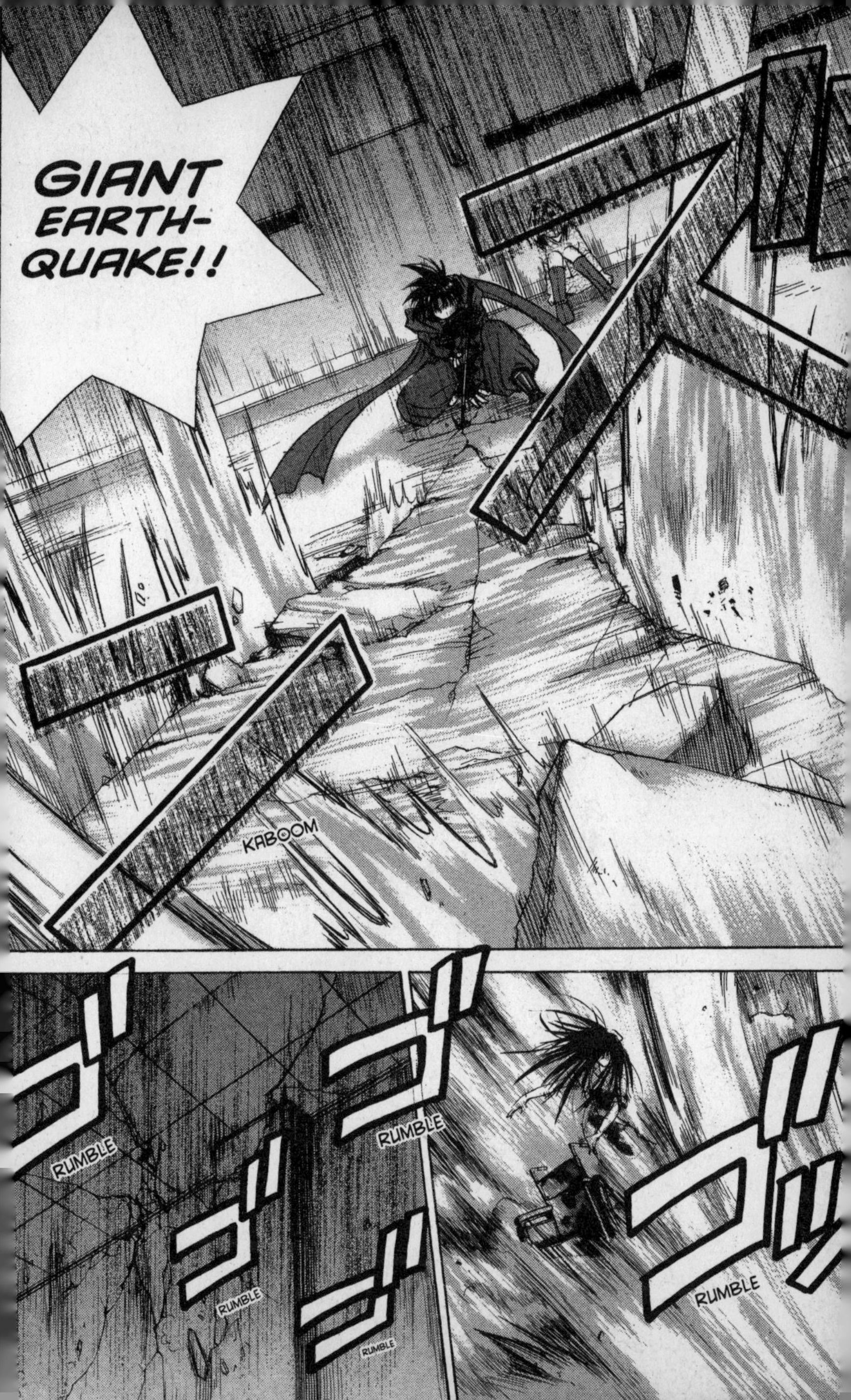
GIANT EARTH-QUAKE!!
KABOOM
RUMBLE
RUMBLE
RUMBLE
RUMBLE
RUMBLE

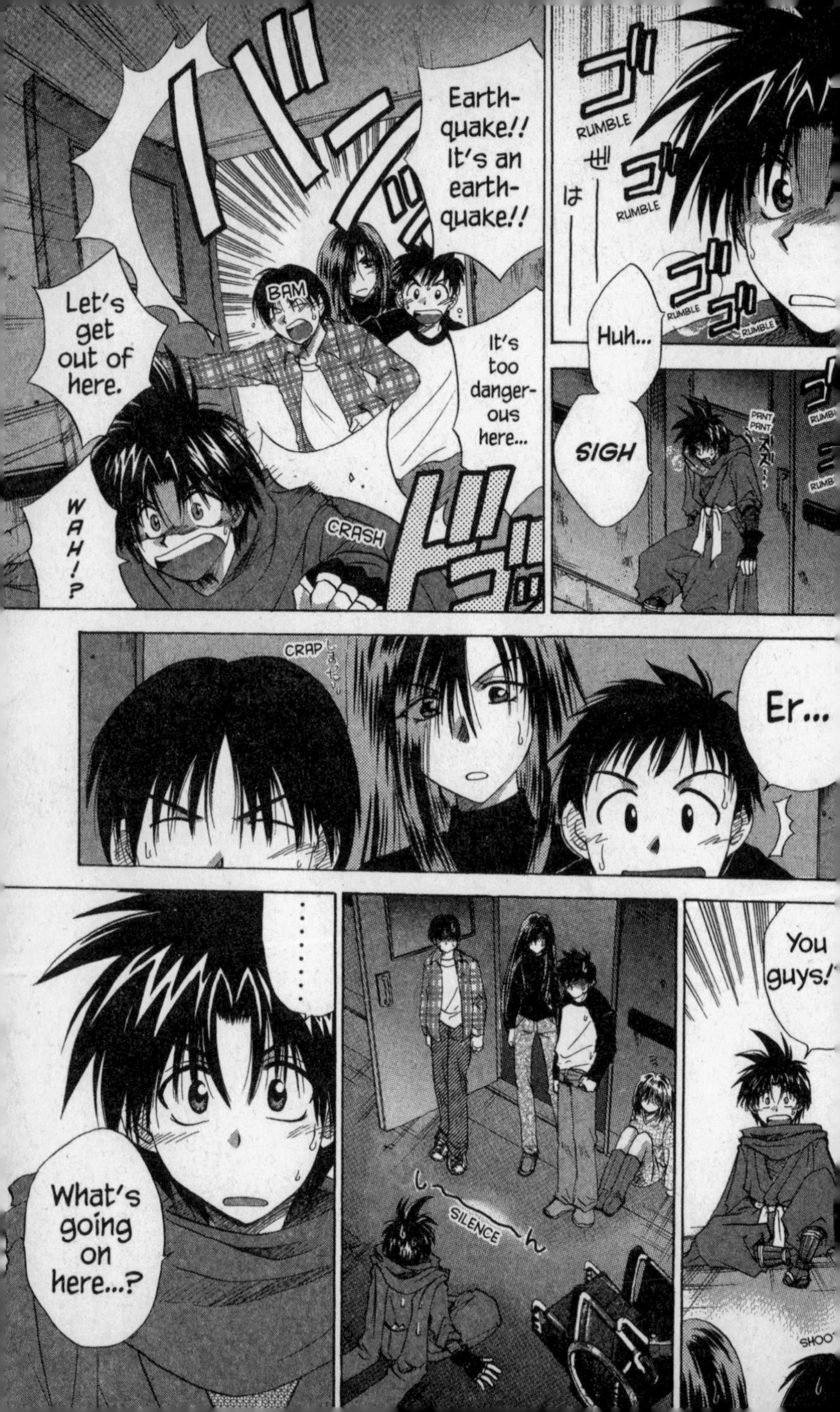

RUMBLE
RUMBLE
RUMBLE
RUMBLE
Huh...
PANT PANT
RUMBLE
RUMBLE
SIGH
Earth-quake!! It's an earth-quake!!
BAM
Let's get out of here.
It's too danger-ous here...
CRASH
WAH!?
Er...
CRAP
You guys!
SHOO
SILENCE
......
What's going on here...?

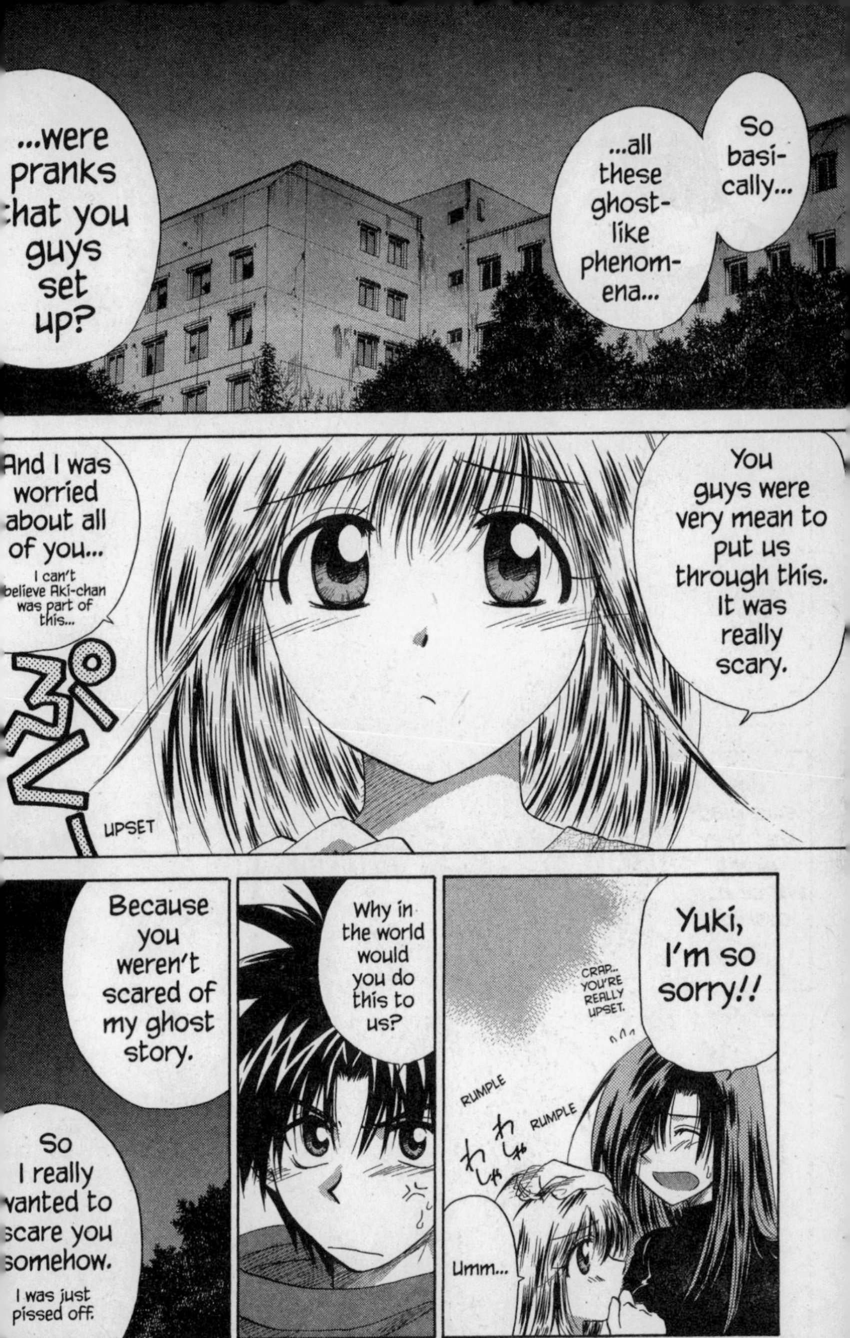
So basically...
...all these ghost-like phenomena...
...were pranks that you guys set up?
You guys were very mean to put us through this. It was really scary.
And I was worried about all of you...
I can't believe Aki-chan was part of this...
UPSET
Yuki, I'm so sorry!!
CRAP... YOU'RE REALLY UPSET.
RUMPLE
RUMPLE
Umm...
Why in the world would you do this to us?
Because you weren't scared of my ghost story.
So I really wanted to scare you somehow.
I was just pissed off.

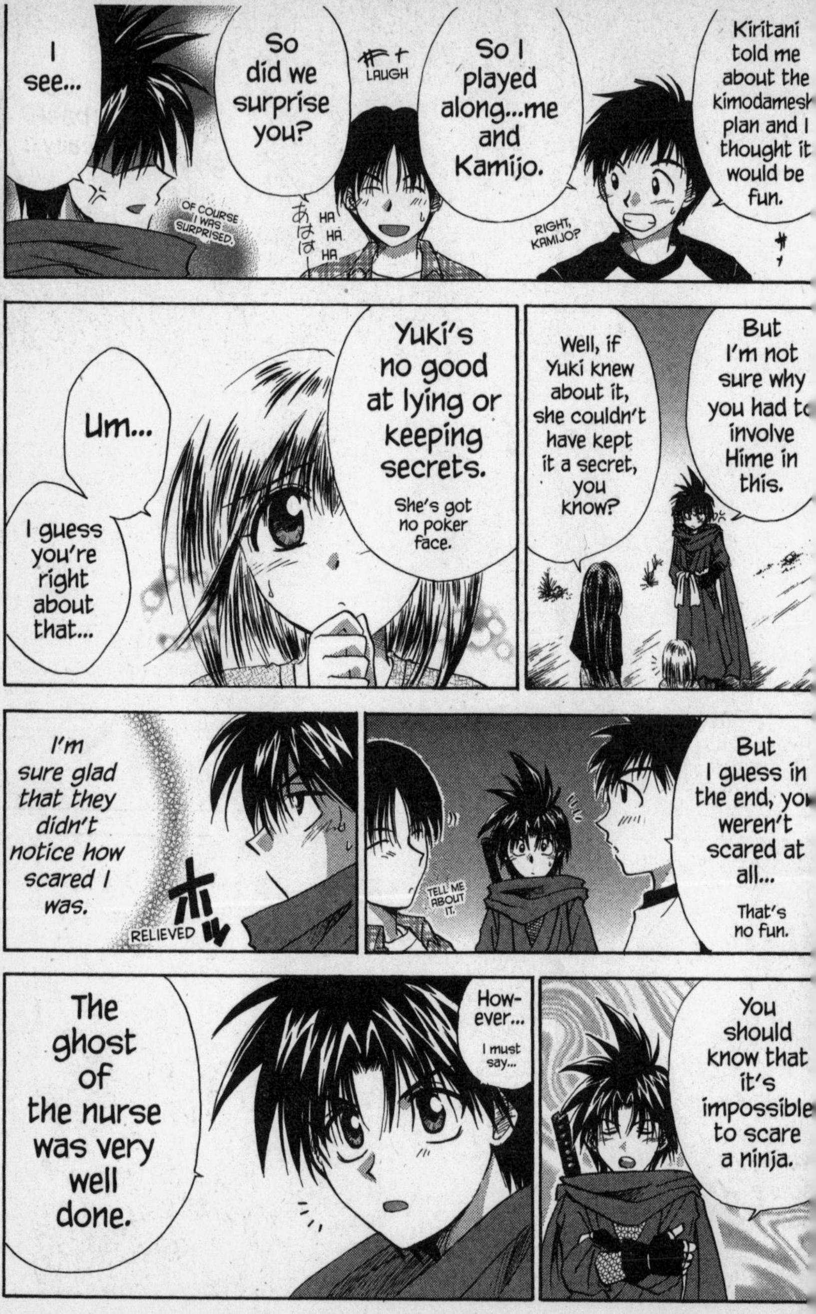
Kiritani told me about the kimodamesh plan and I thought it would be fun.
RIGHT, KAMIJO?
So I played along...me and Kamijo.
LAUGH
So did we surprise you?
HA HA HA
OF COURSE I WAS SURPRISED.
I see...
But I'm not sure why you had t involve Hime in this.
Well, if Yuki knew about it, she couldn't have kept it a secret, you know?
Yuki's no good at lying or keeping secrets.
She's got no poker face.
Um...
I guess you're right about that...
But I guess in the end, yo weren't scared at all...
That's no fun.
TELL ME ABOUT IT.
I'm sure glad that they didn't notice how scared I was.
RELIEVED
You should know that it's impossible to scare a ninja.
How-ever...
I must say...
The ghost of the nurse was very well done.

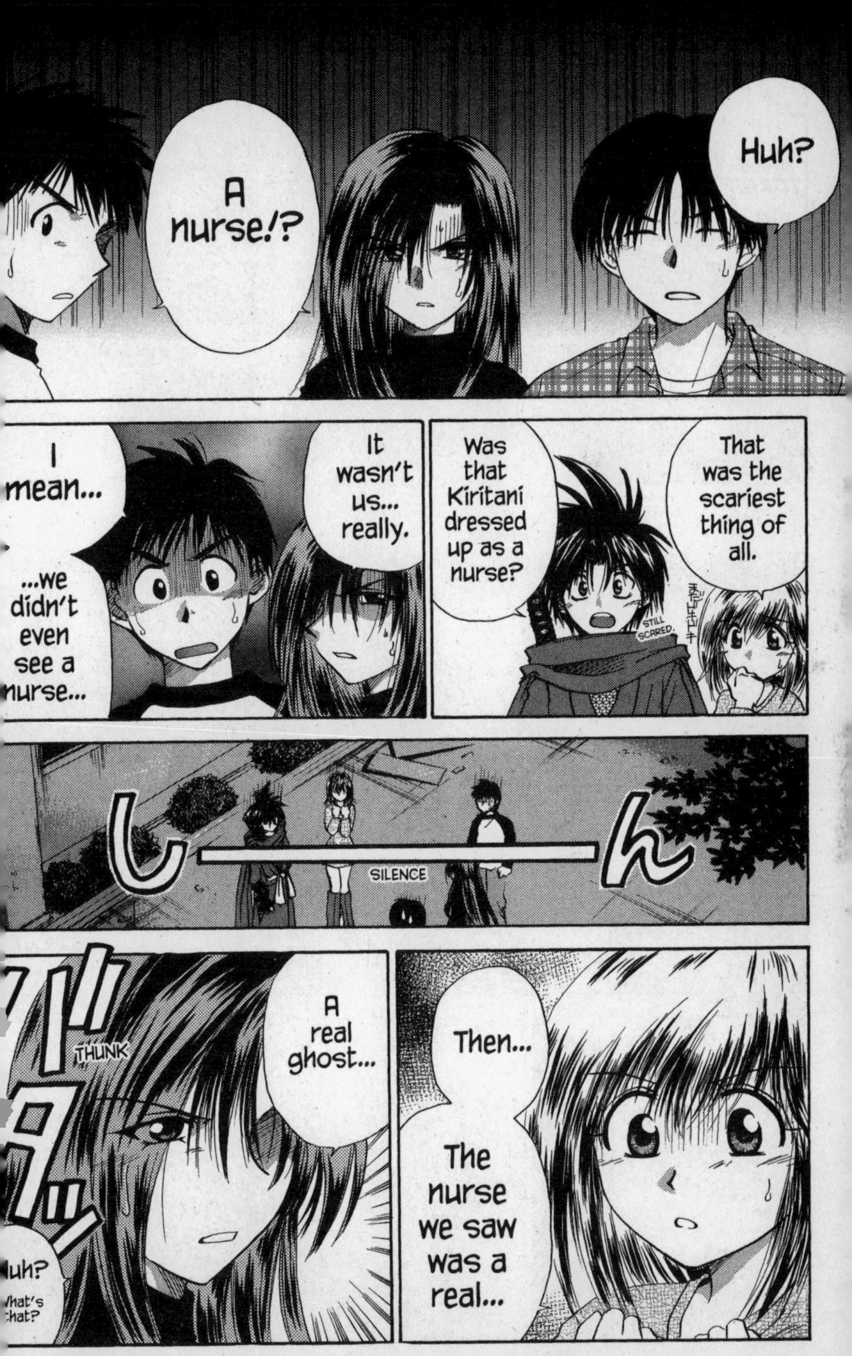
Huh?
A nurse!?
That was the scariest thing of all.
STILL SCARED.
Was that Kiritani dressed up as a nurse?
It wasn't us... really.
I mean...
...we didn't even see a nurse...
SILENCE
Then...
The nurse we saw was a real...
A real ghost...
THUNK
uh?
hat's
hat?

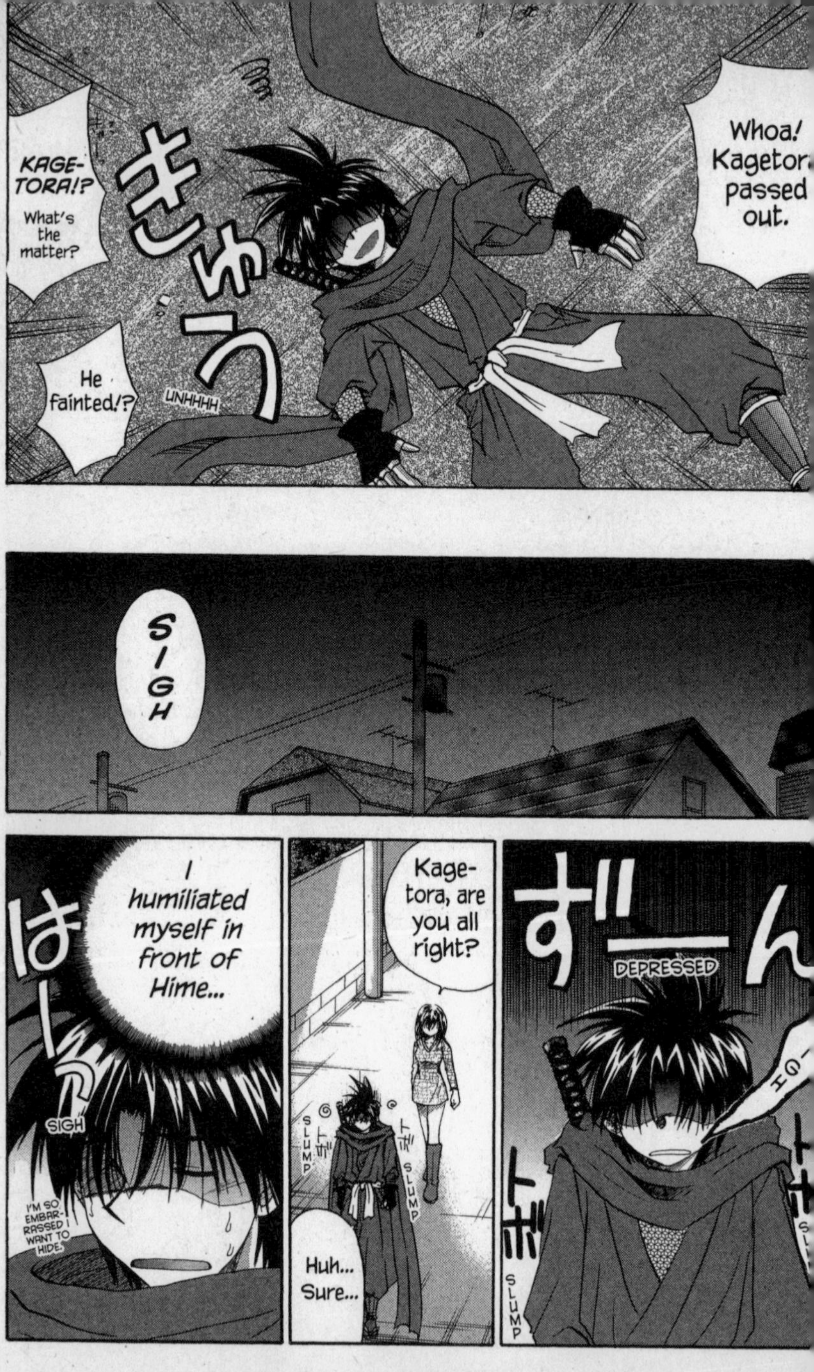

Whoa! Kagetor. passed out.
KAGE-TORA!? What's the matter?
きゅう
UNHHHH
He fainted!?
SIGH
ずーん
DEPRESSED
トボ
SLUMP
Kage-tora, are you all right?
トボ
SLUMP
トボ
SLUMP
Huh... Sure...
はーっ
SIGH
I humiliated myself in front of Hime...
I'M SO EMBAR-RASSED I WANT TO HIDE.

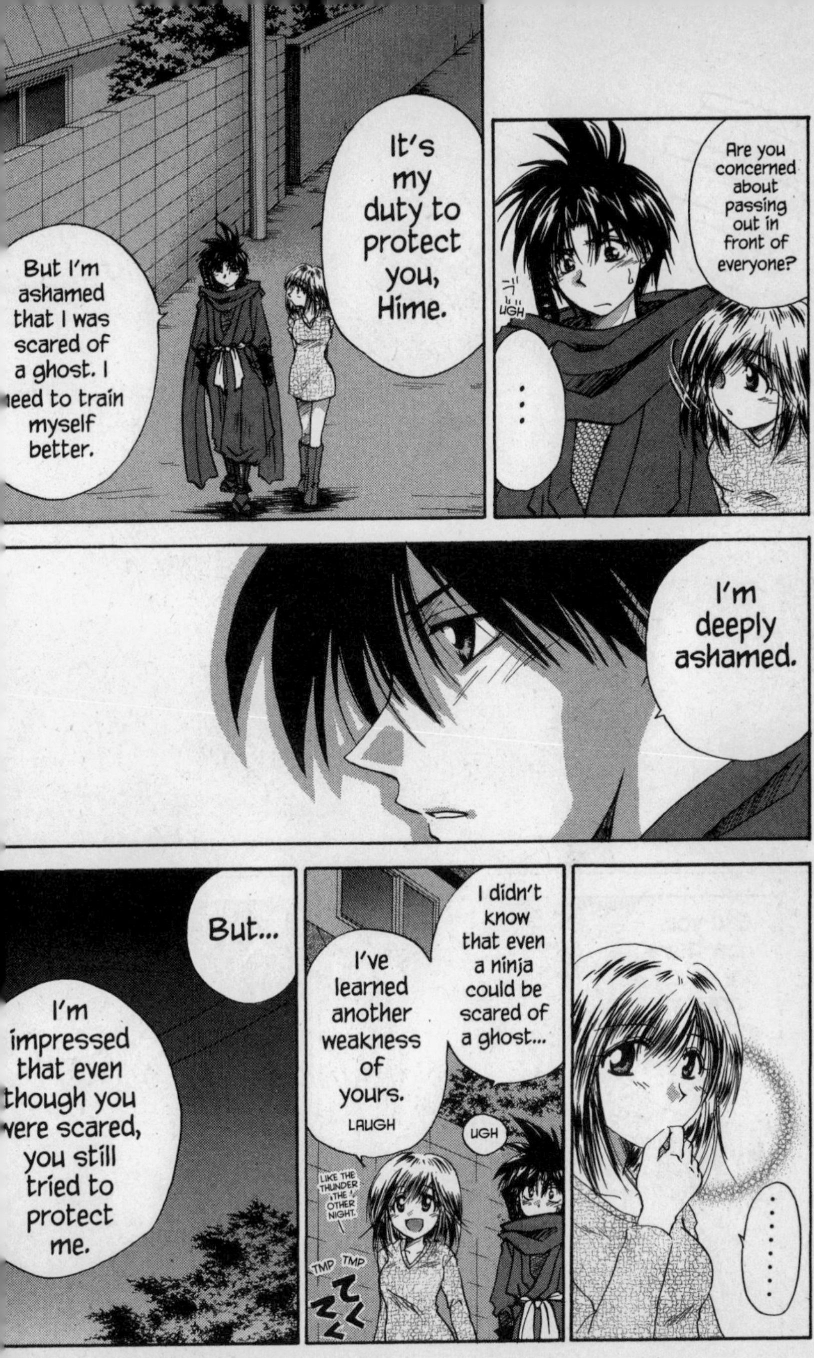

Are you concerned about passing out in front of everyone?
UGH
...
It's my duty to protect you, Hime.
But I'm ashamed that I was scared of a ghost. I need to train myself better.
I'm deeply ashamed.
......
I didn't know that even a ninja could be scared of a ghost...
I've learned another weakness of yours.
LAUGH
UGH
LIKE THE THUNDER THE OTHER NIGHT.
TMP TMP
But...
I'm impressed that even though you were scared, you still tried to protect me.

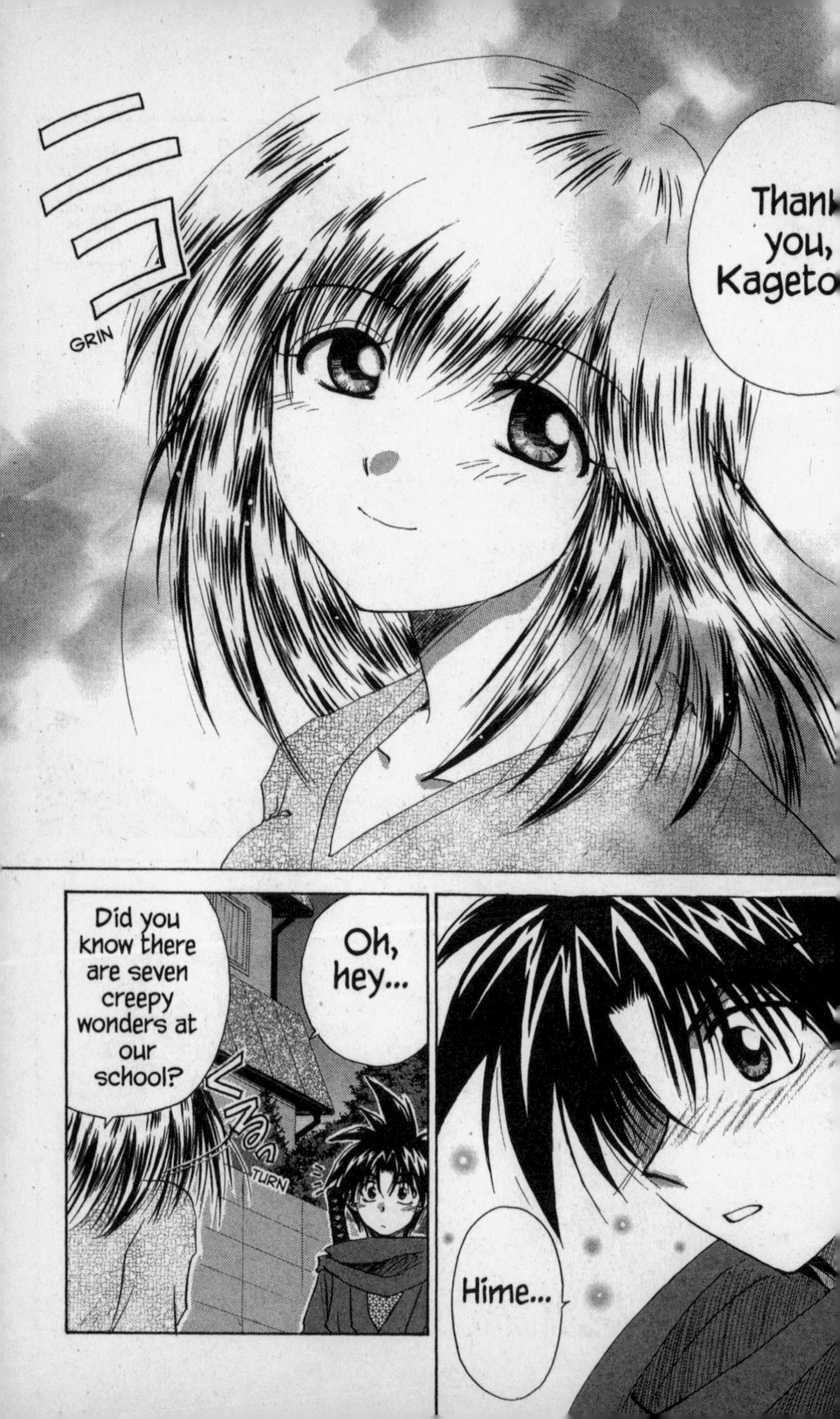
Thank you, Kageto
GRIN
Hime...
Oh, hey...
Did you know there are seven creepy wonders at our school?
TURN

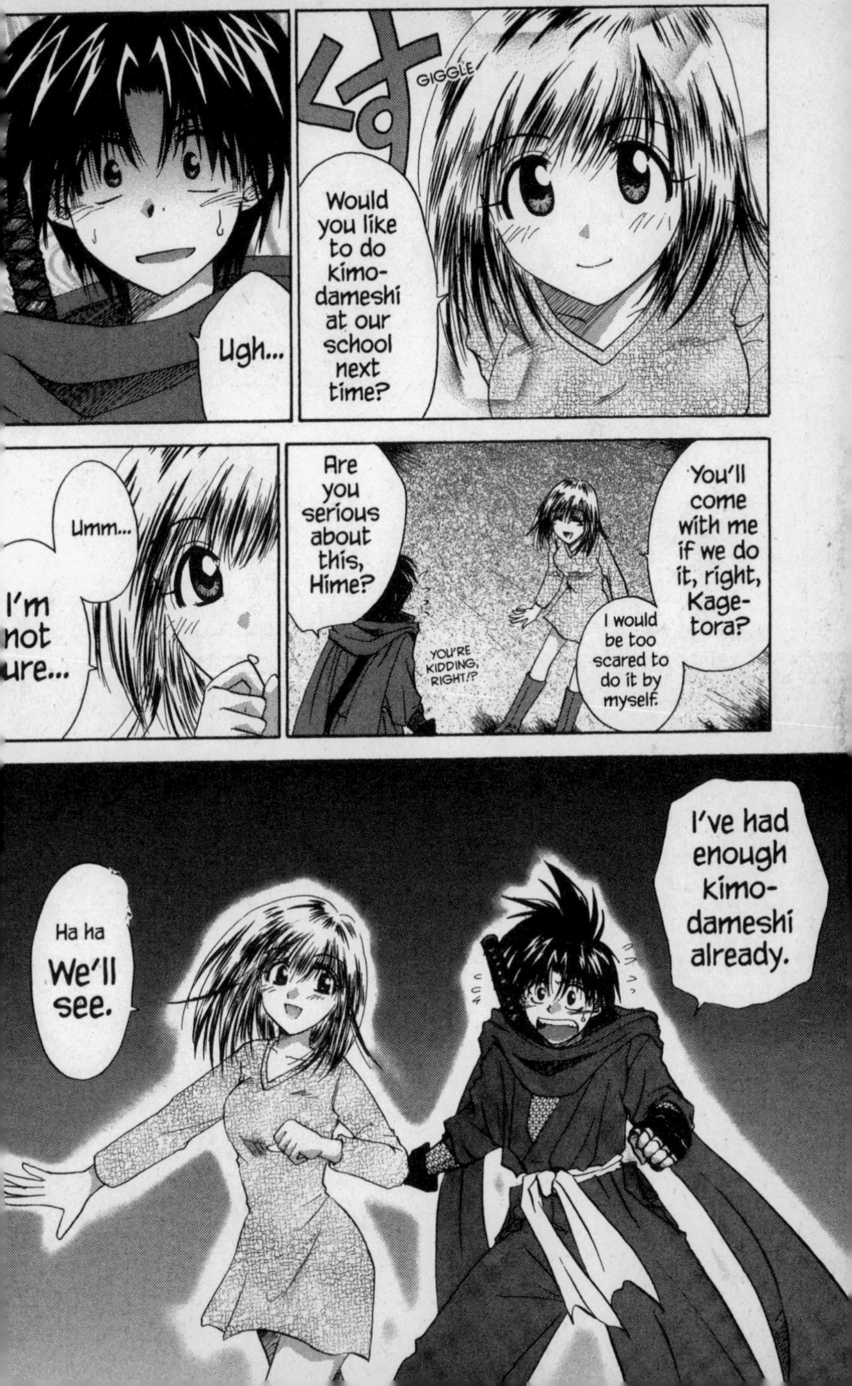
くす
GIGGLE
Would you like to do kimo-dameshi at our school next time?
Ugh...
You'll come with me if we do it, right, Kage-tora?
I would be too scared to do it by myself.
Are you serious about this, Hime?
YOU'RE KIDDING, RIGHT!?
Umm...
I'm not ure...
I've had enough kimo-dameshi already.
Ha ha
We'll see.

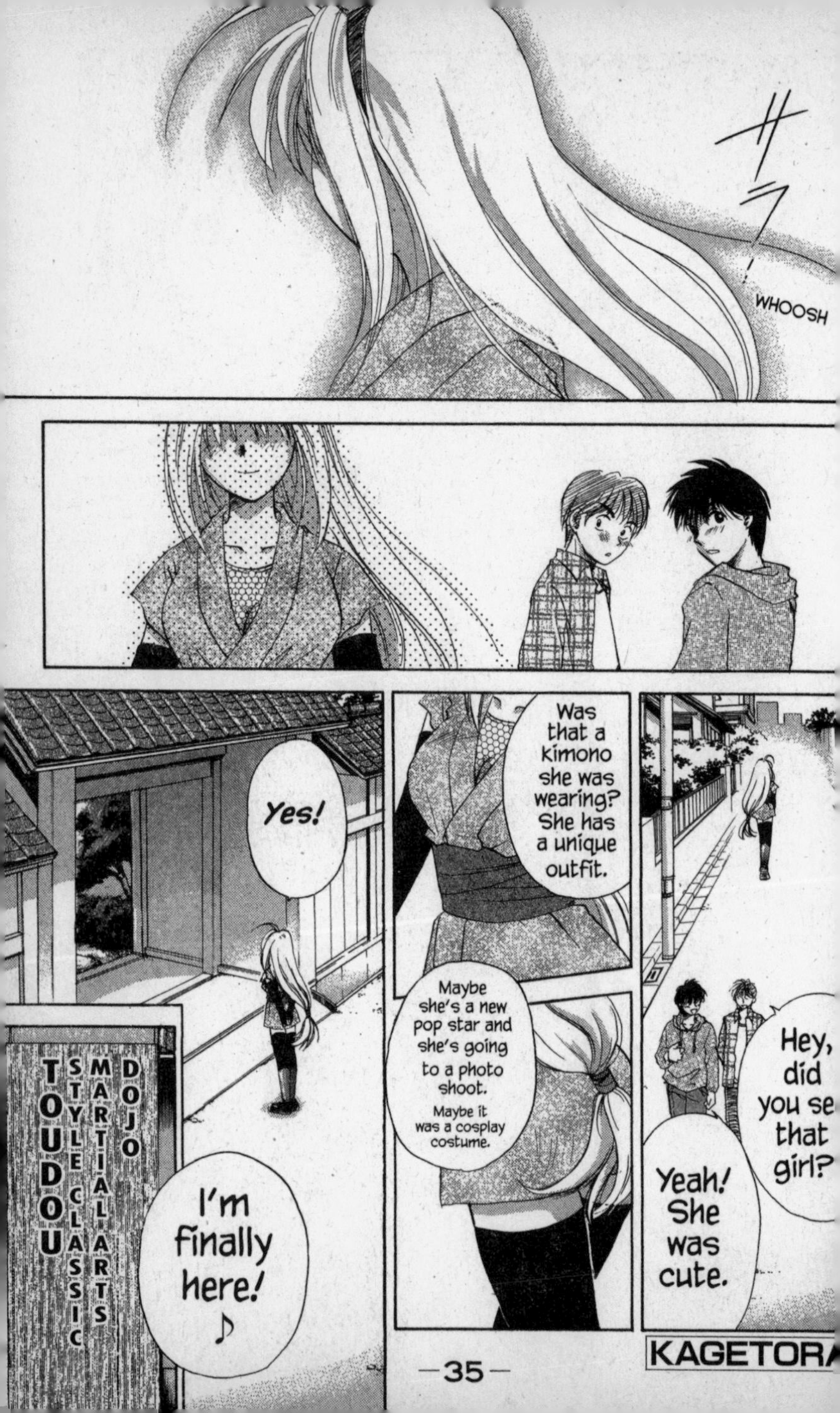
WHOOSH
Hey, did you se that girl?
Yeah! She was cute.
Was that a kimono she was wearing? She has a unique outfit.
Maybe she's a new pop star and she's going to a photo shoot.
Maybe it was a cosplay costume.
Yes!
TOUDOU STYLE CLASSIC MARTIAL ARTS DOJO
I'm finally here! ♪

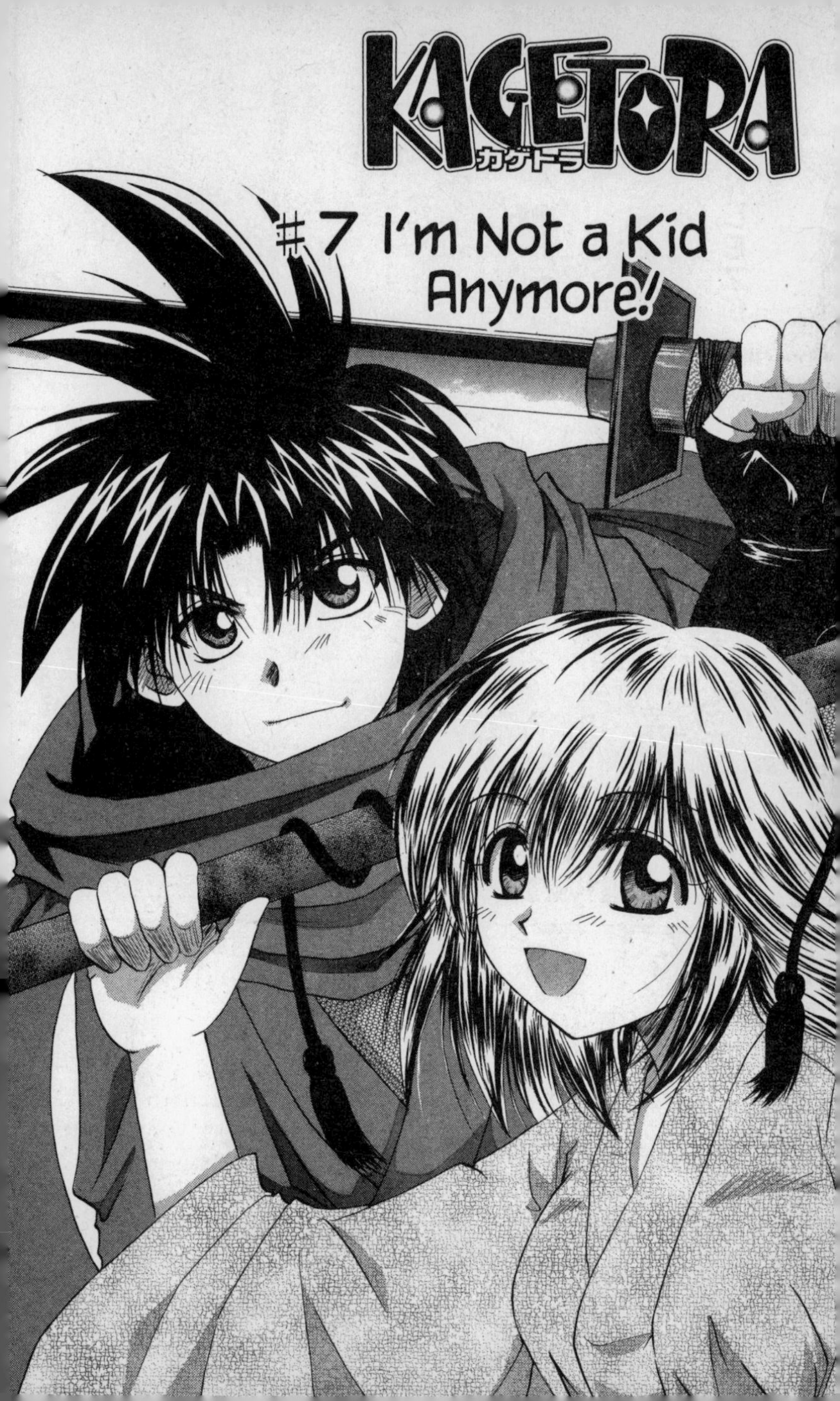
KAGETORA
カゲトラ
#7 I'm Not a Kid Anymore!

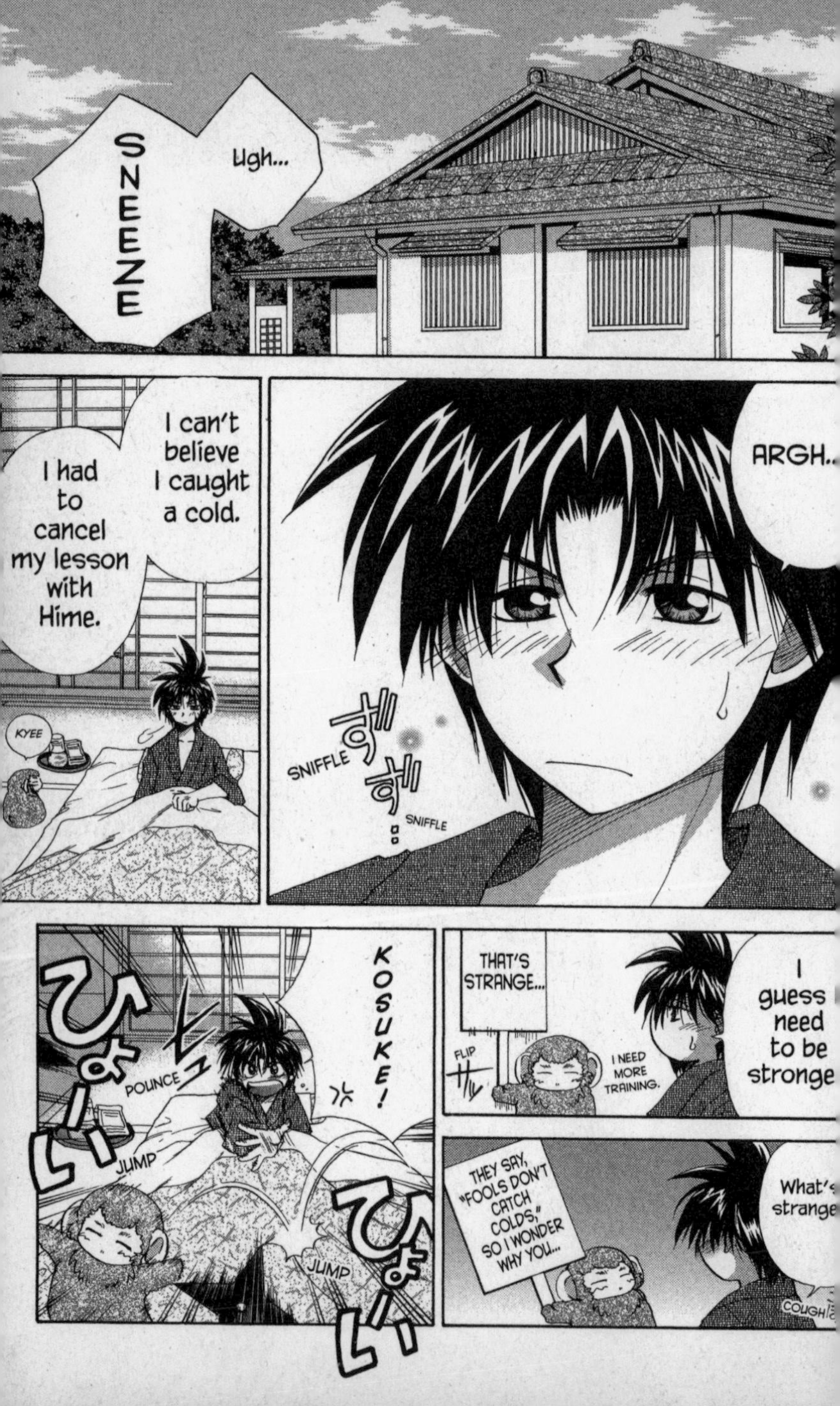
Ugh...
SNEEZE
ARGH..
SNIFFLE
SNIFFLE
I can't believe I caught a cold.
I had to cancel my lesson with Hime.
KYEE
I guess need to be stronge
THAT'S STRANGE...
FLIP
I NEED MORE TRAINING.
What's strange
THEY SAY, "FOOLS DON'T CATCH COLDS," SO I WONDER WHY YOU...
COUGH
KOSUKE!
POUNCE
JUMP
JUMP

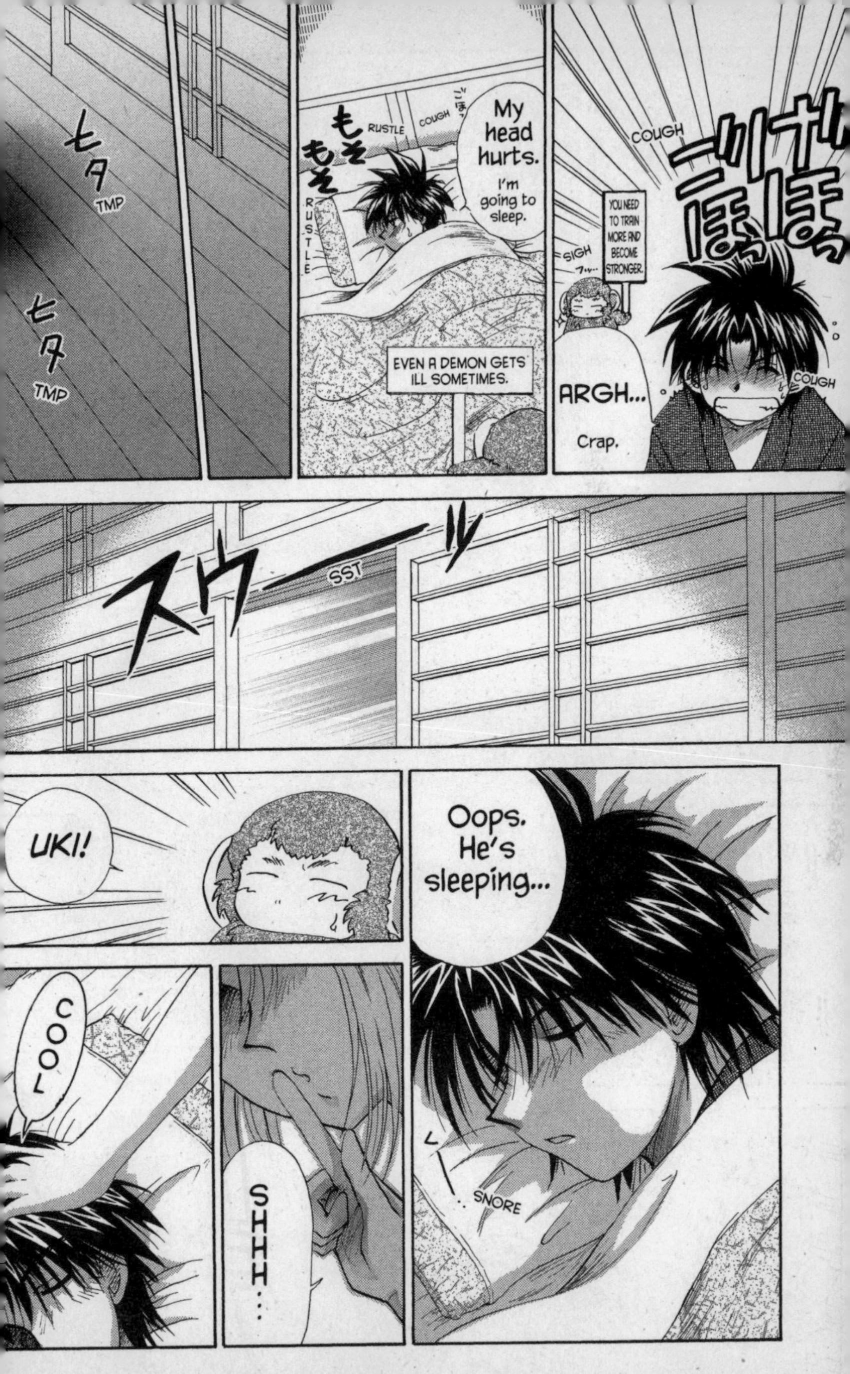
ごほっ ごほっ
COUGH
YOU NEED TO TRAIN MORE AND BECOME STRONGER.
フッ…
SIGH
ARGH...
Crap.
COUGH
ごほっ
COUGH
My head hurts.
I'm going to sleep.
もそもそ
RUSTLE
RUSTLE
EVEN A DEMON GETS ILL SOMETIMES.
ヒタ
TMP
ヒタ
TMP
スウーッ
SST
Oops. He's sleeping...
SNORE
UKI!
SHHH...
COOL

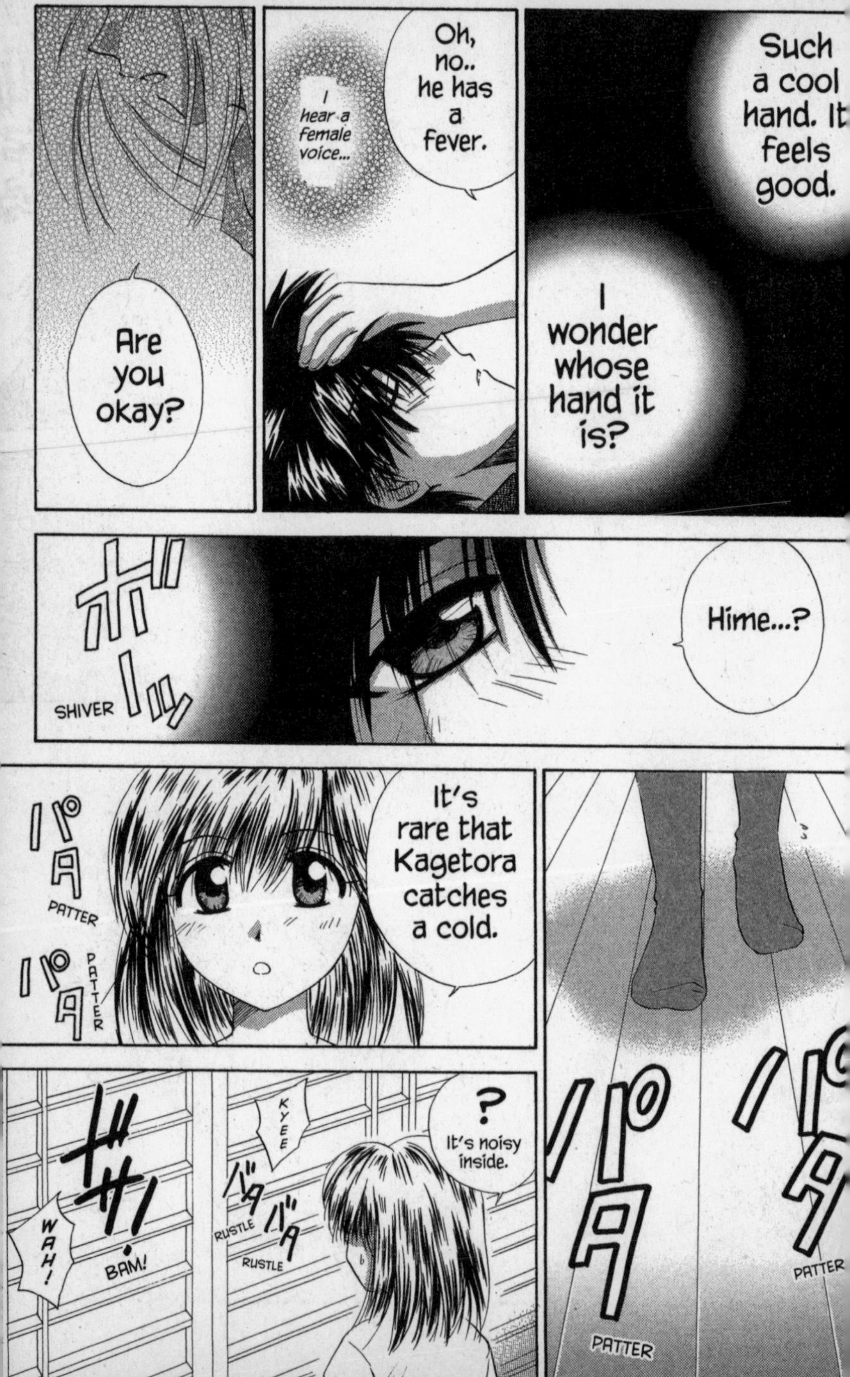
Such a cool hand. It feels good.
I wonder whose hand it is?
Oh, no.. he has a fever.
I hear a female voice...
Are you okay?
Hime...?
SHIVER
PATTER
PATTER
It's rare that Kagetora catches a cold.
PATTER
PATTER
?
It's noisy inside.
KYEE
RUSTLE
RUSTLE
BAM!
WAH!

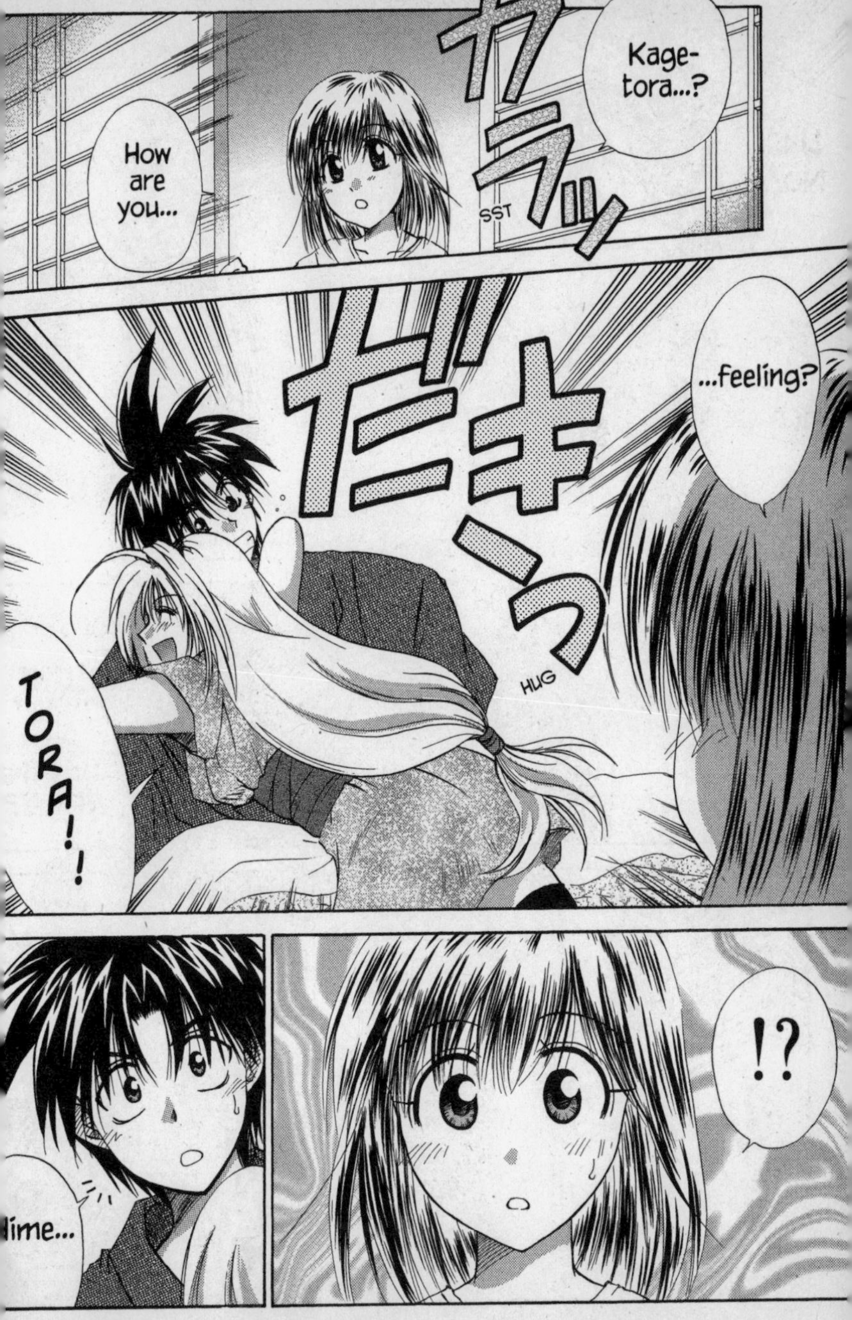
カラッ
SST
Kage-tora...?
How are you...
...feeling?
だきっ
HUG
TORA!!
!?
ime...

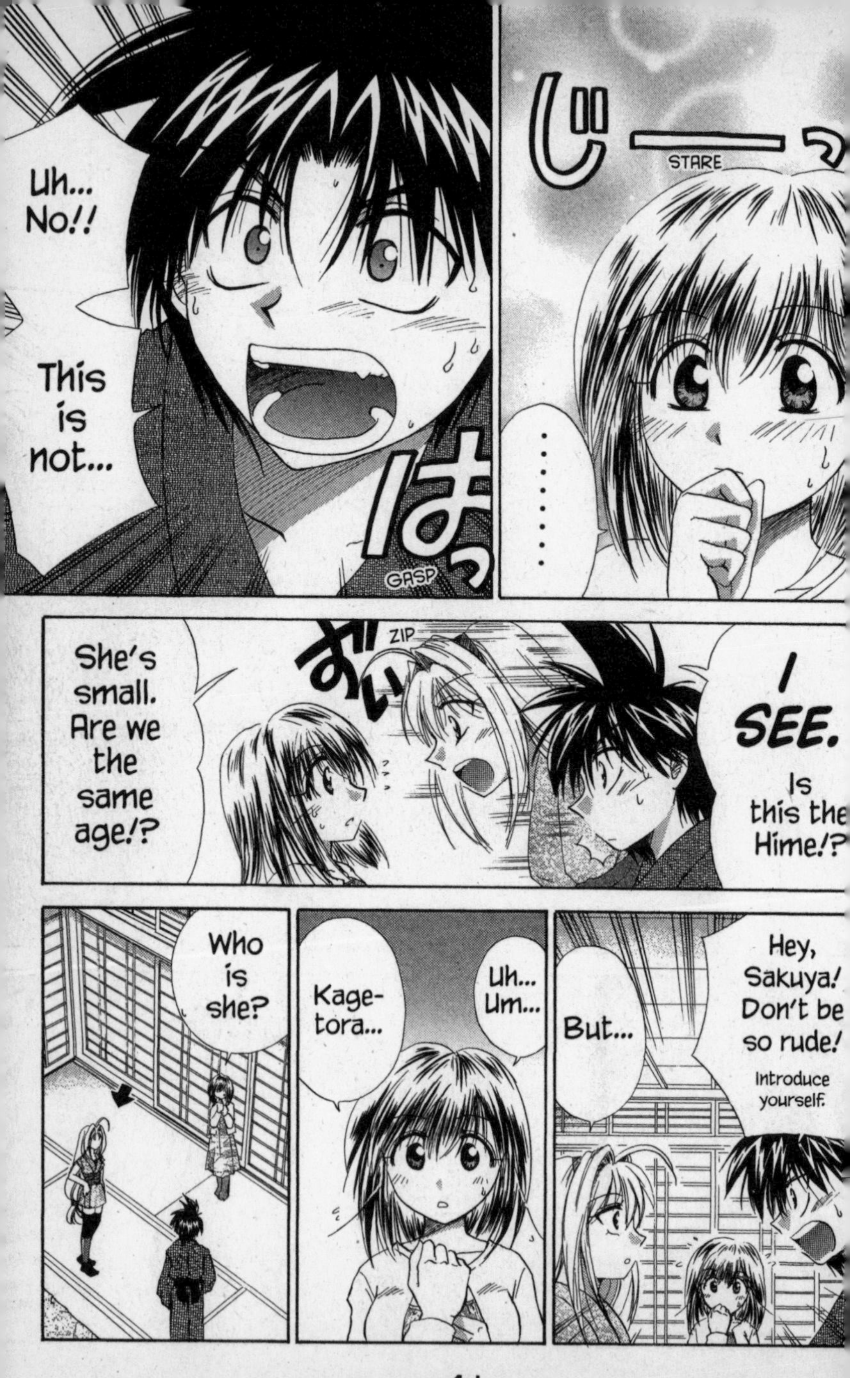
じーっ
STARE
......
Uh... No!!
This is not...
はっ
GASP
I SEE. Is this the Hime!?
ずい
ZIP
She's small. Are we the same age!?
Hey, Sakuya! Don't be so rude! Introduce yourself.
But...
Uh... Um...
Kage-tora...
Who is she?

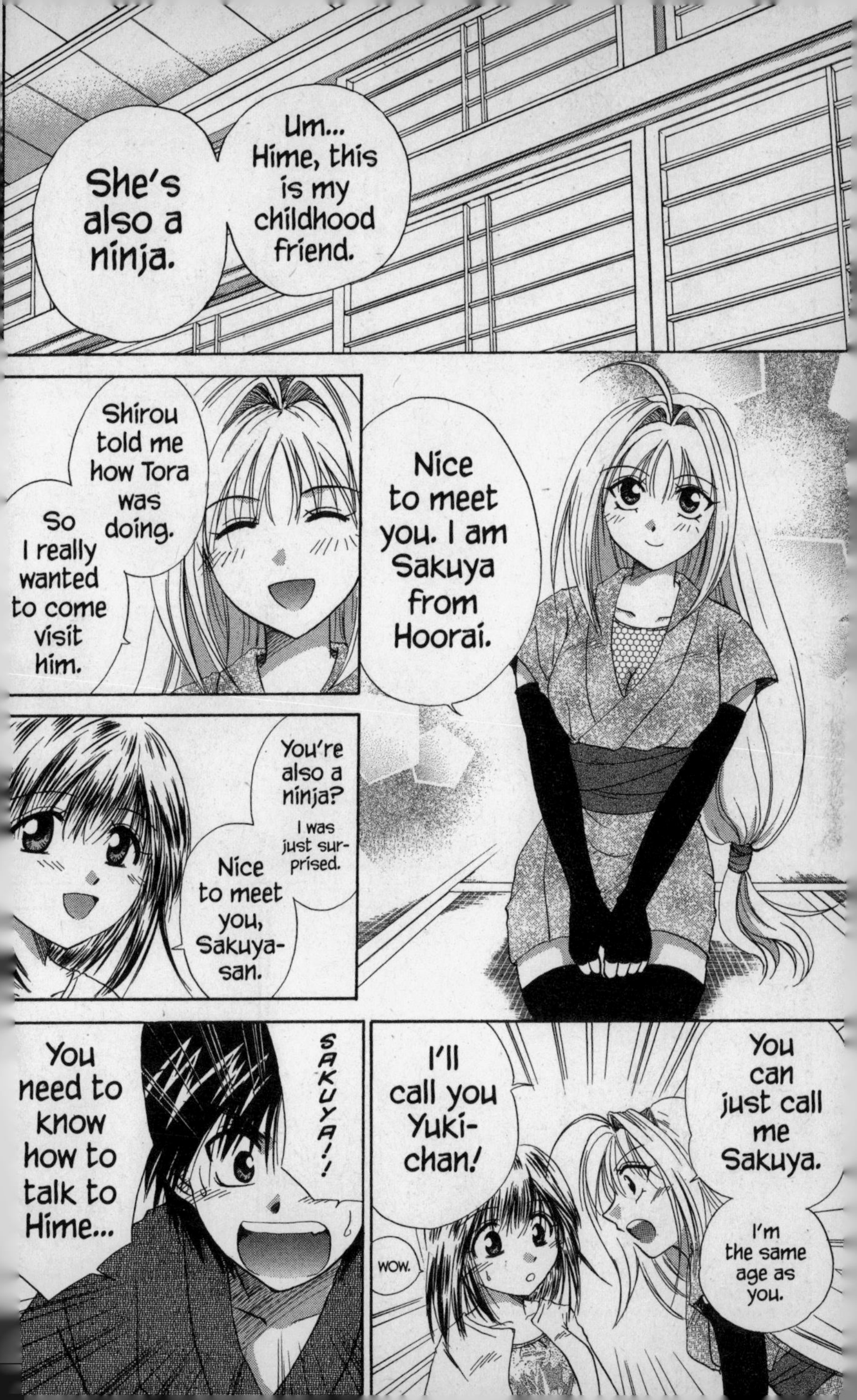
Um... Hime, this is my childhood friend.
She's also a ninja.
Nice to meet you. I am Sakuya from Hoorai.
Shirou told me how Tora was doing.
So I really wanted to come visit him.
You're also a ninja?
I was just surprised.
Nice to meet you, Sakuya-san.
You can just call me Sakuya.
I'm the same age as you.
I'll call you Yuki-chan!
WOW.
SAKUYA!!
You need to know how to talk to Hime...

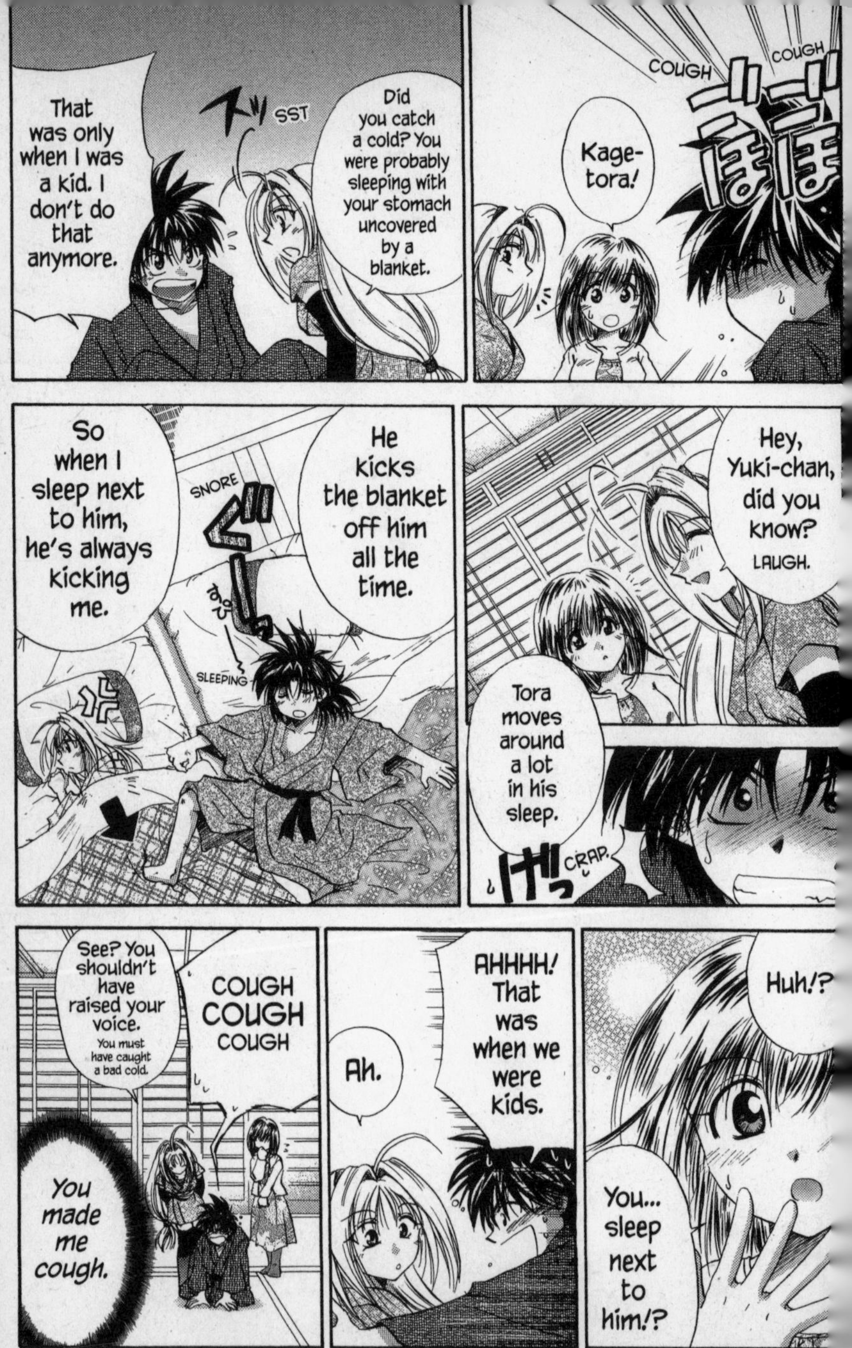
COUGH
COUGH
Kage-tora!
Did you catch a cold? You were probably sleeping with your stomach uncovered by a blanket.
SST
That was only when I was a kid. I don't do that anymore.
Hey, Yuki-chan, did you know?
LAUGH.
Tora moves around a lot in his sleep.
CRAP.
He kicks the blanket off him all the time.
So when I sleep next to him, he's always kicking me.
SNORE
SLEEPING
Huh!?
You... sleep next to him!?
AHHHH! That was when we were kids.
Ah.
COUGH COUGH COUGH
See? You shouldn't have raised your voice.
You must have caught a bad cold.
You made me cough.

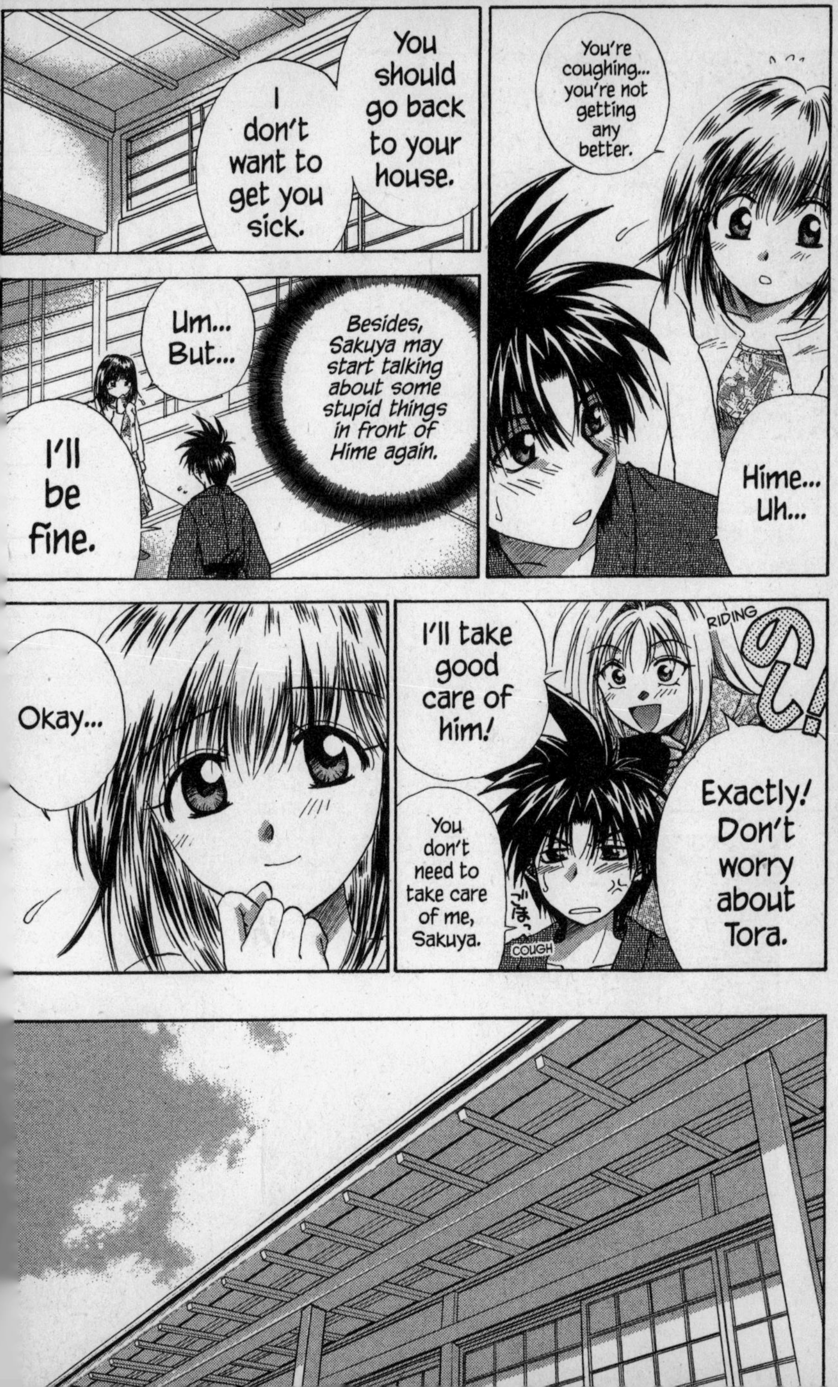
You're coughing... you're not getting any better.
Hime... Uh...
You should go back to your house.
I don't want to get you sick.
Besides, Sakuya may start talking about some stupid things in front of Hime again.
Um... But...
I'll be fine.
RIDING
I'll take good care of him!
Exactly! Don't worry about Tora.
You don't need to take care of me, Sakuya.
COUGH
Okay...

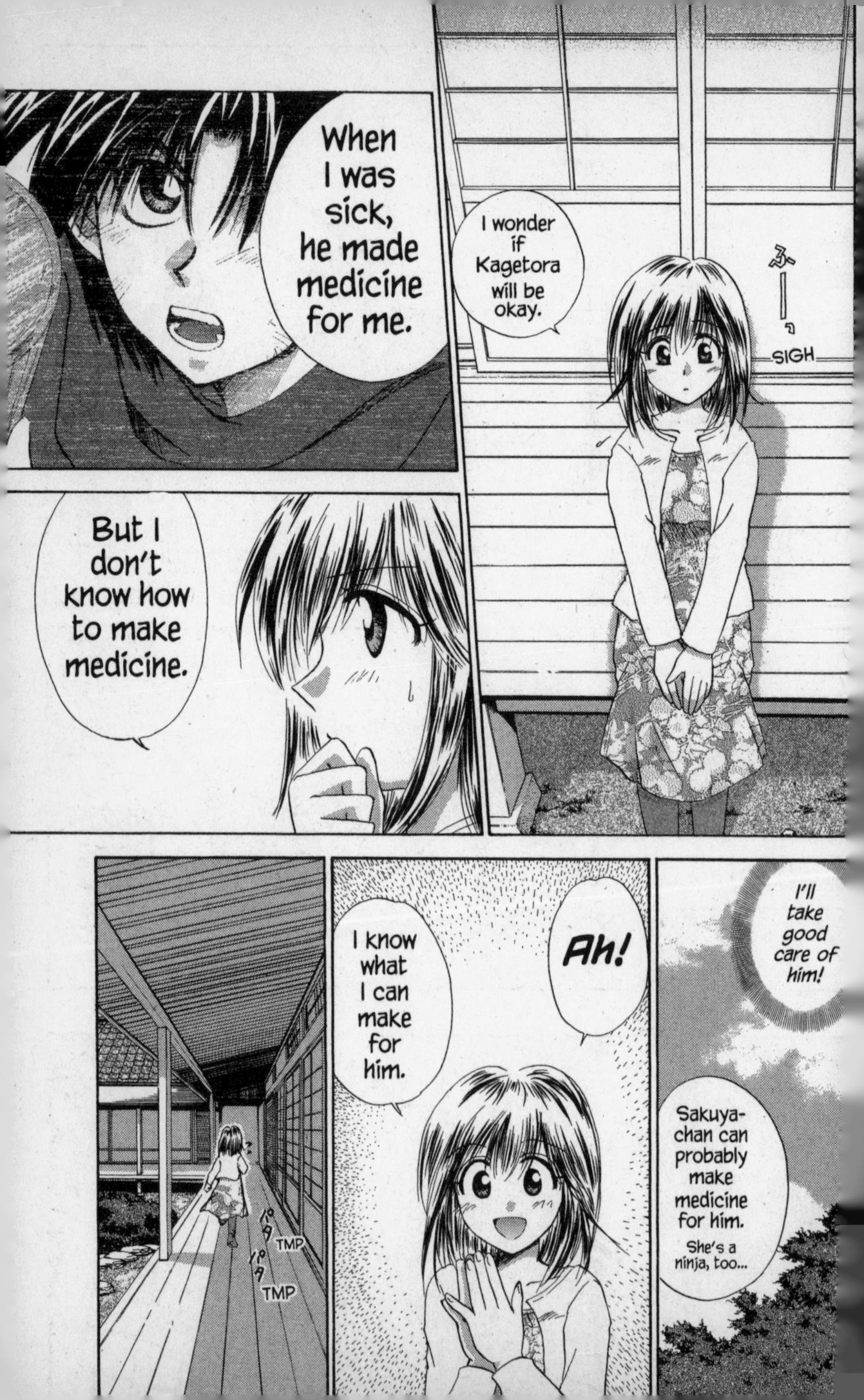
I wonder if Kagetora will be okay.
ふー
SIGH
When I was sick, he made medicine for me.
But I don't know how to make medicine.
I'll take good care of him!
Sakuya-chan can probably make medicine for him.
She's a ninja, too...
Ah!
I know what I can make for him.
パタ
TMP
パタ
TMP

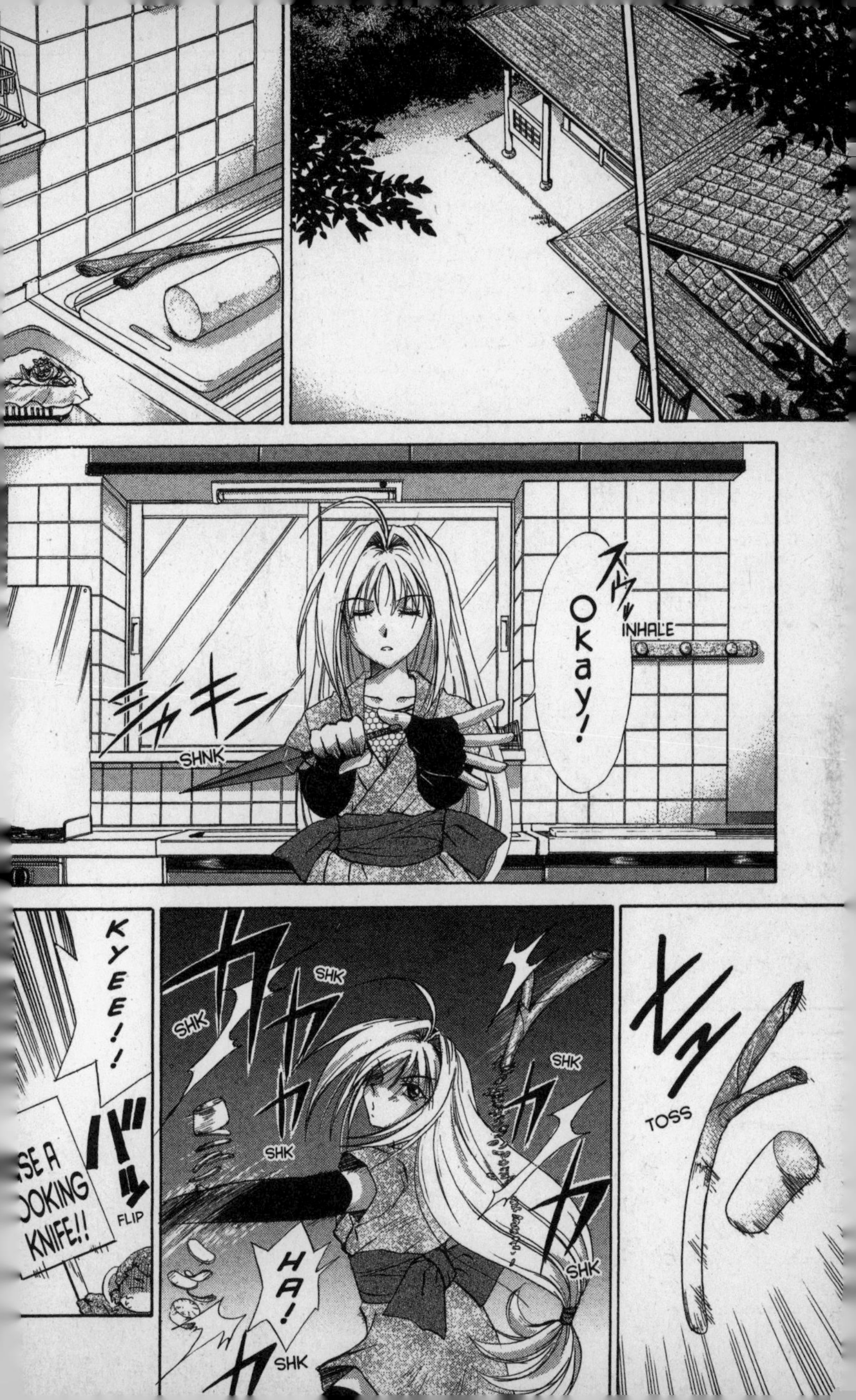

INHALE
Okay!
シャキーン
SHNK
TOSS
SHK
SHK
SHK
SHK
SHK
HA!
SHK
KYEE!!
バッ
FLIP
SE A
OOKING
KNIFE!!

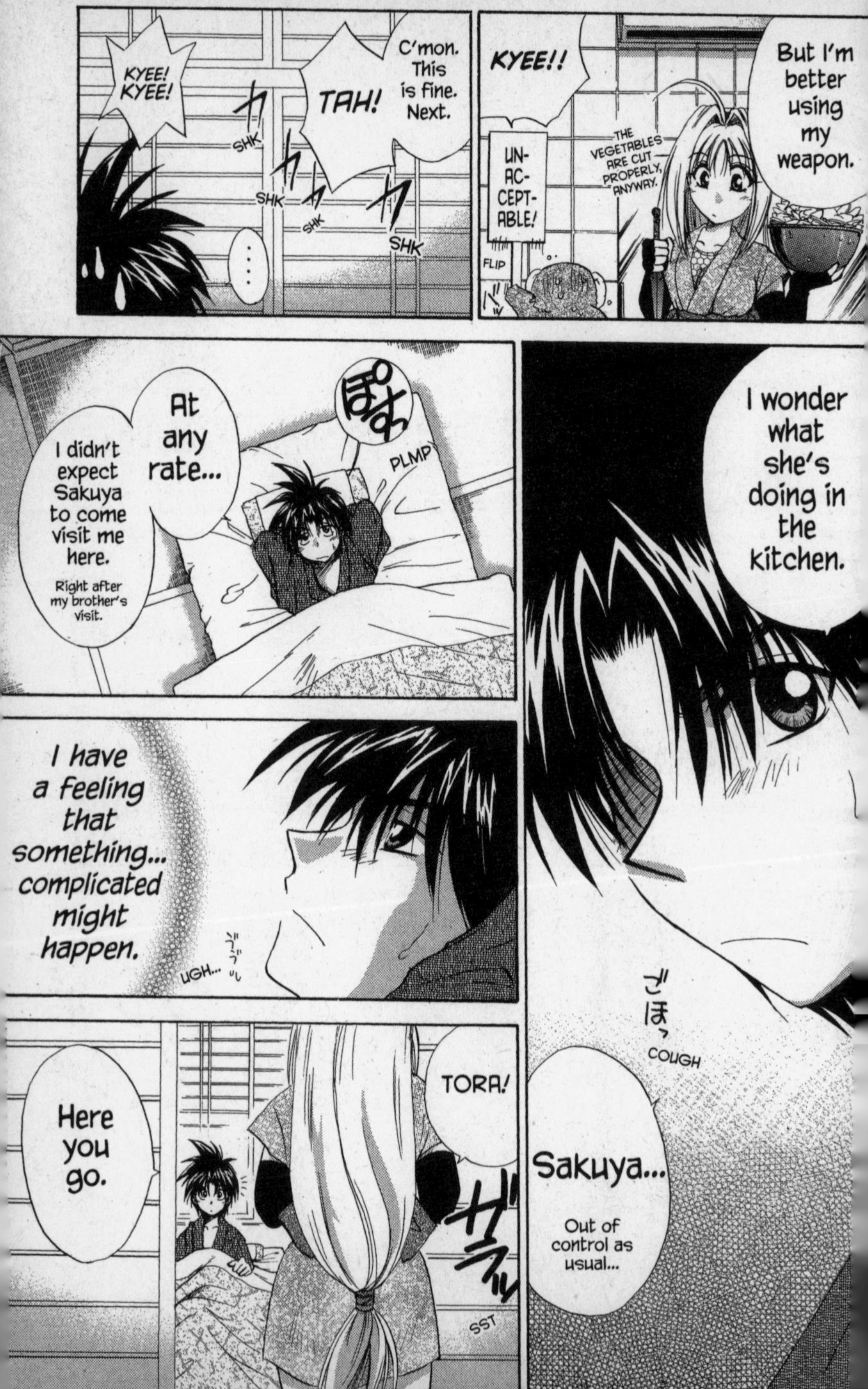
KYEE!!
But I'm better using my weapon.
UN-ACCEPT-ABLE!
THE VEGETABLES ARE CUT PROPERLY, ANYWAY.
FLIP
C'mon. This is fine. Next.
TAH!
KYEE! KYEE!
SHK
SHK
SHK
SHK
...
I wonder what she's doing in the kitchen.
ごほっ
COUGH
Sakuya...
Out of control as usual...
At any rate...
I didn't expect Sakuya to come visit me here.
Right after my brother's visit.
PLMP
I have a feeling that something... complicated might happen.
UGH...
TORA!
Here you go.
SST

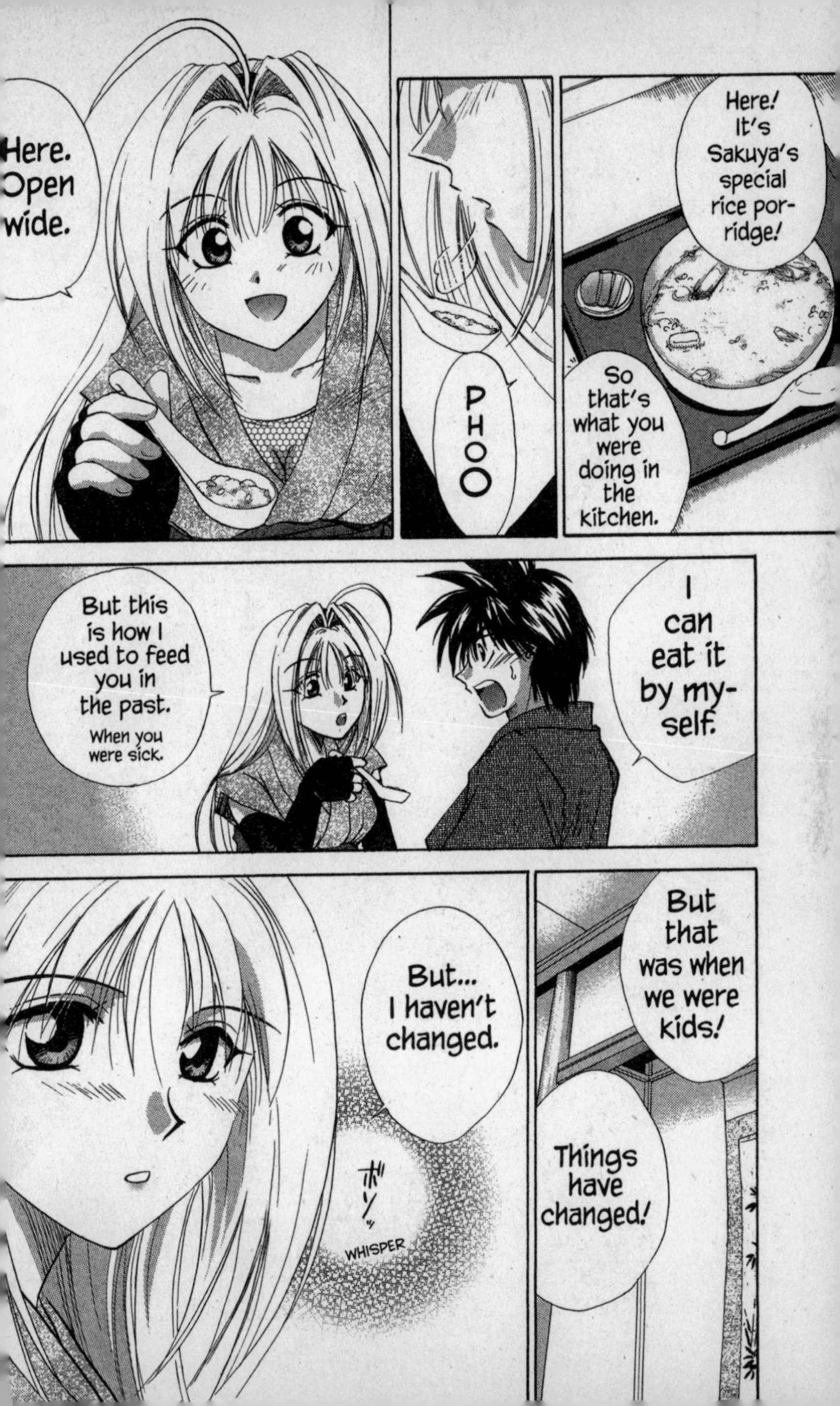
Here! It's Sakuya's special rice porridge!
So that's what you were doing in the kitchen.
PHOO
Here. Open wide.
I can eat it by myself.
But this is how I used to feed you in the past.
When you were sick.
But that was when we were kids!
Things have changed!
But... I haven't changed.
ボソ
WHISPER

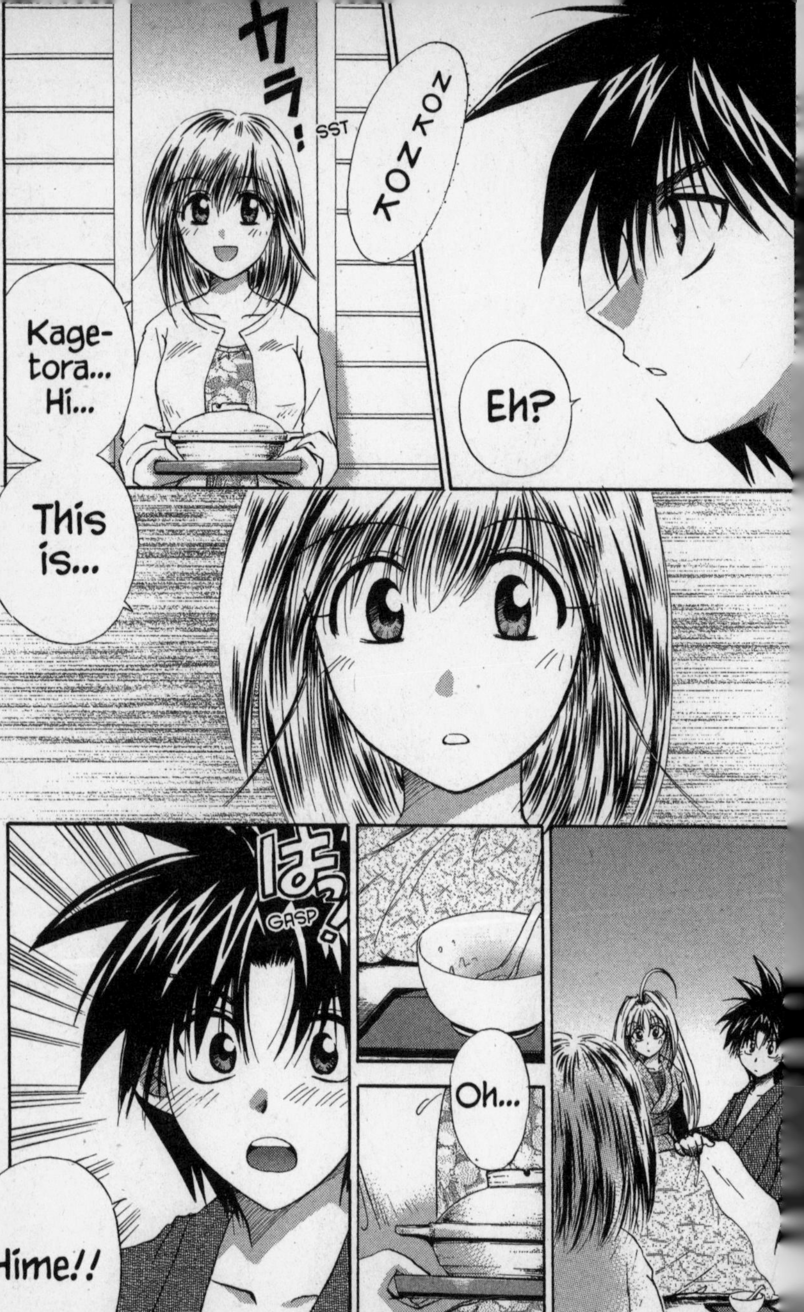
TON TON
Eh?
ヤラ!
SST
Kage-tora... Hi...
This is...
Oh...
はっ!
GASP
Hime!!

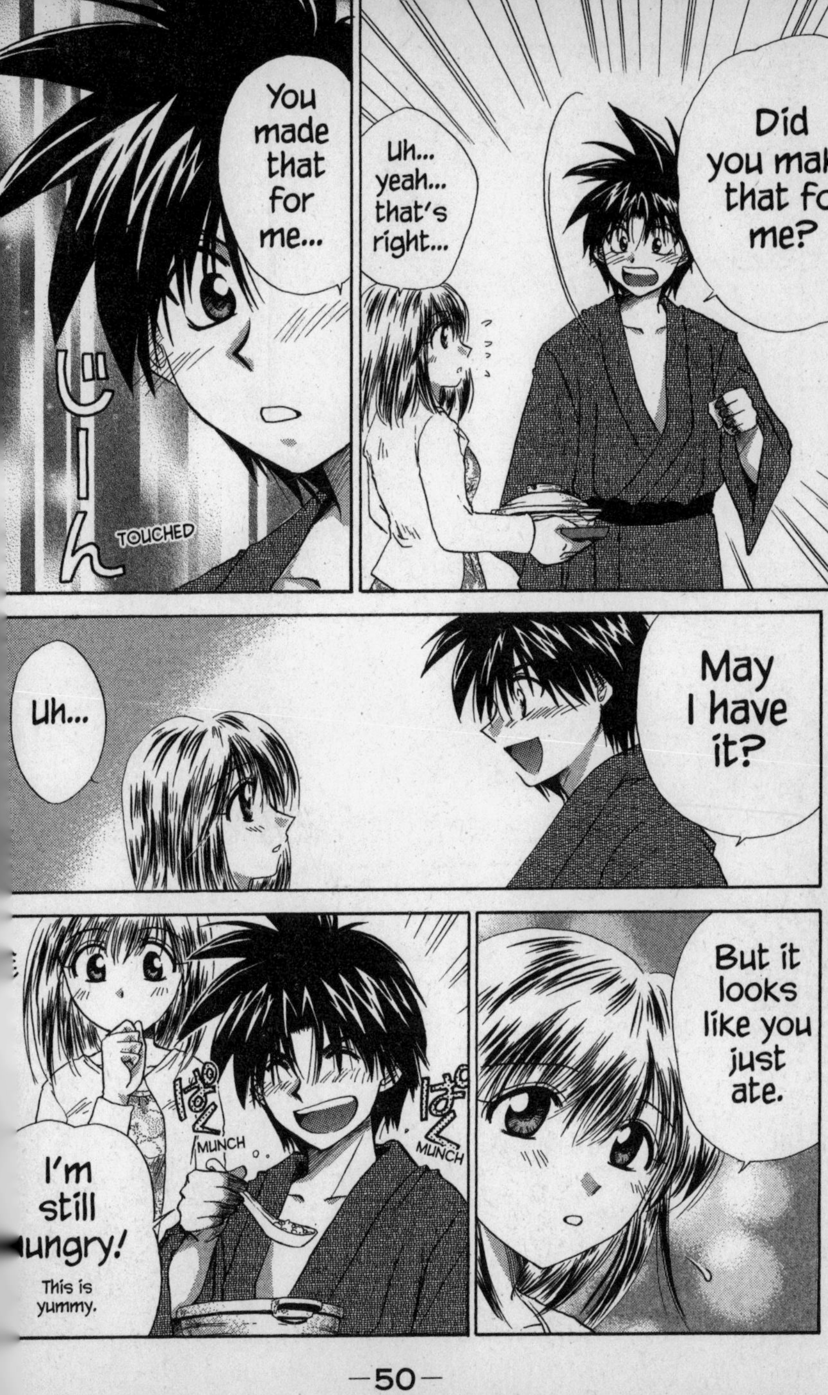

Did you make that for me?
uh... yeah... that's right...
You made that for me...
じーん
TOUCHED
May I have it?
uh...
But it looks like you just ate.
ぱく
MUNCH
ぱく
MUNCH
I'm still ungry!
This is yummy.

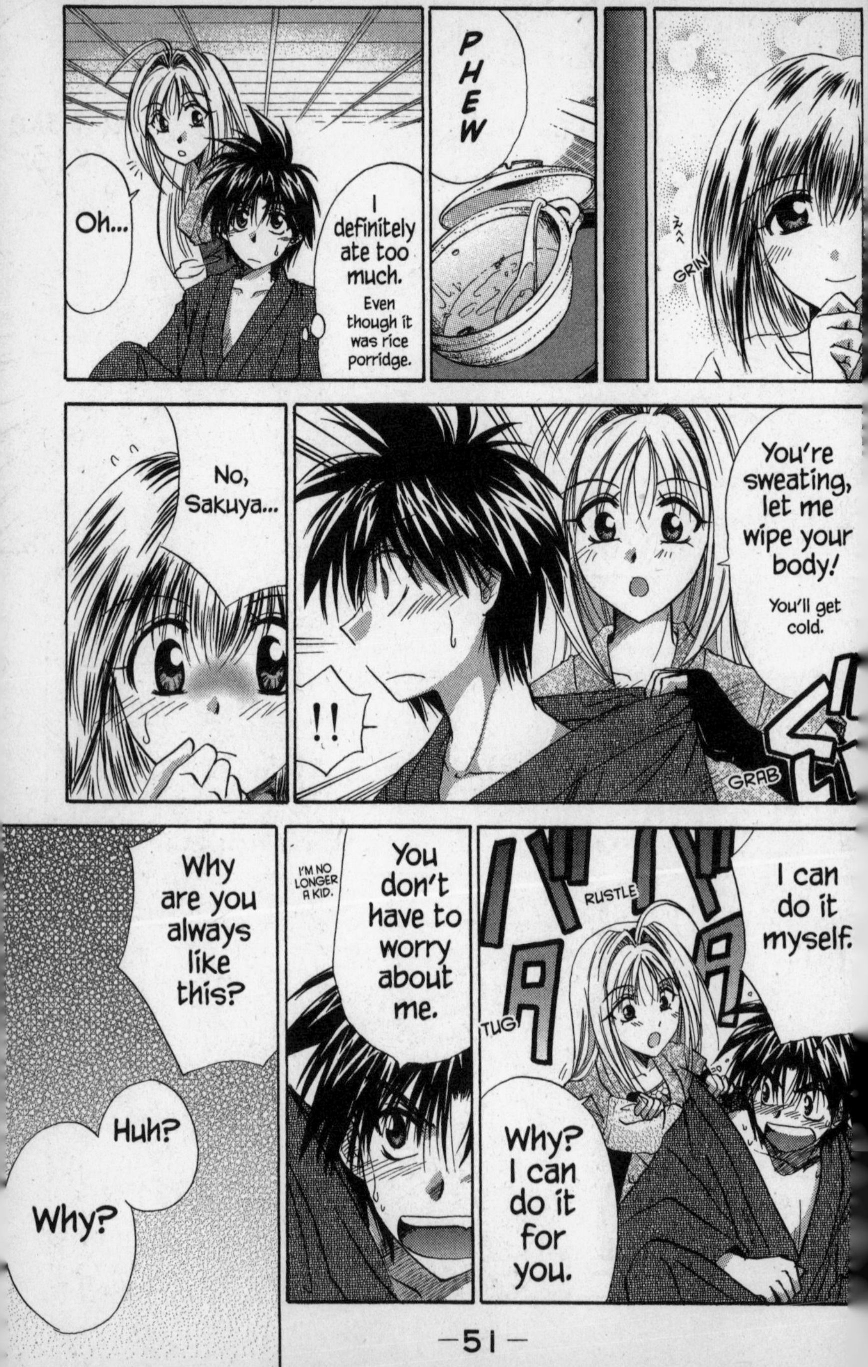
GRIN
PHEW
I definitely ate too much.
Even though it was rice porridge.
Oh...
You're sweating, let me wipe your body!
You'll get cold.
GRAB
!!
No, Sakuya...
I can do it myself.
RUSTLE
TUG
Why? I can do it for you.
You don't have to worry about me.
I'M NO LONGER A KID.
Why are you always like this?
Huh?
Why?

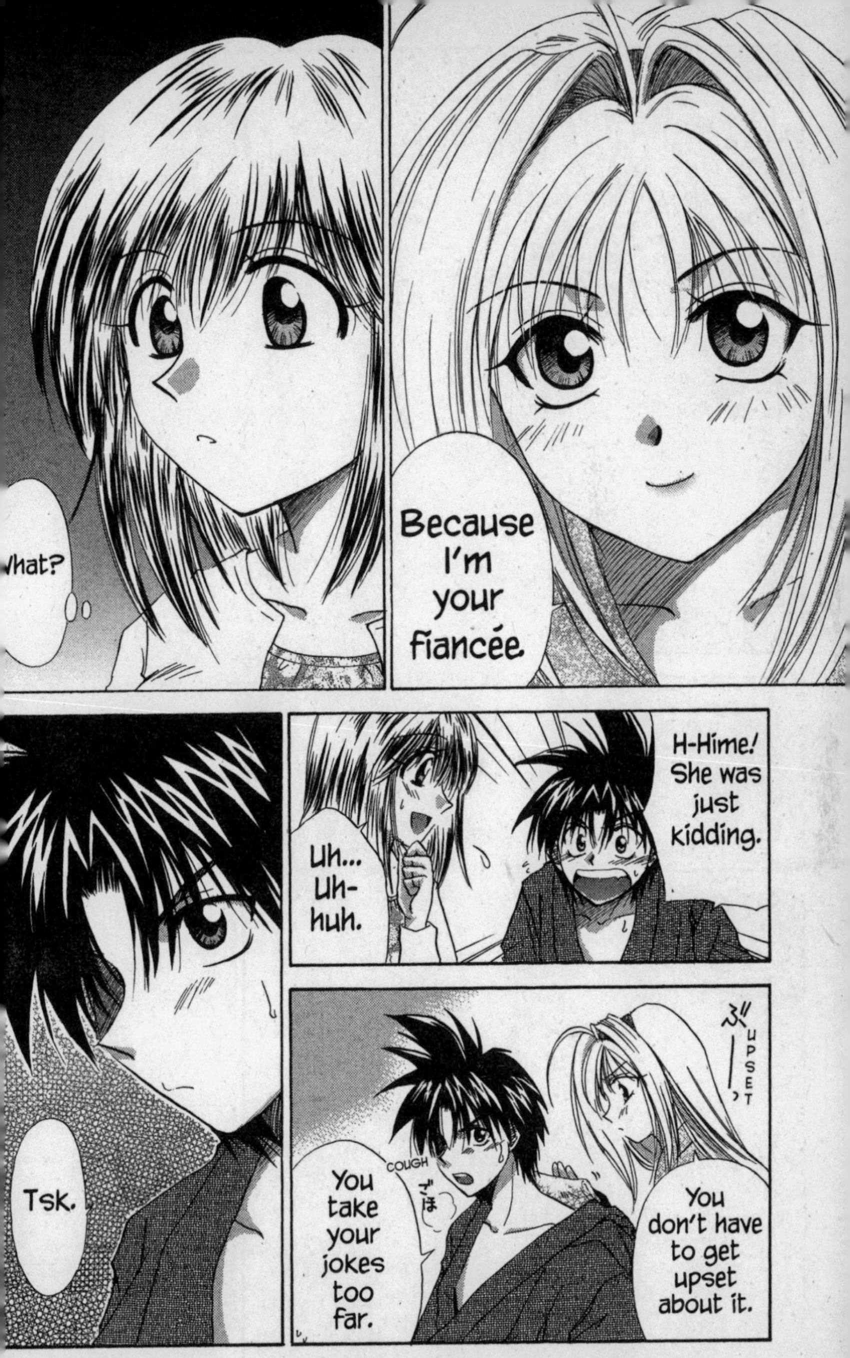
Because I'm your fiancée.
What?
H-Hime! She was just kidding.
Uh... Uh-huh.
ぶー!, UPSET
You don't have to get upset about it.
COUGH ごほ
You take your jokes too far.
Tsk.

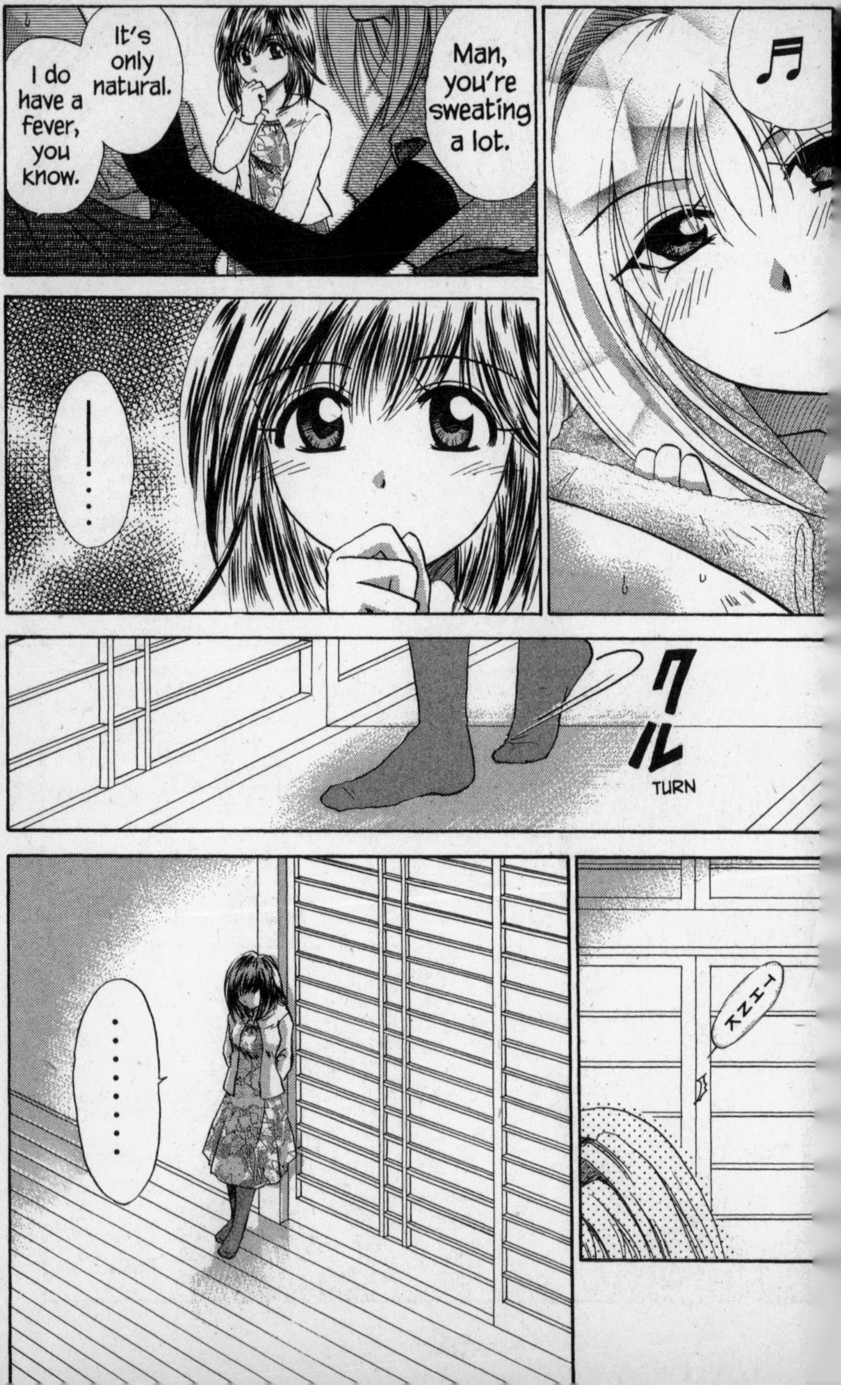
♬
Man, you're sweating a lot.
It's only natural.
I do have a fever, you know.
—....
クル
TURN
....

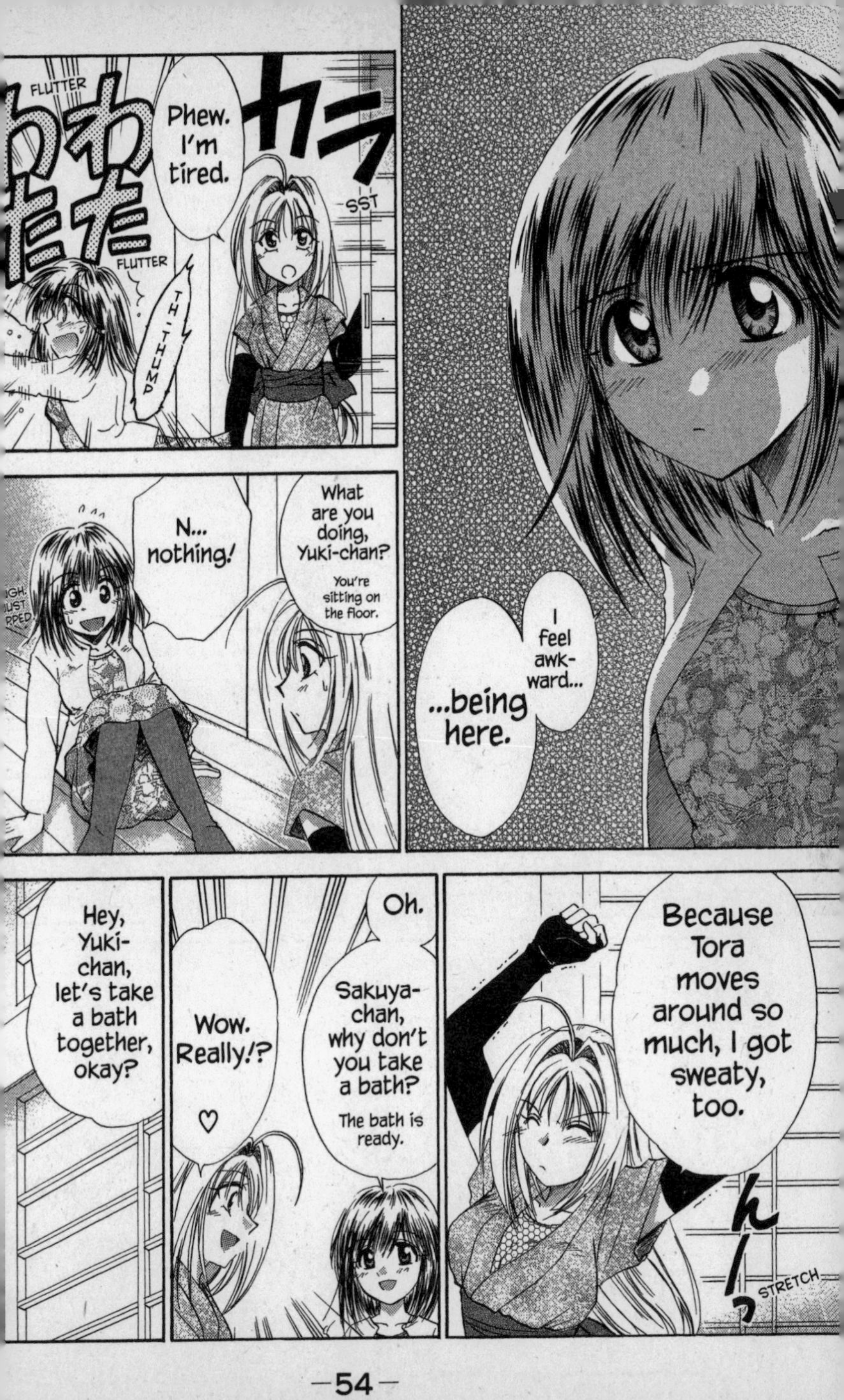
I feel awk-ward...
...being here.
カラ
SST
Phew. I'm tired.
わたわた
FLUTTER
FLUTTER
TH-THUMP
What are you doing, Yuki-chan?
You're sitting on the floor.
N... nothing!
Because Tora moves around so much, I got sweaty, too.
んーっ
STRETCH
Oh.
Sakuya-chan, why don't you take a bath?
The bath is ready.
Wow. Really!?
♡
Hey, Yuki-chan, let's take a bath together, okay?

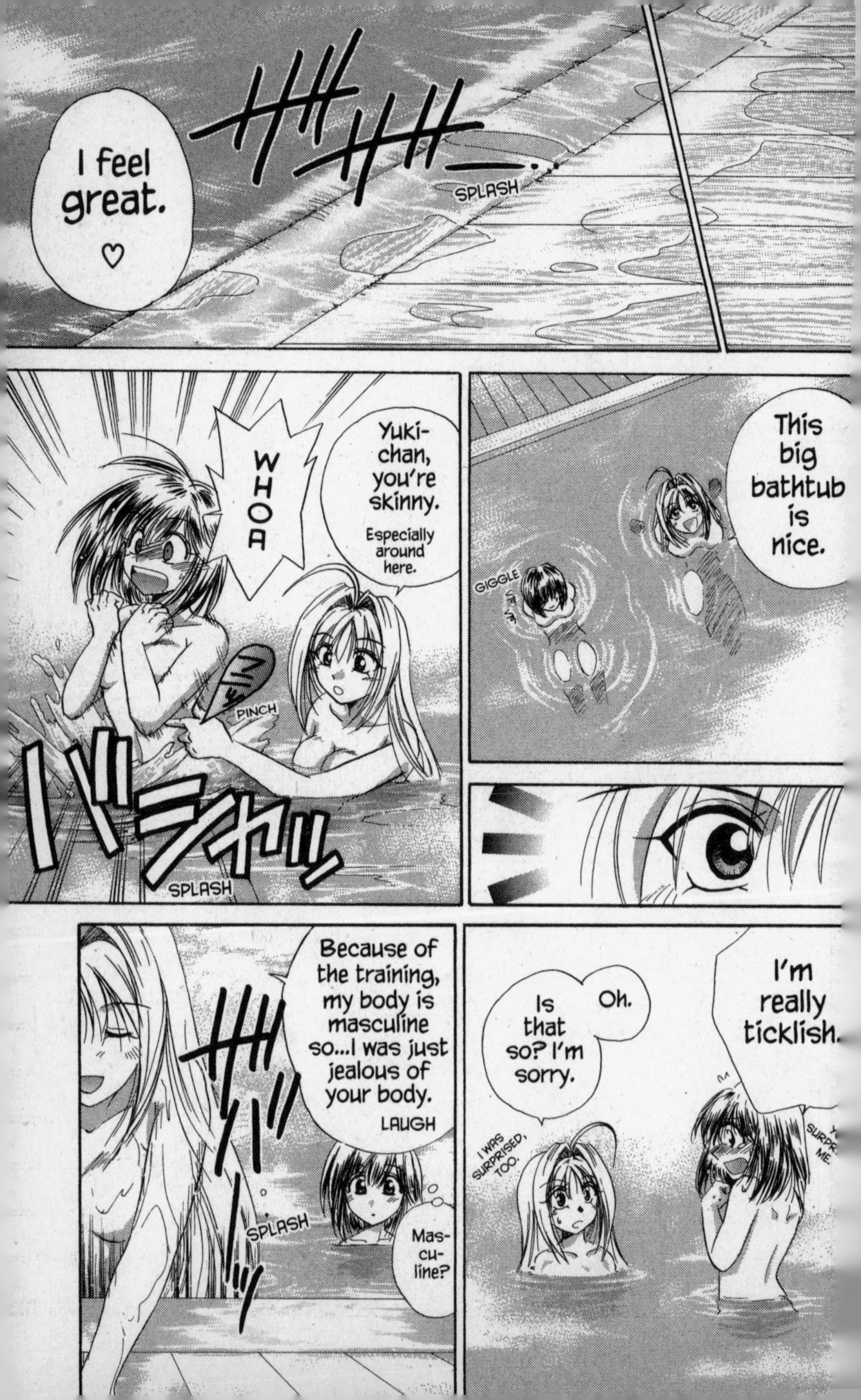
I feel great. ♡
SPLASH
This big bathtub is nice.
GIGGLE
Yuki-chan, you're skinny.
Especially around here.
WHOA
PINCH
SPLASH
I'm really ticklish.
Oh.
Is that so? I'm sorry.
I WAS SURPRISED, TOO.
Because of the training, my body is masculine so...I was just jealous of your body.
LAUGH
SPLASH
Mas-cu-line?

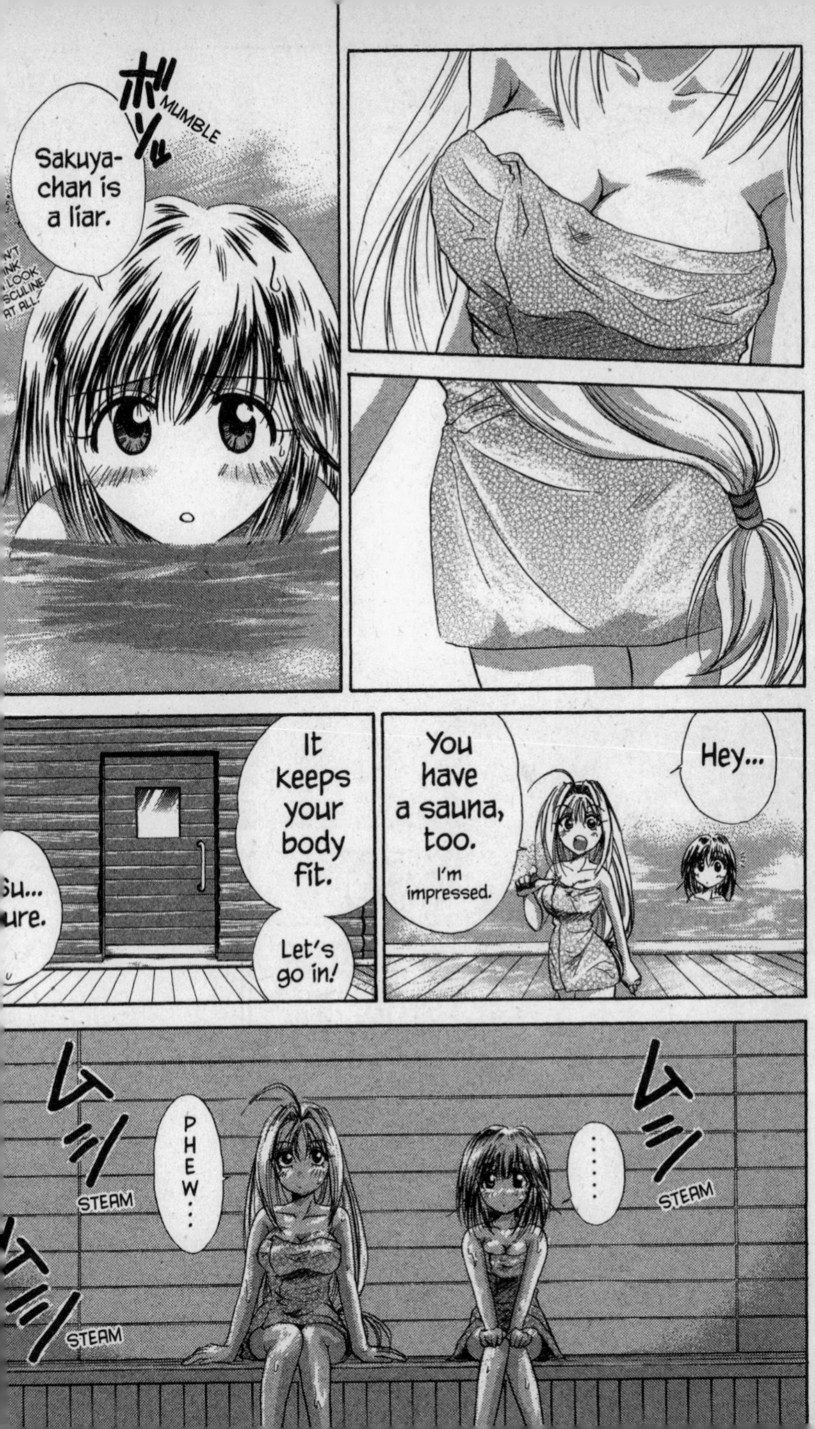
ボソ
MUMBLE
Sakuya-chan is a liar.
Hey...
You have a sauna, too.
I'm impressed.
It keeps your body fit.
Let's go in!
STEAM
......
PHEW...
STEAM
STEAM

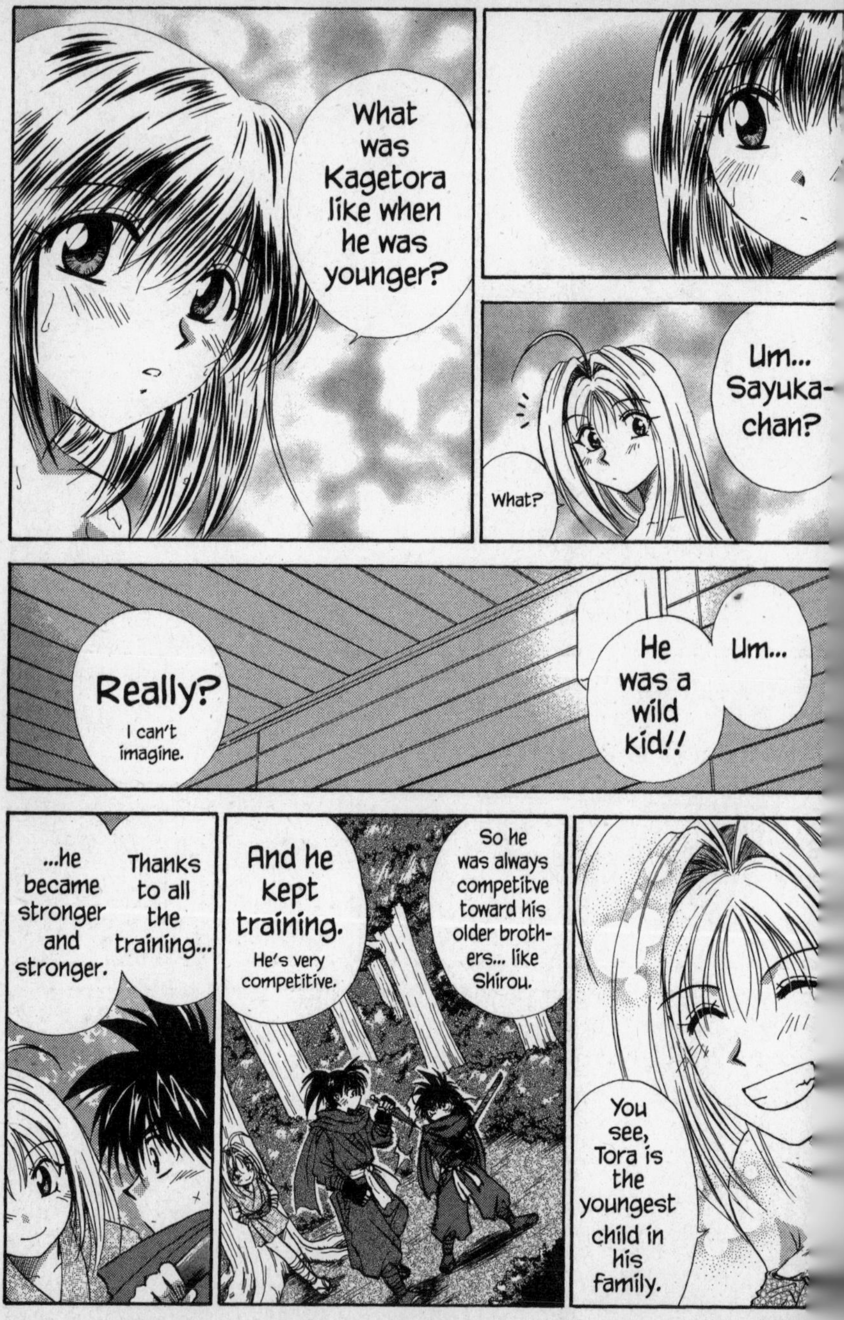
Um... Sayuka-chan?
What?
What was Kagetora like when he was younger?
Um...
He was a wild kid!!
Really?
I can't imagine.
You see, Tora is the youngest child in his family.
So he was always competitve toward his older broth-ers... like Shirou.
And he kept training.
He's very competitive.
Thanks to all the training...
...he became stronger and stronger.

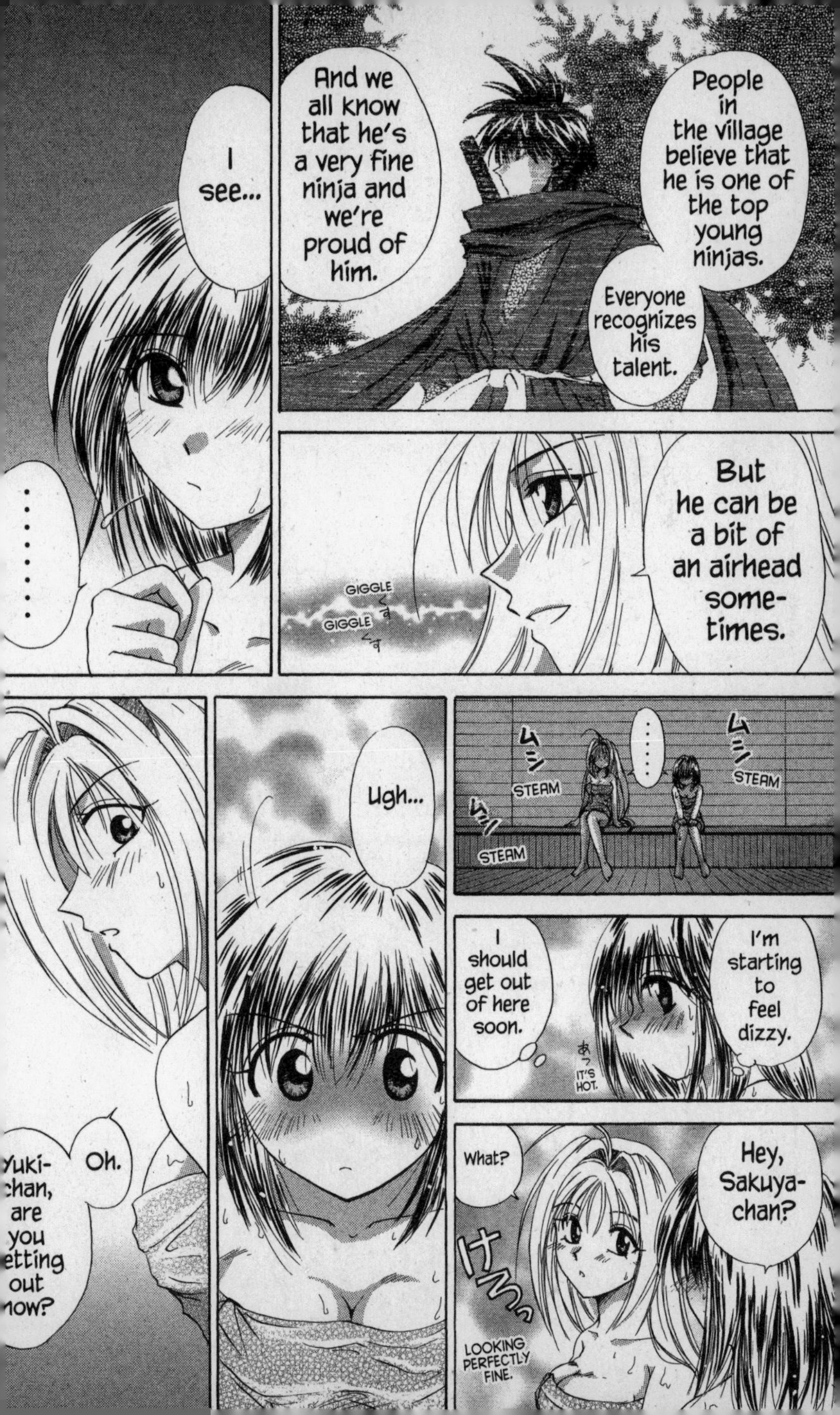
People in the village believe that he is one of the top young ninjas.
Everyone recognizes his talent.
And we all know that he's a very fine ninja and we're proud of him.
But he can be a bit of an airhead sometimes.
GIGGLE くす
GIGGLE くす
I see...
......
......
ムシ STEAM
ムシ STEAM
ムシ STEAM
I'm starting to feel dizzy.
I should get out of here soon.
あつ IT'S HOT.
Hey, Sakuya-chan?
What?
けろっ LOOKING PERFECTLY FINE.
Ugh...
Oh.
Yuki-chan, are you etting out now?

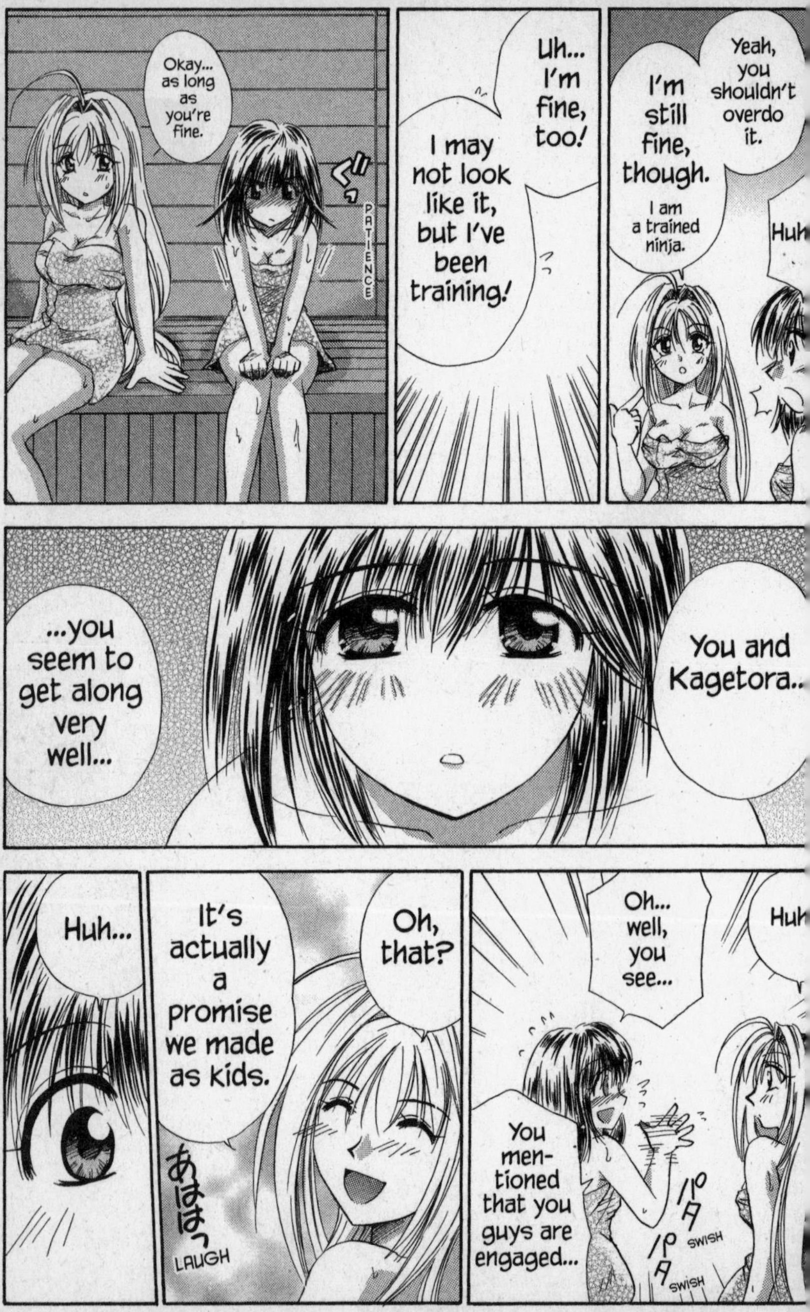
Yeah, you shouldn't overdo it.
Huh
I'm still fine, though.
I am a trained ninja.
Uh... I'm fine, too!
I may not look like it, but I've been training!
Okay... as long as you're fine.
PATIENCE
You and Kagetora...
...you seem to get along very well...
Huh
Oh... well, you see...
You mentioned that you guys are engaged...
パタ SWISH
パタ SWISH
Oh, that?
It's actually a promise we made as kids.
あははっ LAUGH
Huh...

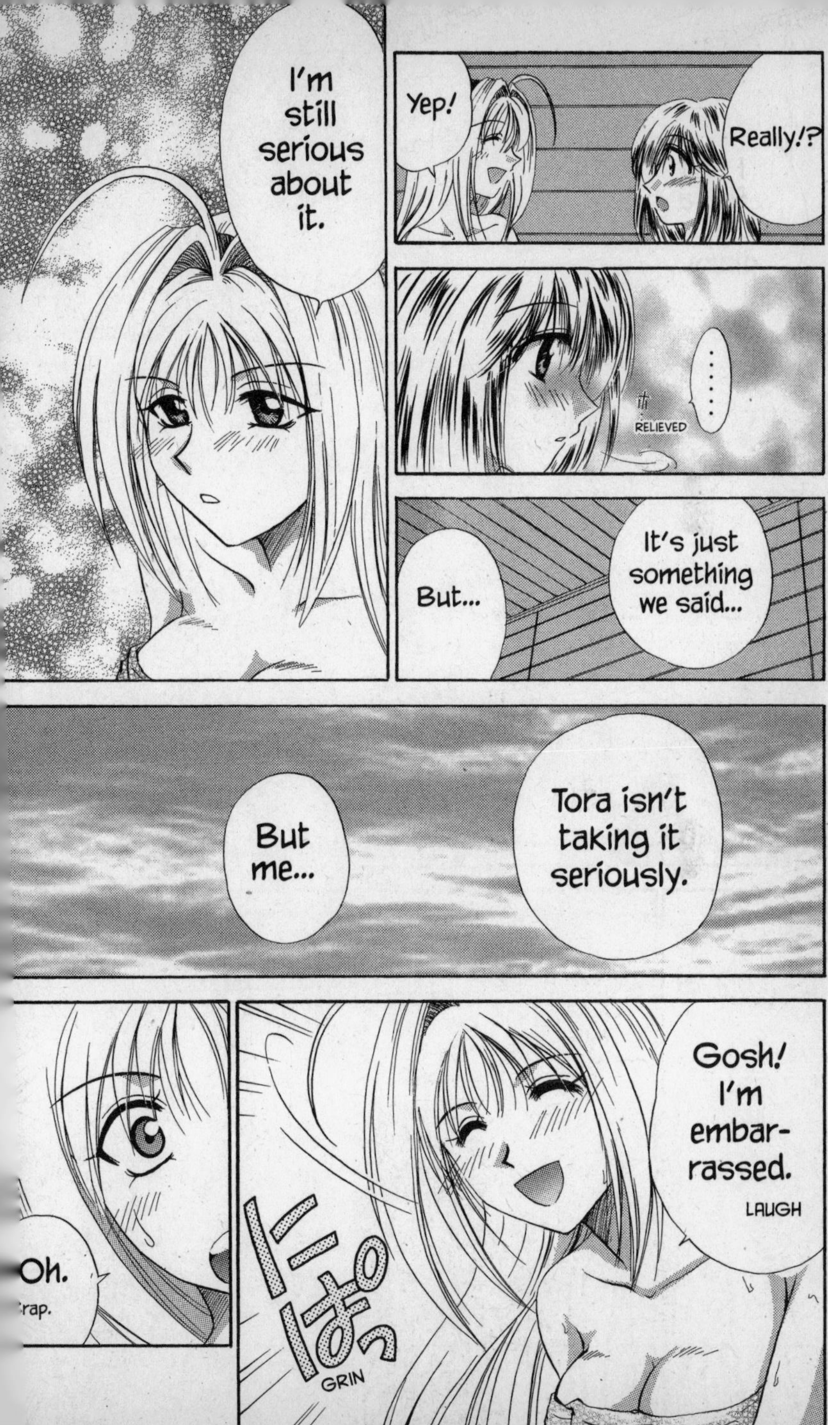
Really!?
Yep!
......
RELIEVED
It's just something we said...
But...
I'm still serious about it.
Tora isn't taking it seriously.
But me...
Gosh! I'm embar-rassed.
LAUGH
にぱっ
GRIN
Oh.
Crap.

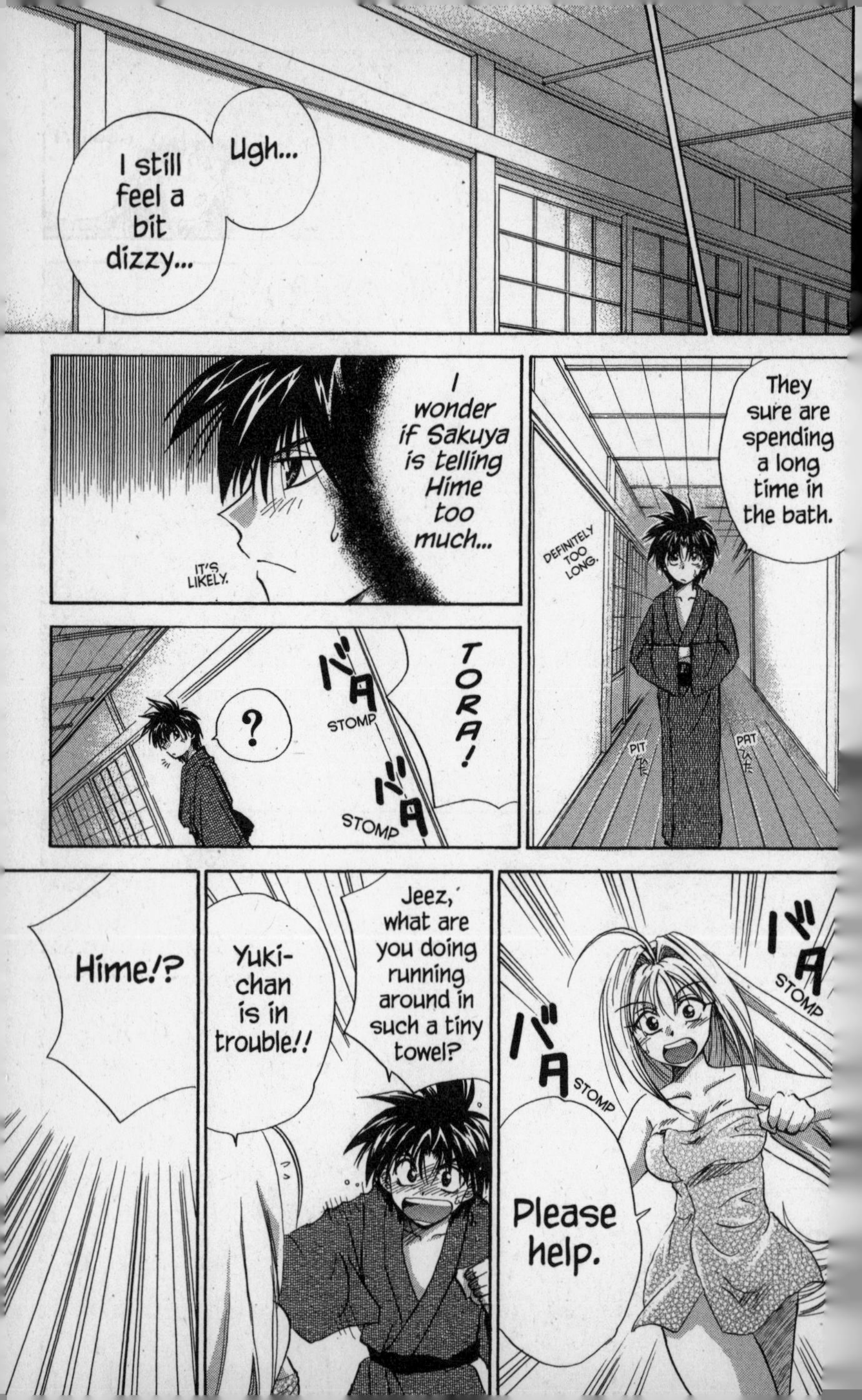
Ugh...
I still feel a bit dizzy...
They sure are spending a long time in the bath.
DEFINITELY TOO LONG.
PIT
PAT
I wonder if Sakuya is telling Hime too much...
IT'S LIKELY.
TORA!
STOMP
STOMP
?
STOMP
STOMP
Please help.
Jeez, what are you doing running around in such a tiny towel?
Yuki-chan is in trouble!!
Hime!?

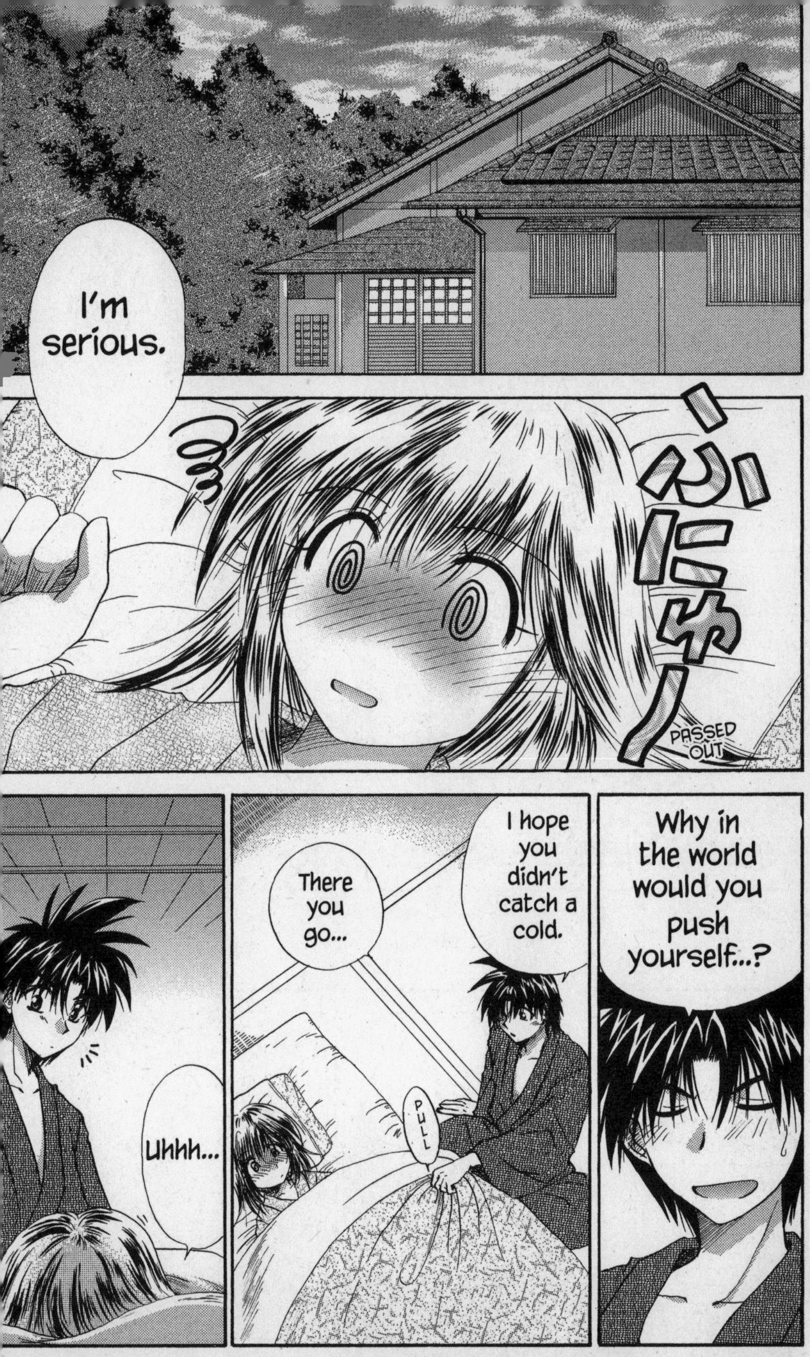
I'm serious.
ふにゅ～
PASSED OUT
Why in the world would you push yourself...?
I hope you didn't catch a cold.
There you go...
PULL
Uhhh...

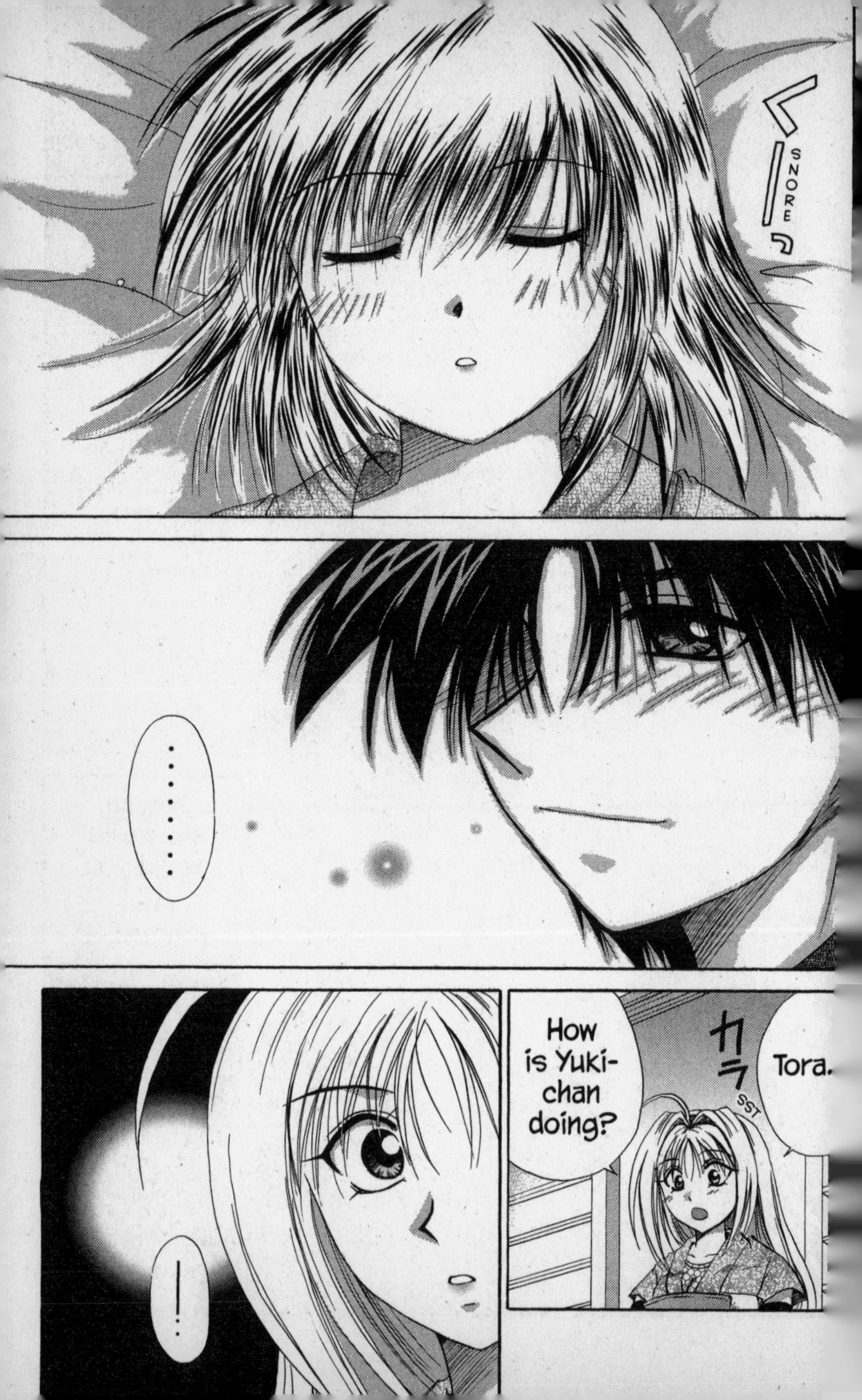
SNORE
......
Tora.
カラ SST
How is Yuki-chan doing?
!

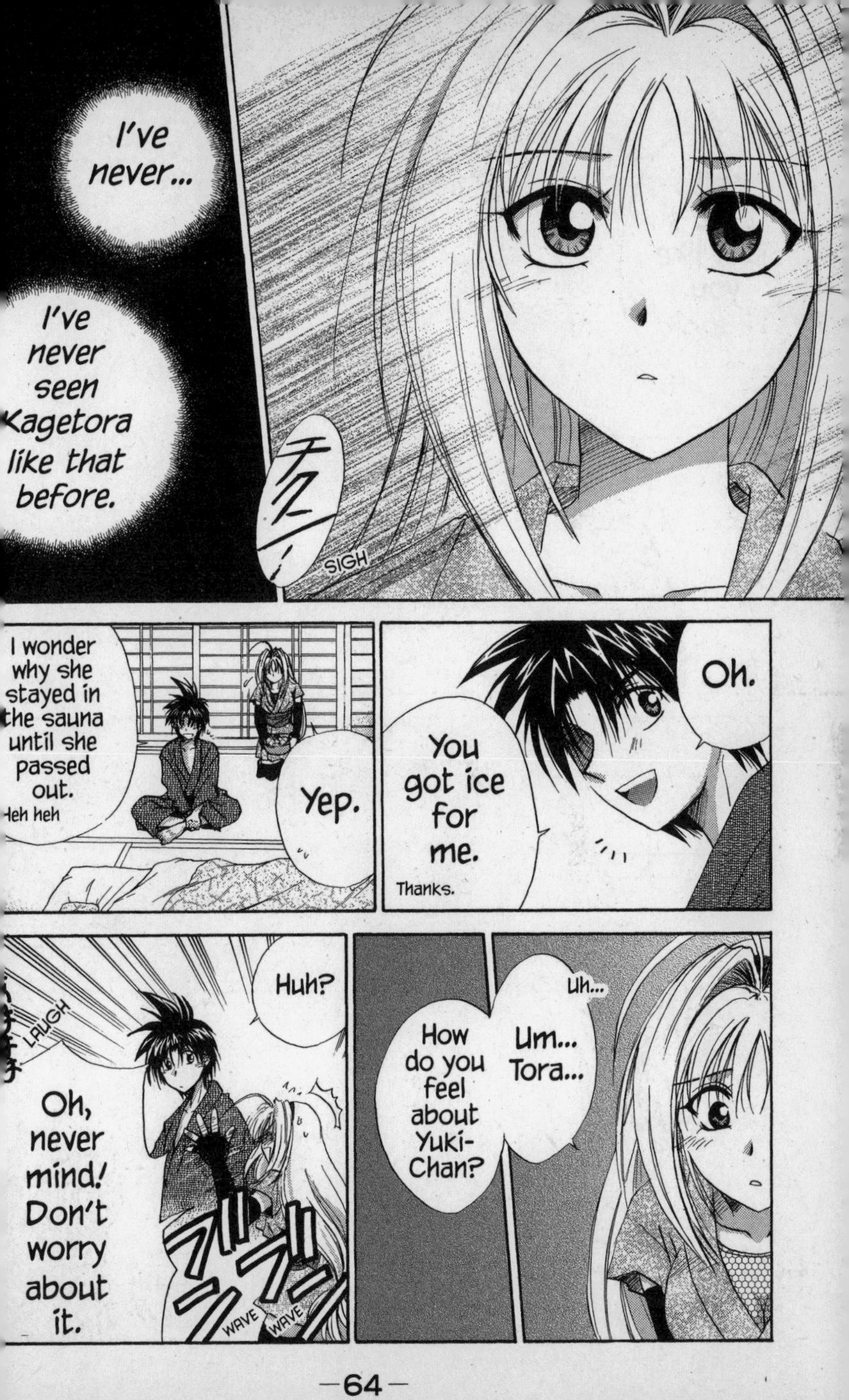
SIGH
I've never...
I've never seen Kagetora like that before.
Oh.
You got ice for me.
Thanks.
Yep.
I wonder why she stayed in the sauna until she passed out.
Heh heh
Uh...
Um... Tora...
How do you feel about Yuki-Chan?
Huh?
LAUGH
Oh, never mind! Don't worry about it.
WAVE WAVE

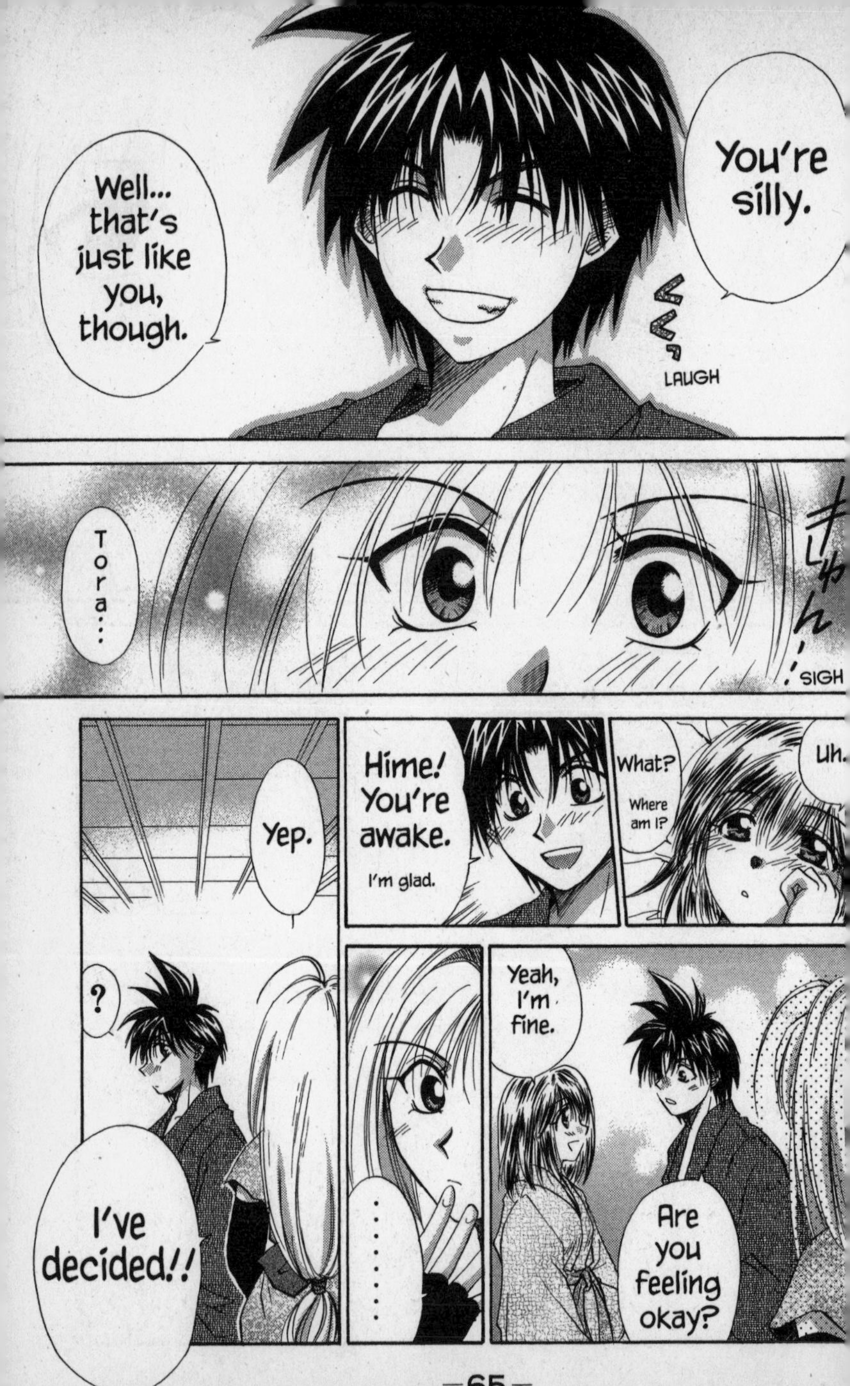
You're silly.
LAUGH
Well... that's just like you, though.
SIGH
Tora...
Uh.
What?
Where am I?
Hime! You're awake.
I'm glad.
Are you feeling okay?
Yeah, I'm fine.
......
Yep.
?
I've decided!!

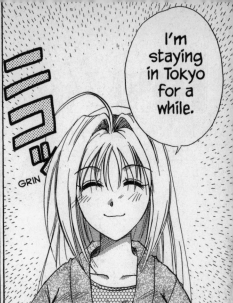

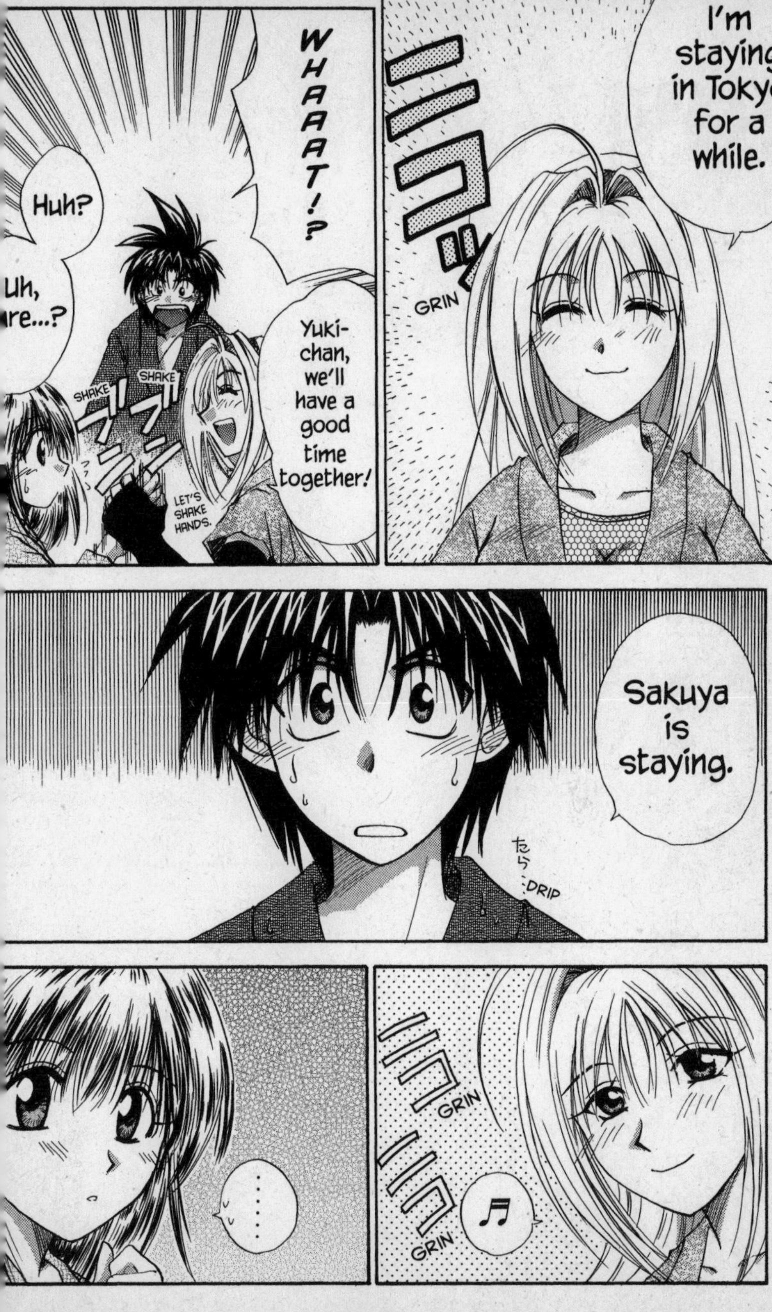
I'm staying in Tokyo for a while.
GRIN
WHAAAT!?
Yuki-chan, we'll have a good time together!
LET'S SHAKE HANDS.
SHAKE
SHAKE
Huh?
uh, re...?
Sakuya is staying.
たら
DRIP
GRIN
GRIN
♪
......

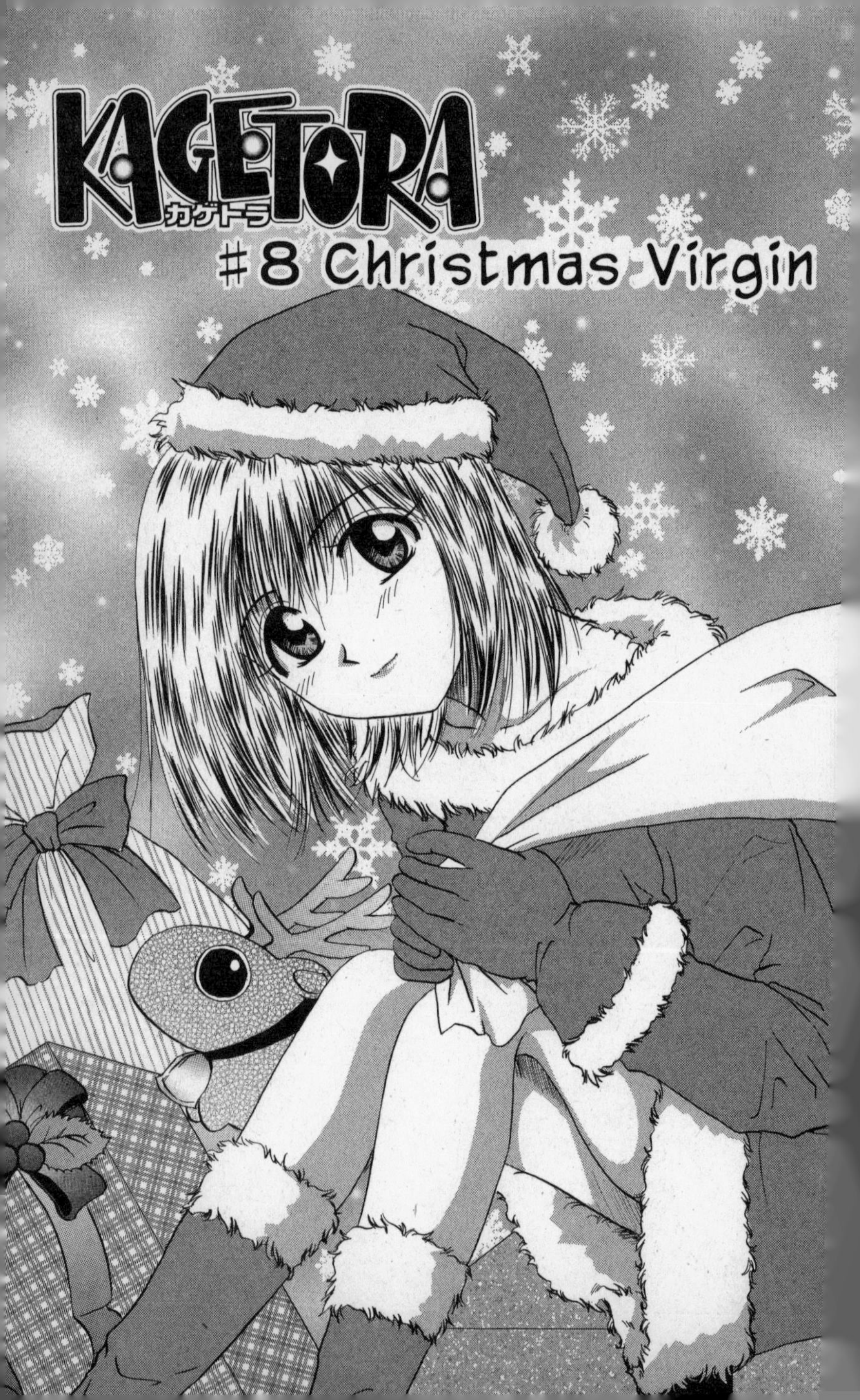
KAGETORA
カゲトラ
#8 Christmas Virgin

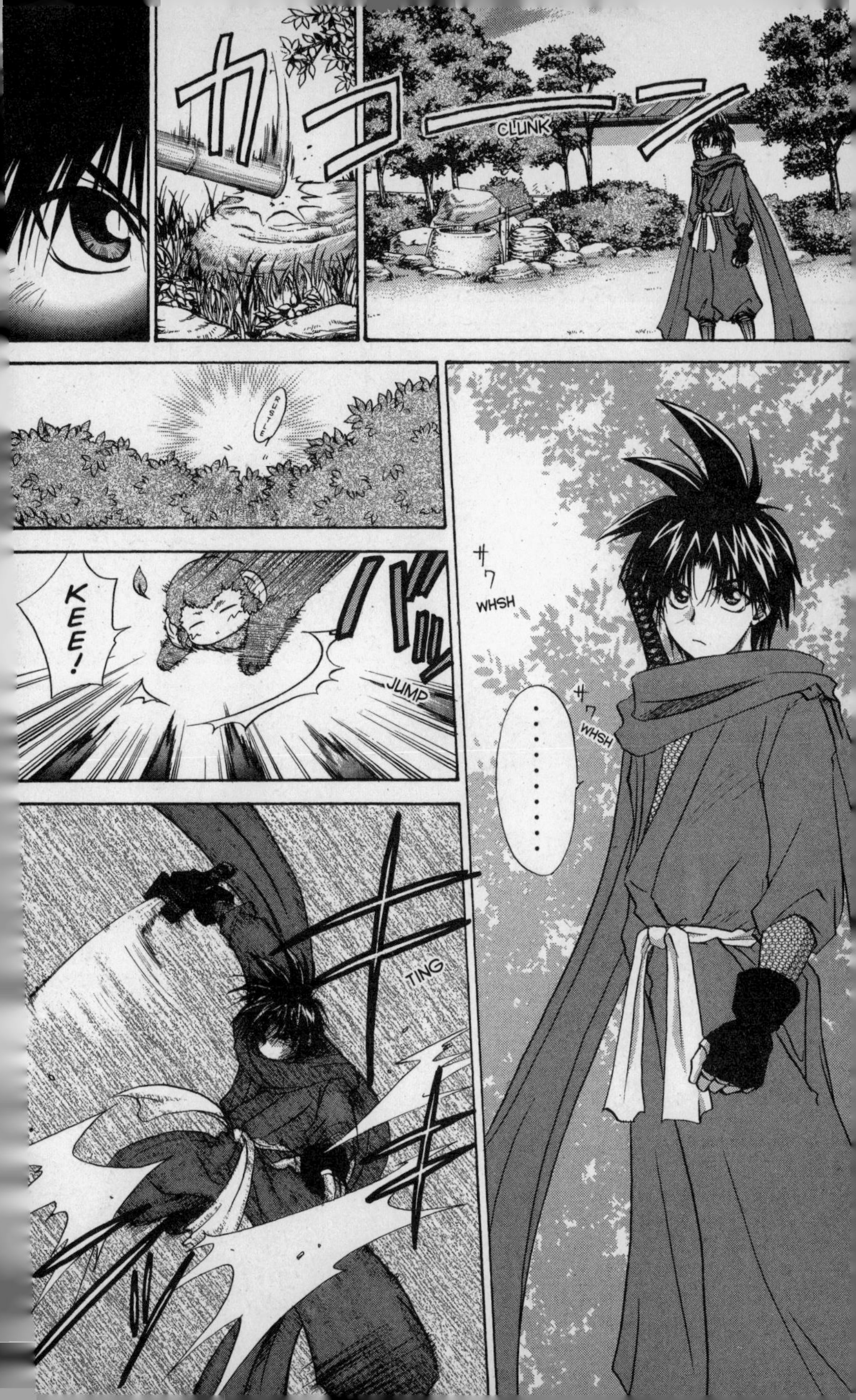

カコーン
CLUNK
WHSH
WHSH
......
RUSTLE
KEE!
JUMP
TING

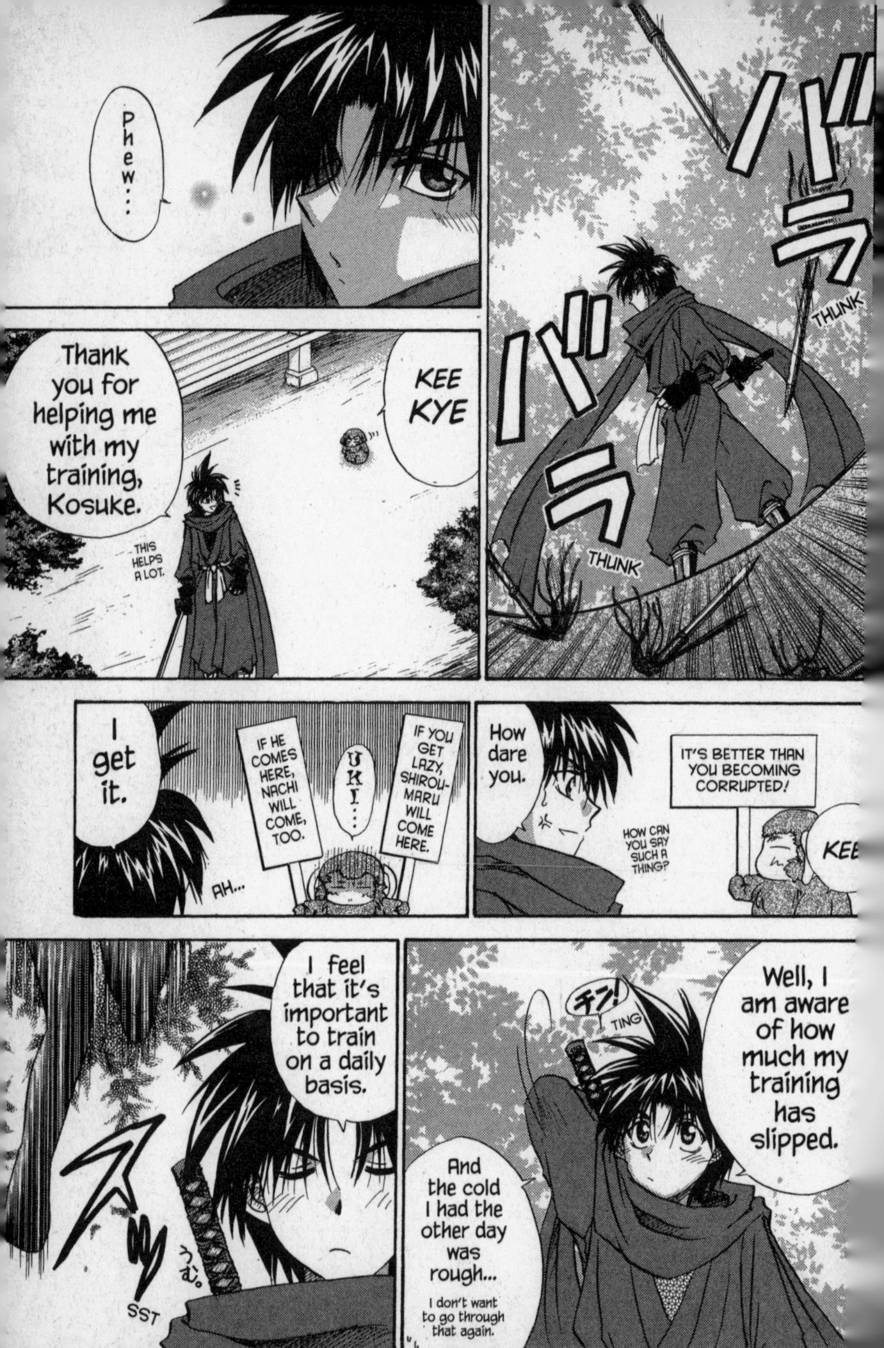
バドラ
THUNK
バドラ
THUNK
Phew...
KEE KYE
Thank you for helping me with my training, Kosuke.
THIS HELPS A LOT.
How dare you.
IT'S BETTER THAN YOU BECOMING CORRUPTED!
HOW CAN YOU SAY SUCH A THING?
KEE
I get it.
IF YOU GET LAZY, SHIROU-MARU WILL COME HERE.
UKI...
IF HE COMES HERE, NACHI WILL COME, TOO.
AH...
チン!
TING
Well, I am aware of how much my training has slipped.
And the cold I had the other day was rough...
I don't want to go through that again.
I feel that it's important to train on a daily basis.
うむ。
SST

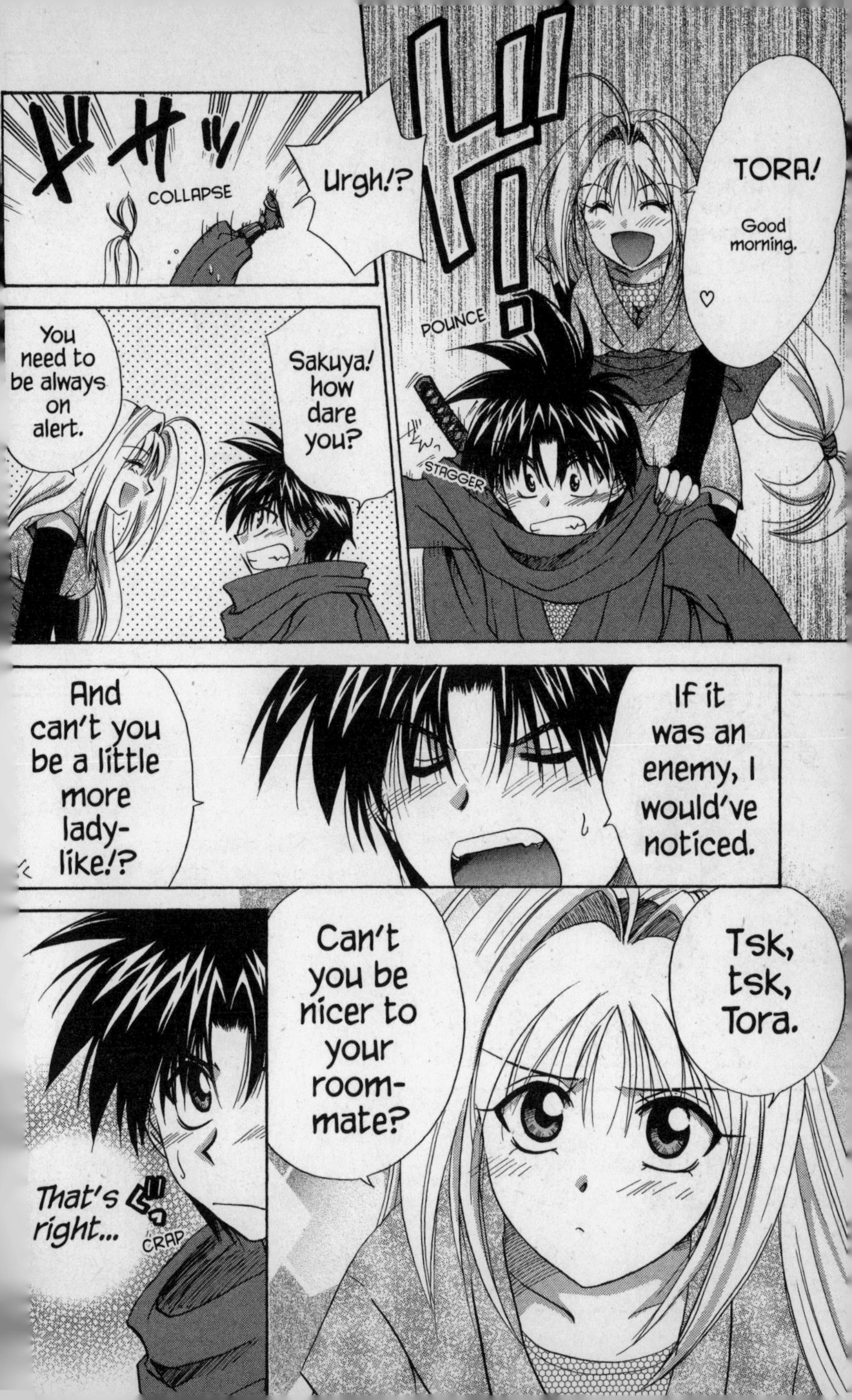
TORA!
Good morning.
POUNCE
STAGGER
Urgh!?
ドサッ
COLLAPSE
Sakuya! how dare you?
You need to be always on alert.
If it was an enemy, I would've noticed.
And can't you be a little more lady-like!?
Tsk, tsk, Tora.
Can't you be nicer to your roommate?
That's right...
CRAP

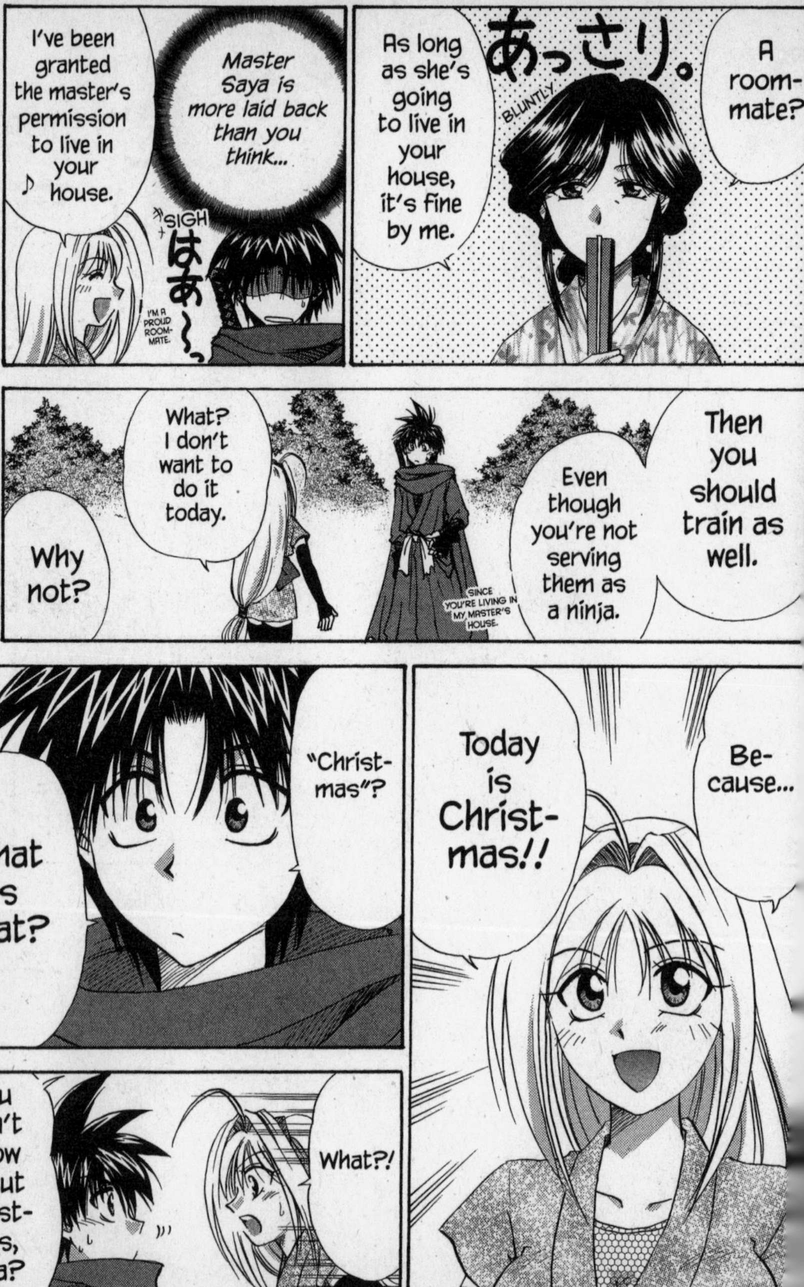
A roommate?
あっさり。
BLUNTLY
As long as she's going to live in your house, it's fine by me.
I've been granted the master's permission to live in your house. ♪
Master Saya is more laid back than you think...
SIGH
はあ～っ
I'M A PROUD ROOMMATE.
Then you should train as well.
Even though you're not serving them as a ninja.
SINCE YOU'RE LIVING IN MY MASTER'S HOUSE.
What? I don't want to do it today.
Why not?
Be-cause...
Today is Christ-mas!!
"Christ-mas"?
What is that?
What?!
You don't know about Christ-mas, Tora?

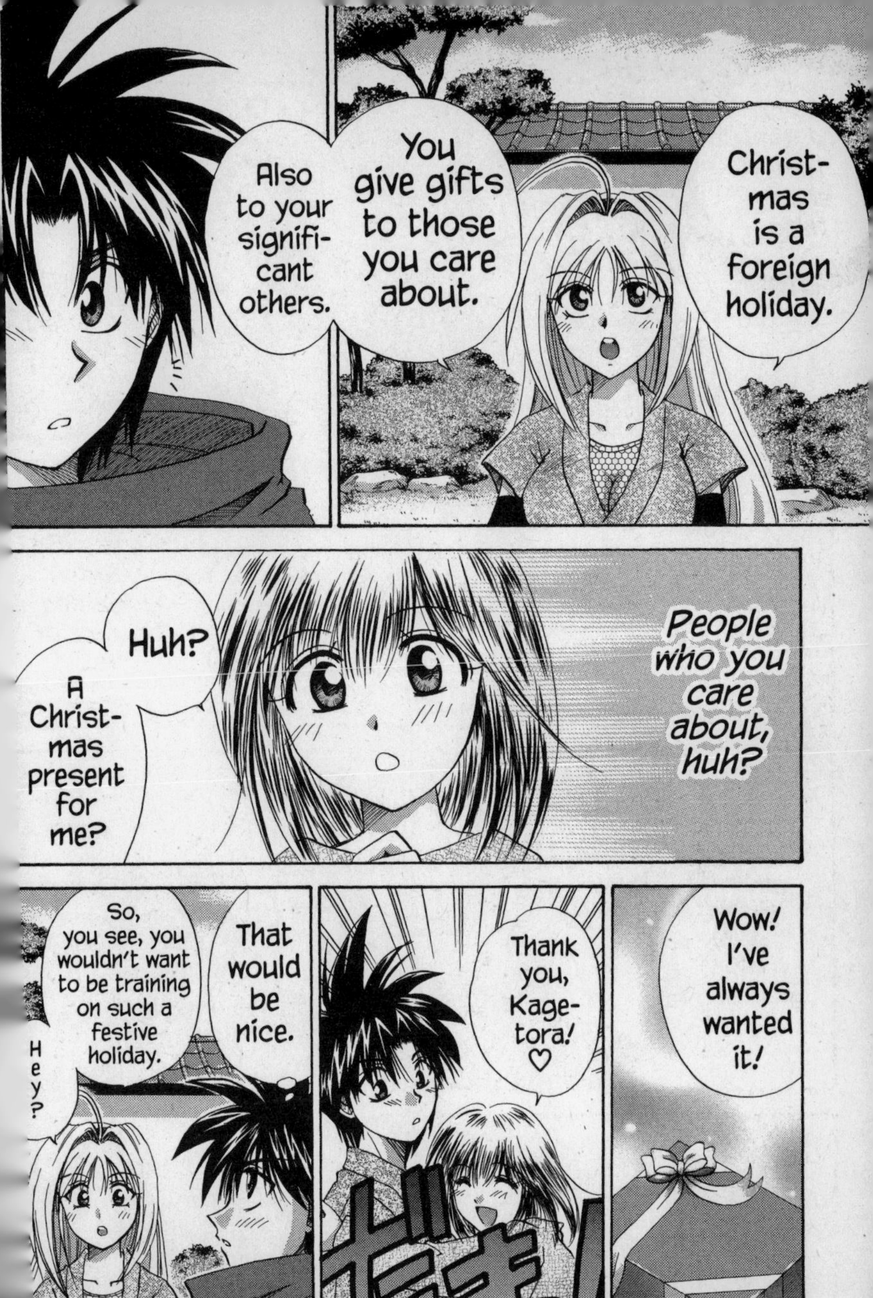
Christmas is a foreign holiday.
You give gifts to those you care about.
Also to your significant others.
People who you care about, huh?
Huh?
A Christmas present for me?
Wow! I've always wanted it!
Thank you, Kagetora! ♡
HUG
That would be nice.
So, you see, you wouldn't want to be training on such a festive holiday.
Hey?

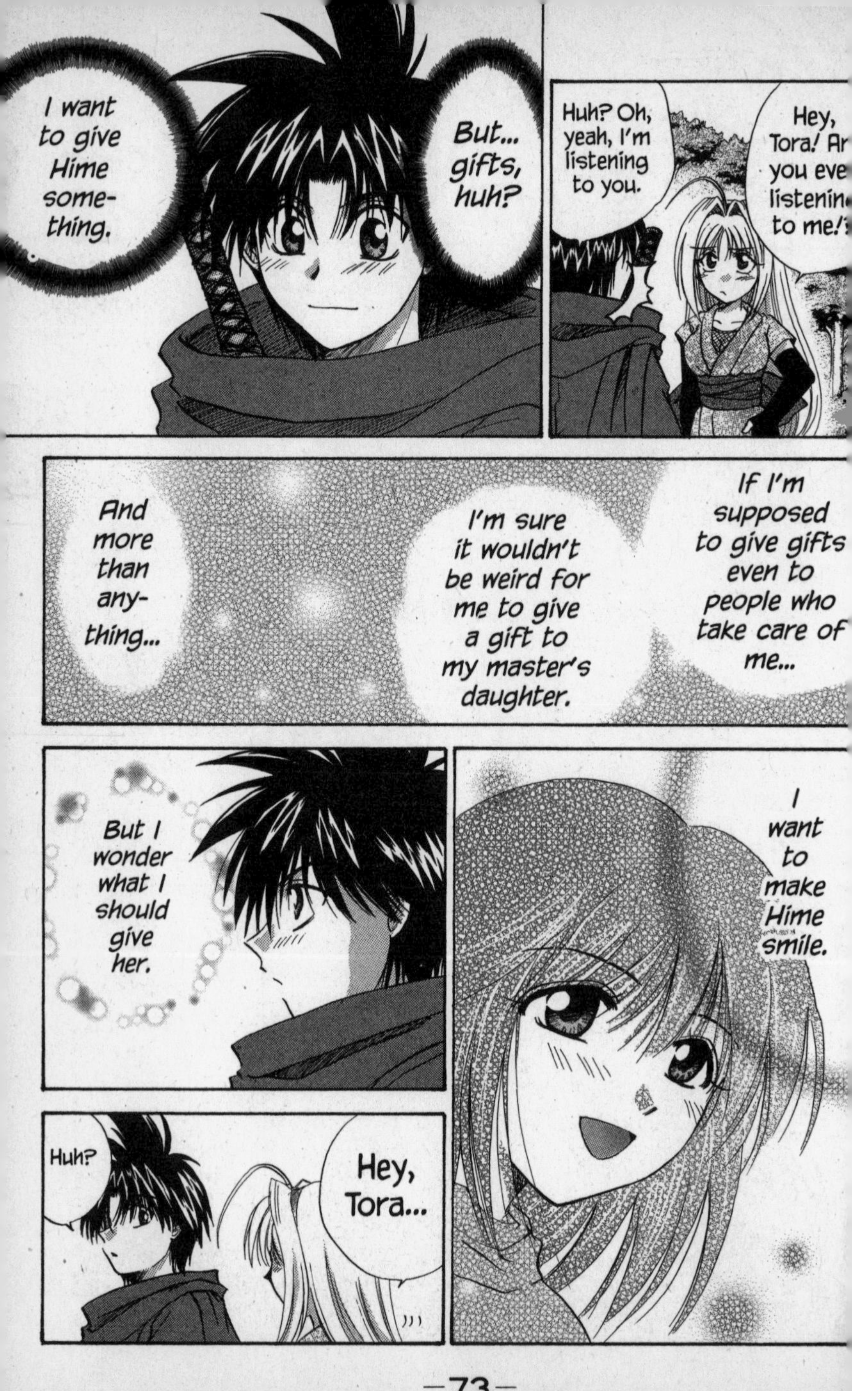
Hey, Tora! Ar you eve listenin to me!
Huh? Oh, yeah, I'm listening to you.
But... gifts, huh?
I want to give Hime something.
If I'm supposed to give gifts even to people who take care of me...
I'm sure it wouldn't be weird for me to give a gift to my master's daughter.
And more than anything...
I want to make Hime smile.
But I wonder what I should give her.
Hey, Tora...
Huh?

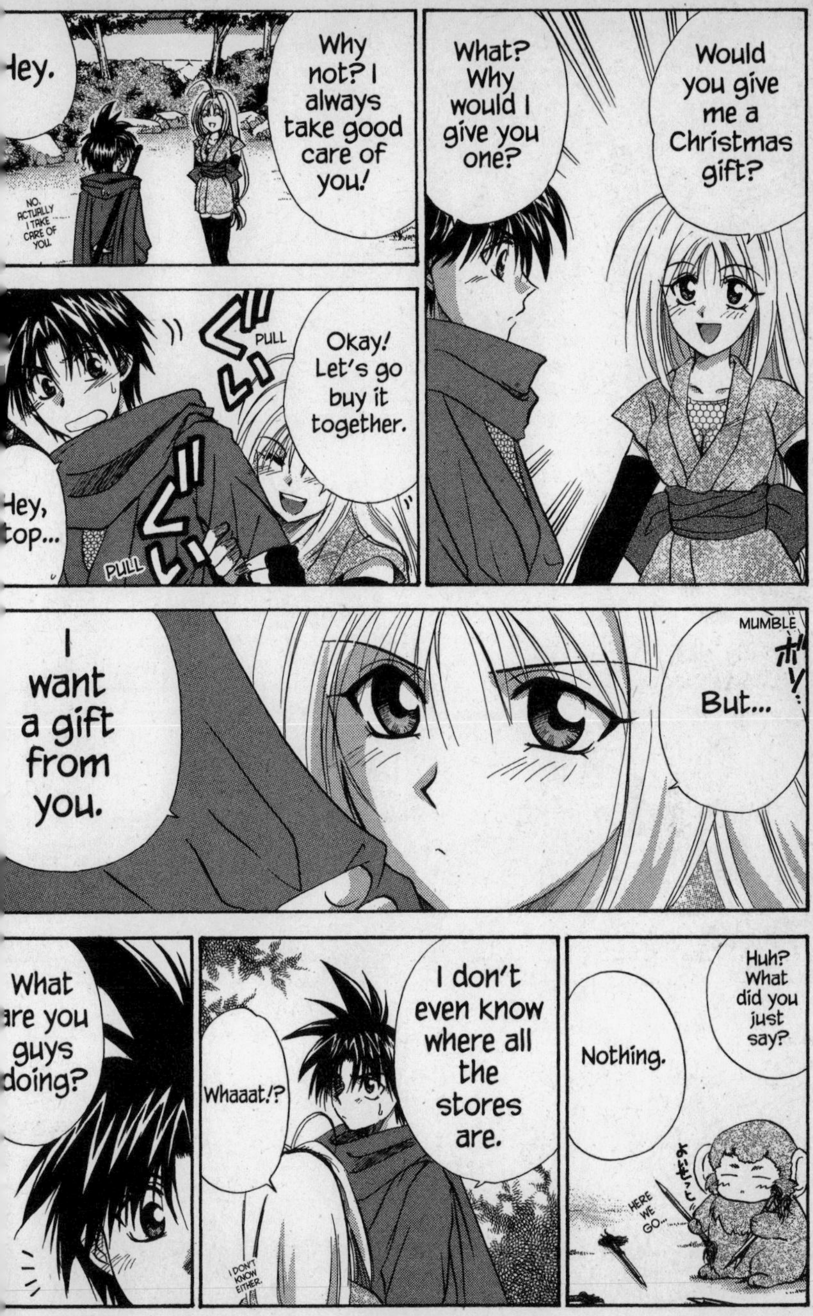
Would you give me a Christmas gift?
What? Why would I give you one?
Why not? I always take good care of you!
Hey.
NO, ACTUALLY I TAKE CARE OF YOU.
Okay! Let's go buy it together.
PULL
Hey, top...
PULL
MUMBLE
But...
I want a gift from you.
Huh? What did you just say?
Nothing.
HERE WE GO...
I don't even know where all the stores are.
Whaaat!?
I DON'T KNOW EITHER.
What re you guys doing?

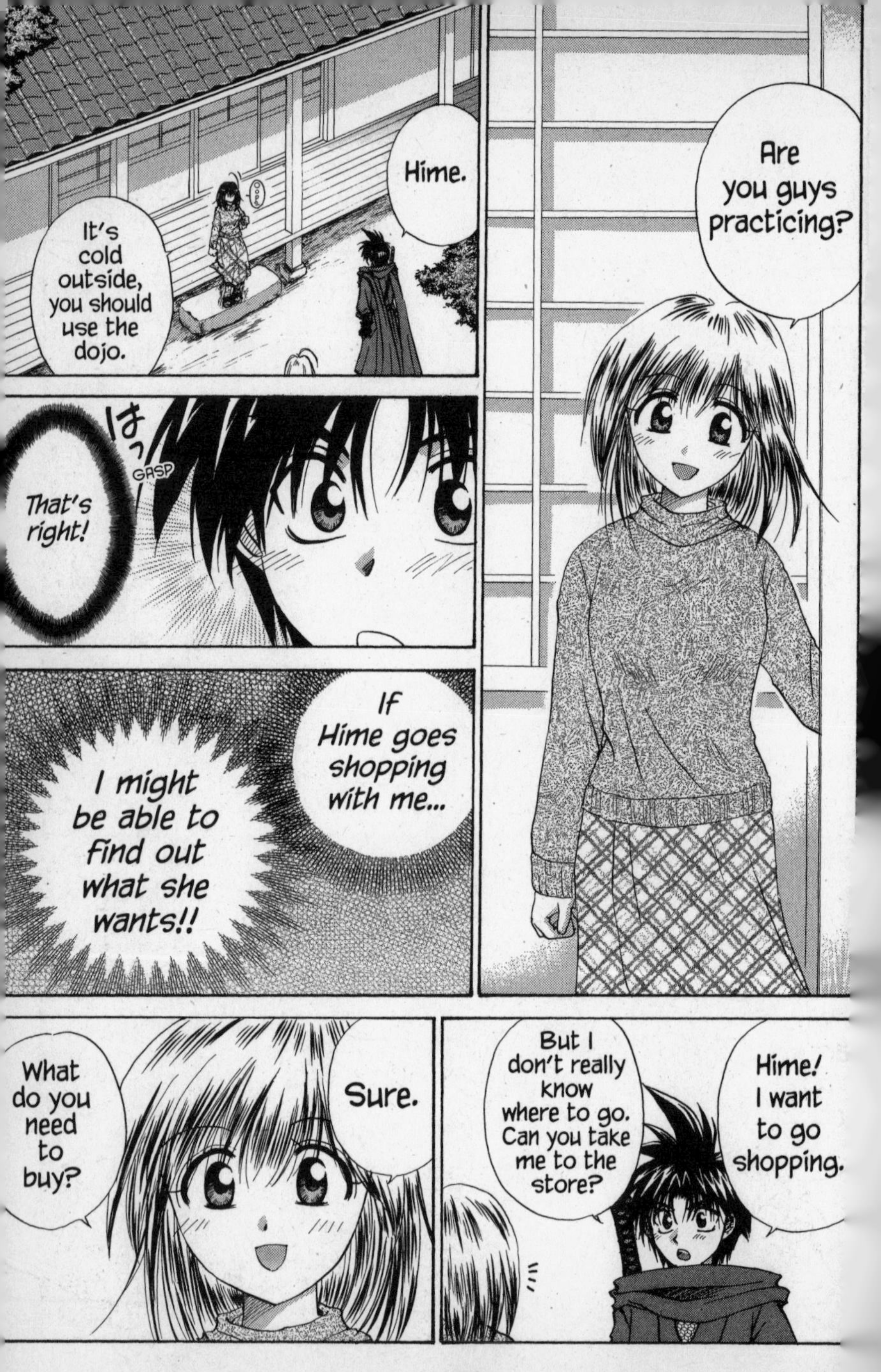

Are you guys practicing?
Hime.
It's cold outside, you should use the dojo.
GASP
That's right!
If Hime goes shopping with me...
I might be able to find out what she wants!!
Hime! I want to go shopping.
But I don't really know where to go. Can you take me to the store?
Sure.
What do you need to buy?

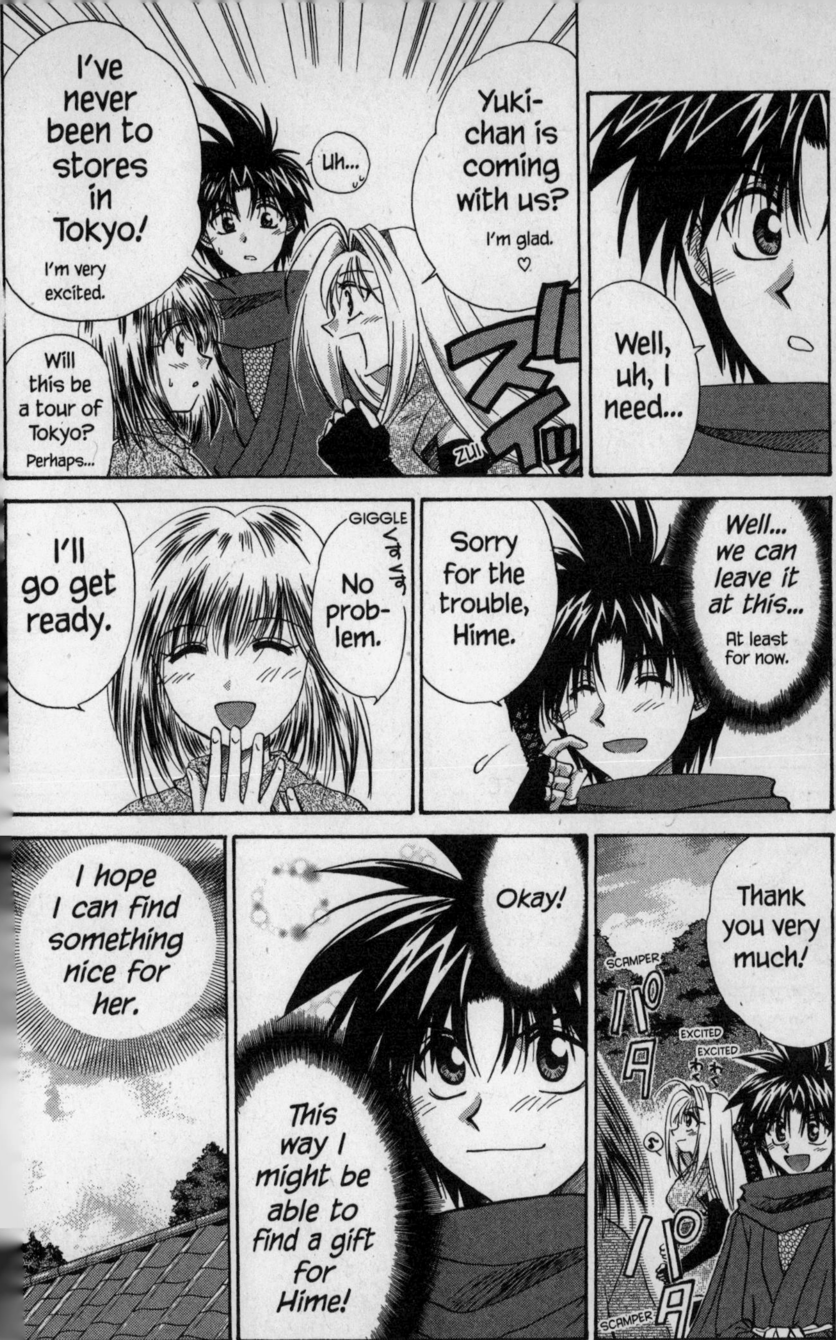

Well, uh, I need...
Yuki-chan is coming with us?
I'm glad. ♡
ZUI
uh...
I've never been to stores in Tokyo!
I'm very excited.
Will this be a tour of Tokyo?
Perhaps...
Well... we can leave it at this...
At least for now.
Sorry for the trouble, Hime.
GIGGLE
No prob-lem.
I'll go get ready.
Thank you very much!
SCAMPER
EXCITED
EXCITED
SCAMPER
Okay!
This way I might be able to find a gift for Hime!
I hope I can find something nice for her.

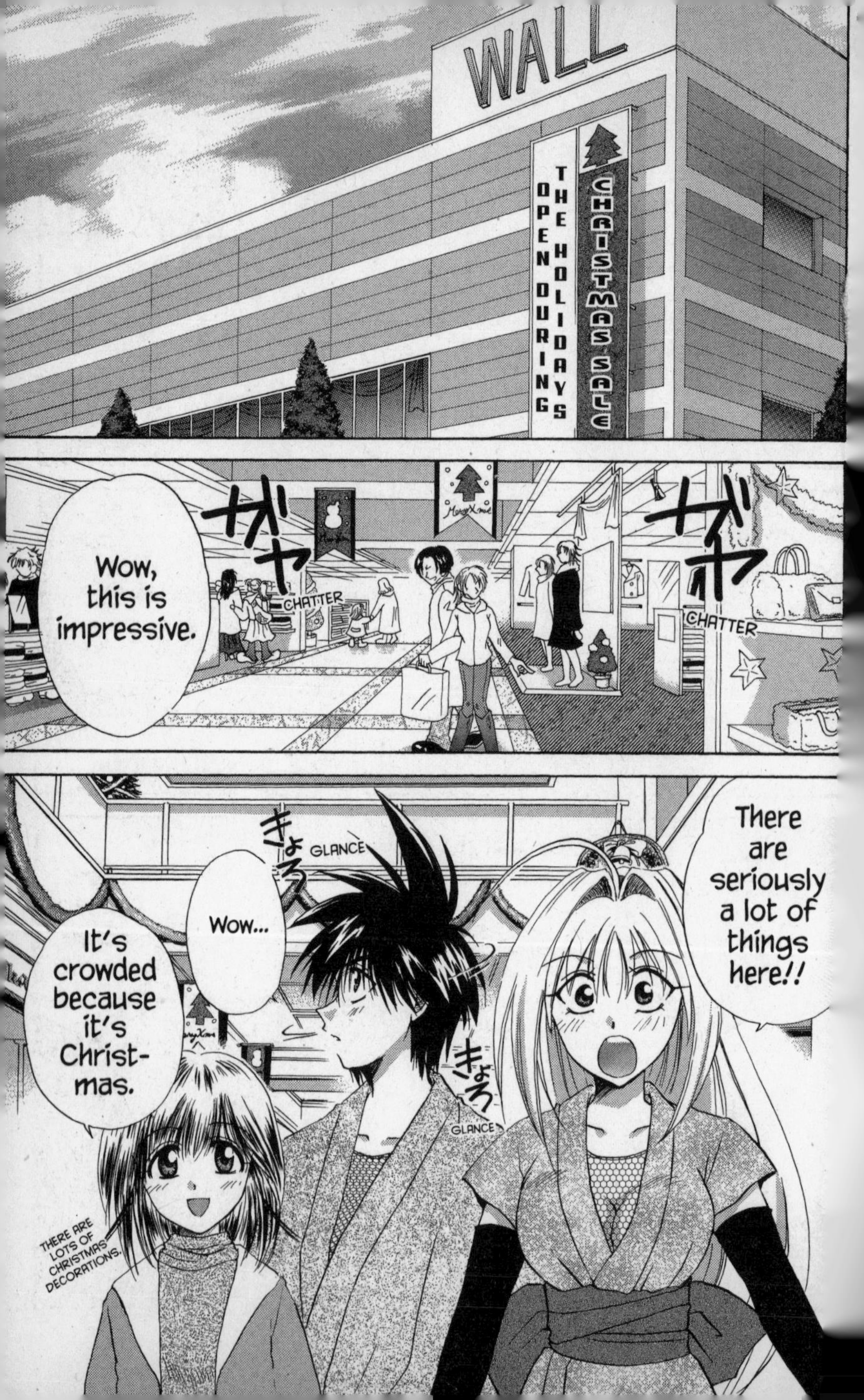
WALL
CHRISTMAS SALE
THE HOLIDAYS
OPEN DURING
ザワ
CHATTER
ガヤ
CHATTER
Wow, this is impressive.
There are seriously a lot of things here!!
きょろ
GLANCE
Wow...
きょろ
GLANCE
It's crowded because it's Christ-mas.
THERE ARE LOTS OF CHRISTMAS DECORATIONS.

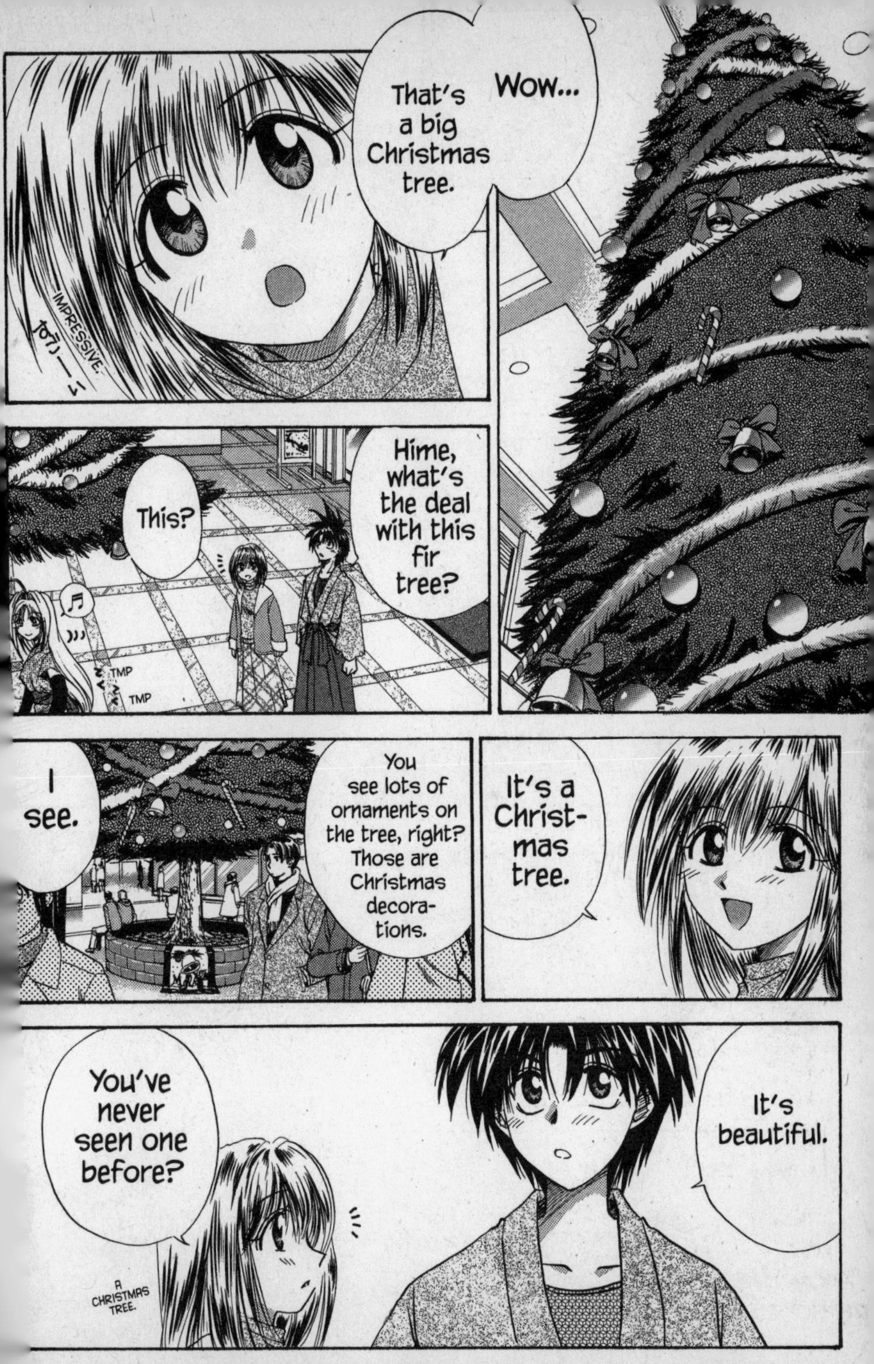
Wow...
That's a big Christmas tree.
IMPRESSIVE.
Hime, what's the deal with this fir tree?
This?
TMP
TMP
It's a Christmas tree.
You see lots of ornaments on the tree, right? Those are Christmas decorations.
I see.
It's beautiful.
You've never seen one before?
A CHRISTMAS TREE.

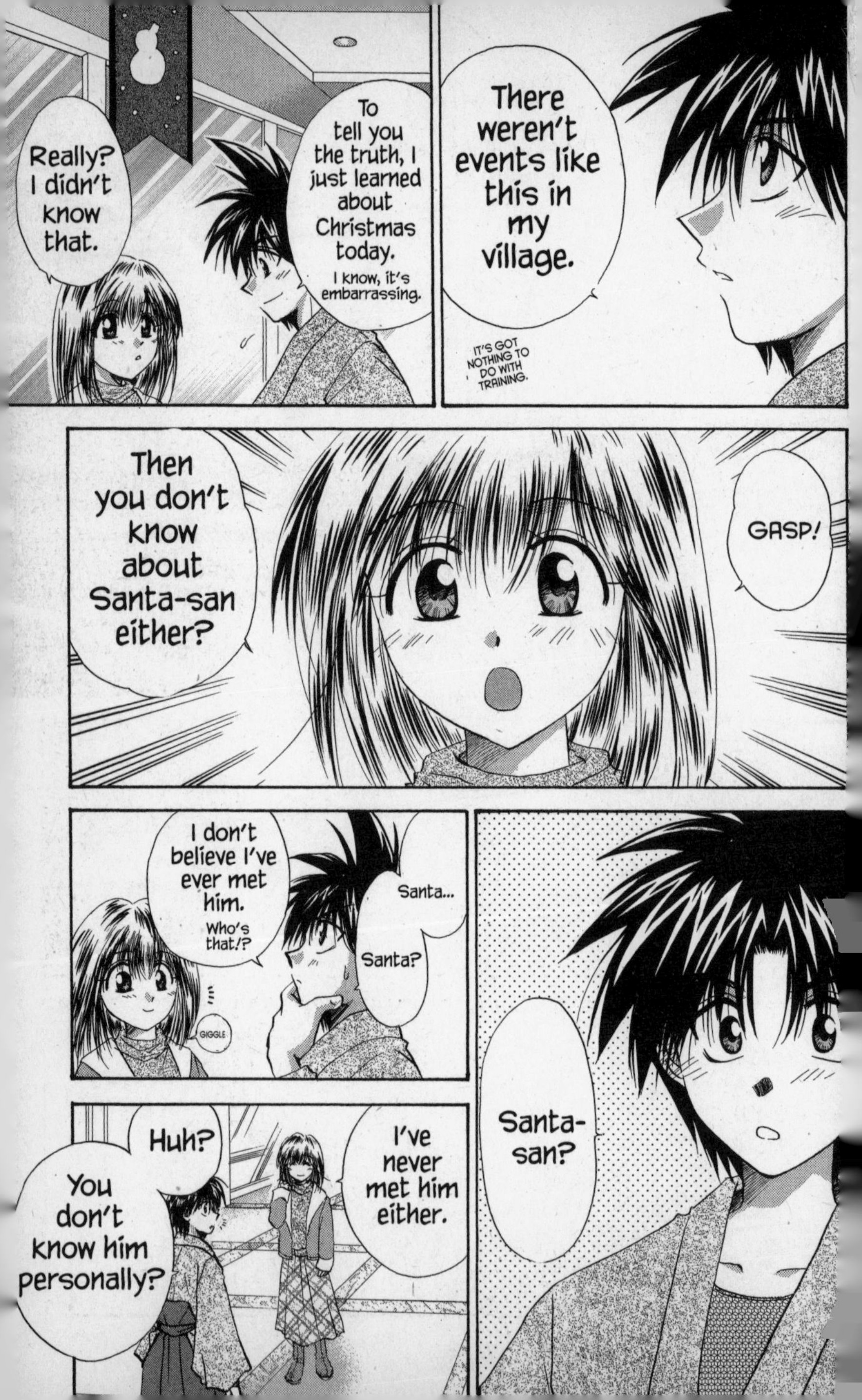
There weren't events like this in my village.
IT'S GOT NOTHING TO DO WITH TRAINING.
To tell you the truth, I just learned about Christmas today.
I know, it's embarrassing.
Really? I didn't know that.
GASP!
Then you don't know about Santa-san either?
Santa-san?
Santa...
Santa?
I don't believe I've ever met him.
Who's that!?
GIGGLE
I've never met him either.
Huh?
You don't know him personally?

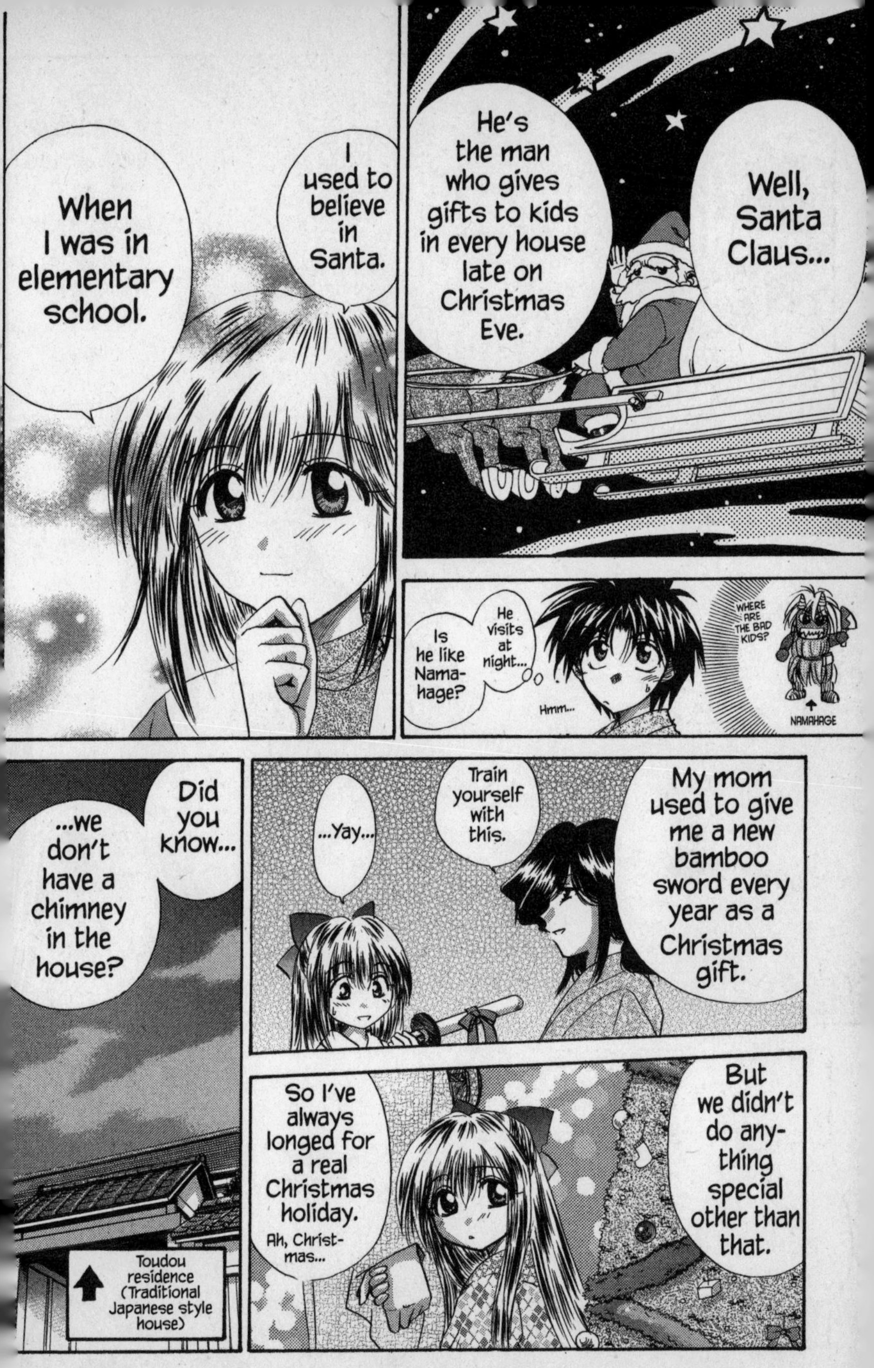
Well, Santa Claus...
He's the man who gives gifts to kids in every house late on Christmas Eve.
WHERE ARE THE BAD KIDS?
NAMAHAGE
He visits at night...
Is he like Namahage?
Hmm...
I used to believe in Santa.
When I was in elementary school.
My mom used to give me a new bamboo sword every year as a Christmas gift.
Train yourself with this.
...Yay...
But we didn't do anything special other than that.
So I've always longed for a real Christmas holiday.
Ah, Christmas...
Did you know...
...we don't have a chimney in the house?
Toudou residence (Traditional Japanese style house)

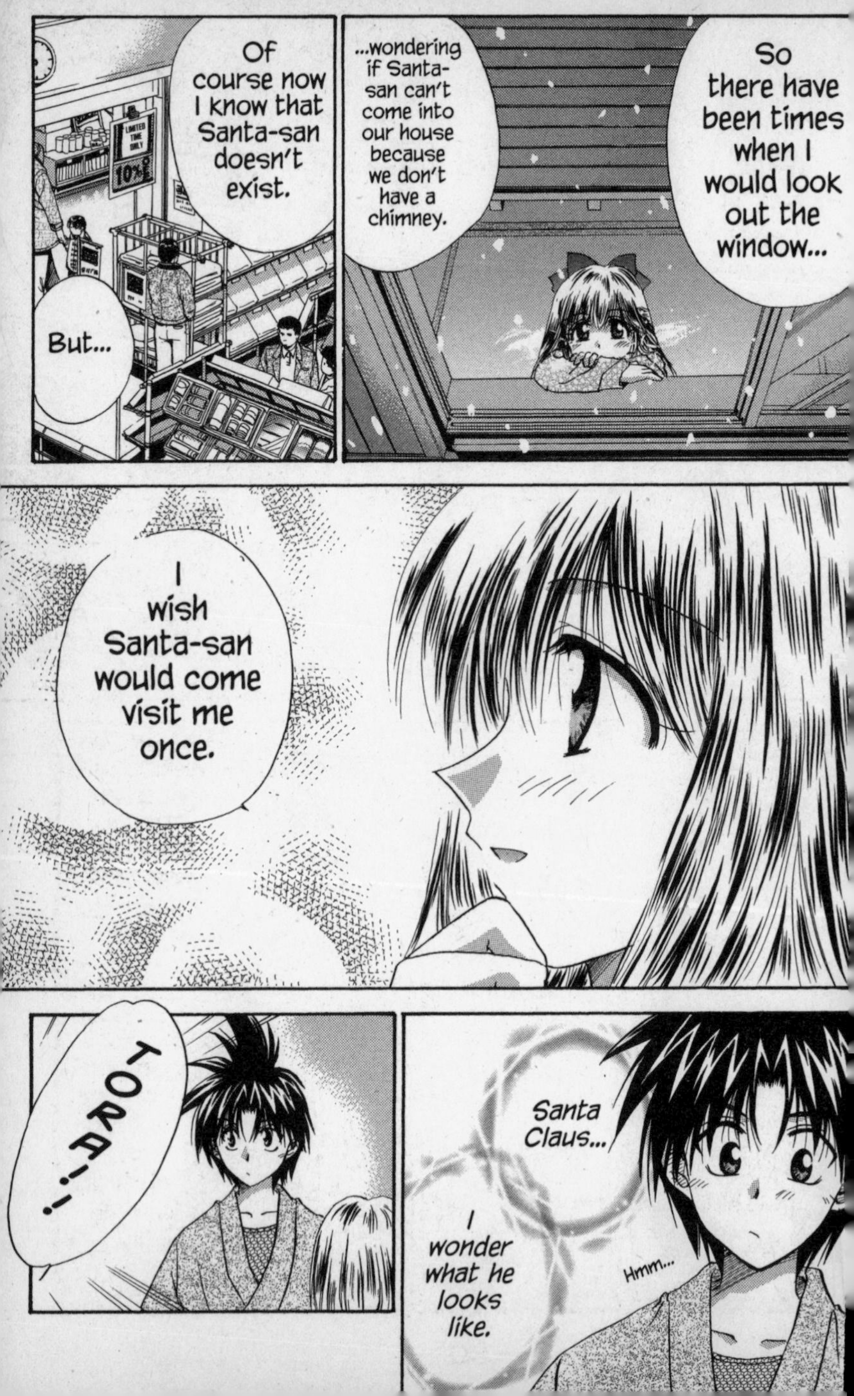
So there have been times when I would look out the window...
...wondering if Santa-san can't come into our house because we don't have a chimney.
Of course now I know that Santa-san doesn't exist.
But...
I wish Santa-san would come visit me once.
Santa Claus...
I wonder what he looks like.
Hmm...
TORA-!!

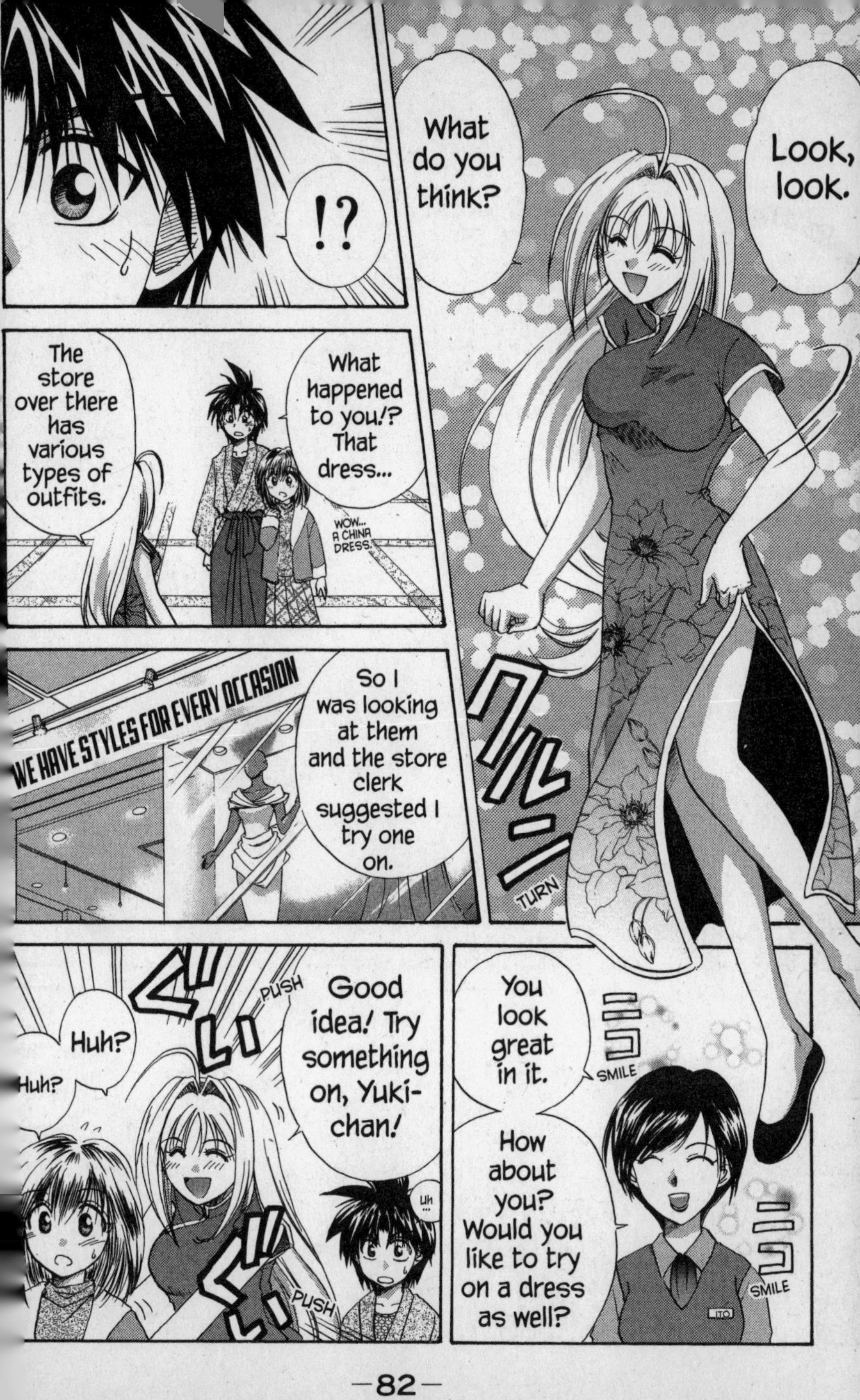
Look, look.
What do you think?
TURN
!?
What happened to you!? That dress...
The store over there has various types of outfits.
WOW... A CHINA DRESS.
So I was looking at them and the store clerk suggested I try one on.
WE HAVE STYLES FOR EVERY OCCASION
SMILE
You look great in it.
How about you? Would you like to try on a dress as well?
SMILE
ITO
Good idea! Try something on, Yuki-chan!
PUSH
Huh?
Huh?
uh...
PUSH

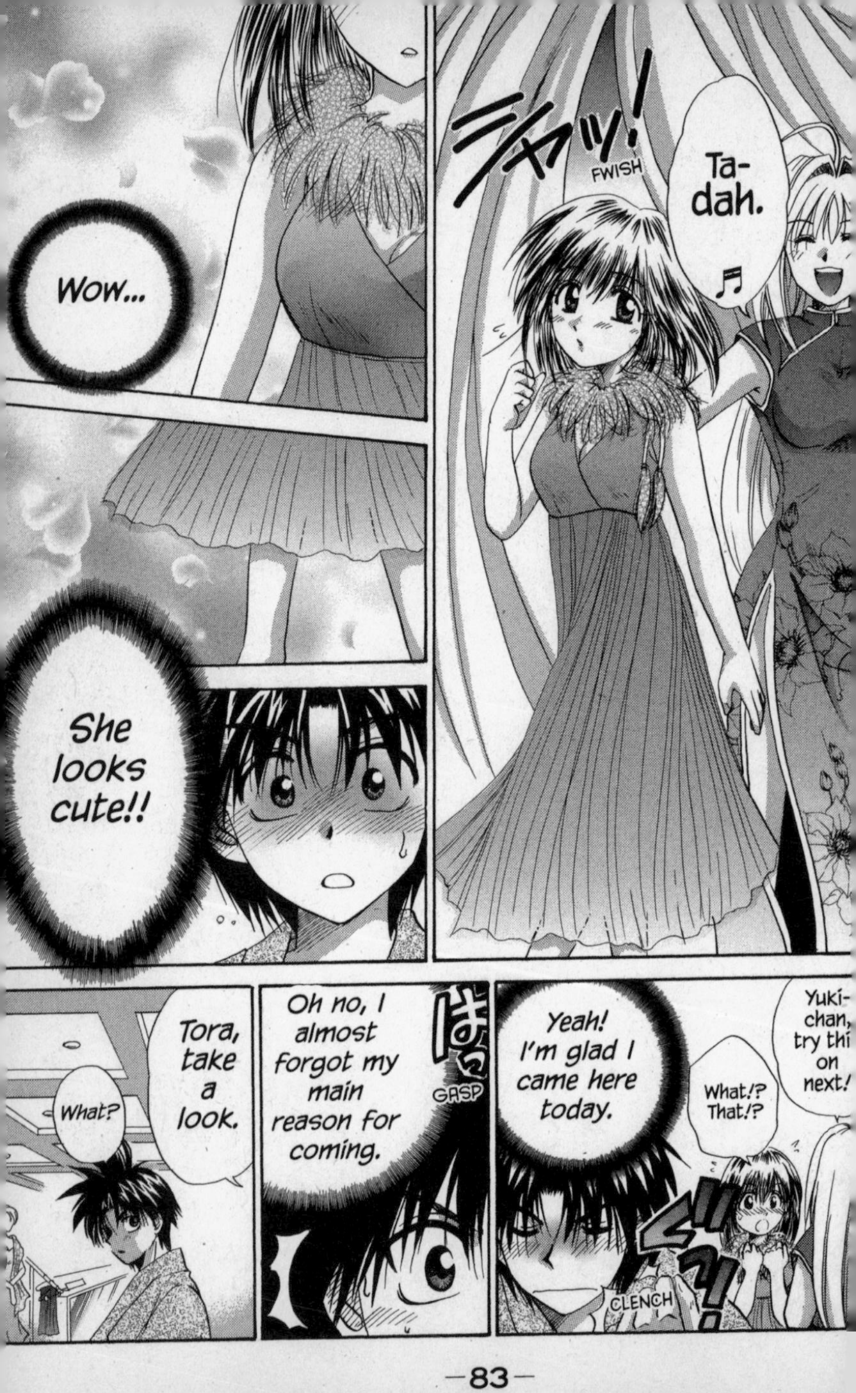
シャッ!
FWISH
Ta-dah. ♪
Wow...
She looks cute!!
Yuki-chan, try thi on next!
What!? That!?
CLENCH
Yeah! I'm glad I came here today.
GASP
Oh no, I almost forgot my main reason for coming.
Tora, take a look.
What?

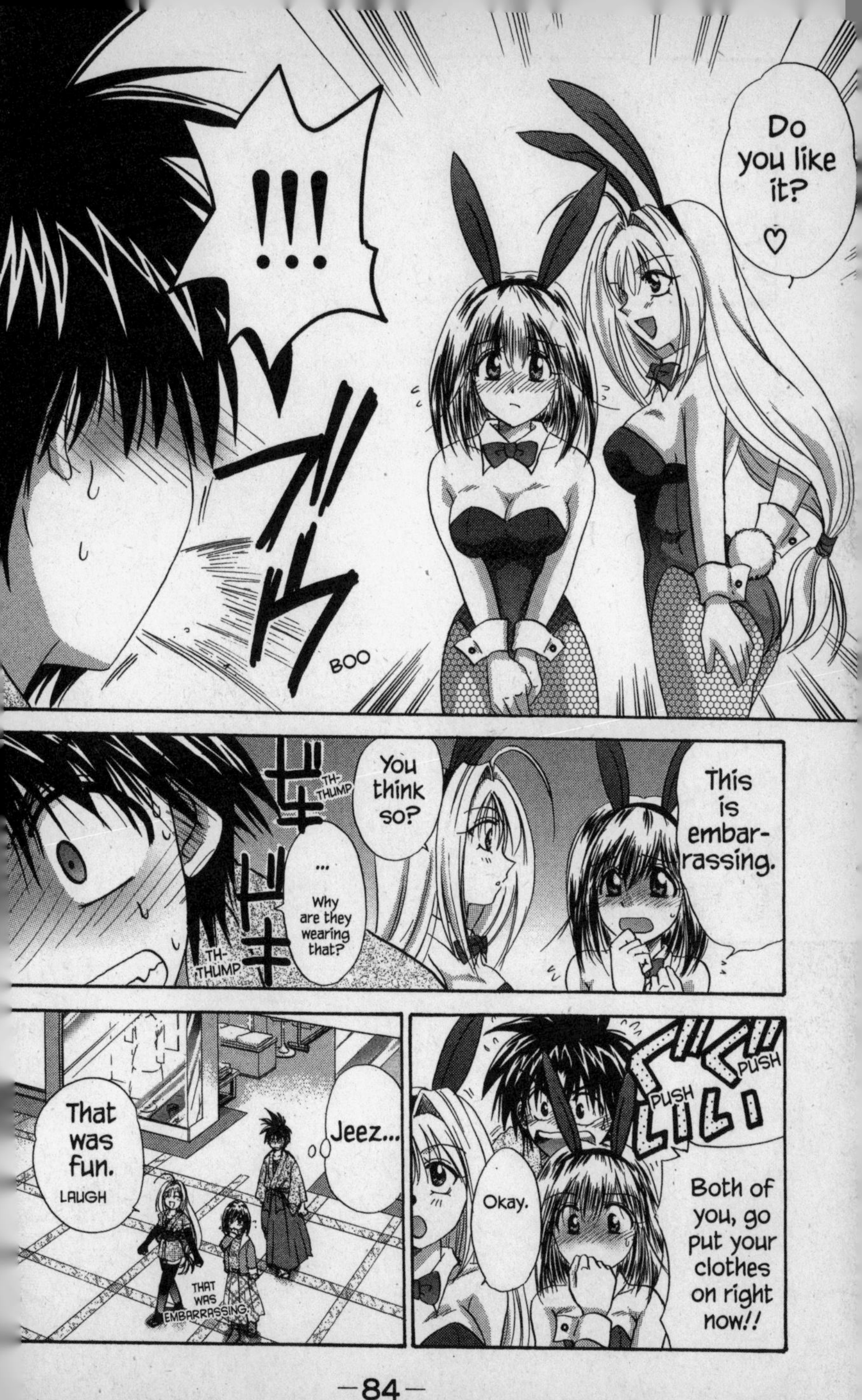
Do you like it? ♡
!!!
BOO
This is embarrassing.
You think so?
TH-THUMP
... Why are they wearing that?
TH-THUMP
PUSH
PUSH
Both of you, go put your clothes on right now!!
Okay.
Jeez...
That was fun.
LAUGH
THAT WAS EMBARRASSING

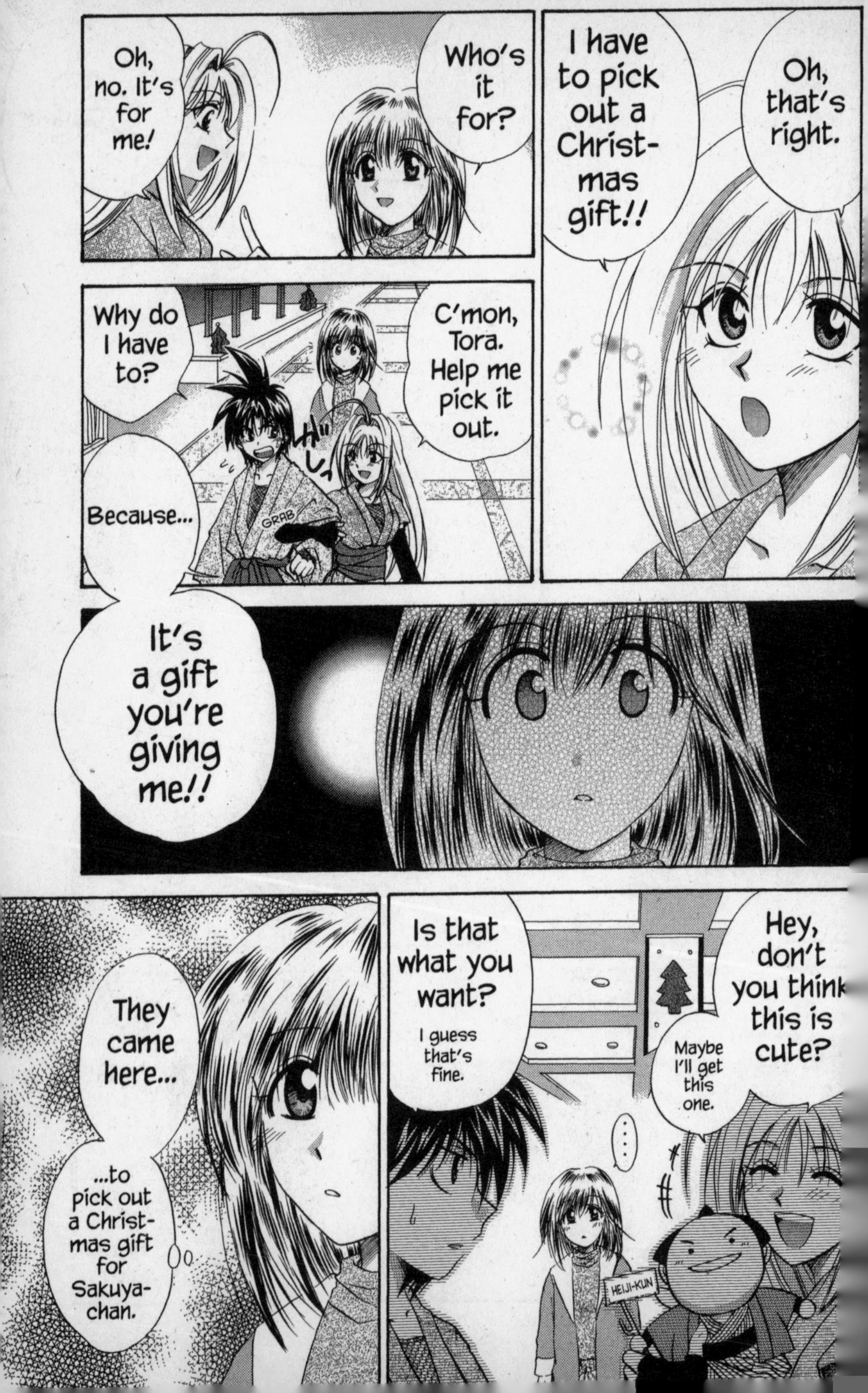
Oh, that's right.
I have to pick out a Christmas gift!!
Who's it for?
Oh, no. It's for me!
C'mon, Tora. Help me pick it out.
Why do I have to?
GRAB
Because...
It's a gift you're giving me!!
Hey, don't you think this is cute?
Maybe I'll get this one.
Is that what you want?
I guess that's fine.
...
HEIJI-KUN
They came here...
...to pick out a Christmas gift for Sakuya-chan.

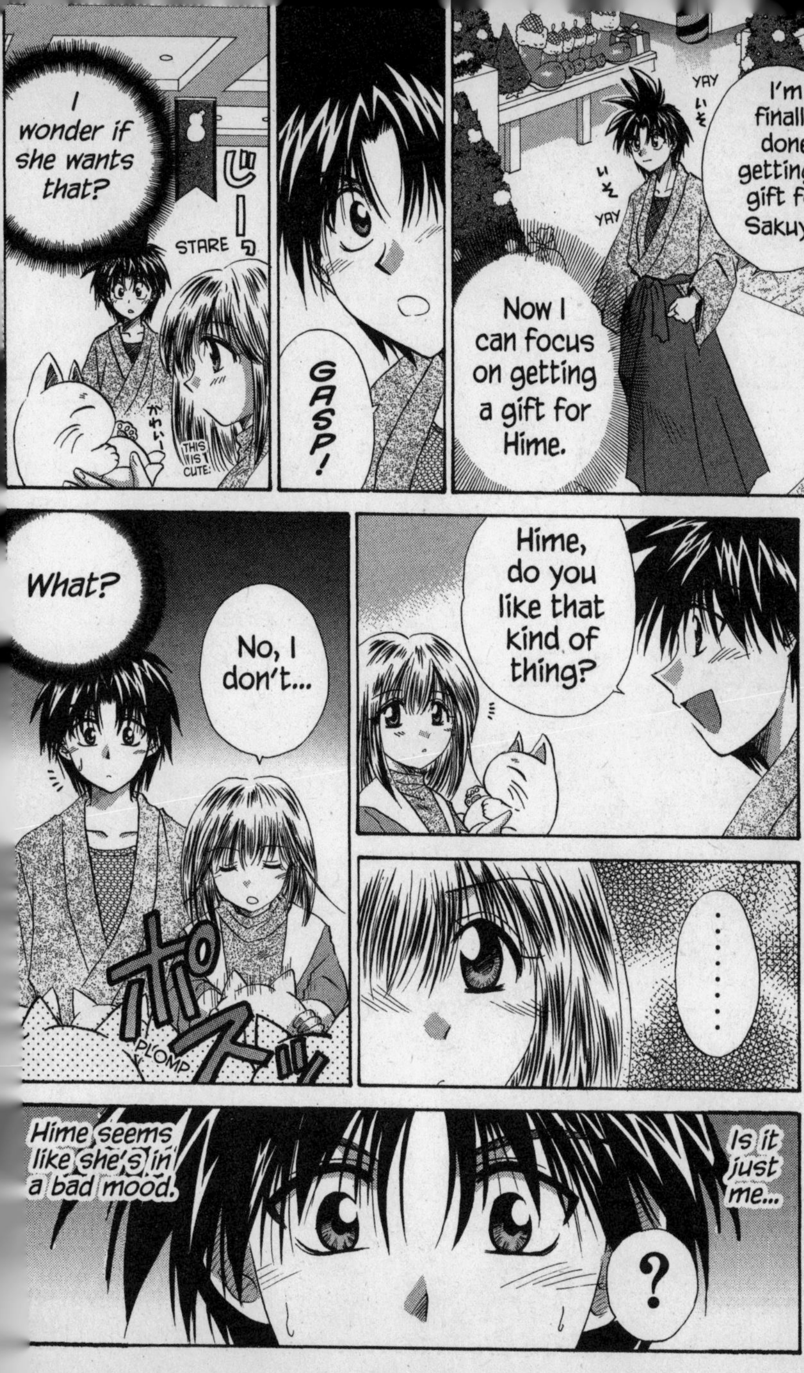
YAY
I'm finally done getting a gift for Sakuya.
YAY
Now I can focus on getting a gift for Hime.
GASP!
I wonder if she wants that?
STARE
THIS IS CUTE
Hime, do you like that kind of thing?
......
What?
No, I don't...
PLOMP
Is it just me...
Hime seems like she's in a bad mood.
?

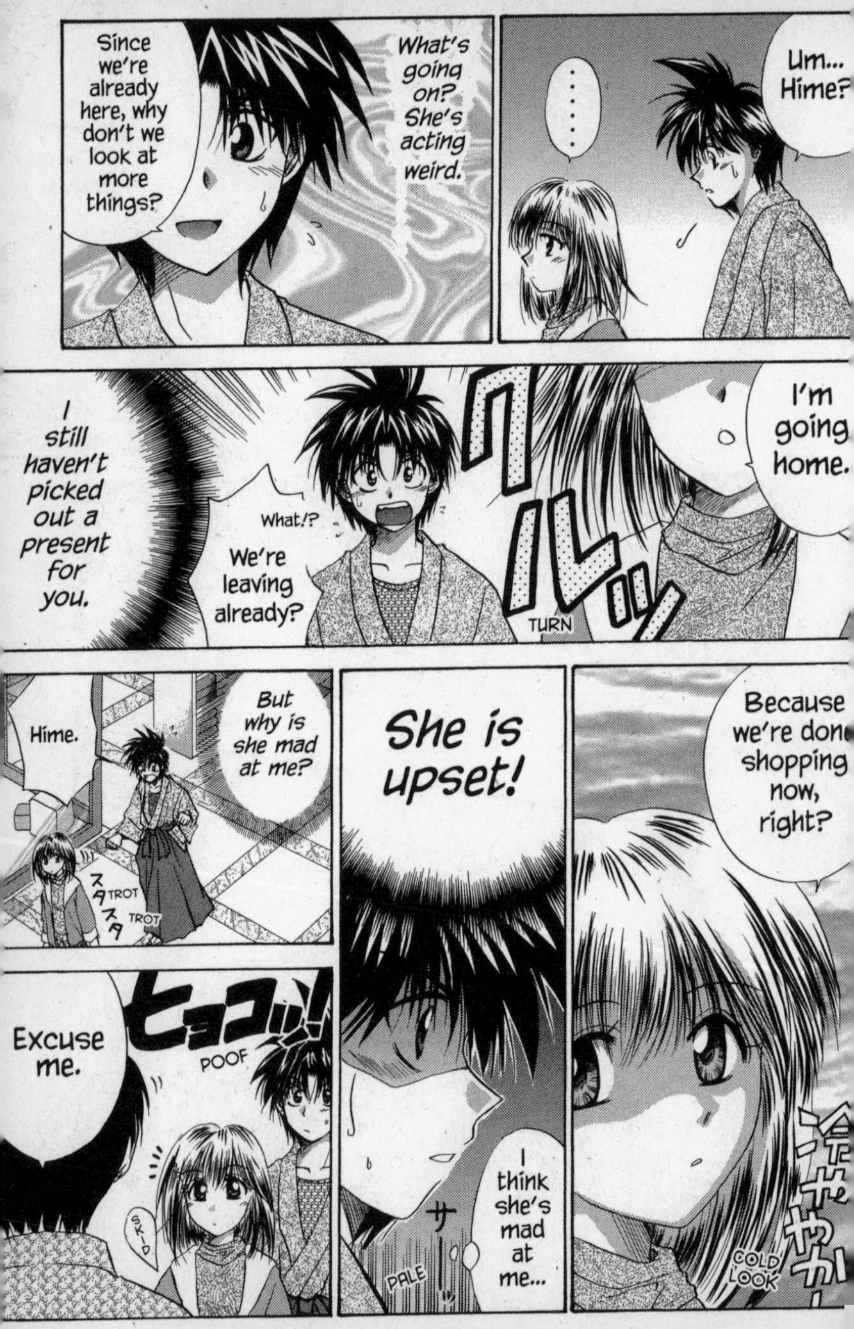
Um... Hime?
......
What's going on? She's acting weird.
Since we're already here, why don't we look at more things?
I'm going home.
TURN
What!?
We're leaving already?
I still haven't picked out a present for you.
Because we're don shopping now, right?
COLD LOOK
She is upset!
I think she's mad at me...
PALE
But why is she mad at me?
Hime.
TROT
TROT
Excuse me.
POOF
SKID

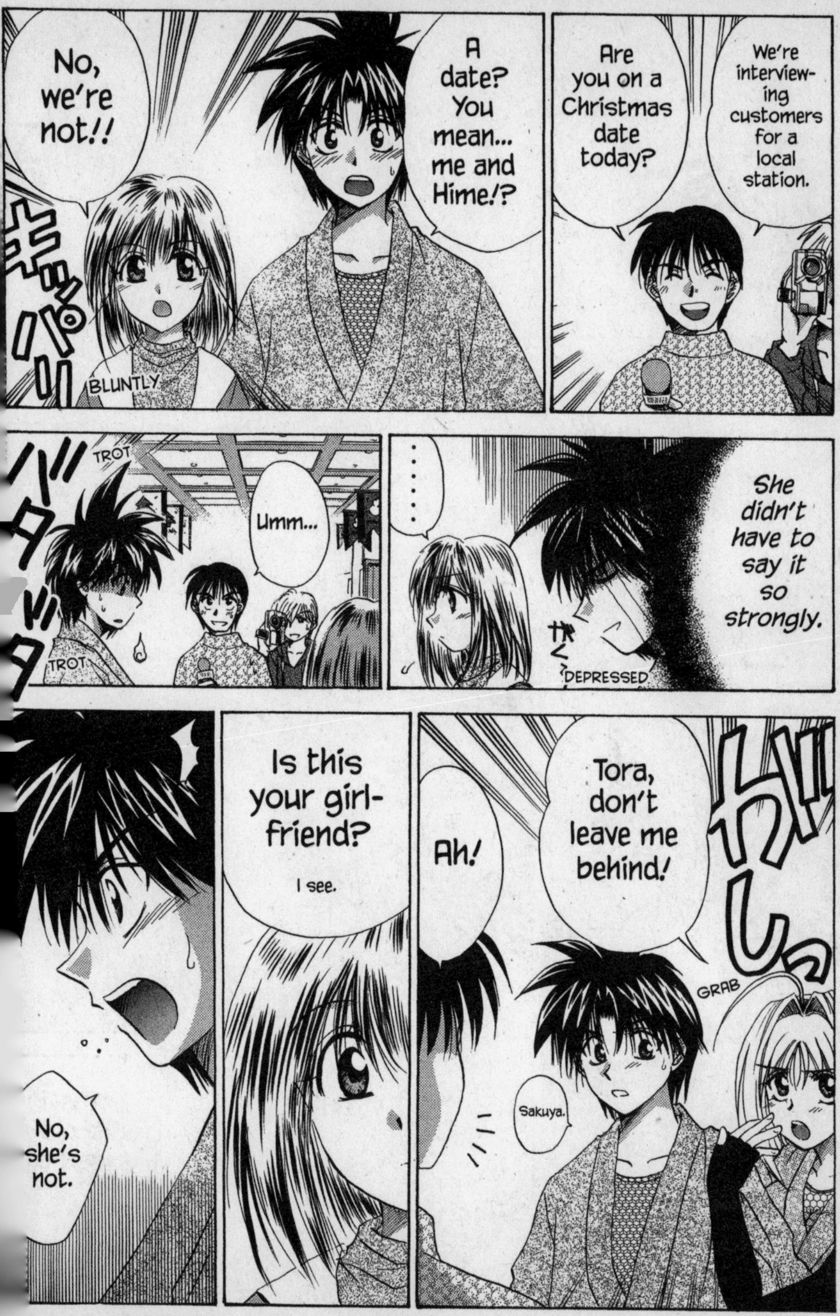
We're interview-ing customers for a local station.
Are you on a Christmas date today?
A date? You mean... me and Hime!?
No, we're not!!
BLUNTLY
She didn't have to say it so strongly.
DEPRESSED
......
Umm...
TROT
TROT
Tora, don't leave me behind!
GRAB
Ah!
Sakuya.
Is this your girl-friend?
I see.
No, she's not.

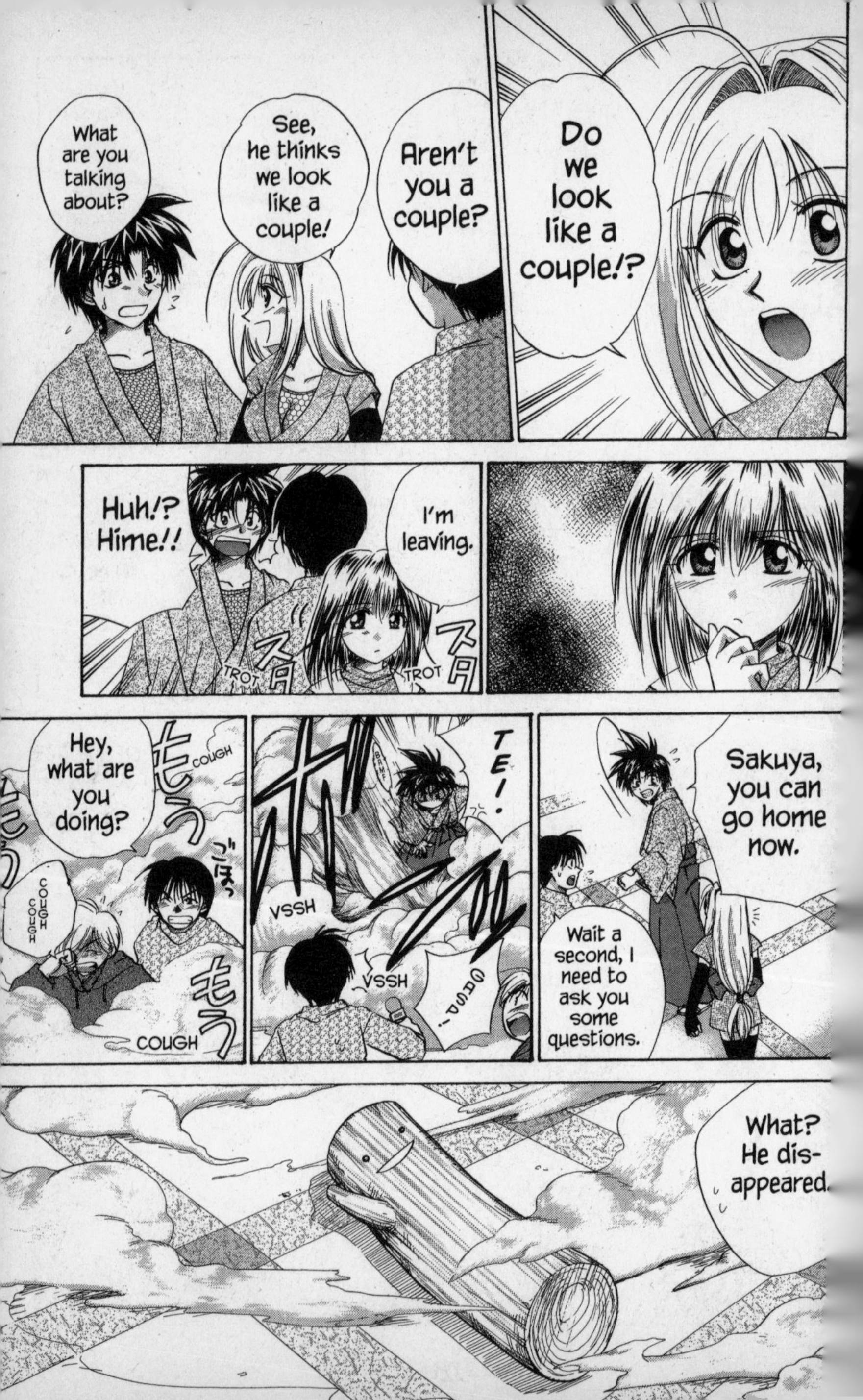
Do we look like a couple!?
Aren't you a couple?
See, he thinks we look like a couple!
What are you talking about?
I'm leaving.
スタ
TROT
スタ
TROT
Huh!? Hime!!
Sakuya, you can go home now.
Wait a second, I need to ask you some questions.
TE!
BAMF
VSSH
VSSH
Hey, what are you doing?
もう
COUGH
ごほっ
COUGH COUGH
もう
COUGH
What? He dis- appeared.

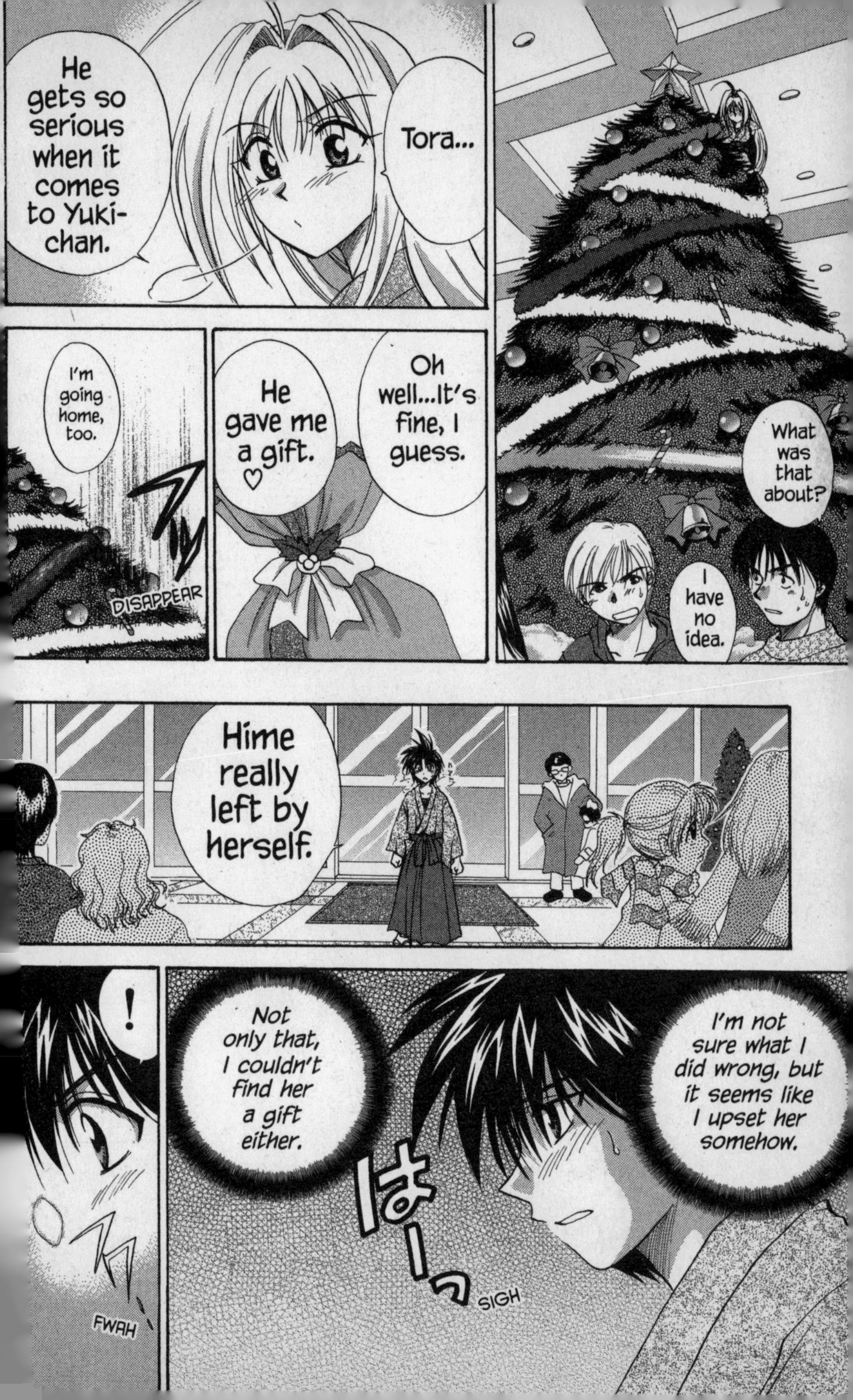
What was that about?
I have no idea.
Tora...
He gets so serious when it comes to Yuki-chan.
Oh well...It's fine, I guess.
He gave me a gift. ♡
I'm going home, too.
DISAPPEAR
Hime really left by herself.
I'm not sure what I did wrong, but it seems like I upset her somehow.
Not only that, I couldn't find her a gift either.
SIGH
!
FWAH

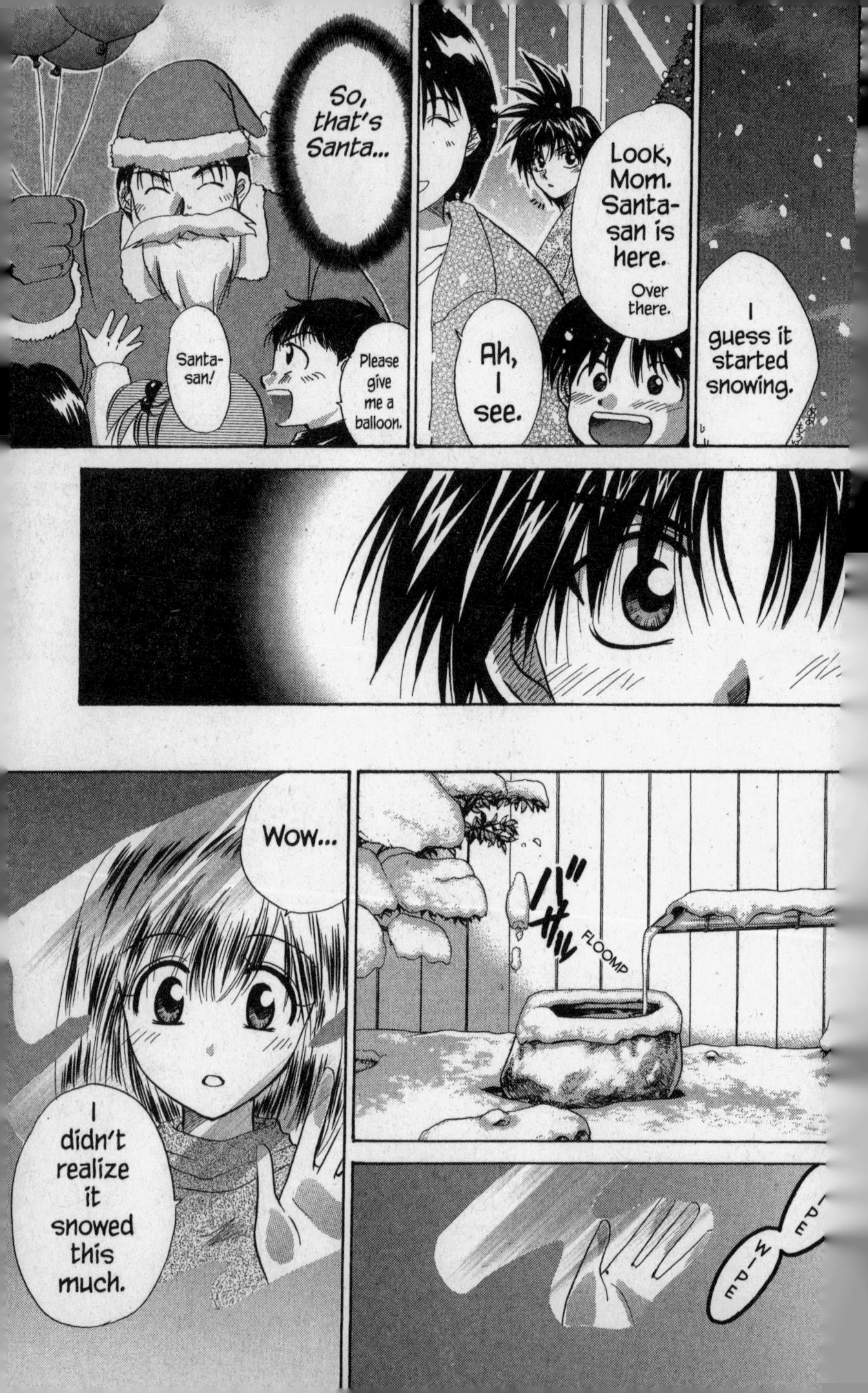
I guess it started snowing.
Look, Mom. Santa-san is here.
Over there.
Ah, I see.
So, that's Santa...
Please give me a balloon.
Santa-san!
FLOOMP
WIDE
Wow...
I didn't realize it snowed this much.

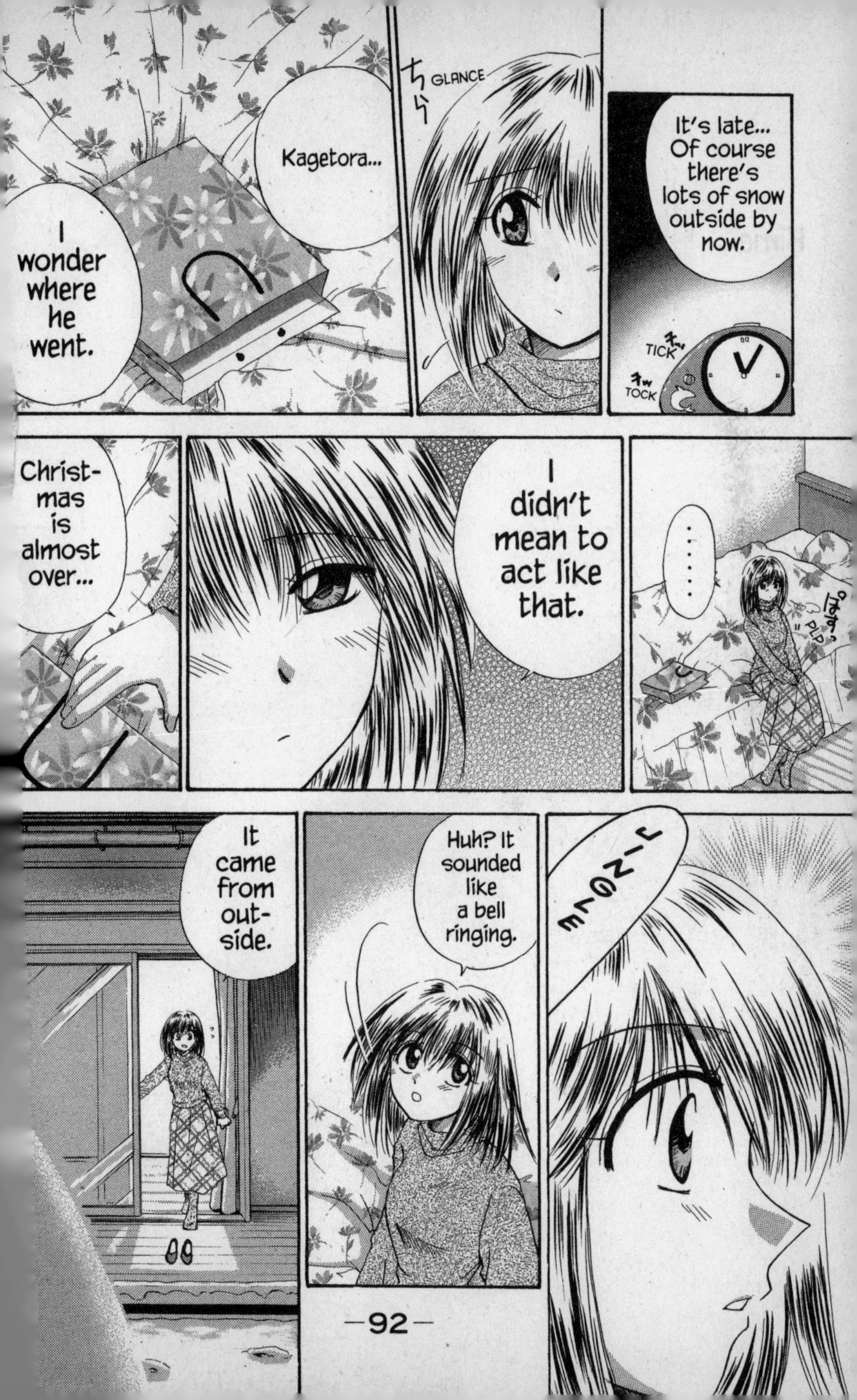
It's late... Of course there's lots of snow outside by now.
TICK
TOCK
GLANCE
Kagetora...
I wonder where he went.
......
PLP
I didn't mean to act like that.
Christmas is almost over...
Huh? It sounded like a bell ringing.
It came from outside.

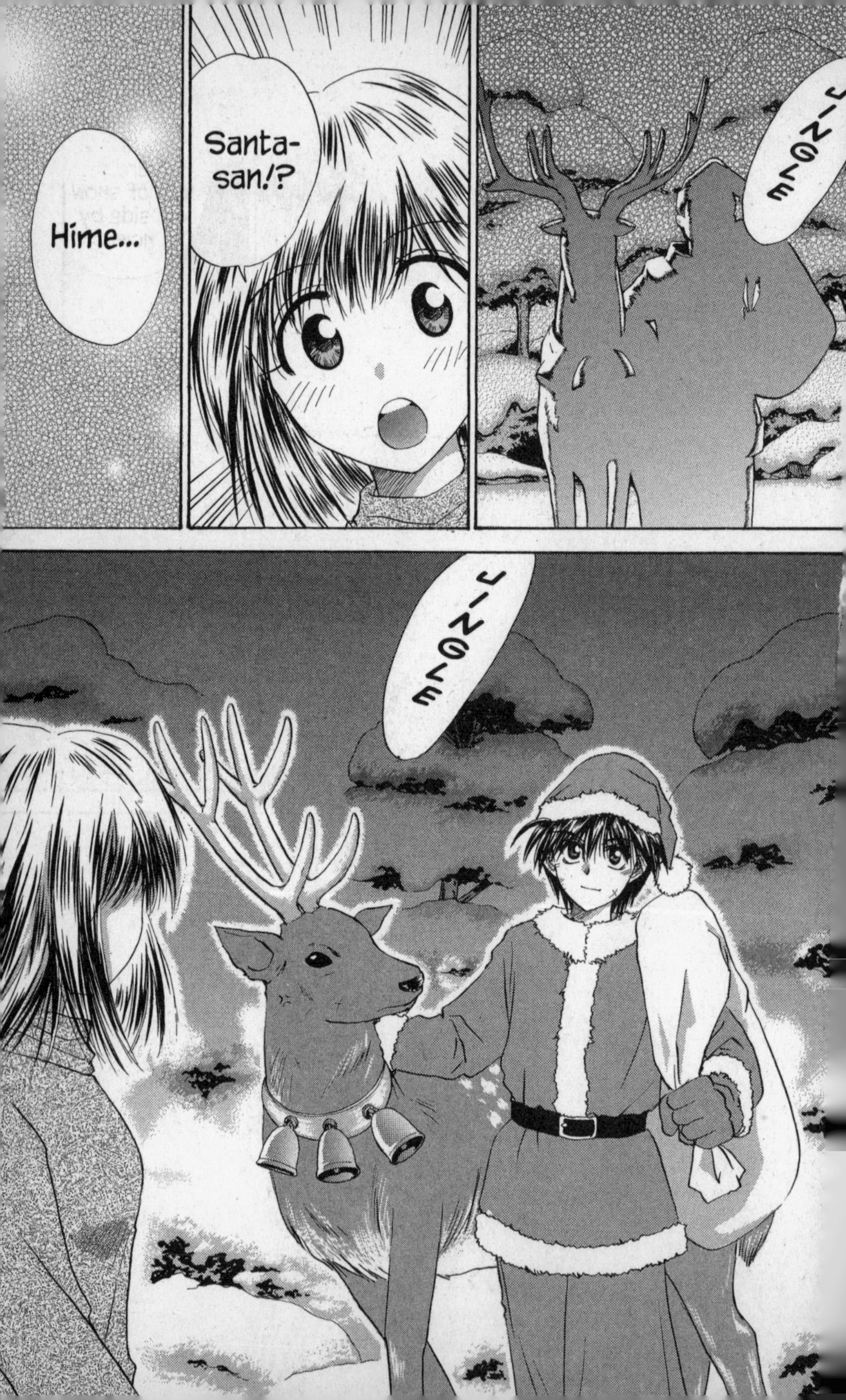
JINGLE
Santa-san!?
Hime...
JINGLE

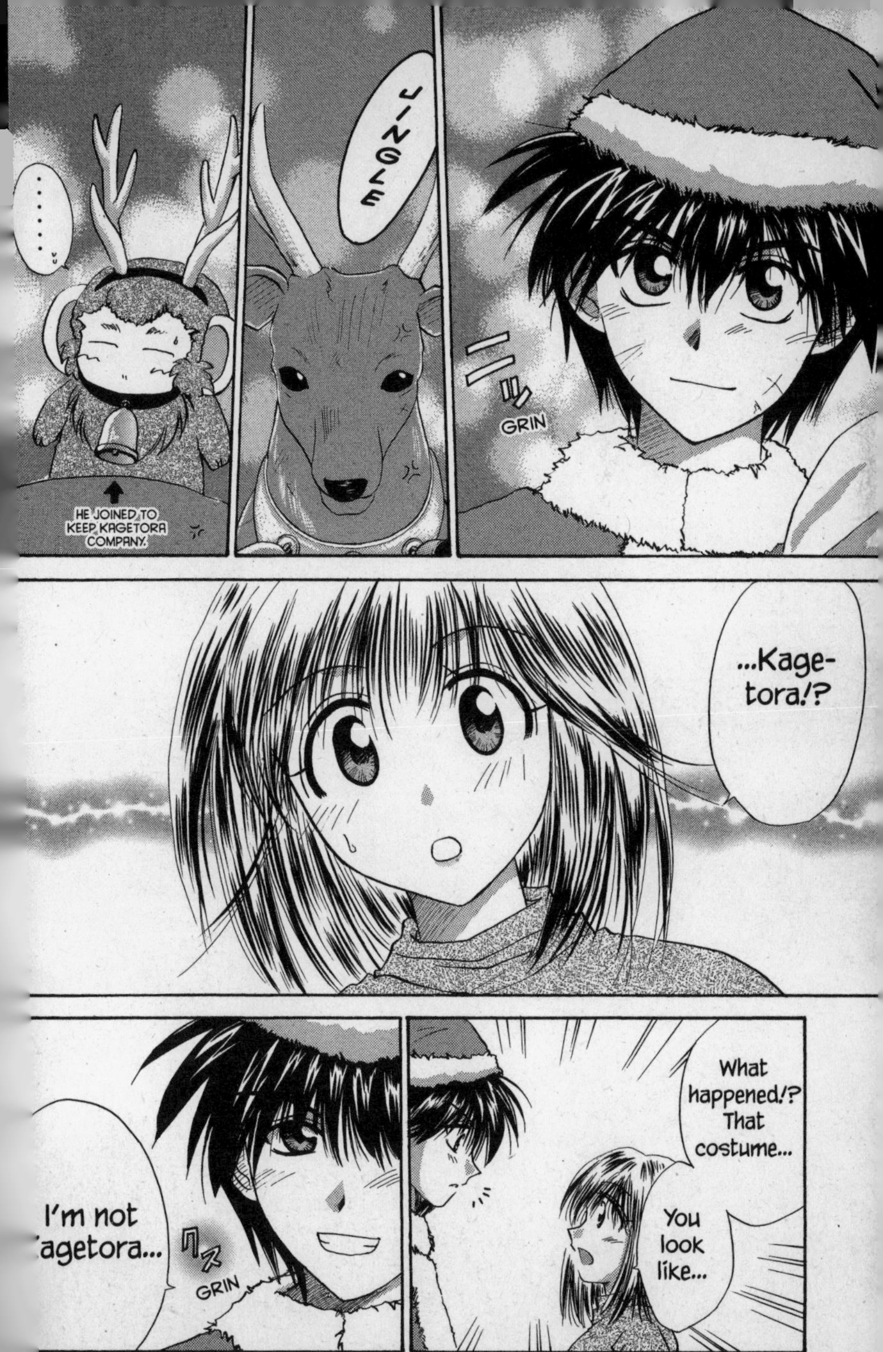
GRIN
JINGLE
......
HE JOINED TO KEEP KAGETORA COMPANY.
...Kage-tora!?
What happened!? That costume...
You look like...
I'm not
agetora...
GRIN

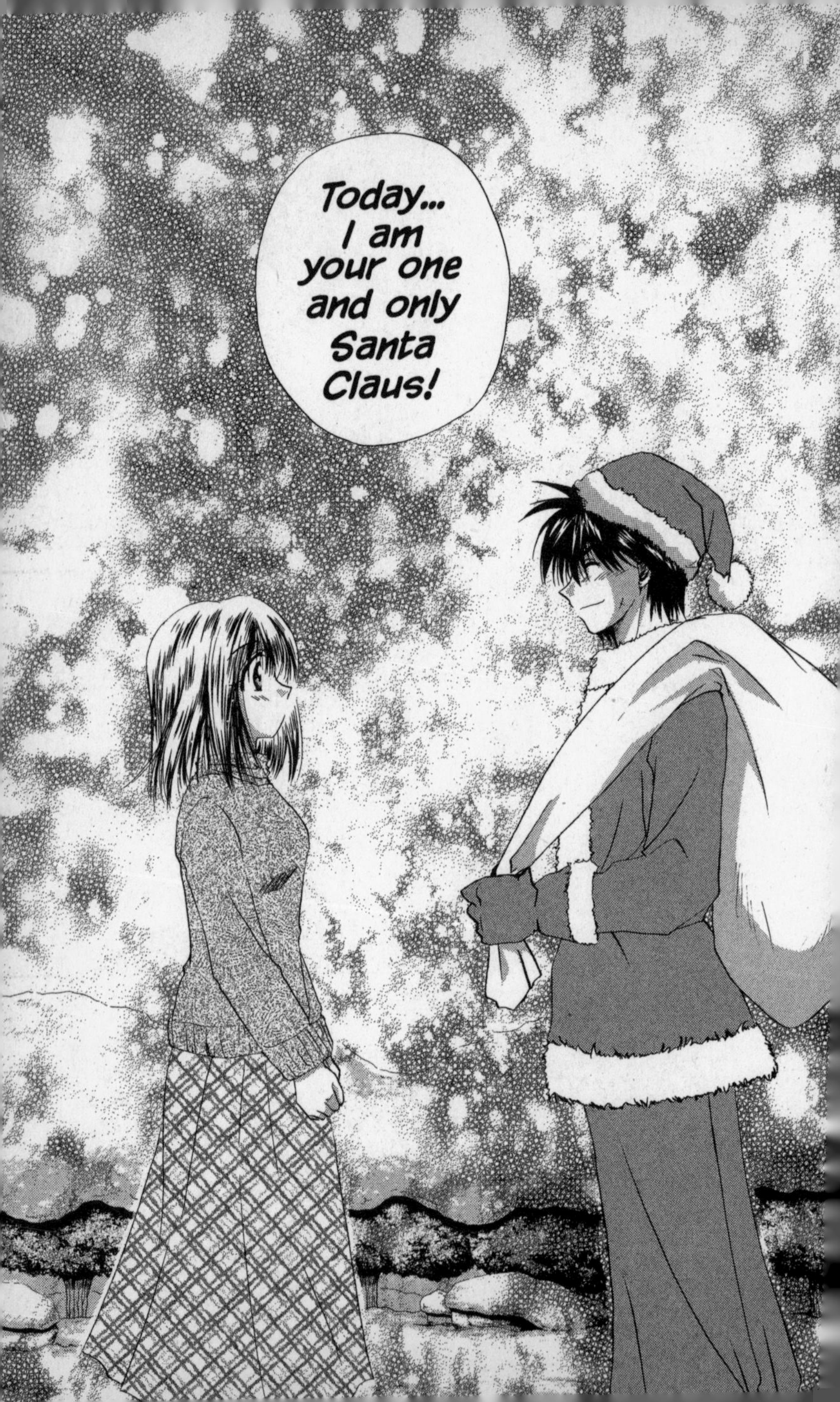
Today... I am your one and only Santa Claus!

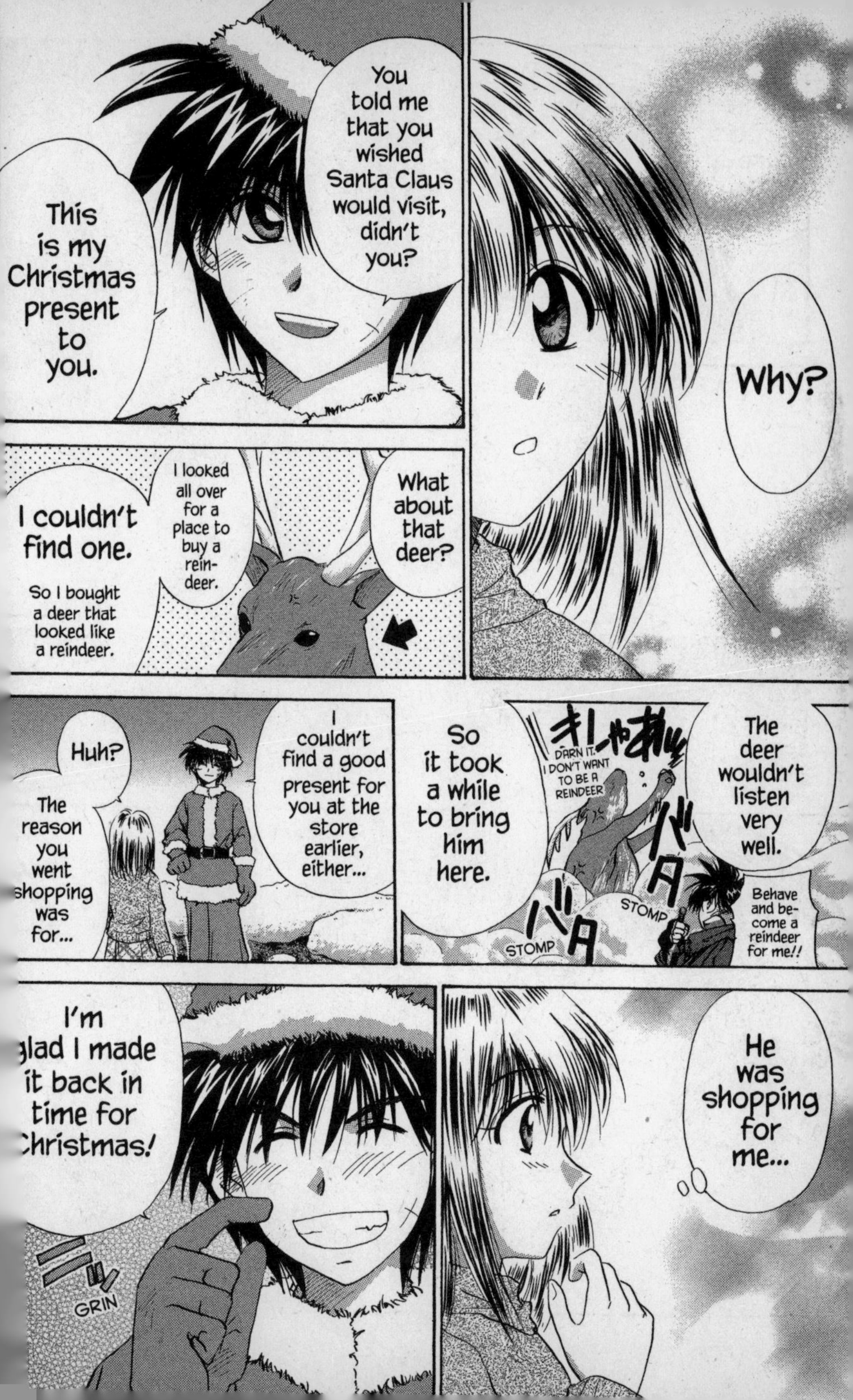
Why?
You told me that you wished Santa Claus would visit, didn't you?
This is my Christmas present to you.
What about that deer?
I looked all over for a place to buy a reindeer.
I couldn't find one.
So I bought a deer that looked like a reindeer.
The deer wouldn't listen very well.
DARN IT. I DON'T WANT TO BE A REINDEER
So it took a while to bring him here.
STOMP
STOMP
Behave and become a reindeer for me!!
I couldn't find a good present for you at the store earlier, either...
Huh?
The reason you went shopping was for...
He was shopping for me...
I'm glad I made it back in time for Christmas!
GRIN

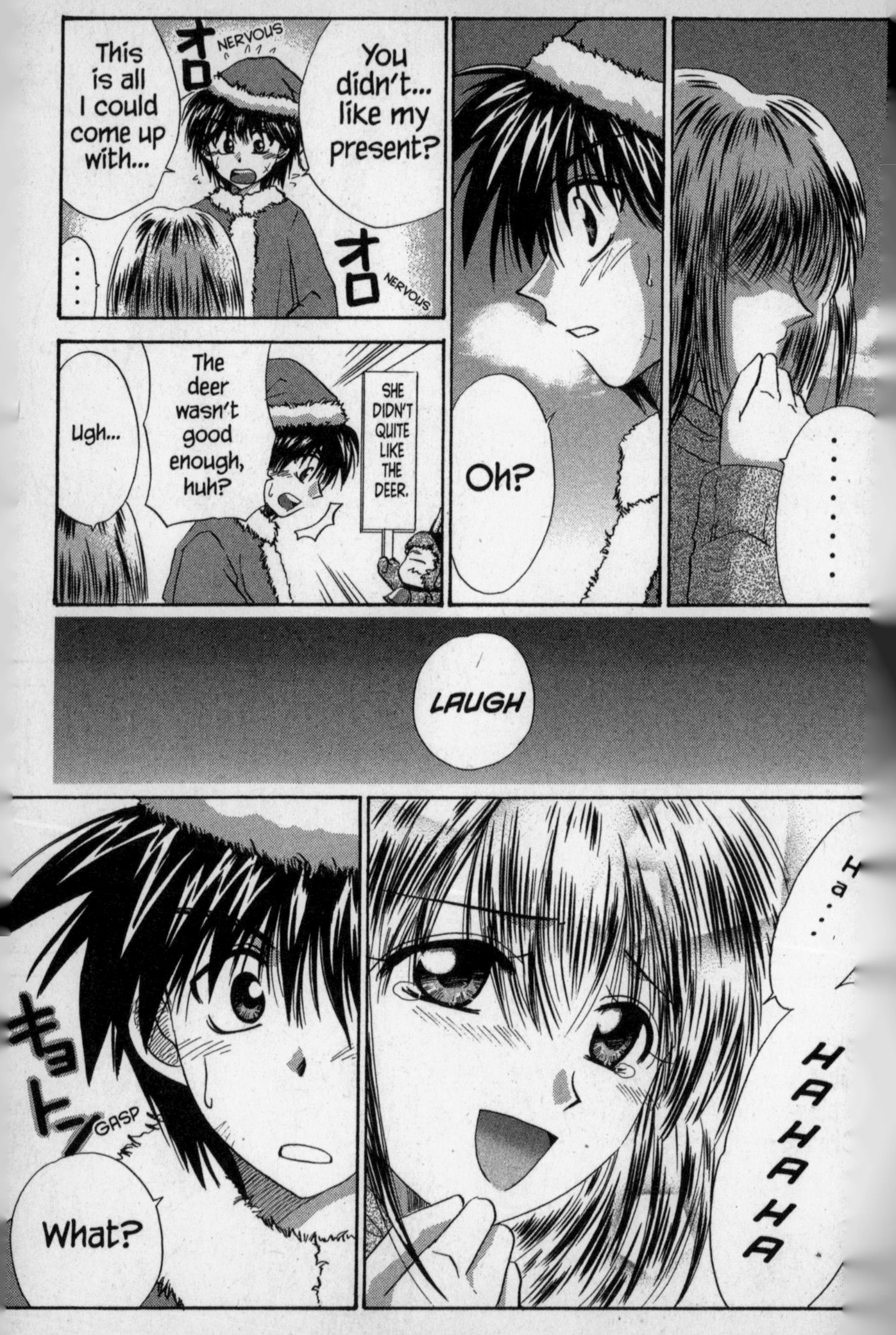
......
Oh?
オロ NERVOUS
You didn't... like my present?
This is all I could come up with...
オロ NERVOUS
...
SHE DIDN'T QUITE LIKE THE DEER.
The deer wasn't good enough, huh?
Ugh...
LAUGH
Ha...
HAHAHAHA
キョトン GASP
What?

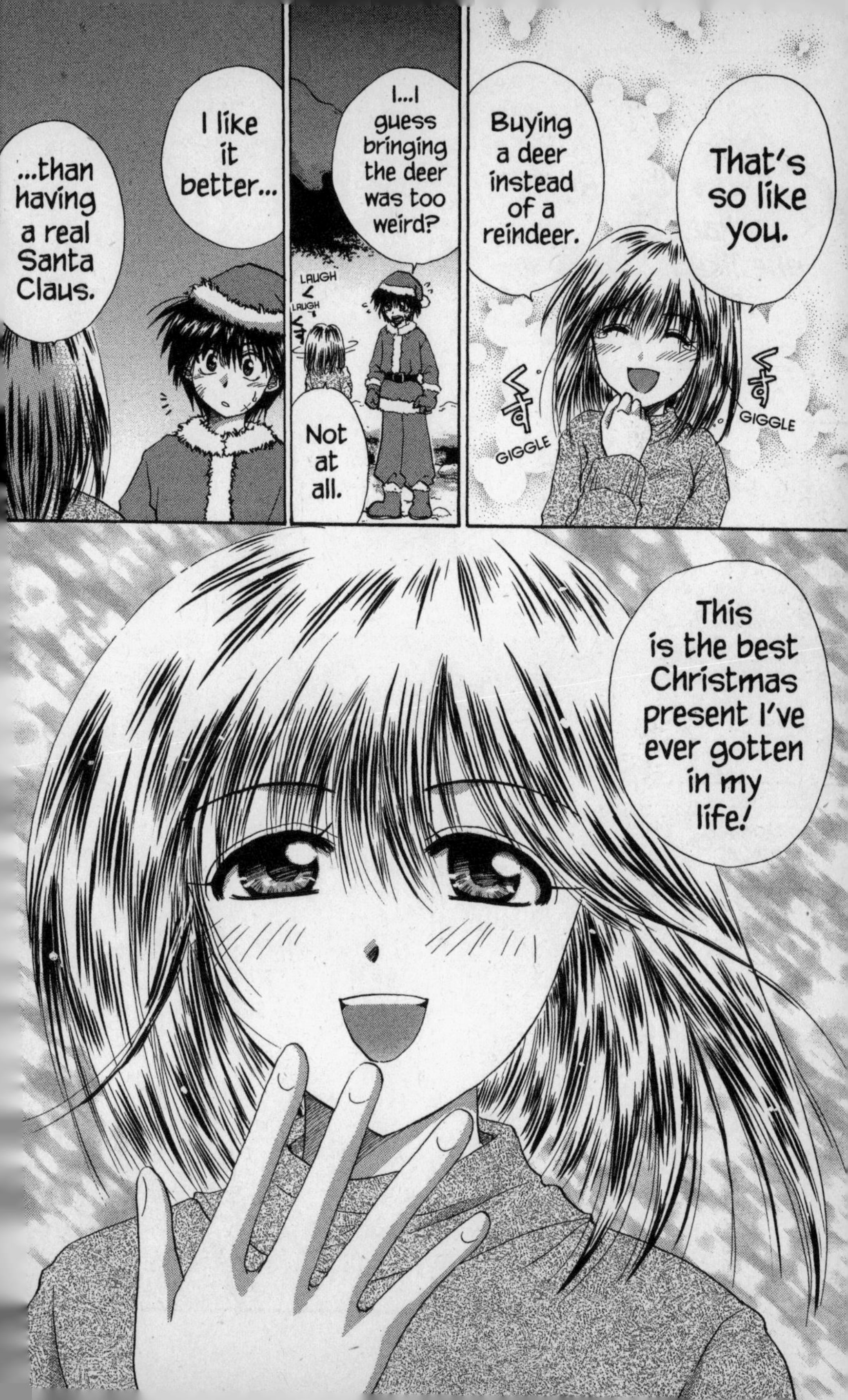
That's so like you.
Buying a deer instead of a reindeer.
くす GIGGLE
くす GIGGLE
I...I guess bringing the deer was too weird?
LAUGH LAUGH
Not at all.
I like it better...
...than having a real Santa Claus.
This is the best Christmas present I've ever gotten in my life!

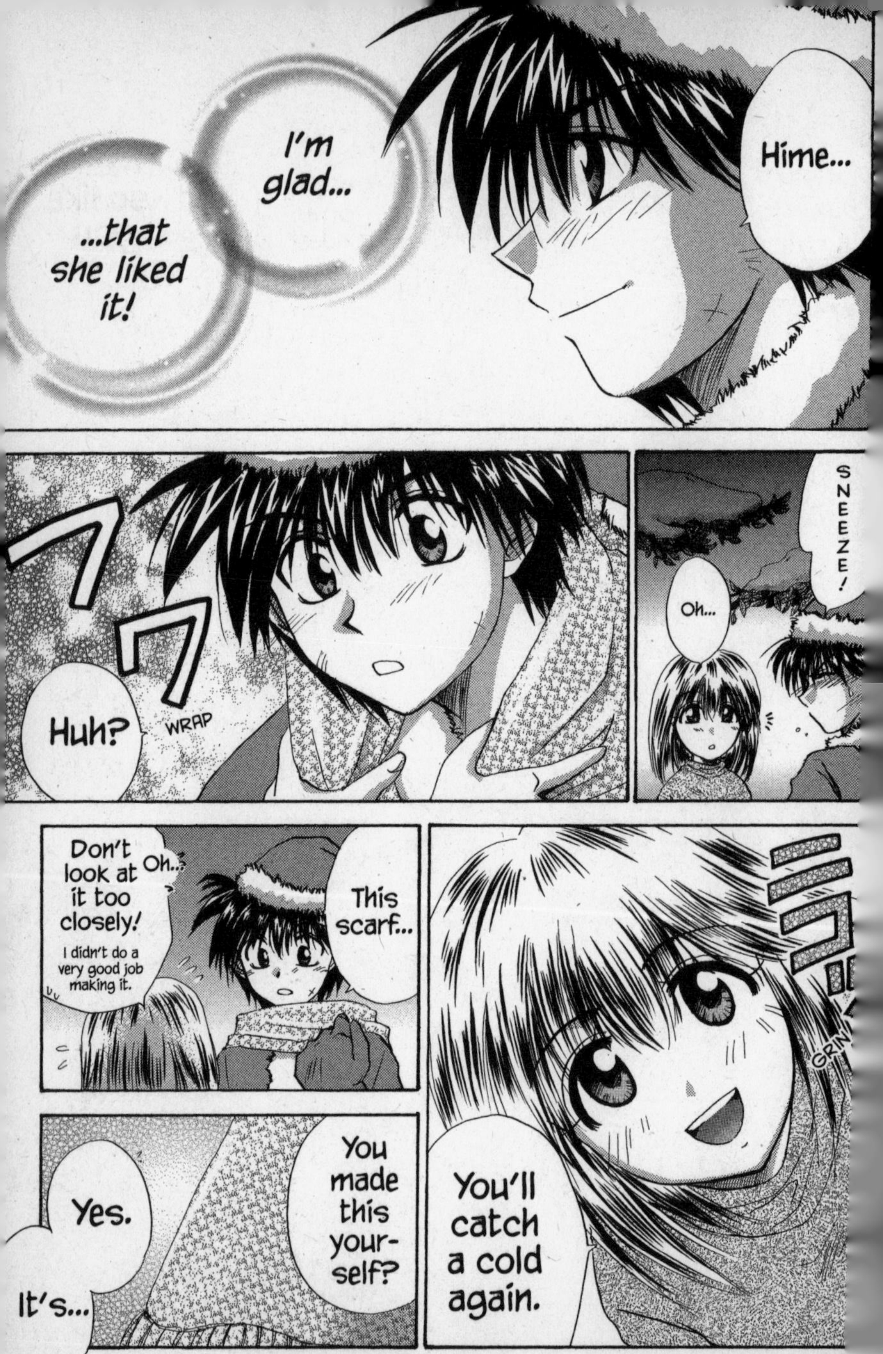
Hime...
I'm glad...
...that she liked it!
SNEEZE!
Oh...
Huh?
WRAP
You'll catch a cold again.
GRIN
This scarf...
Oh...
Don't look at it too closely!
I didn't do a very good job making it.
You made this yourself?
Yes.
It's...

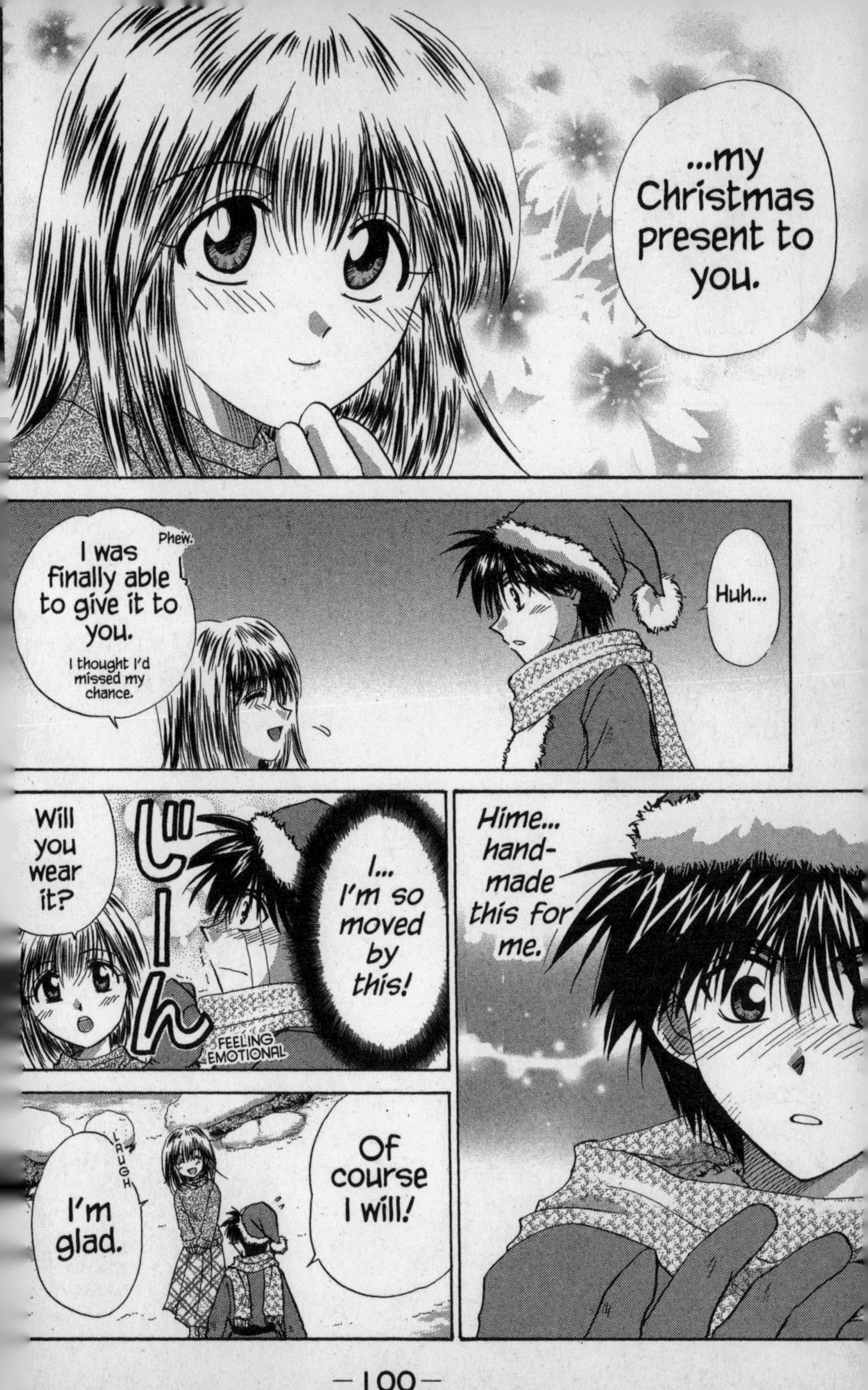
...my Christmas present to you.
Huh...
Phew.
I was finally able to give it to you.
I thought I'd missed my chance.
Hime... hand-made this for me.
I... I'm so moved by this!
じーん
FEELING EMOTIONAL
Will you wear it?
Of course I will!
LAUGH
I'm glad.

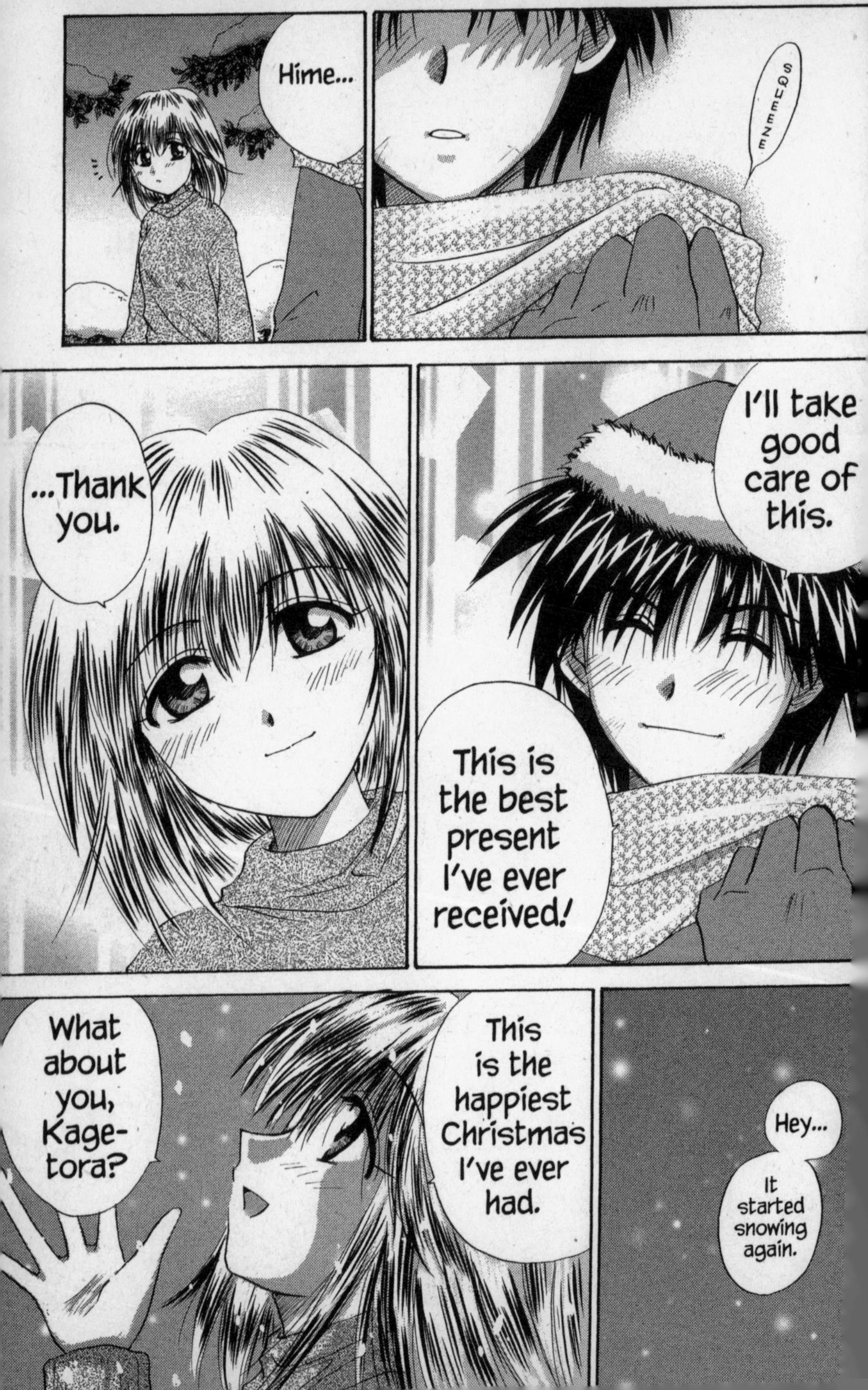
SQUEEZE
Hime...
I'll take good care of this.
This is the best present I've ever received!
...Thank you.
Hey...
It started snowing again.
This is the happiest Christmas I've ever had.
What about you, Kage-tora?

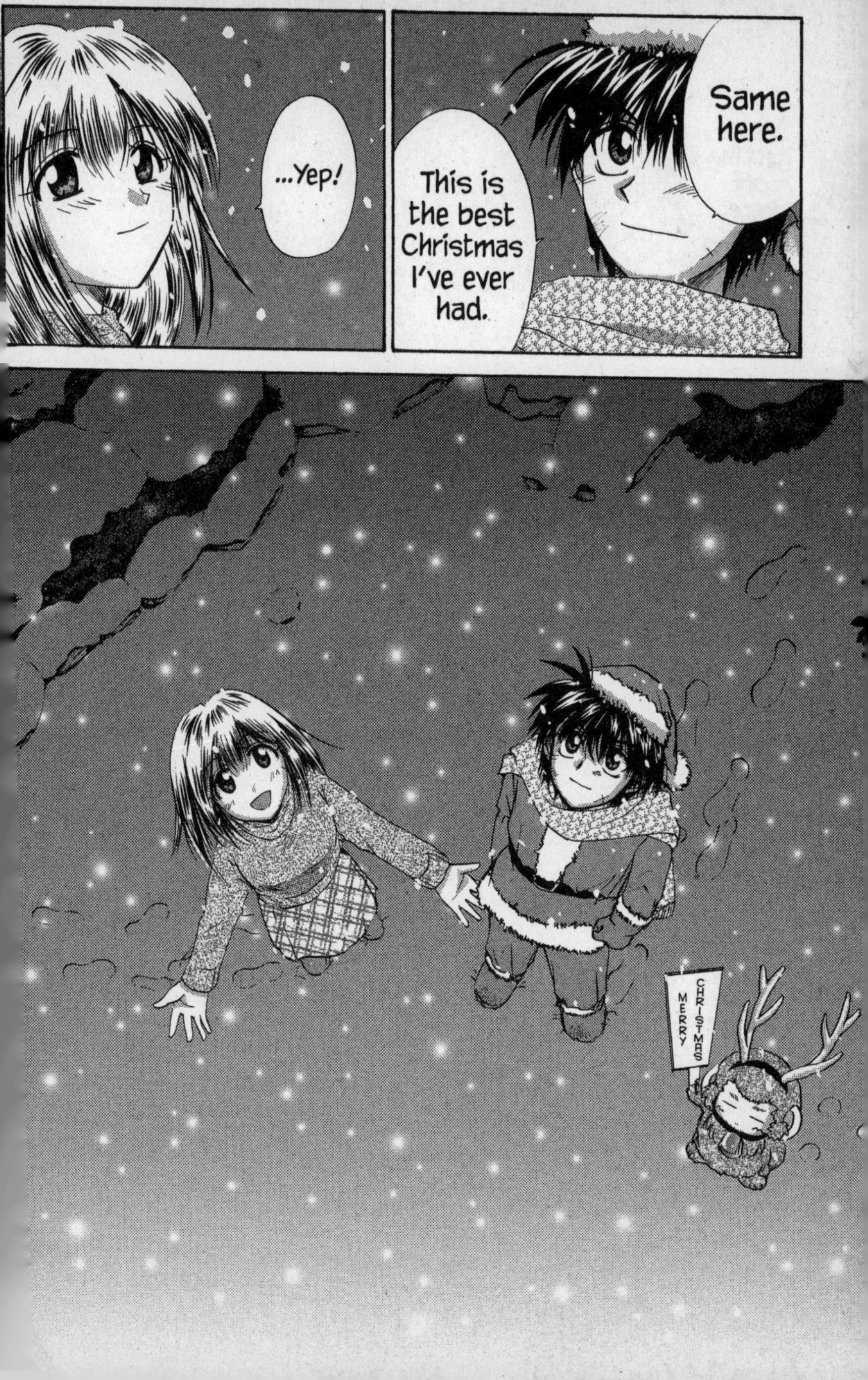
Same here.
This is the best Christmas I've ever had.
...Yep!
MERRY CHRISTMAS

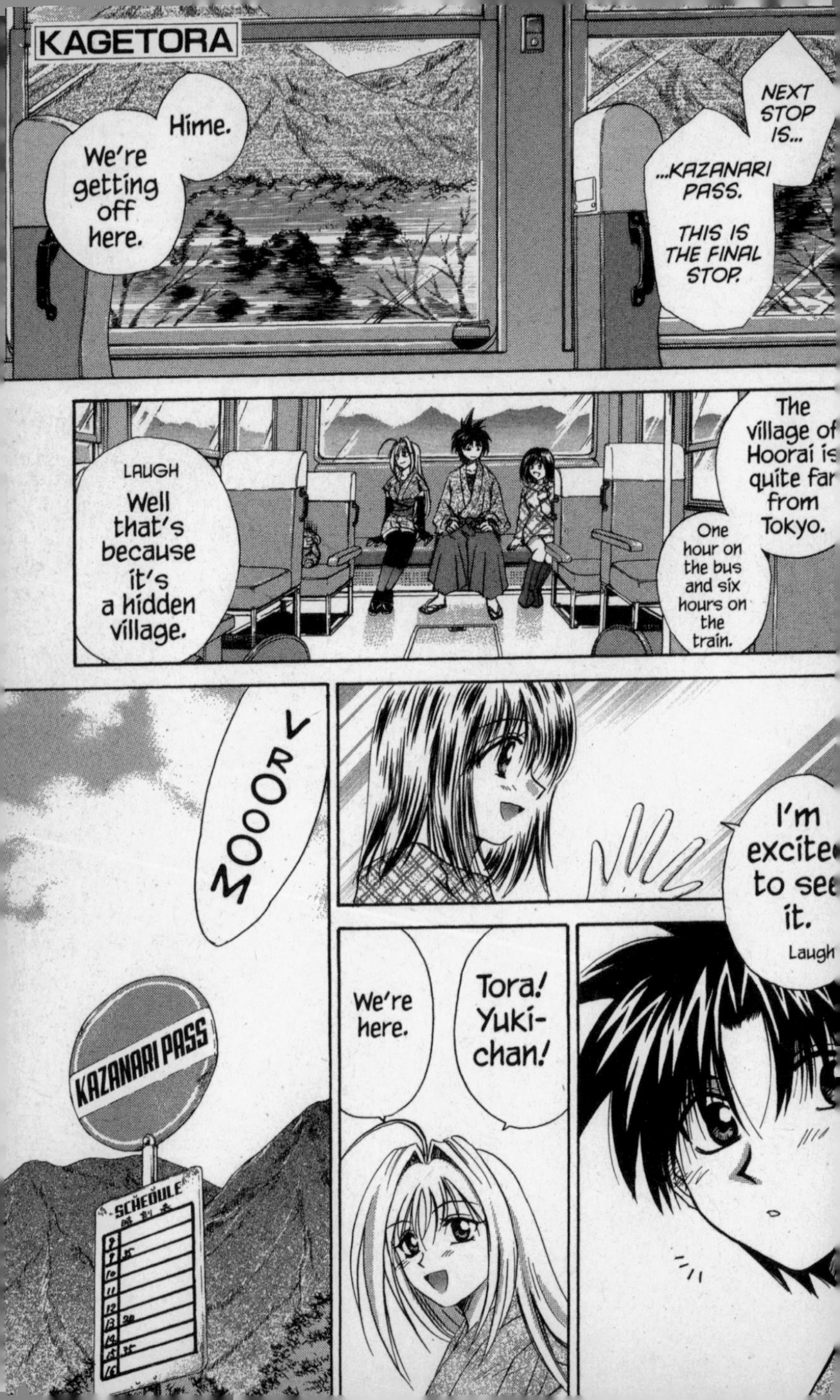
NEXT STOP IS...
...KAZANARI PASS.
THIS IS THE FINAL STOP.
Hime.
We're getting off here.
The village of Hoorai is quite far from Tokyo.
One hour on the bus and six hours on the train.
LAUGH
Well that's because it's a hidden village.
I'm excite to see it.
Laugh
Tora! Yuki-chan!
We're here.
VROOOOM
KAZANARI PASS
SCHEDULE

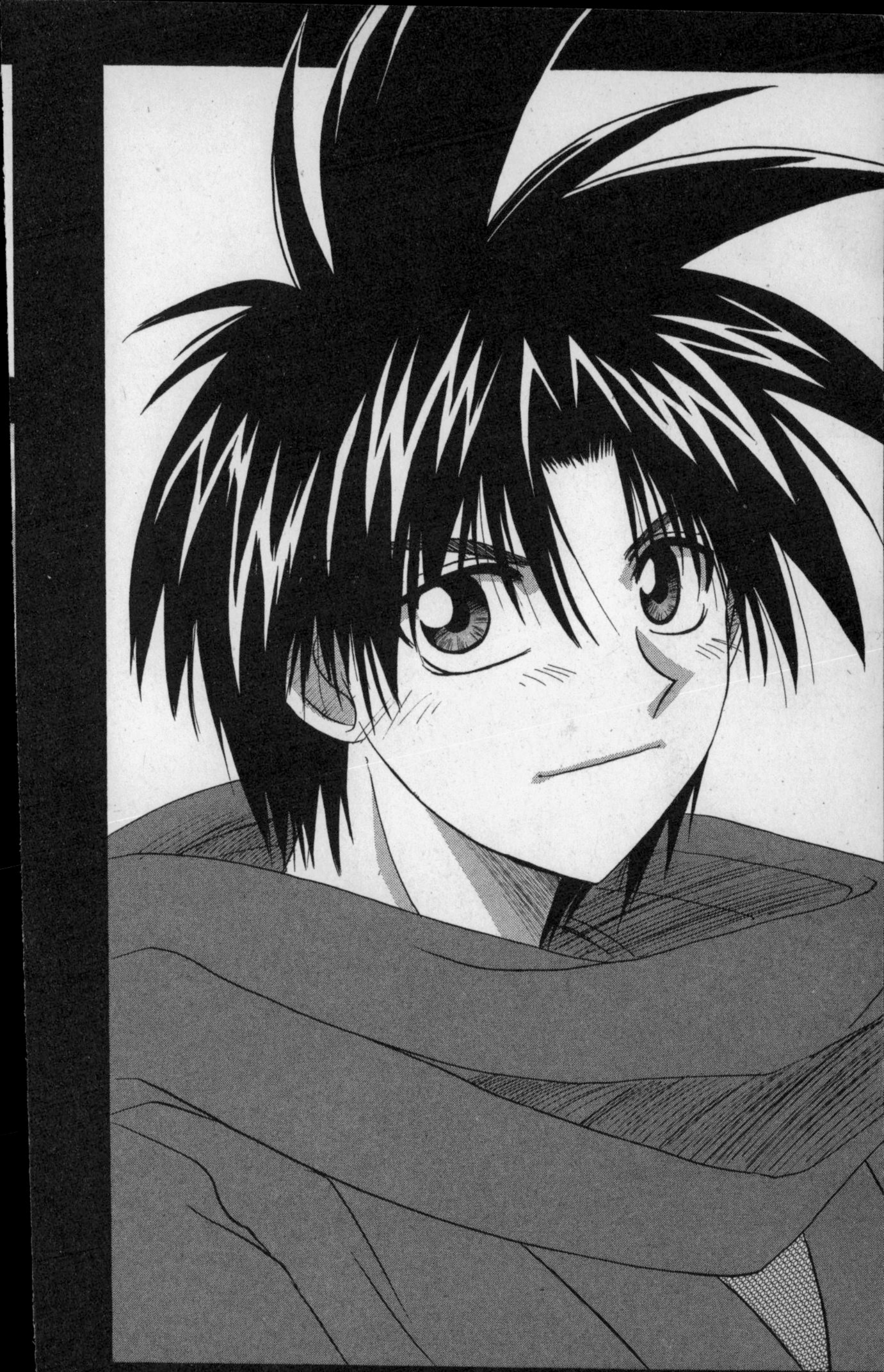

KAGETORA カゲトラ

#9 A Secret Just Between Us

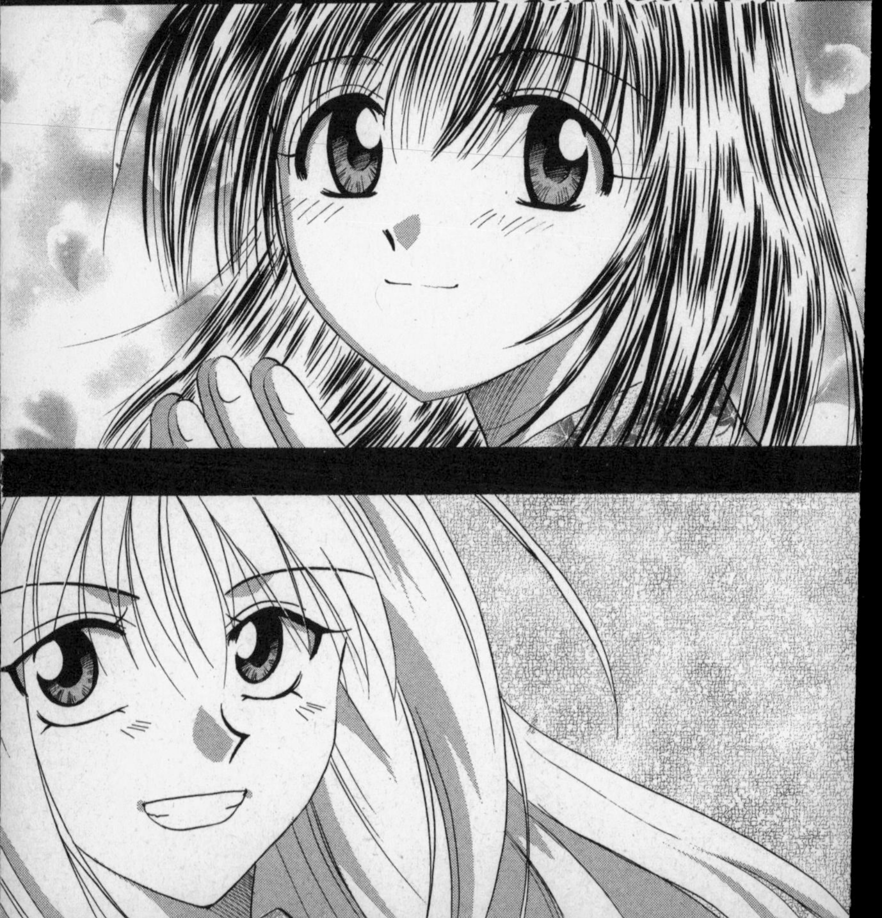

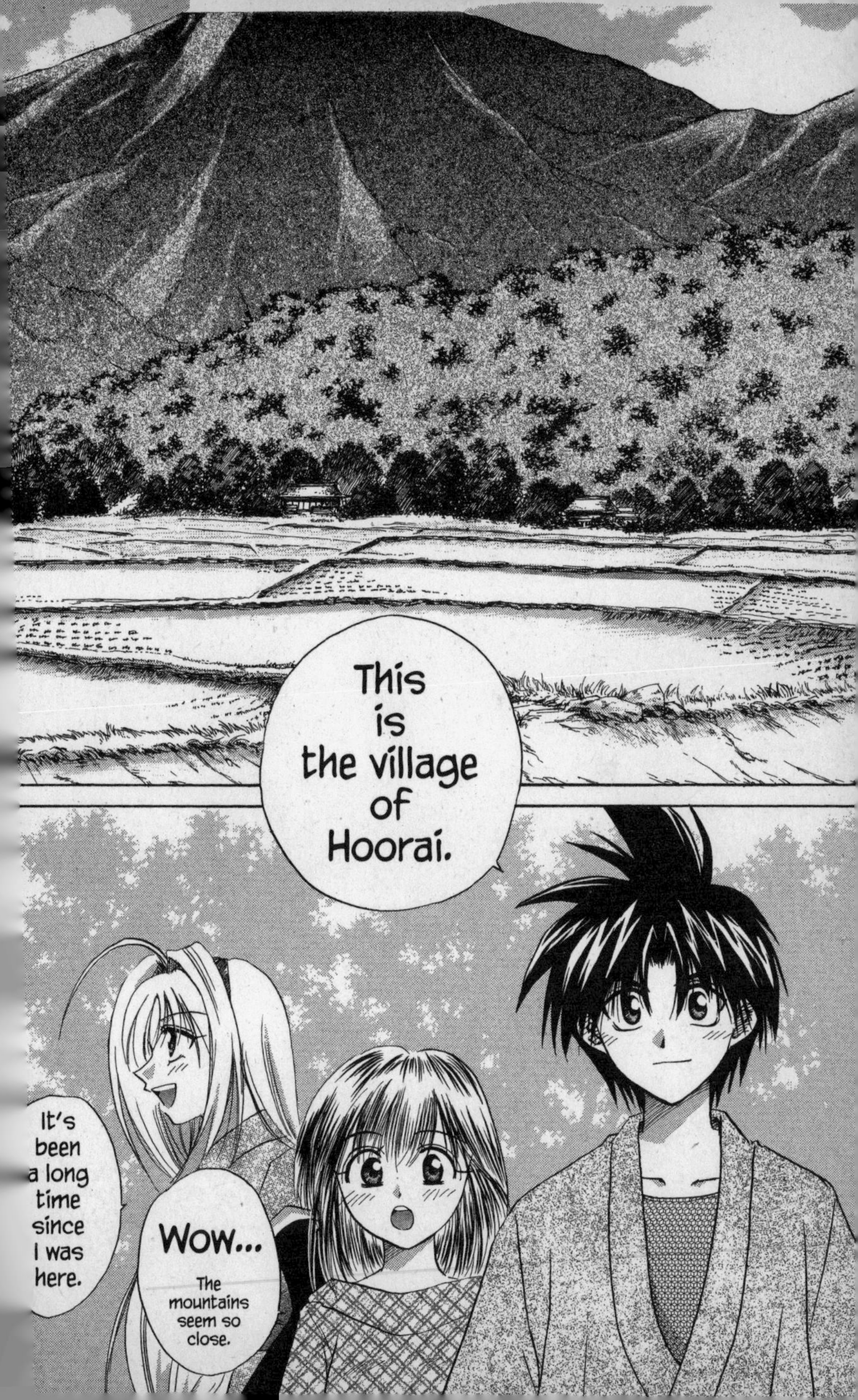
This is the village of Hoorai.
Wow...
The mountains seem so close.
It's been a long time since I was here.

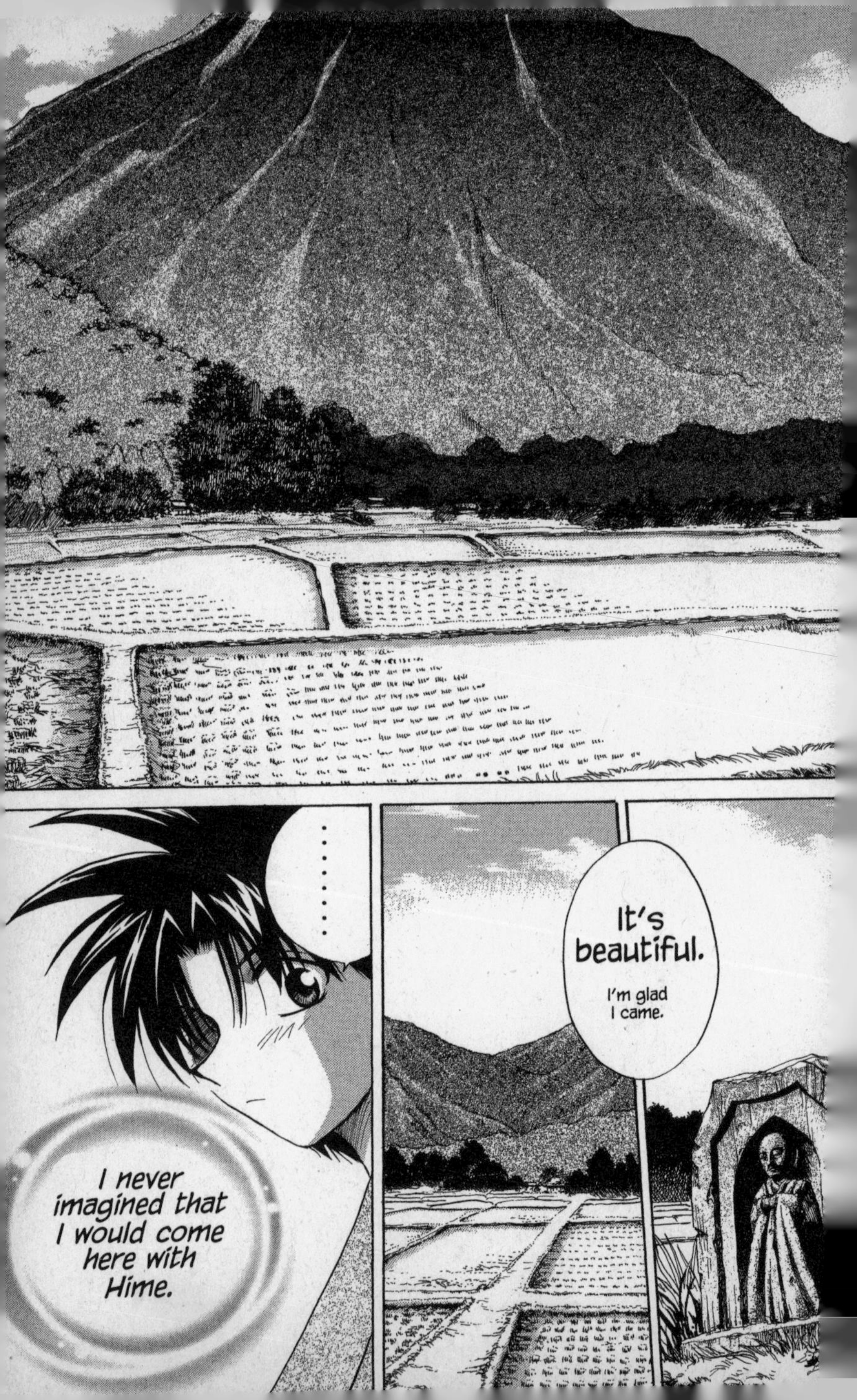
It's beautiful.
I'm glad I came.
......
I never imagined that I would come here with Hime.

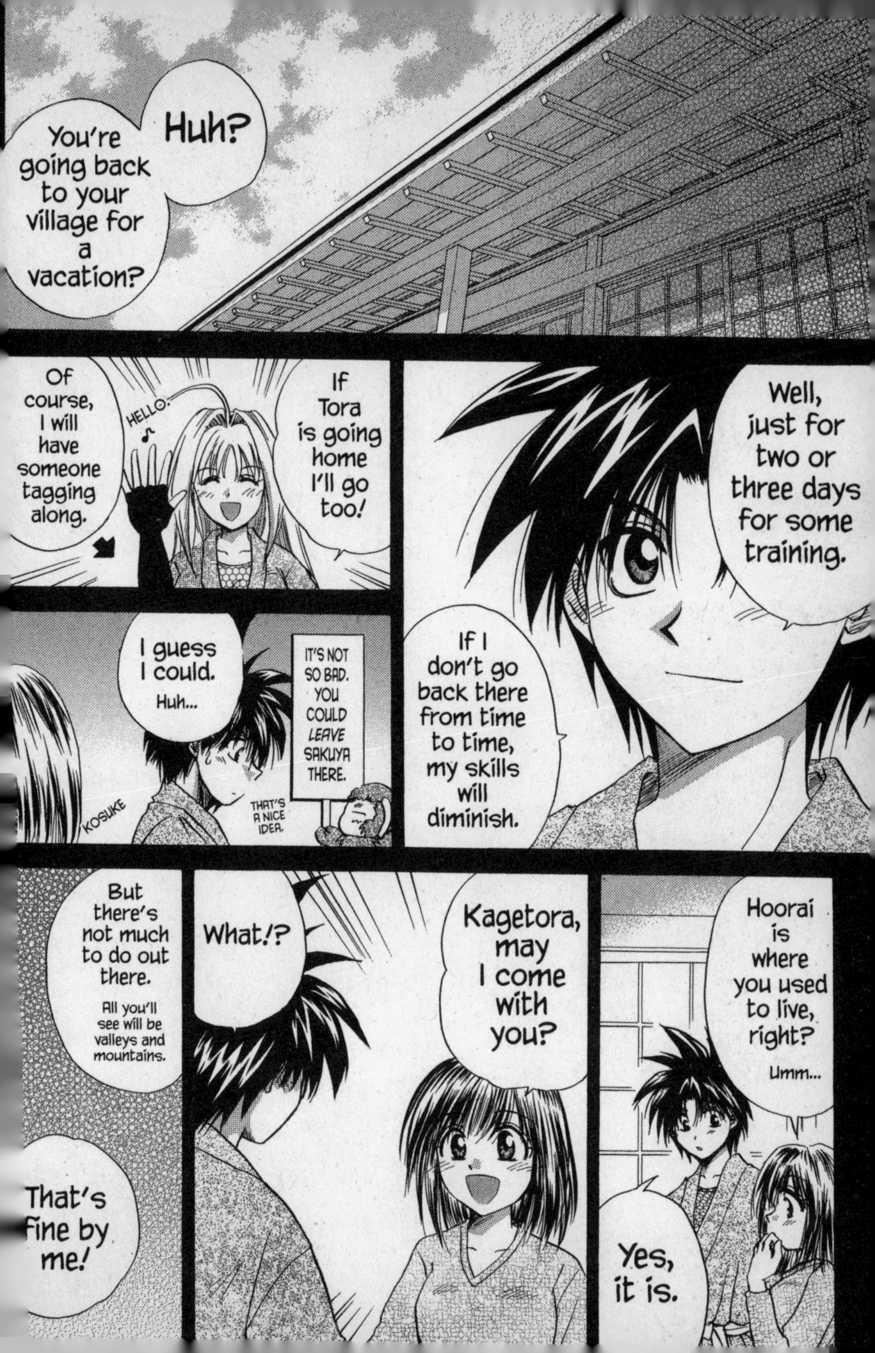
Huh?
You're going back to your village for a vacation?
Well, just for two or three days for some training.
If I don't go back there from time to time, my skills will diminish.
If Tora is going home I'll go too!
HELLO ♪
Of course, I will have someone tagging along.
IT'S NOT SO BAD. YOU COULD *LEAVE* SAKUYA THERE.
I guess I could.
Huh...
THAT'S A NICE IDEA.
KOSUKE
Hoorai is where you used to live, right?
Umm...
Yes, it is.
Kagetora, may I come with you?
What!?
But there's not much to do out there.
All you'll see will be valleys and mountains.
That's fine by me!

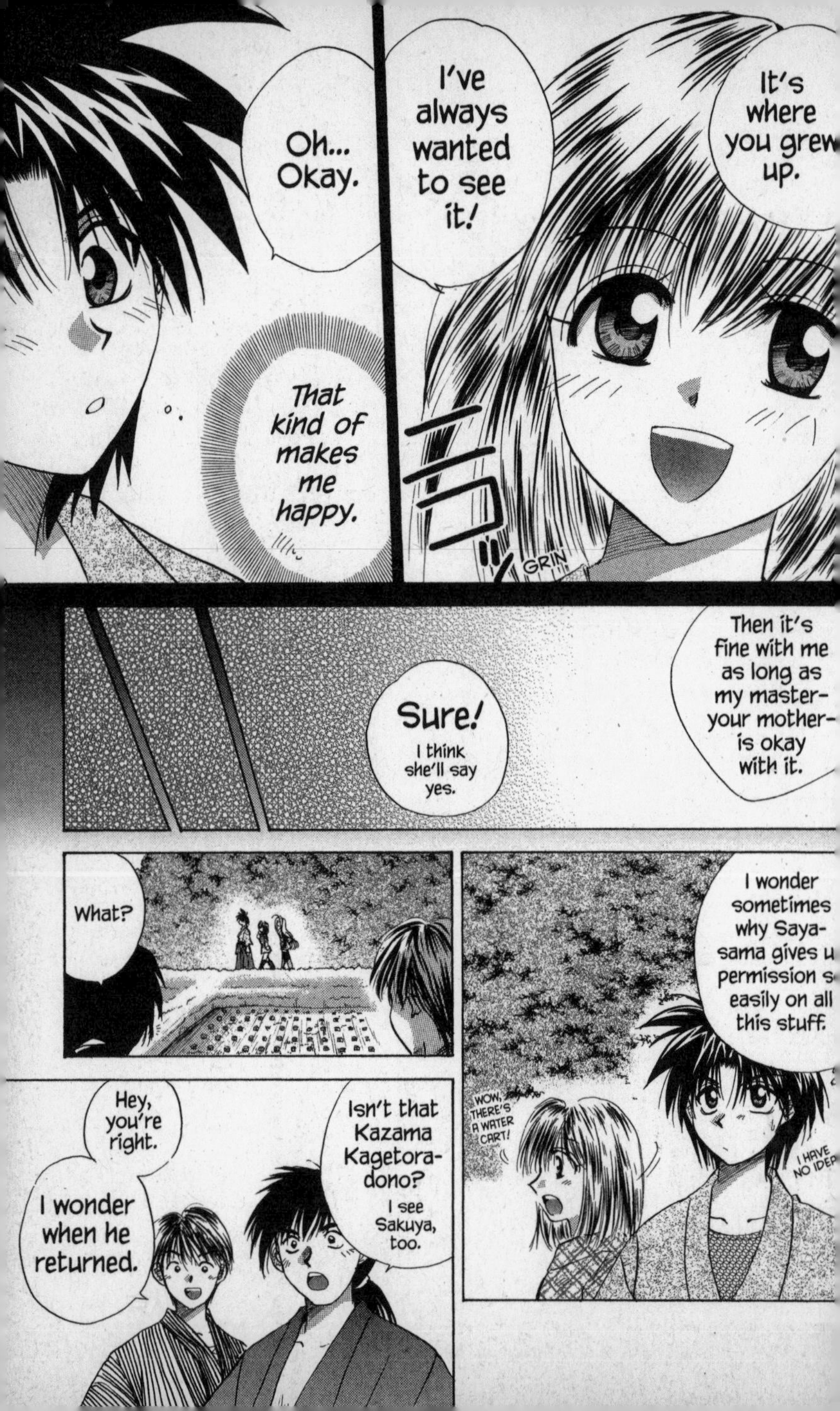

It's where you grew up.
I've always wanted to see it!
GRIN
Oh... Okay.
That kind of makes me happy.
Then it's fine with me as long as my master—your mother—is okay with it.
Sure! I think she'll say yes.
I wonder sometimes why Saya-sama gives u permission s easily on all this stuff.
I HAVE NO IDE
WOW, THERE'S A WATER CART!
What?
Isn't that Kazama Kagetora-dono? I see Sakuya, too.
Hey, you're right.
I wonder when he returned.

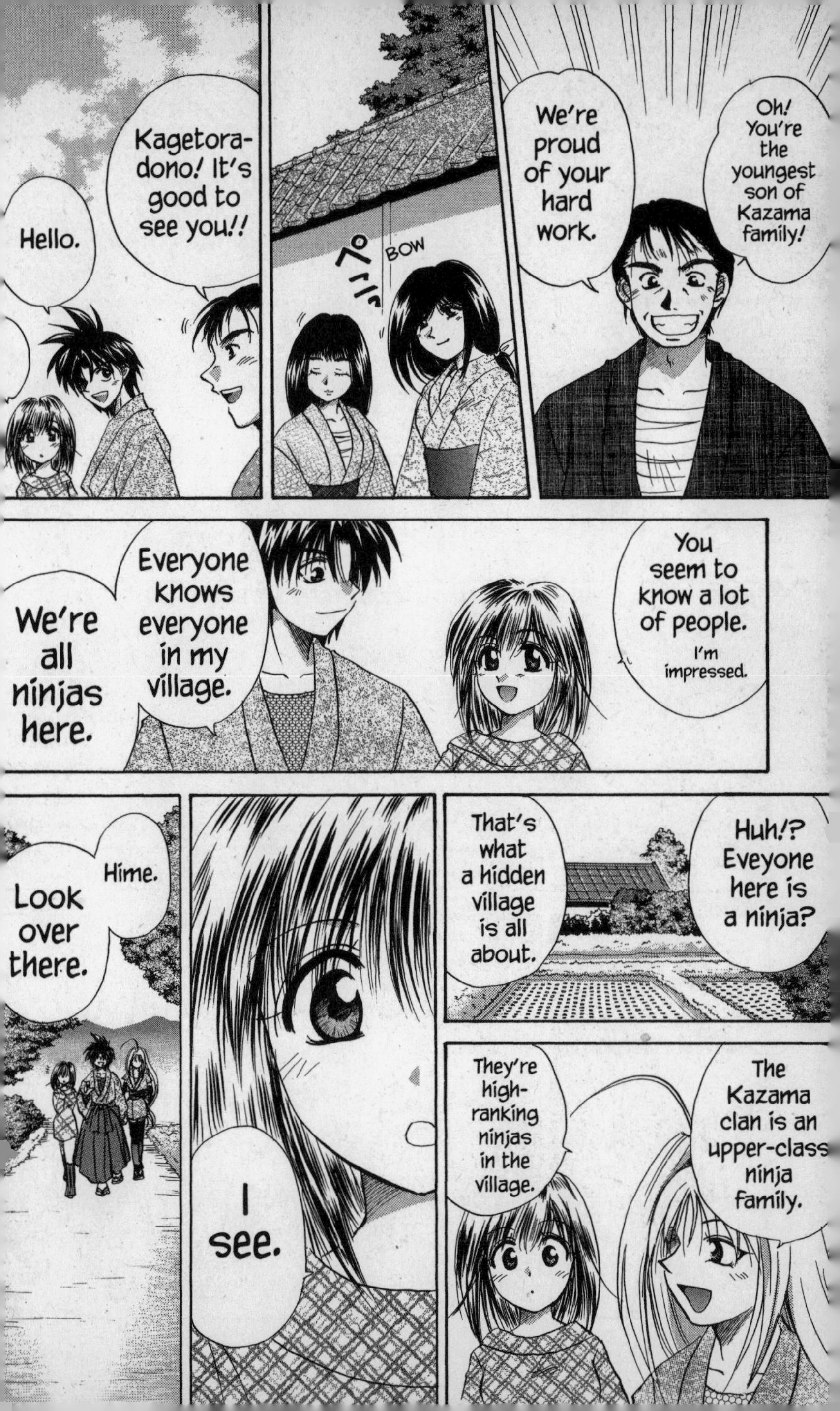
Oh! You're the youngest son of Kazama family!
We're proud of your hard work.
BOW
Kagetora-dono! It's good to see you!!
Hello.
You seem to know a lot of people.
I'm impressed.
Everyone knows everyone in my village.
We're all ninjas here.
Huh!? Eveyone here is a ninja?
That's what a hidden village is all about.
The Kazama clan is an upper-class ninja family.
They're high-ranking ninjas in the village.
I see.
Hime.
Look over there.

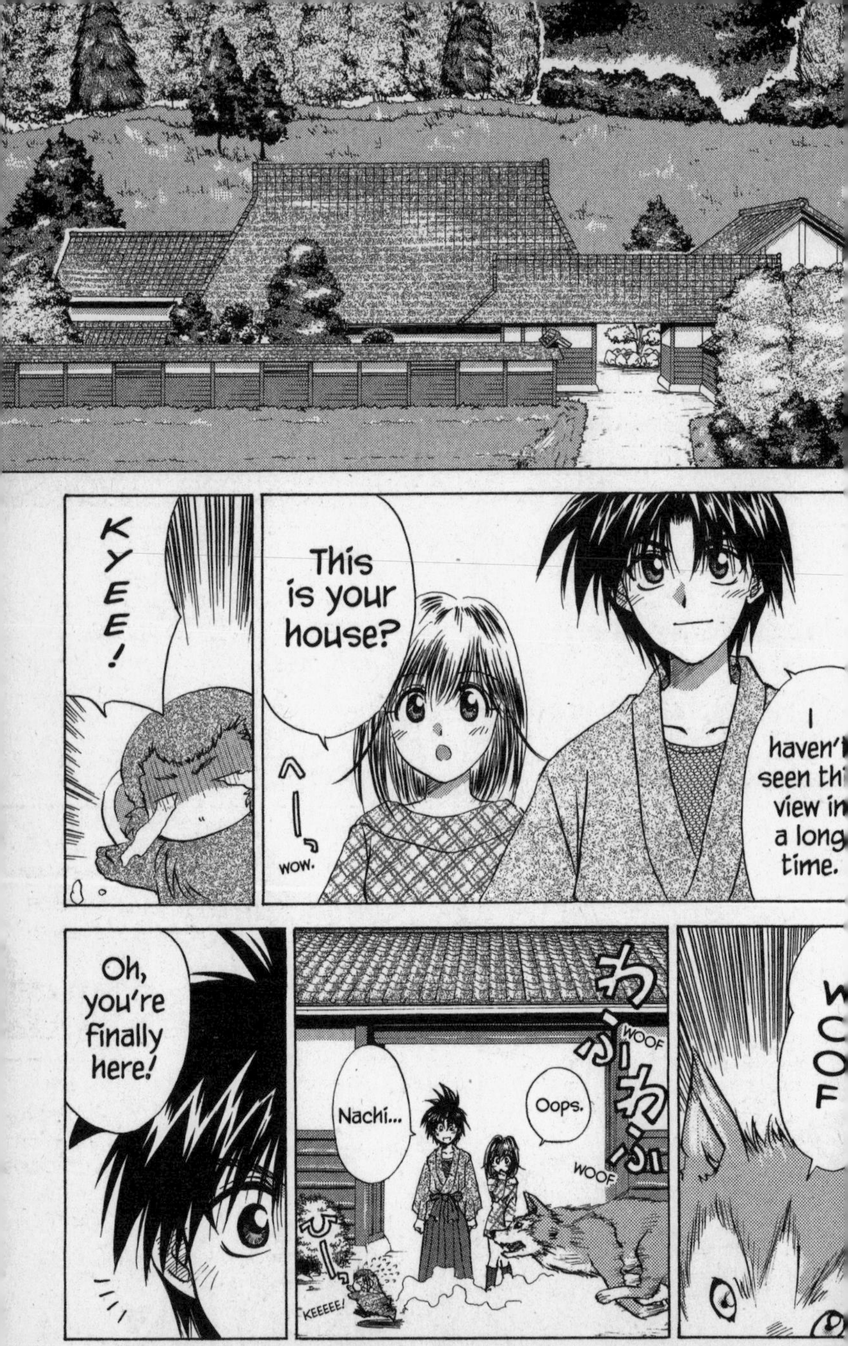
I haven't seen this view in a long time.
This is your house?
へー
WOW.
KYEE!
WOOF
わふわふ
WOOF
WOOF
Oops.
Nachi...
ひー
KEEEEE!
Oh, you're finally here!

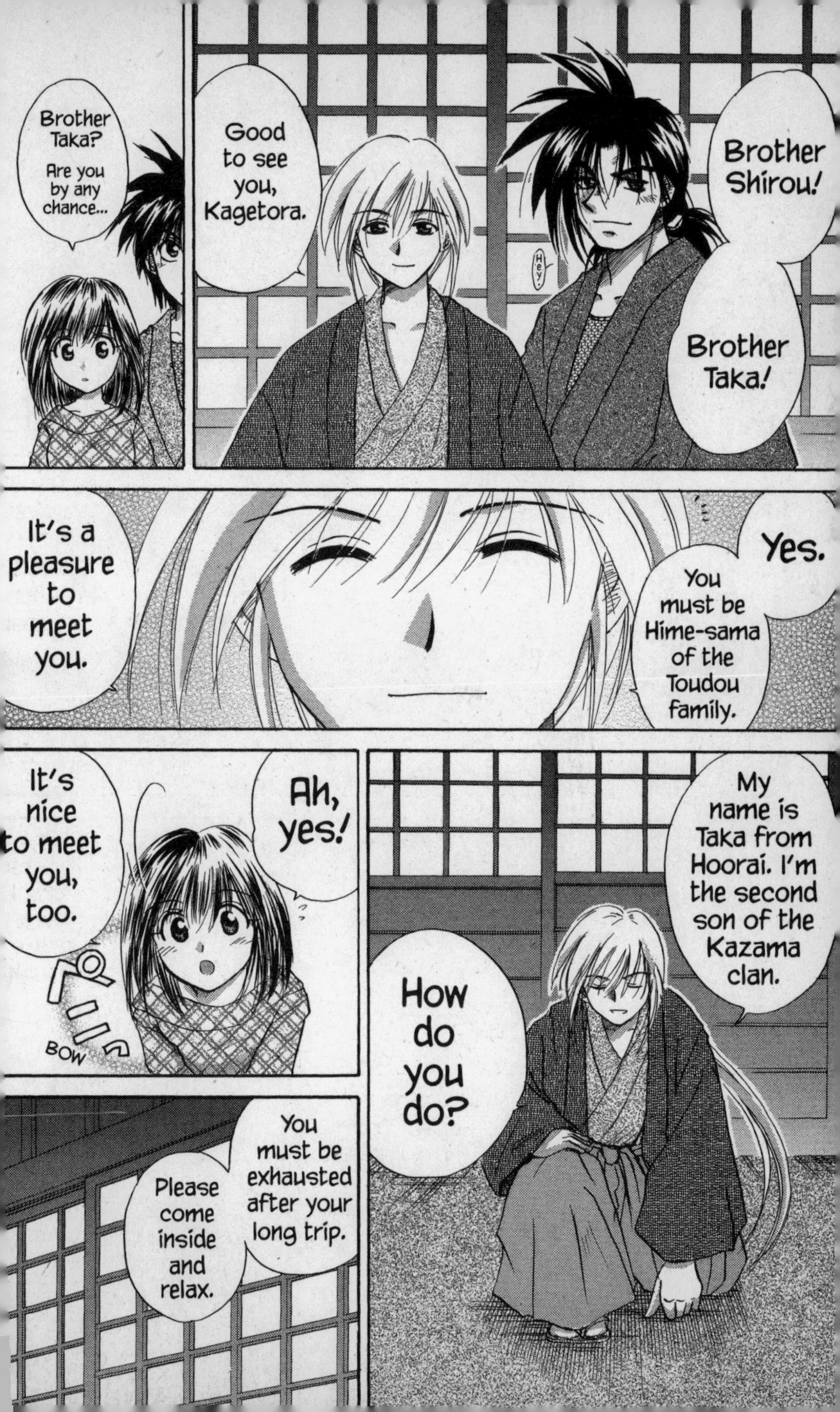
Brother Shirou!
Brother Taka!
Hey
Good to see you, Kagetora.
Brother Taka? Are you by any chance...
Yes.
You must be Hime-sama of the Toudou family.
It's a pleasure to meet you.
My name is Taka from Hoorai. I'm the second son of the Kazama clan.
How do you do?
Ah, yes!
It's nice to meet you, too.
BOW
You must be exhausted after your long trip.
Please come inside and relax.

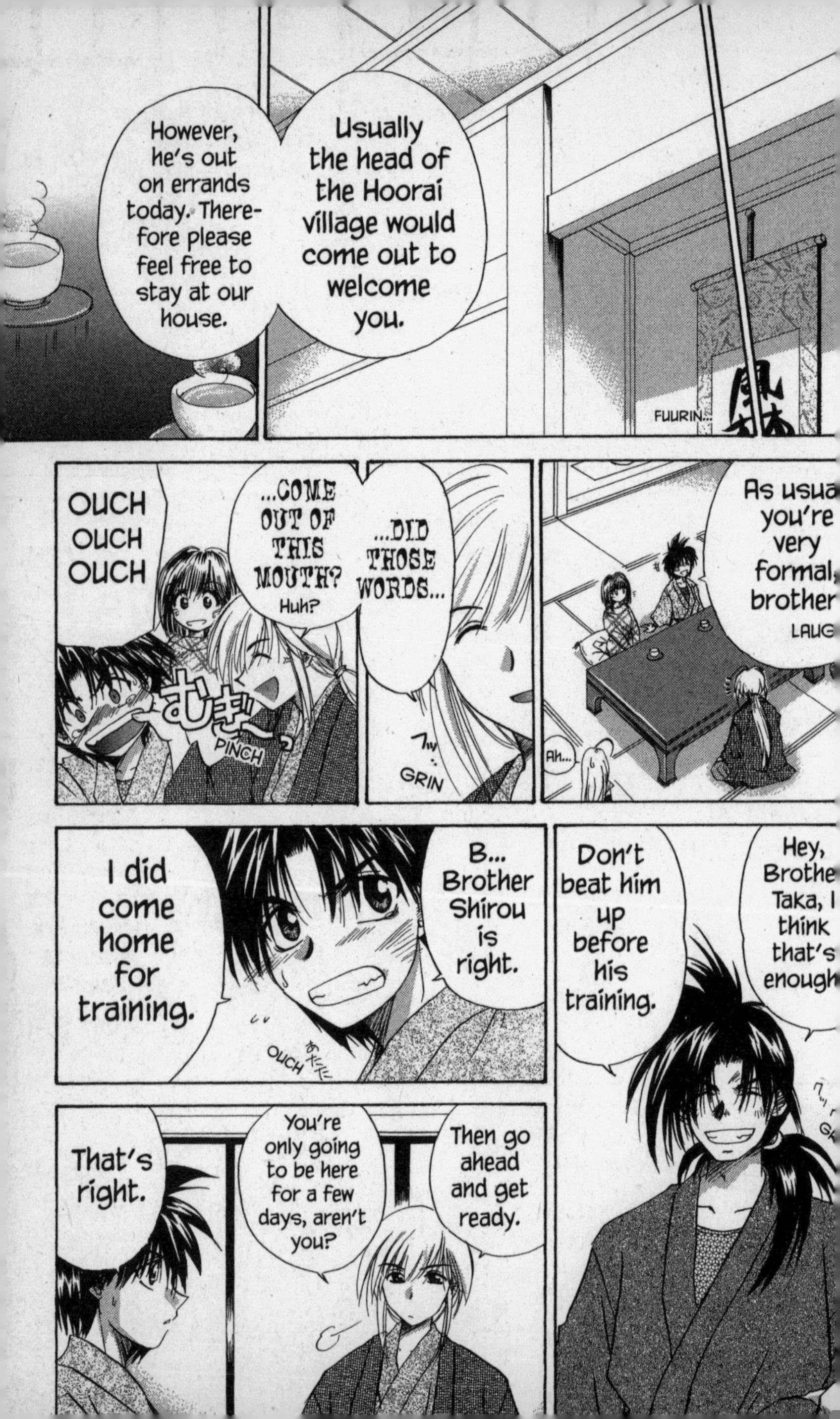
Usually the head of the Hoorai village would come out to welcome you.
However, he's out on errands today. Therefore please feel free to stay at our house.
FUURIN...
As usua you're very formal, brother
LAUG
Ah...
...DID THOSE WORDS...
...COME OUT OF THIS MOUTH? Huh?
GRIN
OUCH OUCH OUCH
PINCH
Hey, Brothe Taka, I think that's enough
Don't beat him up before his training.
B... Brother Shirou is right.
I did come home for training.
OUCH
Then go ahead and get ready.
You're only going to be here for a few days, aren't you?
That's right.

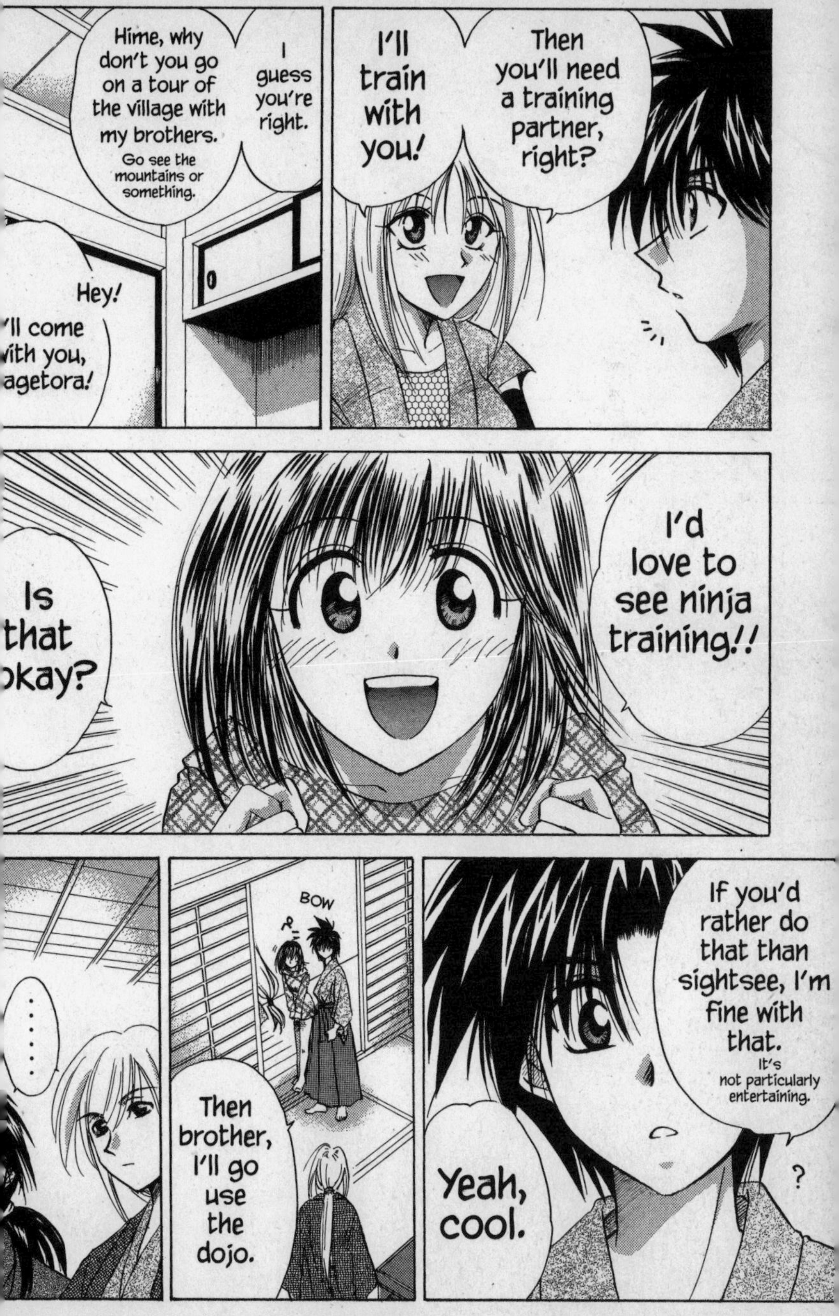

Then you'll need a training partner, right?
I'll train with you!
I guess you're right.
Hime, why don't you go on a tour of the village with my brothers.
Go see the mountains or something.
Hey!
'll come ith you, agetora!
I'd love to see ninja training!!
Is that okay?
If you'd rather do that than sightsee, I'm fine with that.
It's not particularly entertaining.
?
Yeah, cool.
BOW
Then brother, I'll go use the dojo.
......

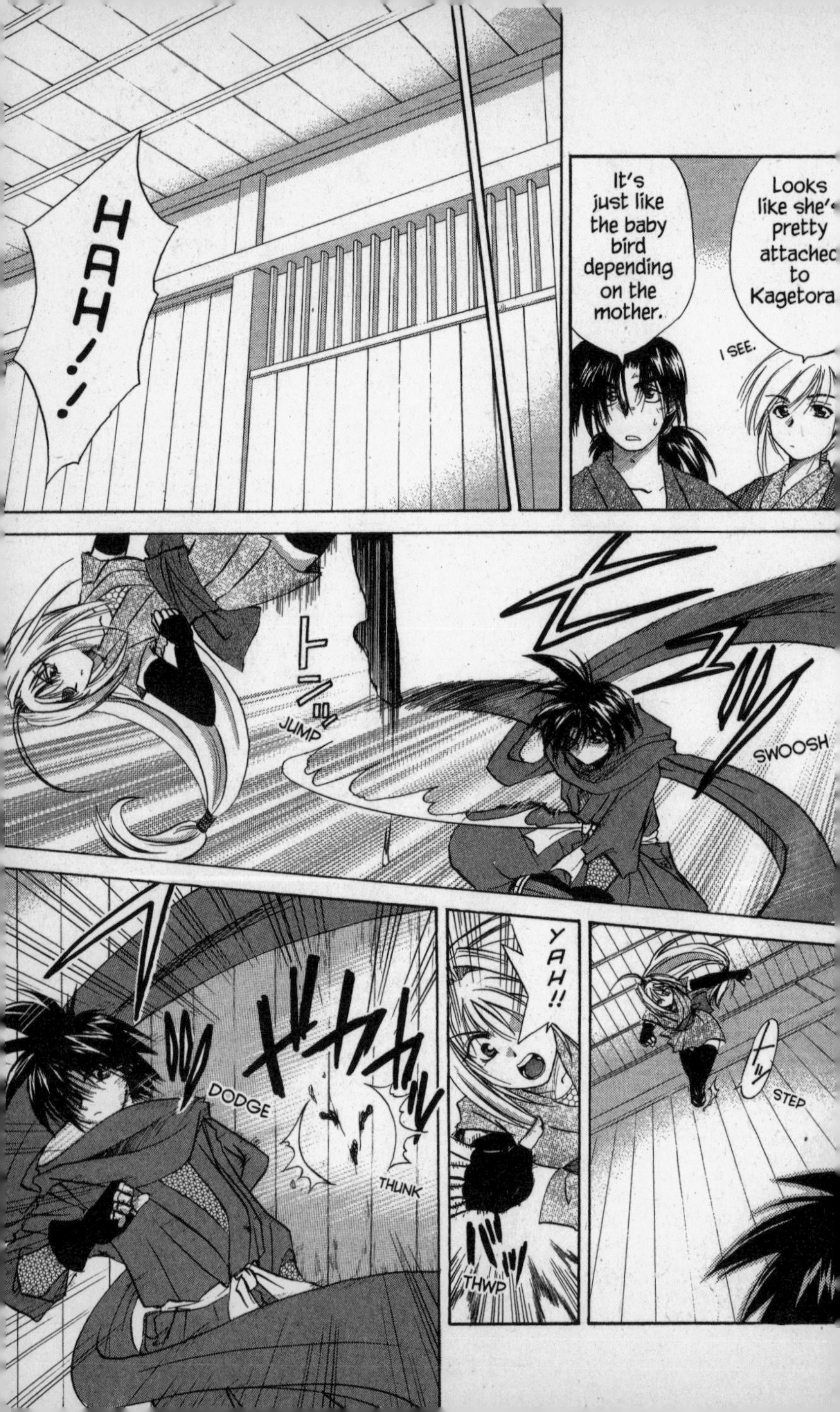
Looks like she' pretty attache to Kagetora
I SEE.
It's just like the baby bird depending on the mother.
HAH!!
SWOOSH
JUMP
STEP
YAH!!
THWP
DODGE
THUNK

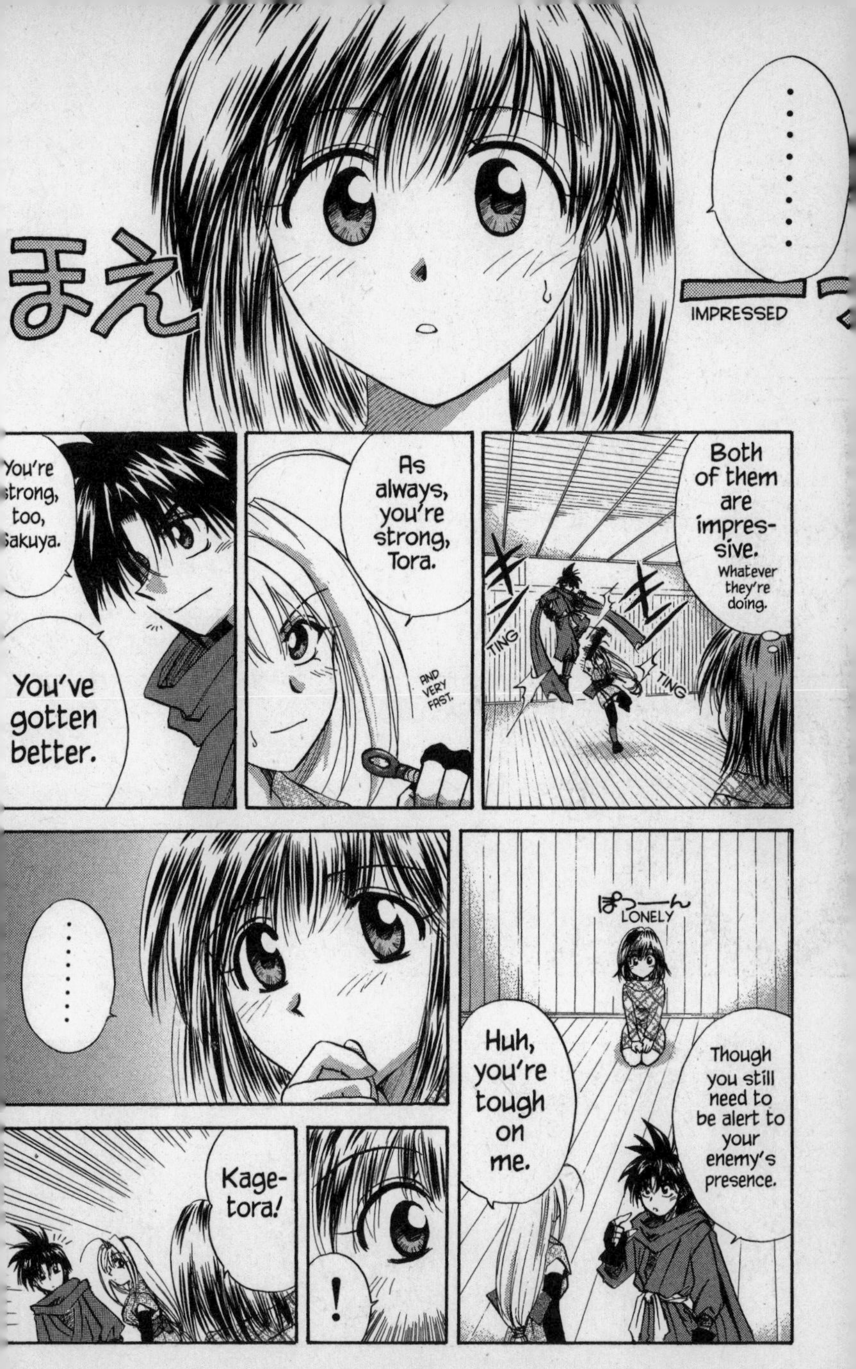

......
まえーっ
IMPRESSED
Both of them are impres-sive.
Whatever they're doing.
TING
TING
As always, you're strong, Tora.
AND VERY FAST.
You're strong, too, Sakuya.
You've gotten better.
ぽつーん
LONELY
Though you still need to be alert to your enemy's presence.
Huh, you're tough on me.
......
!
Kage-tora!

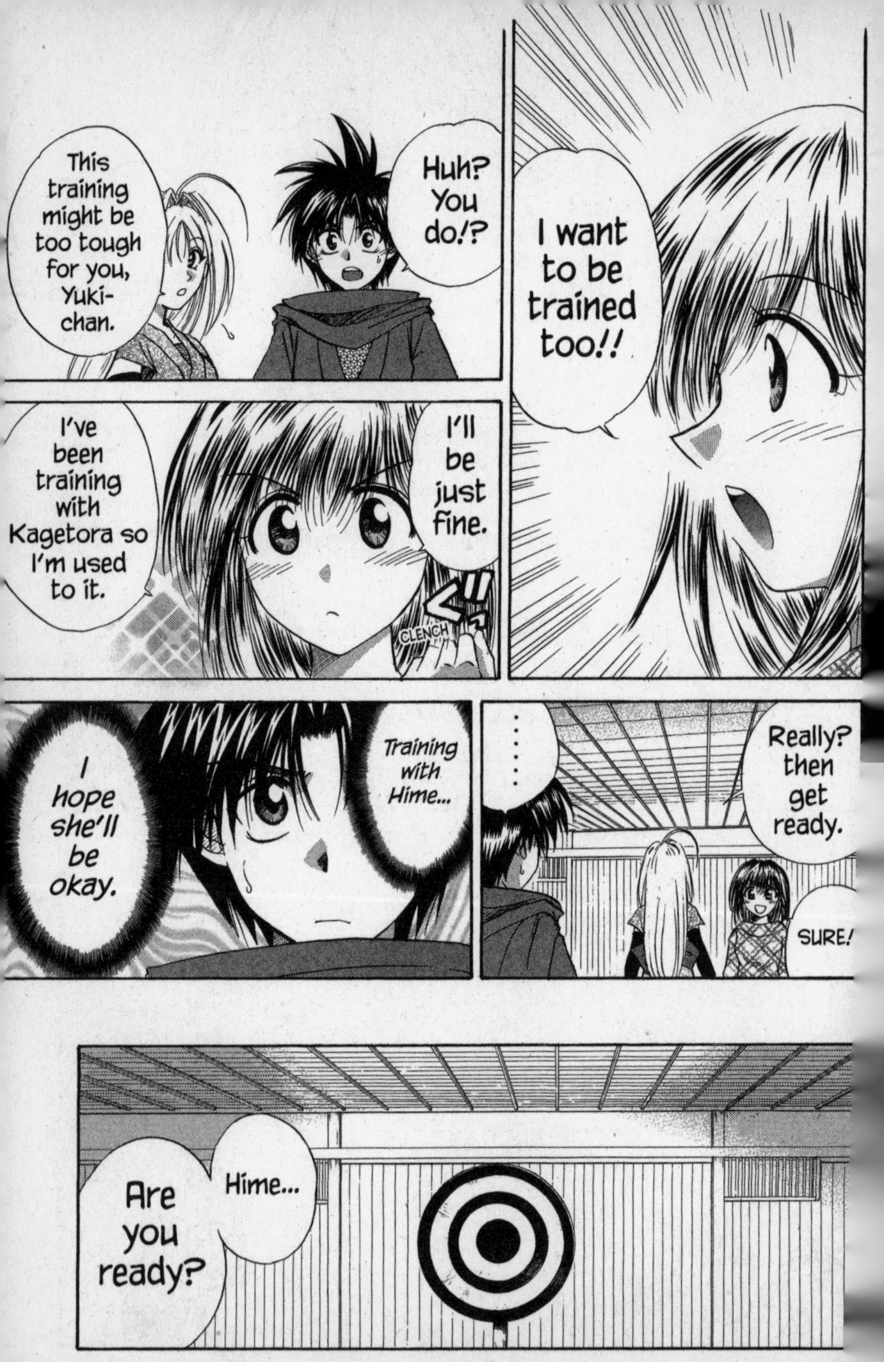
I want to be trained too!!
Huh? You do!?
This training might be too tough for you, Yuki-chan.
I'll be just fine.
I've been training with Kagetora so I'm used to it.
CLENCH
Really? then get ready.
......
SURE!
Training with Hime...
I hope she'll be okay.
Hime...
Are you ready?

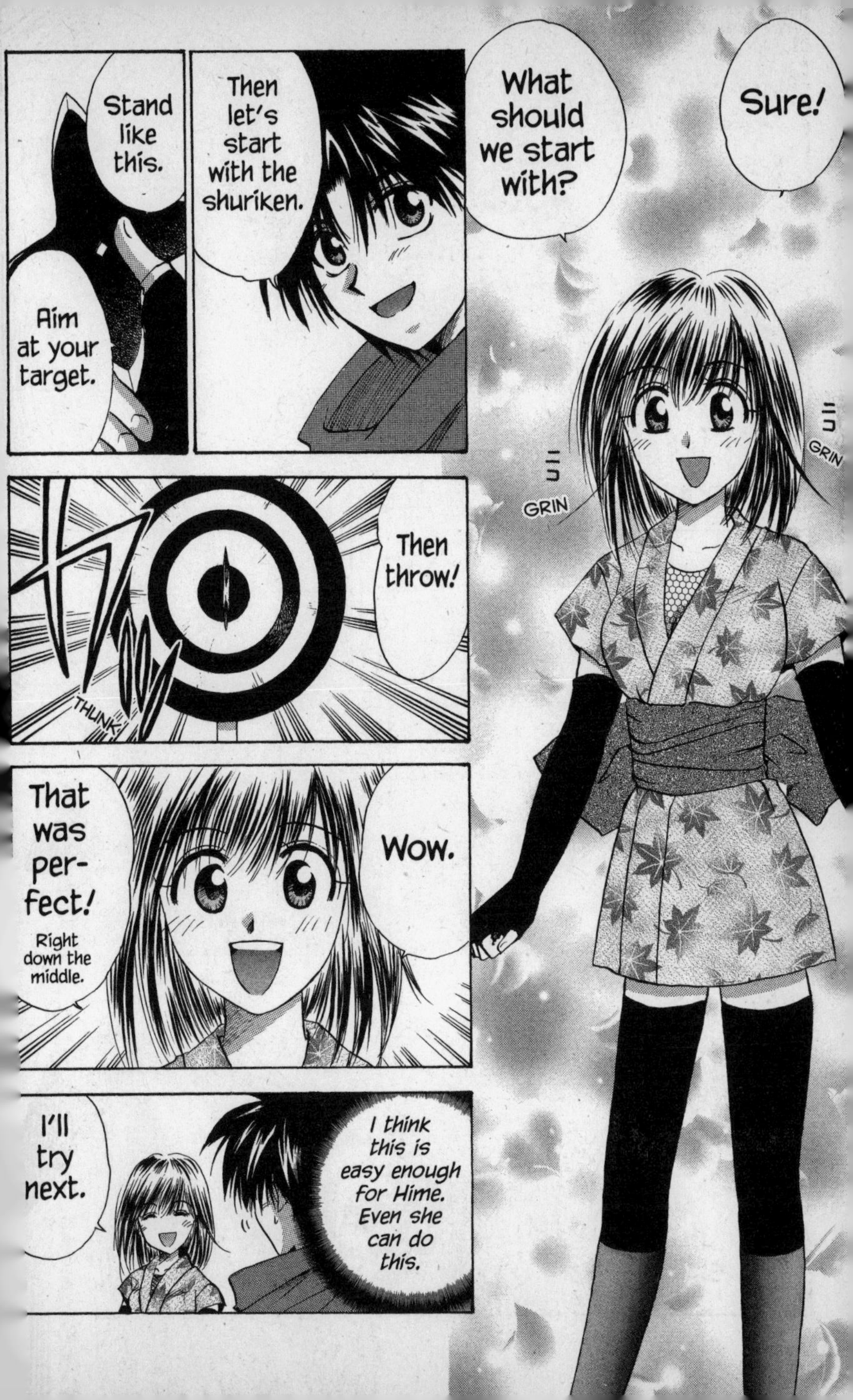
Sure!
What should we start with?
GRIN
GRIN
Then let's start with the shuriken.
Stand like this.
Aim at your target.
Then throw!
THUNK
Wow.
That was perfect!
Right down the middle.
I think this is easy enough for Hime. Even she can do this.
I'll try next.

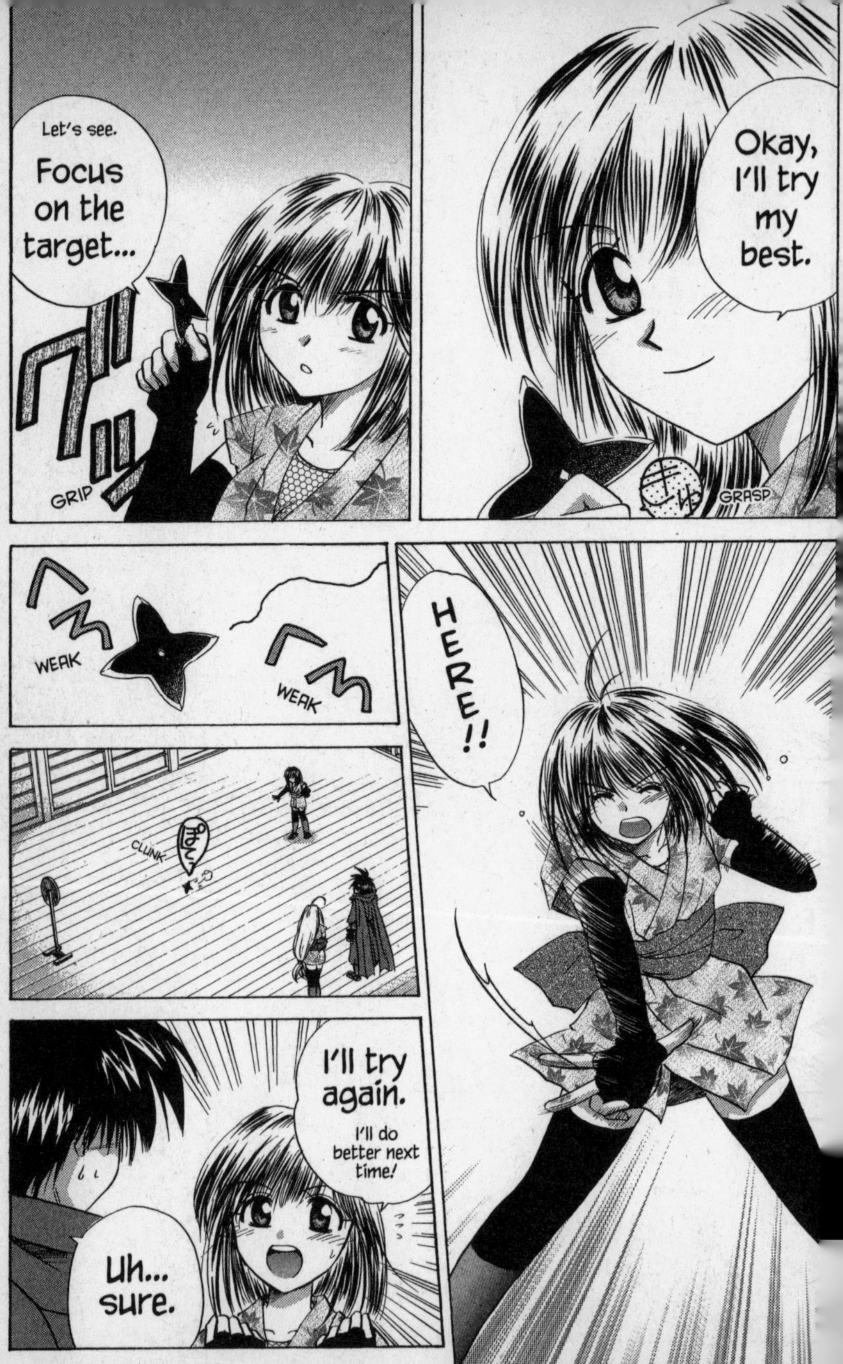
Okay, I'll try my best.
GRASP
Let's see.
Focus on the target...
GRIP
HERE!!
WEAK
WEAK
CLUNK
I'll try again.
I'll do better next time!
Uh... sure.

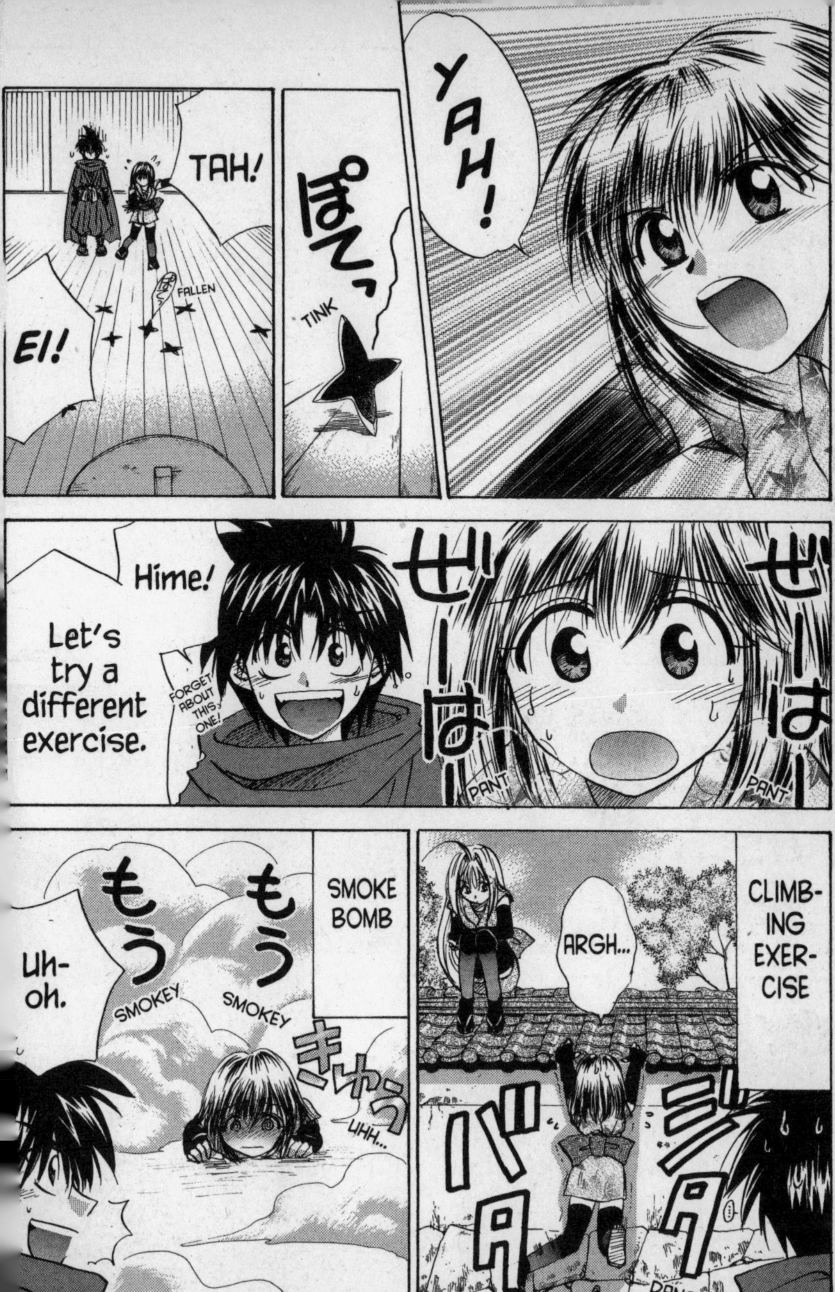
YAH!
ぽてっ
TINK
TAH!
FALLEN
EI!
ぜーはー
PANT
ぜーはー
PANT
Hime!
Let's try a different exercise.
FORGET ABOUT THIS ONE!
CLIMBING EXERCISE
ARGH...
ジタ
DANGLE
バタ
STRUGGLE
SMOKE BOMB
もう
SMOKEY
もう
SMOKEY
きゅう
UHH...
Uh-oh.

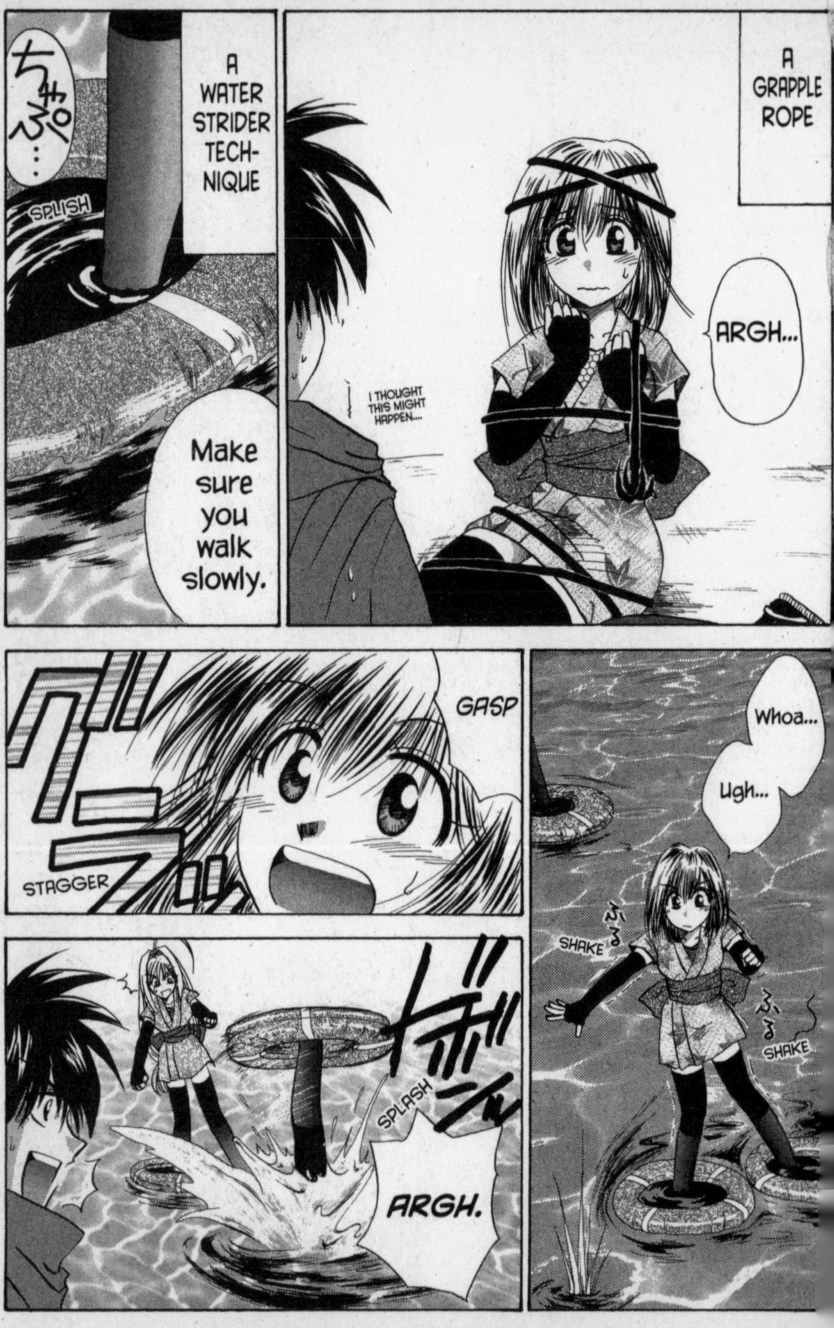
A GRAPPLE ROPE
ARGH...
I THOUGHT THIS MIGHT HAPPEN....
A WATER STRIDER TECH-NIQUE
ちゃぷん…
SPLISH
Make sure you walk slowly.
Whoa...
Ugh...
ふる
SHAKE
ふる
SHAKE
GASP
STAGGER
SPLASH
ARGH.

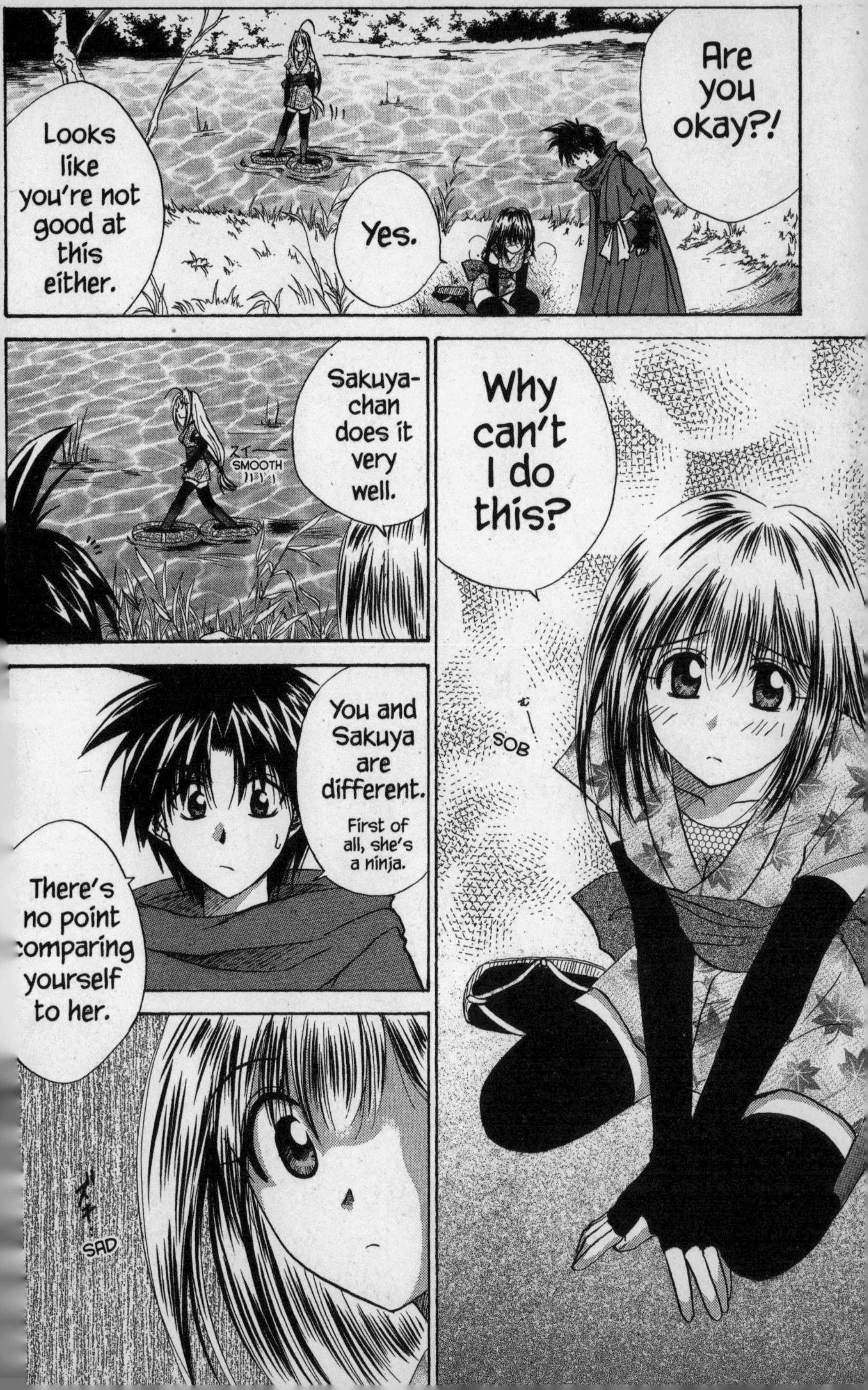
Are you okay?!
Yes.
Looks like you're not good at this either.
Why can't I do this?
SOB
Sakuya-chan does it very well.
SMOOTH
You and Sakuya are different.
First of all, she's a ninja.
There's no point comparing yourself to her.
SAD

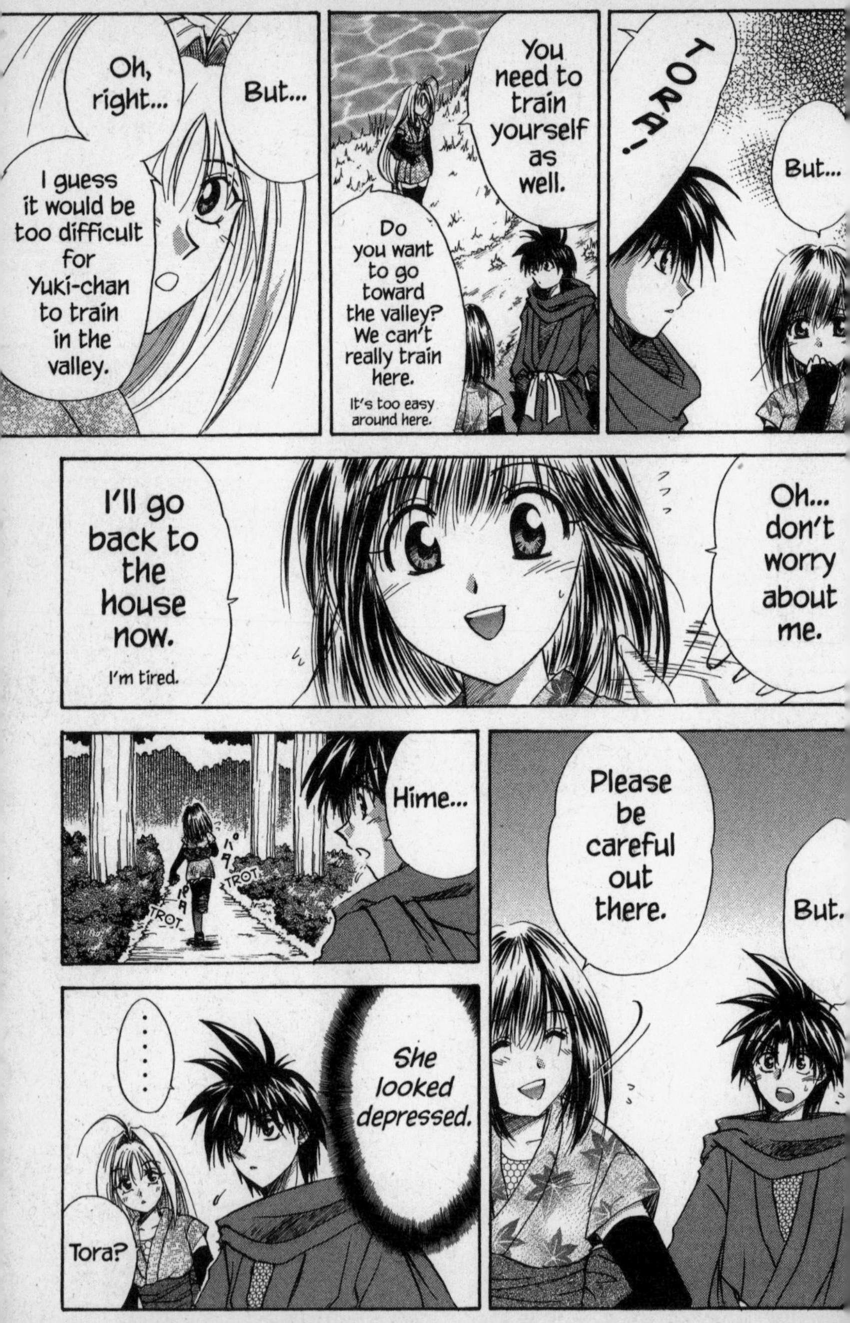
TORA-!
But...
You need to train yourself as well.
Do you want to go toward the valley? We can't really train here.
It's too easy around here.
But...
Oh, right...
I guess it would be too difficult for Yuki-chan to train in the valley.
Oh... don't worry about me.
I'll go back to the house now.
I'm tired.
But.
Please be careful out there.
Hime...
TROT
TROT
She looked depressed.
......
Tora?

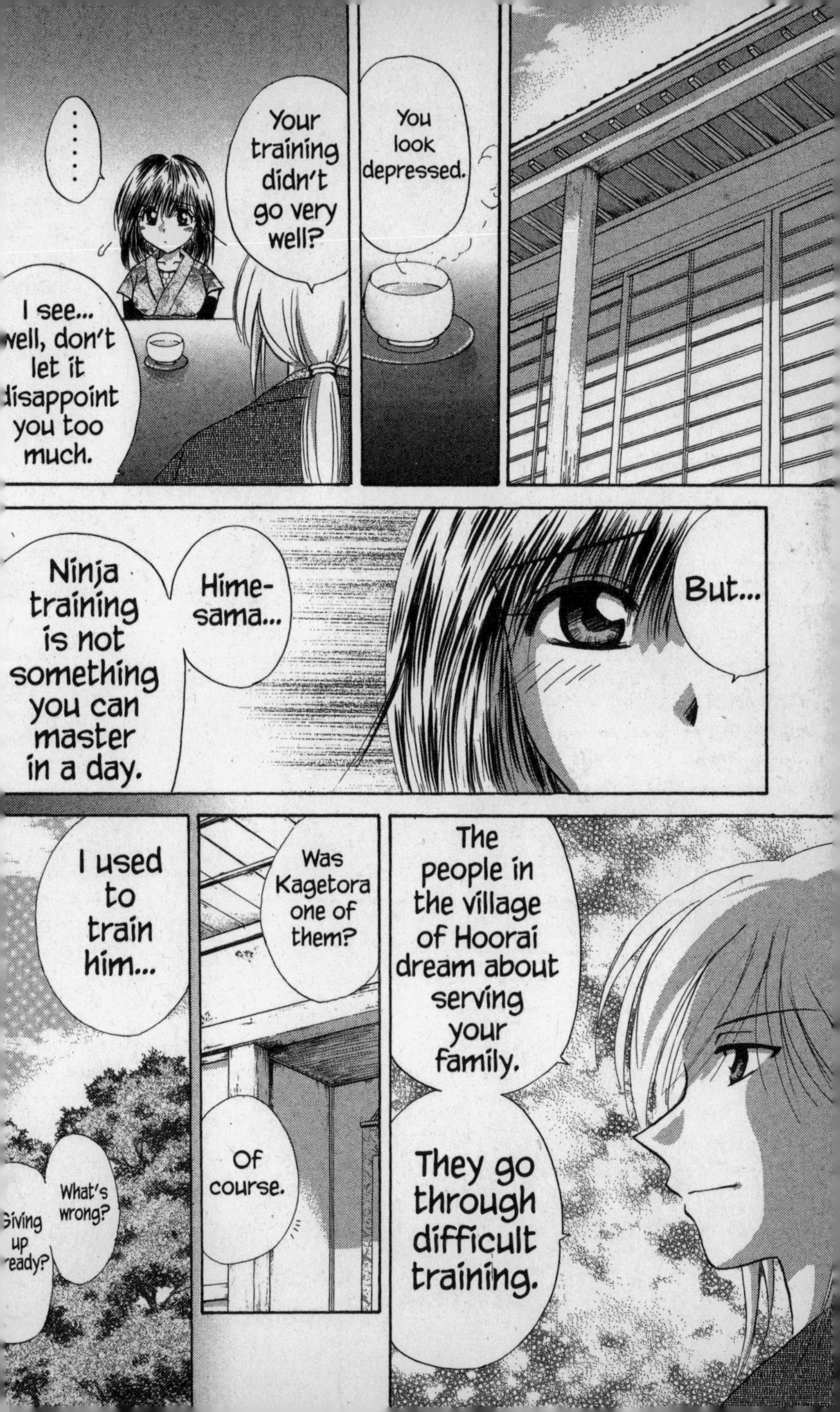
You look depressed.
Your training didn't go very well?
......
I see... well, don't let it disappoint you too much.
But...
Hime-sama...
Ninja training is not something you can master in a day.
The people in the village of Hoorai dream about serving your family.
They go through difficult training.
Was Kagetora one of them?
Of course.
I used to train him...
What's wrong?
Giving up ready?

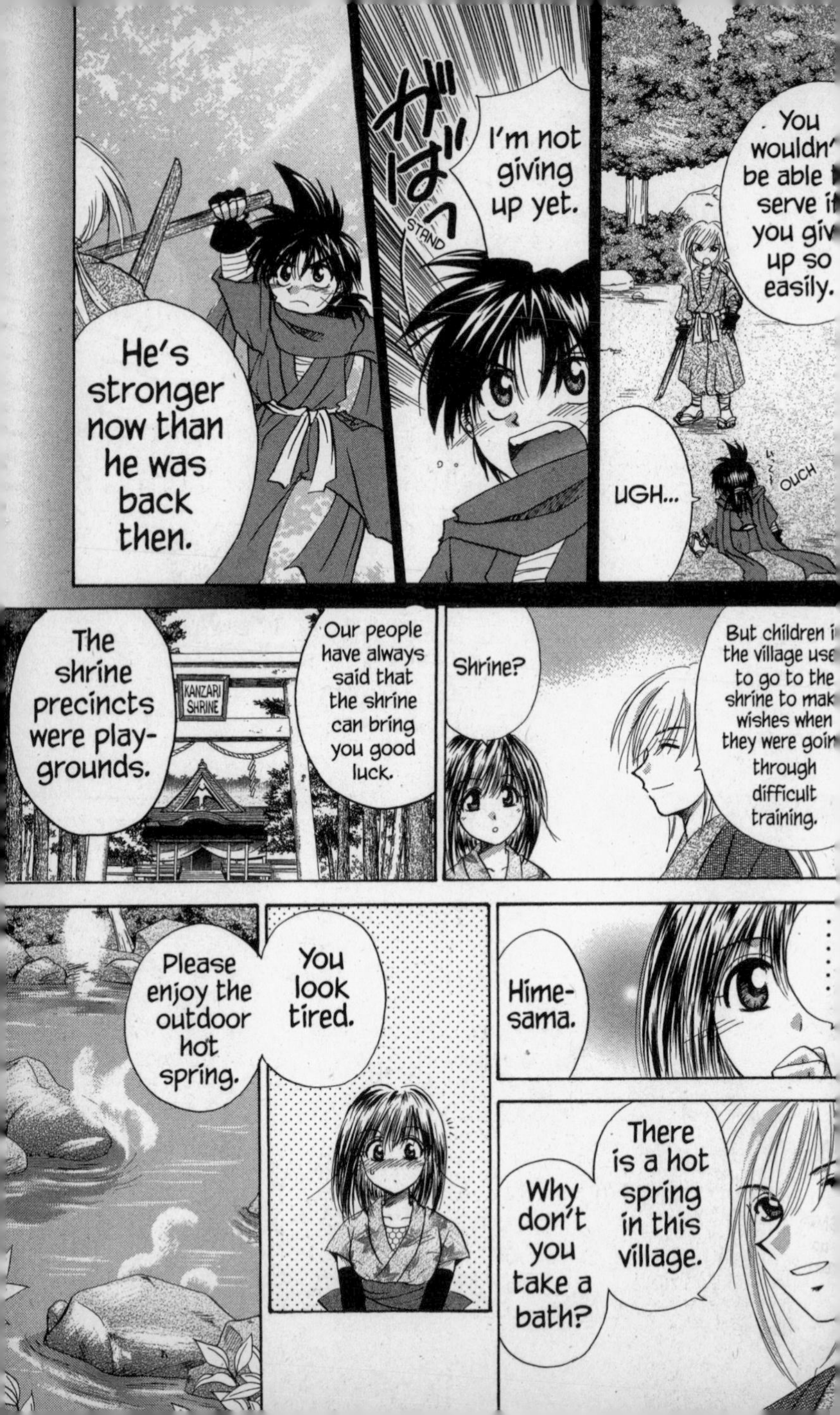
You wouldn’ be able t serve i you giv up so easily.
UGH...
OUCH
がばっ
STAND
I’m not giving up yet.
He’s stronger now than he was back then.
But children i the village use to go to the shrine to mak wishes when they were goin through difficult training.
Shrine?
Our people have always said that the shrine can bring you good luck.
KANZARI SHRINE
The shrine precincts were play-grounds.
Hime-sama.
There is a hot spring in this village.
Why don’t you take a bath?
You look tired.
Please enjoy the outdoor hot spring.

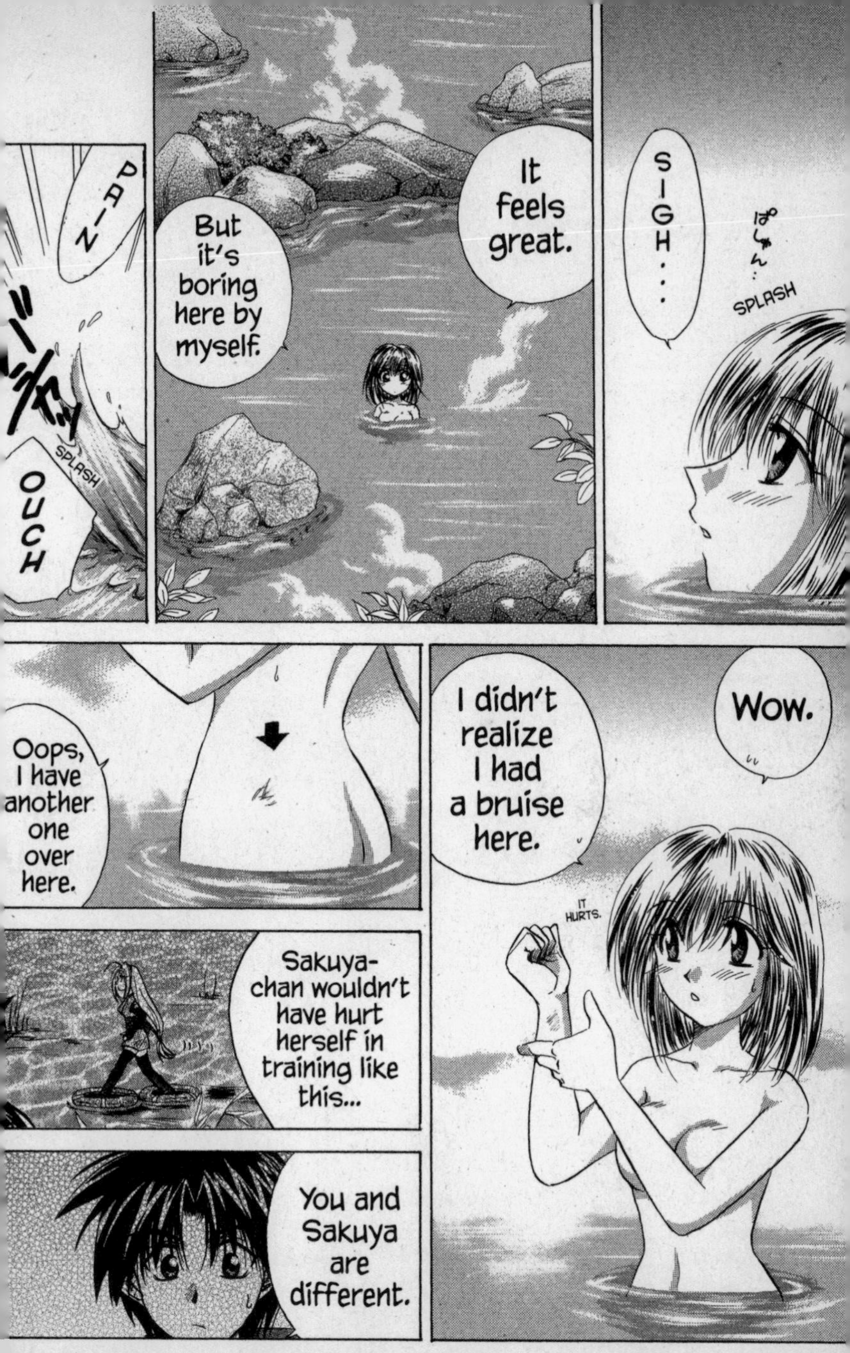
SIGH...
ぱしゃん..
SPLASH
It feels great.
But it's boring here by myself.
PAIN
SPLASH
OUCH
Wow.
I didn't realize I had a bruise here.
IT HURTS.
Oops, I have another one over here.
Sakuya-chan wouldn't have hurt herself in training like this...
You and Sakuya are different.

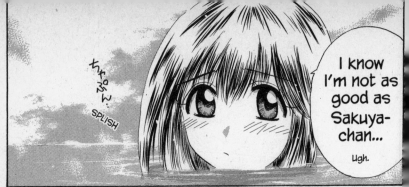

I know I'm not as good as Sakuya-chan...

Ugh.

SPLISH

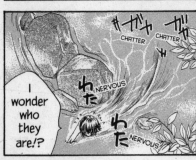

CHATTER CHATTER

NERVOUS

I wonder who they are!?

NERVOUS

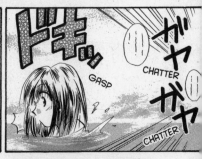

GASP

CHATTER

CHATTER

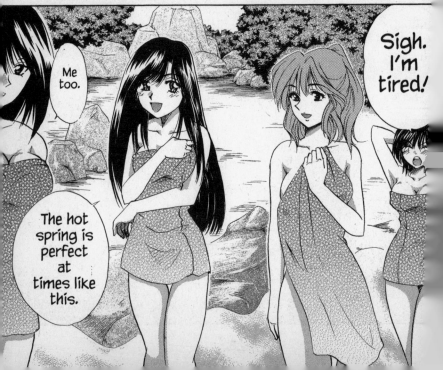

Sigh. I'm tired!

Me too.

The hot spring is perfect at times like this.

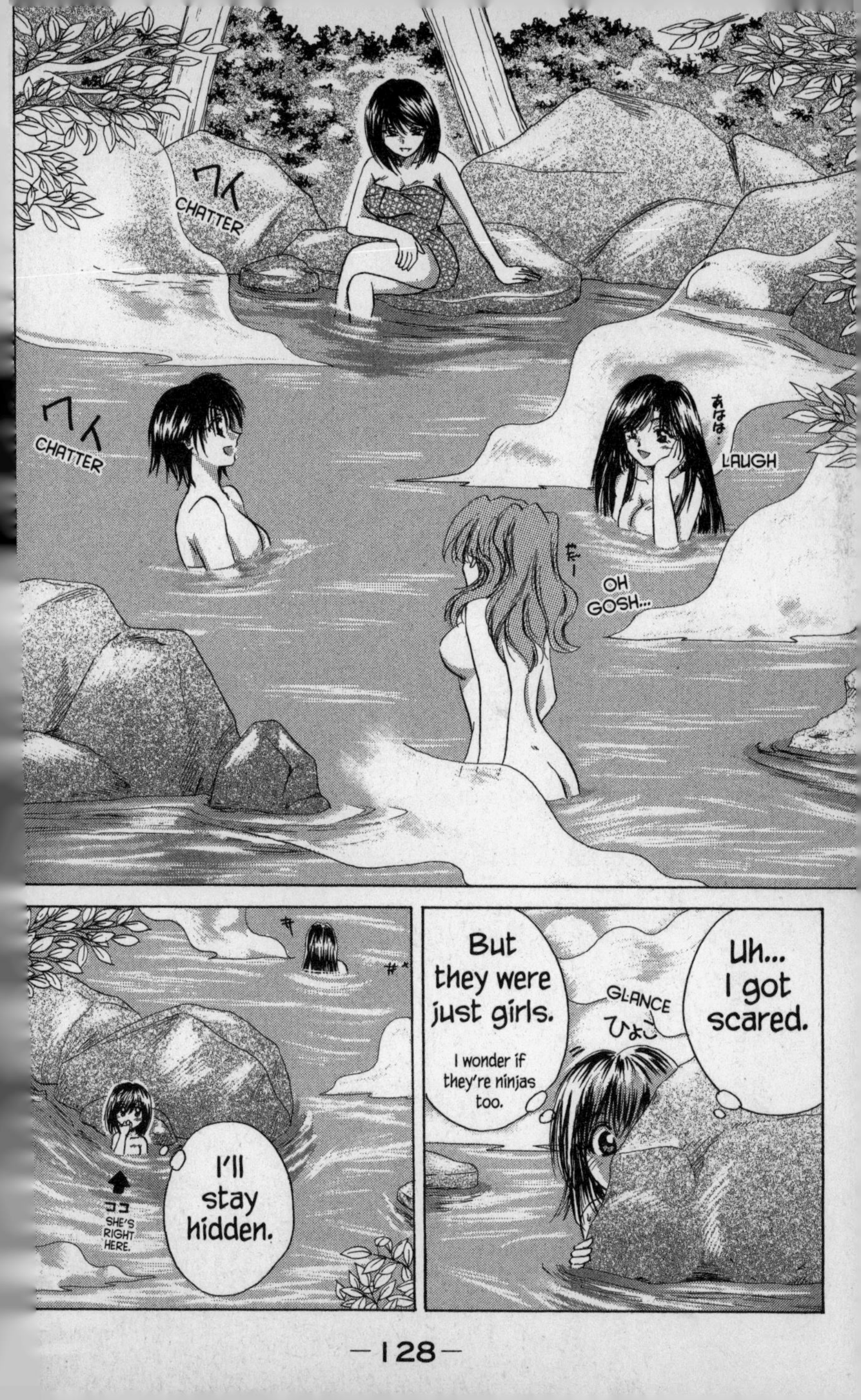
ワイ
CHATTER
あはは…
LAUGH
ワイ
CHATTER
OH GOSH...
Uh... I got scared.
GLANCE
ひょこ
But they were just girls.
I wonder if they're ninjas too.
I'll stay hidden.
ココ
SHE'S RIGHT HERE.

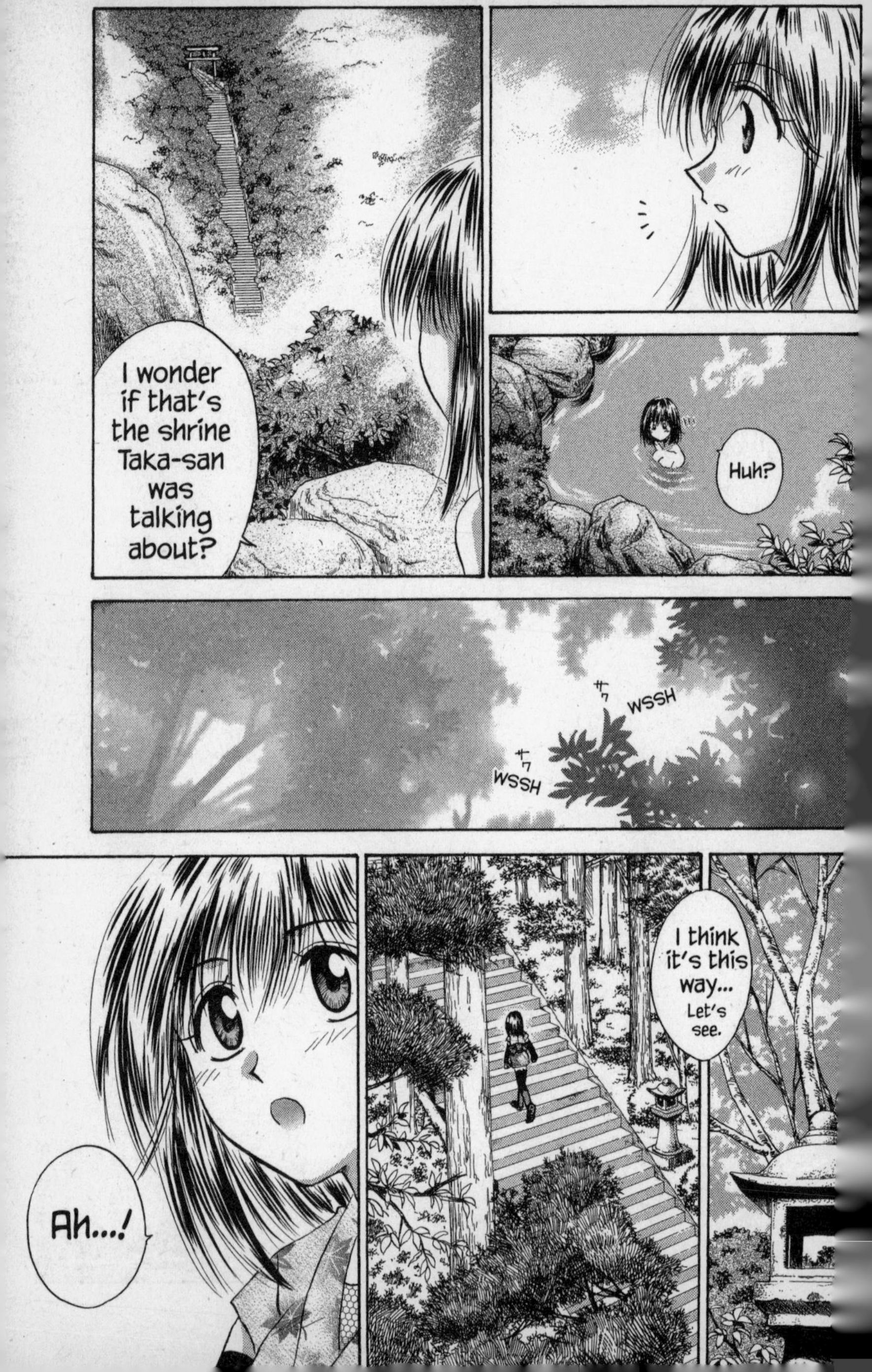
Huh?
I wonder if that's the shrine Taka-san was talking about?
WSSH
WSSH
I think it's this way... Let's see.
Ah...!

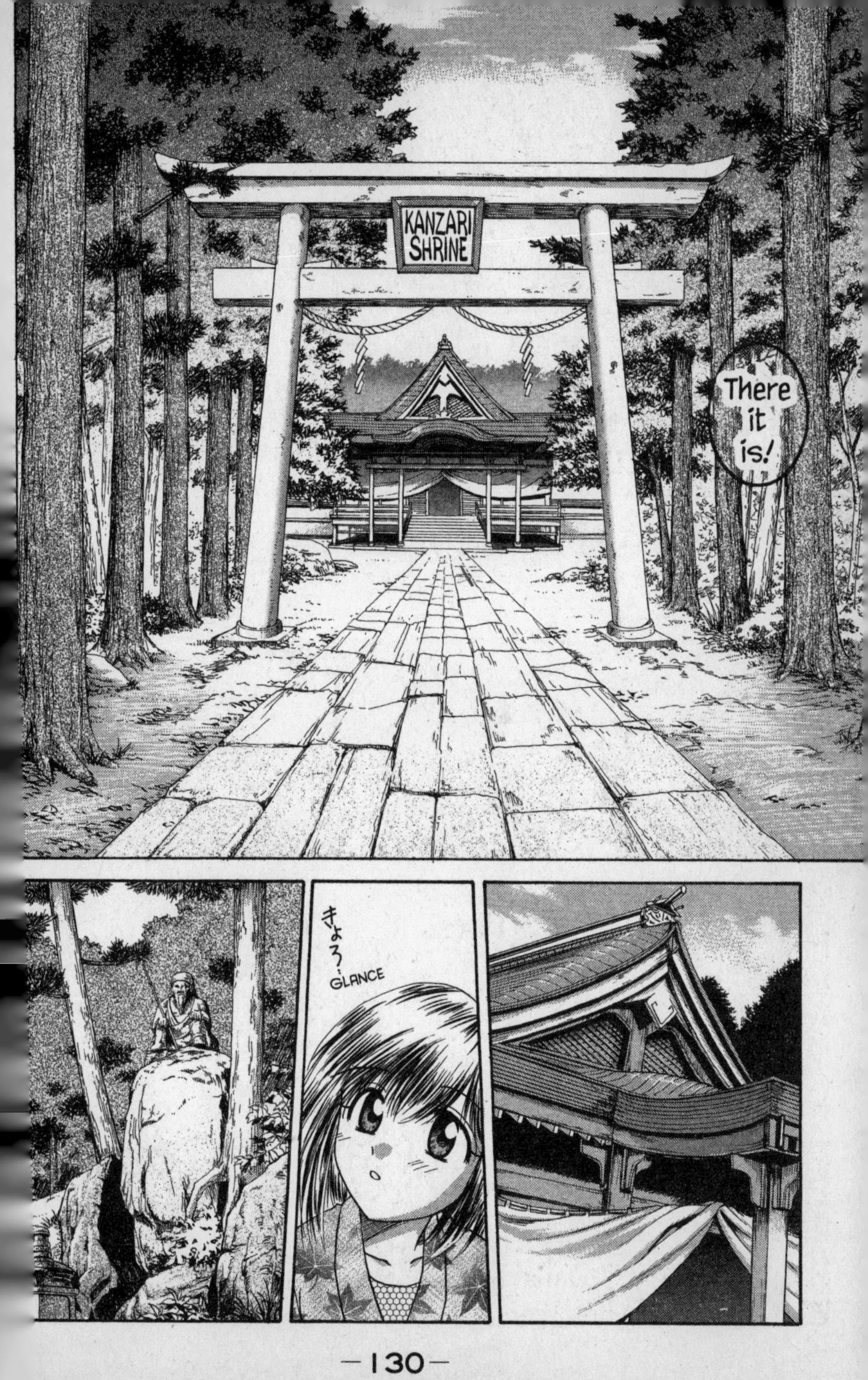
KANZARI SHRINE
There it is!
きょろ
GLANCE

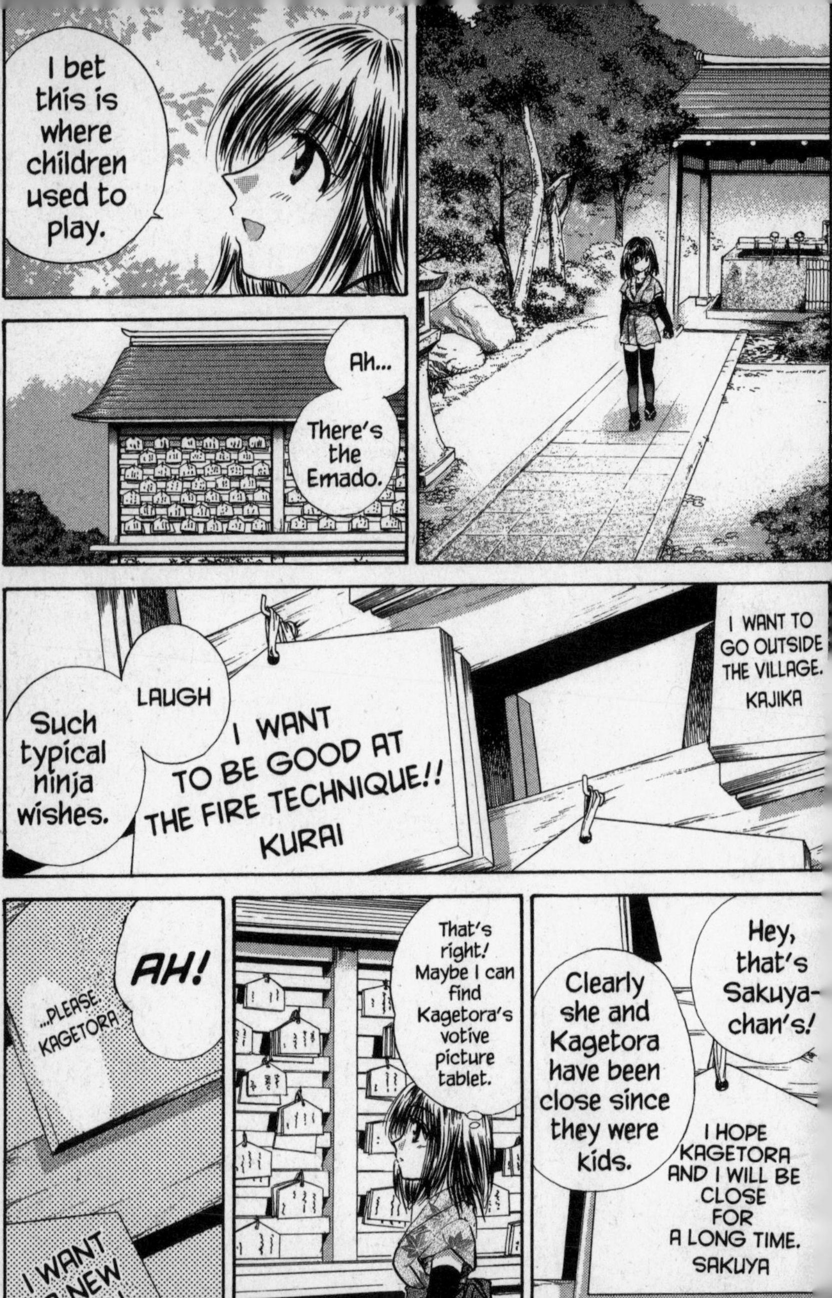
I bet this is where children used to play.
Ah...
There's the Emado.
I WANT TO GO OUTSIDE THE VILLAGE. KAJIKA
I WANT TO BE GOOD AT THE FIRE TECHNIQUE!! KURAI
LAUGH
Such typical ninja wishes.
Hey, that's Sakuya-chan's!
Clearly she and Kagetora have been close since they were kids.
I HOPE KAGETORA AND I WILL BE CLOSE FOR A LONG TIME. SAKUYA
That's right! Maybe I can find Kagetora's votive picture tablet.
AH!
...PLEASE. KAGETORA
I WANT A NEW CHAIN.

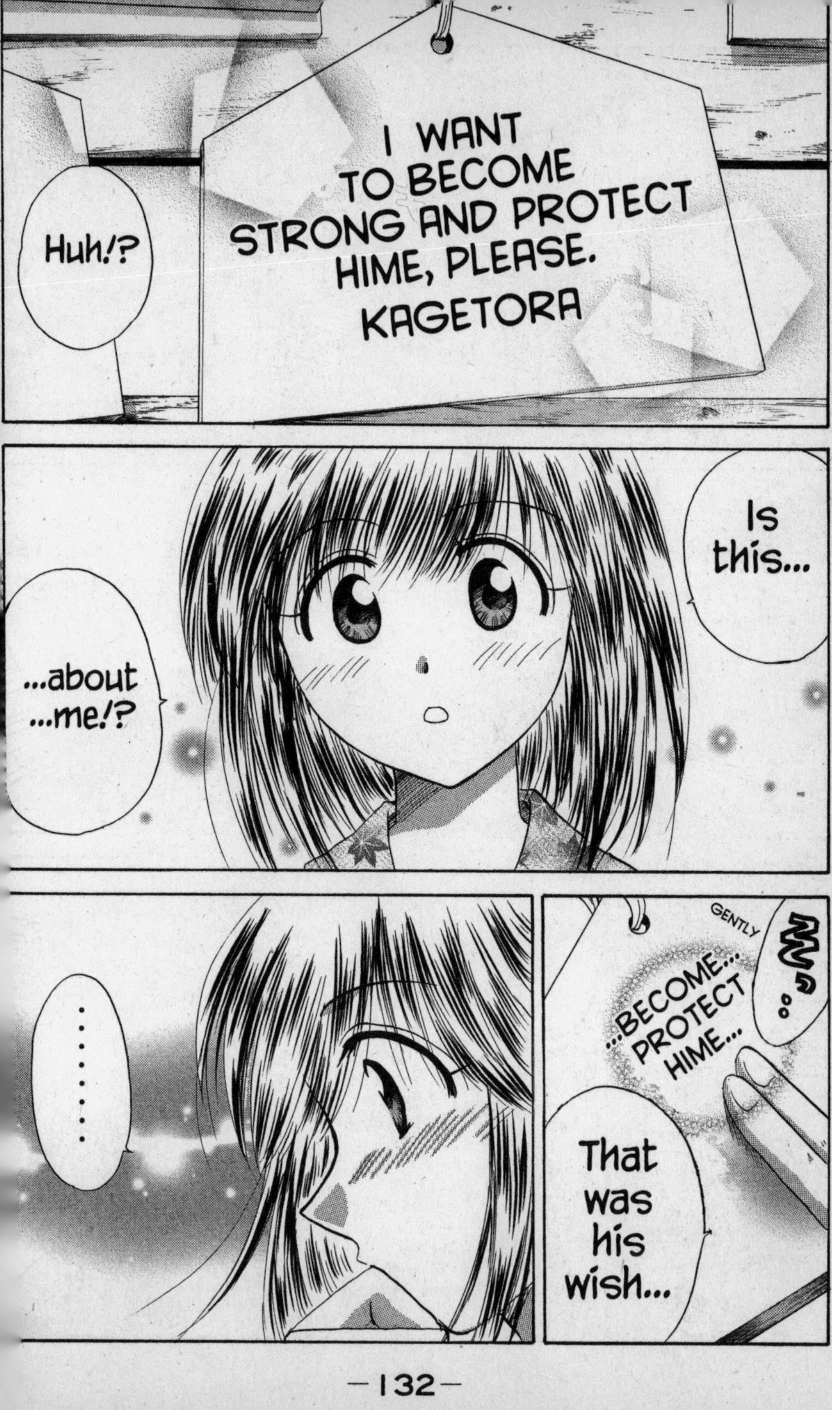
I WANT TO BECOME STRONG AND PROTECT HIME, PLEASE. KAGETORA
Huh!?
Is this...
...about ...me!?
GENTLY
...BECOME... PROTECT HIME...
That was his wish...
....

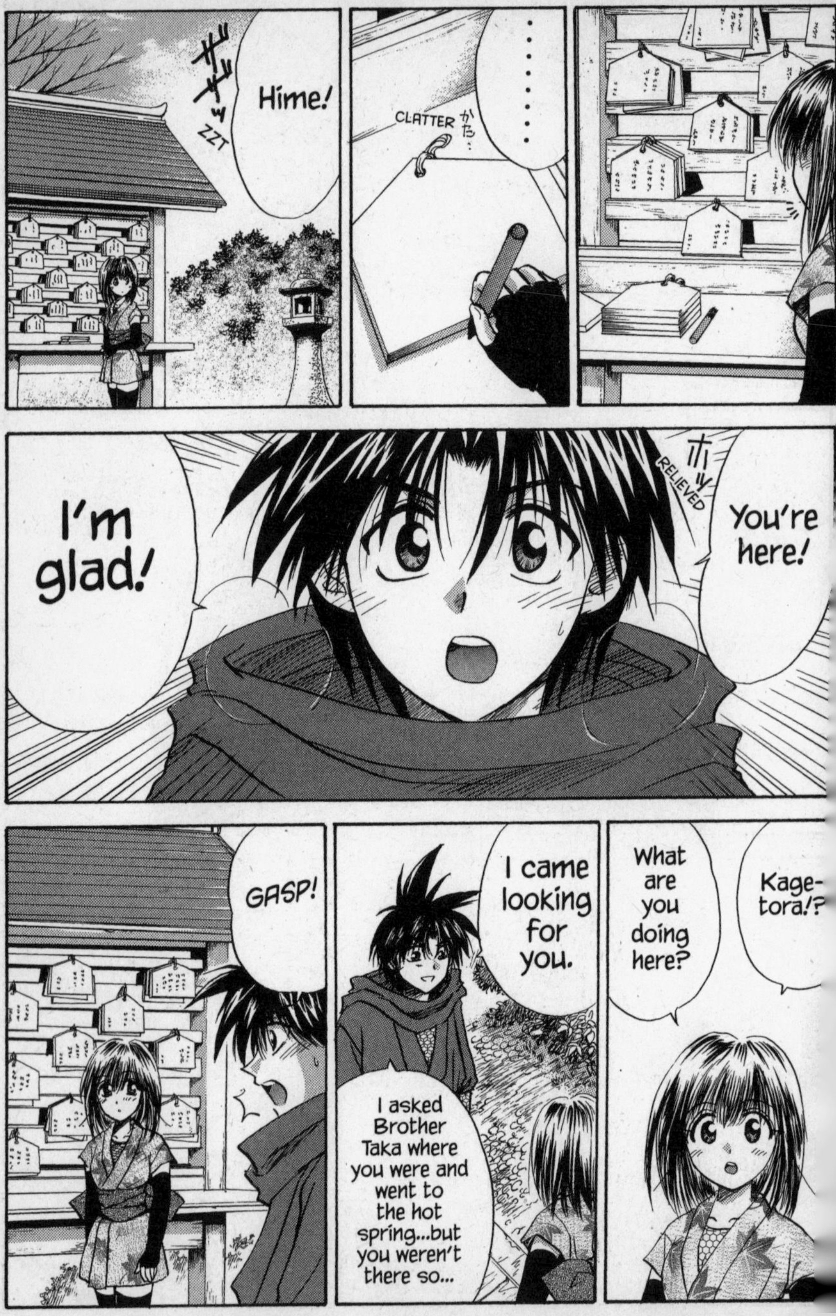
......
CLATTER かた…
Hime!
ZZT
RELIEVED ホッ
You're here!
I'm glad!
Kage-tora!?
What are you doing here?
I came looking for you.
I asked Brother Taka where you were and went to the hot spring...but you weren't there so...
GASP!

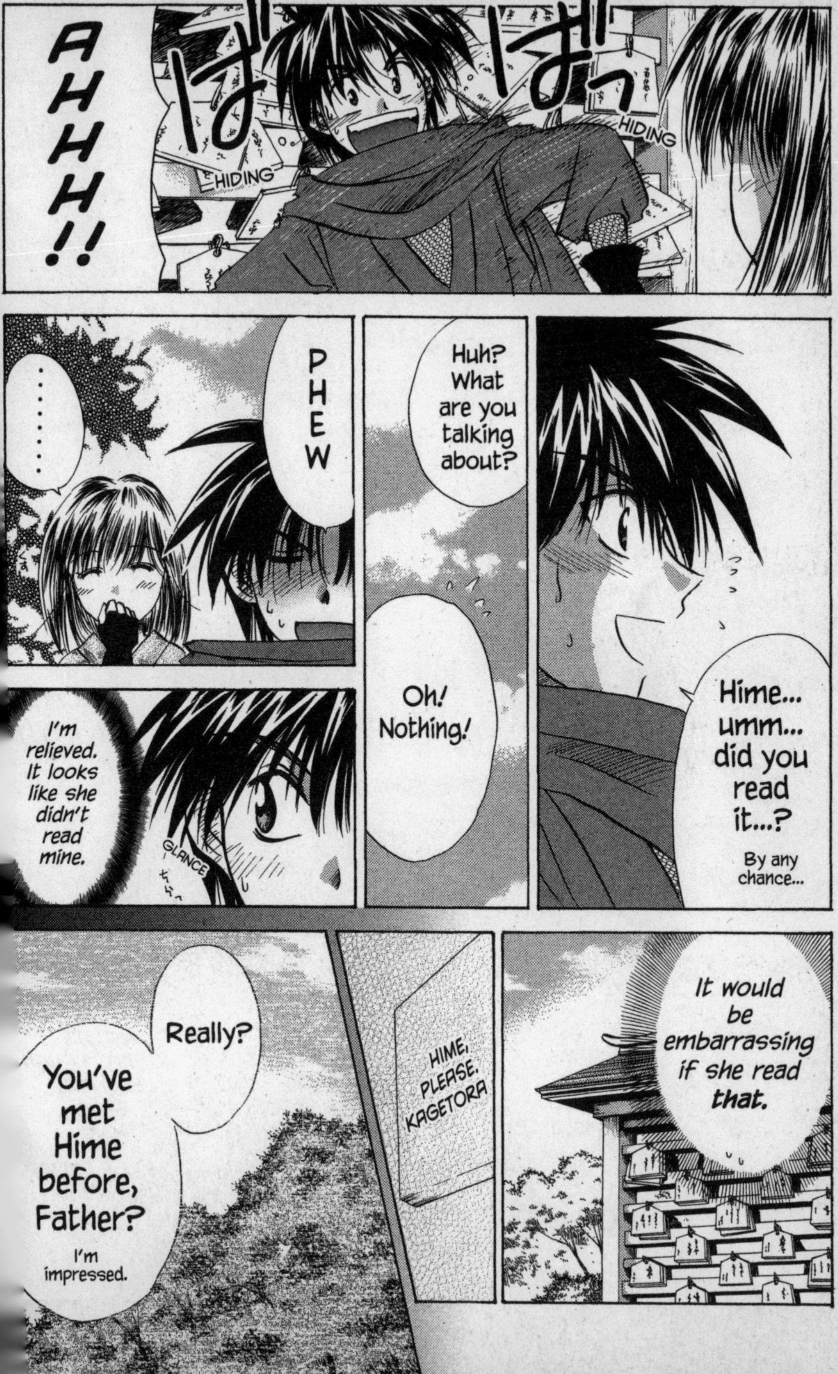
HIDING
HIDING
AHHHH!!
Hime... umm... did you read it...?
By any chance...
Huh? What are you talking about?
Oh! Nothing!
PHEW
......
I'm relieved. It looks like she didn't read mine.
GLANCE
It would be embarrassing if she read that.
HIME, PLEASE. KAGETORA
Really?
You've met Hime before, Father?
I'm impressed.

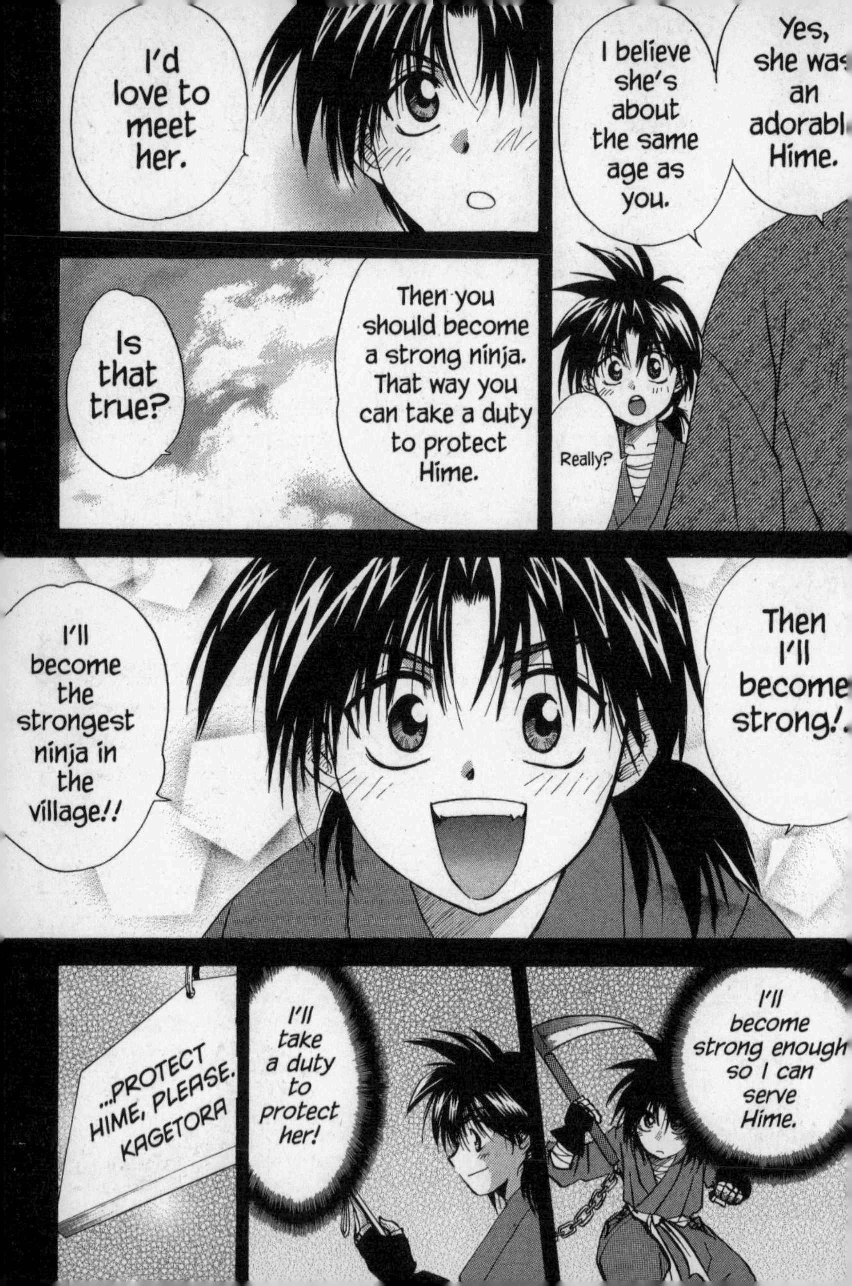
Yes, she was an adorabl Hime.
I believe she's about the same age as you.
I'd love to meet her.
Really?
Then you should become a strong ninja. That way you can take a duty to protect Hime.
Is that true?
Then I'll become strong!.
I'll become the strongest ninja in the village!!
I'll become strong enough so I can serve Hime.
I'll take a duty to protect her!
...PROTECT HIME, PLEASE. KAGETORA

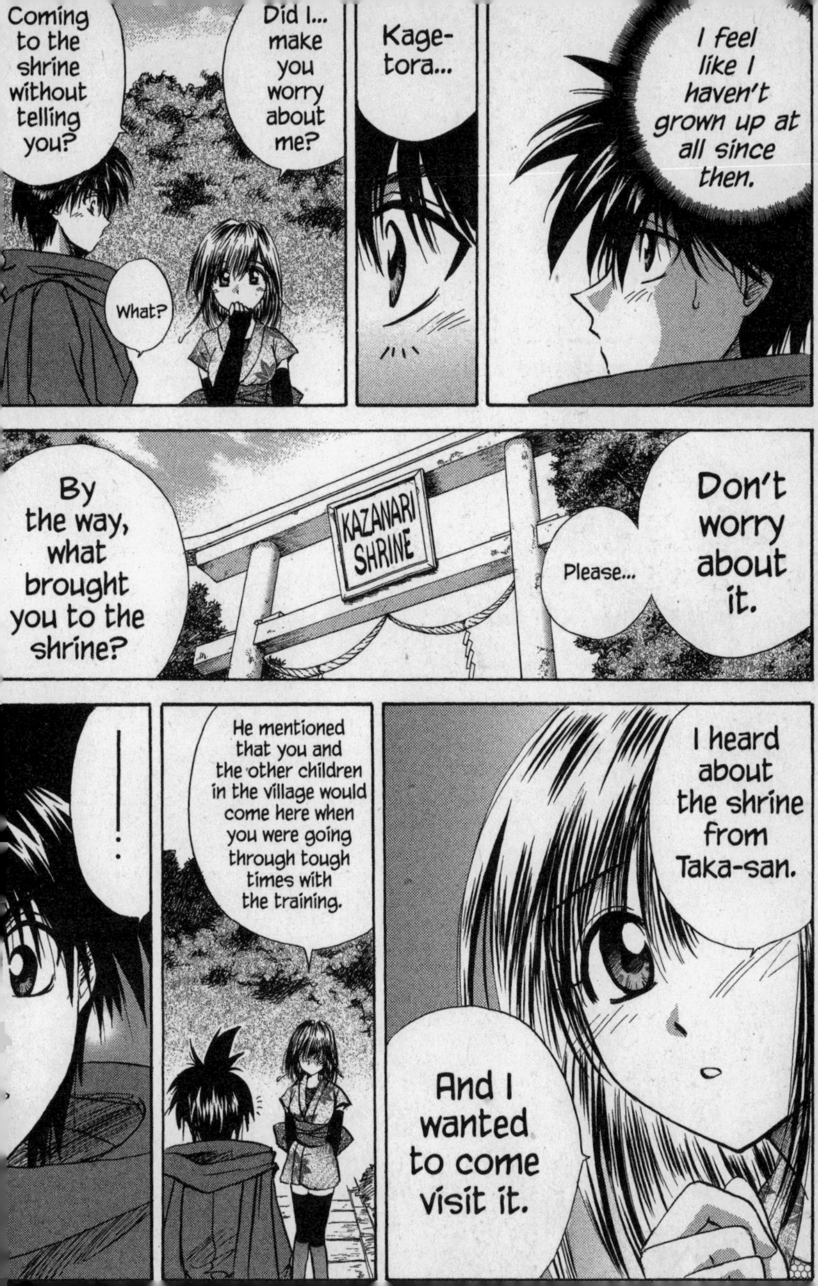
I feel like I haven't grown up at all since then.
Kage-tora...
Did I... make you worry about me?
Coming to the shrine without telling you?
What?
Don't worry about it.
Please...
KAZANARI SHRINE
By the way, what brought you to the shrine?
I heard about the shrine from Taka-san.
And I wanted to come visit it.
He mentioned that you and the other children in the village would come here when you were going through tough times with the training.
—!

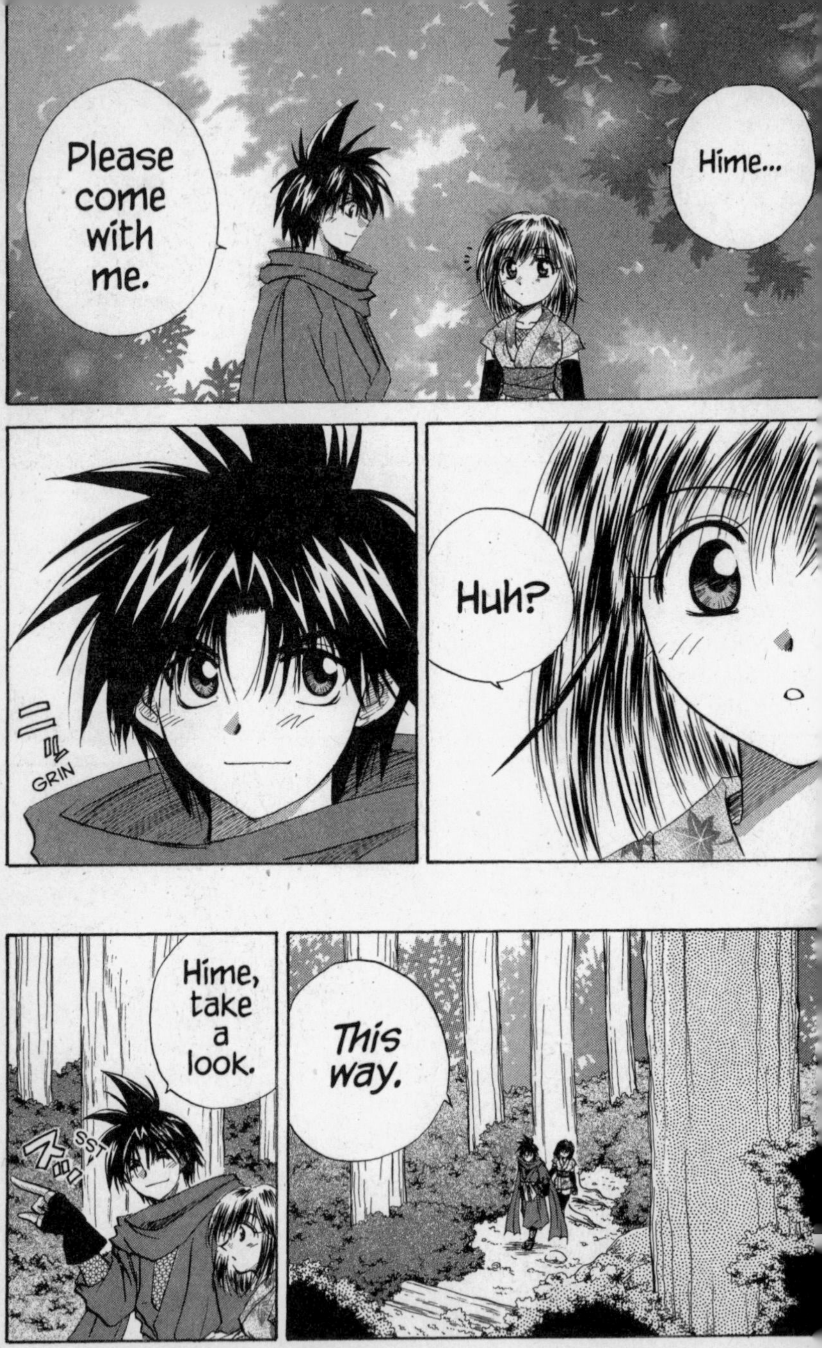
Hime...
Please come with me.
Huh?
GRIN
This way.
Hime, take a look.
SST

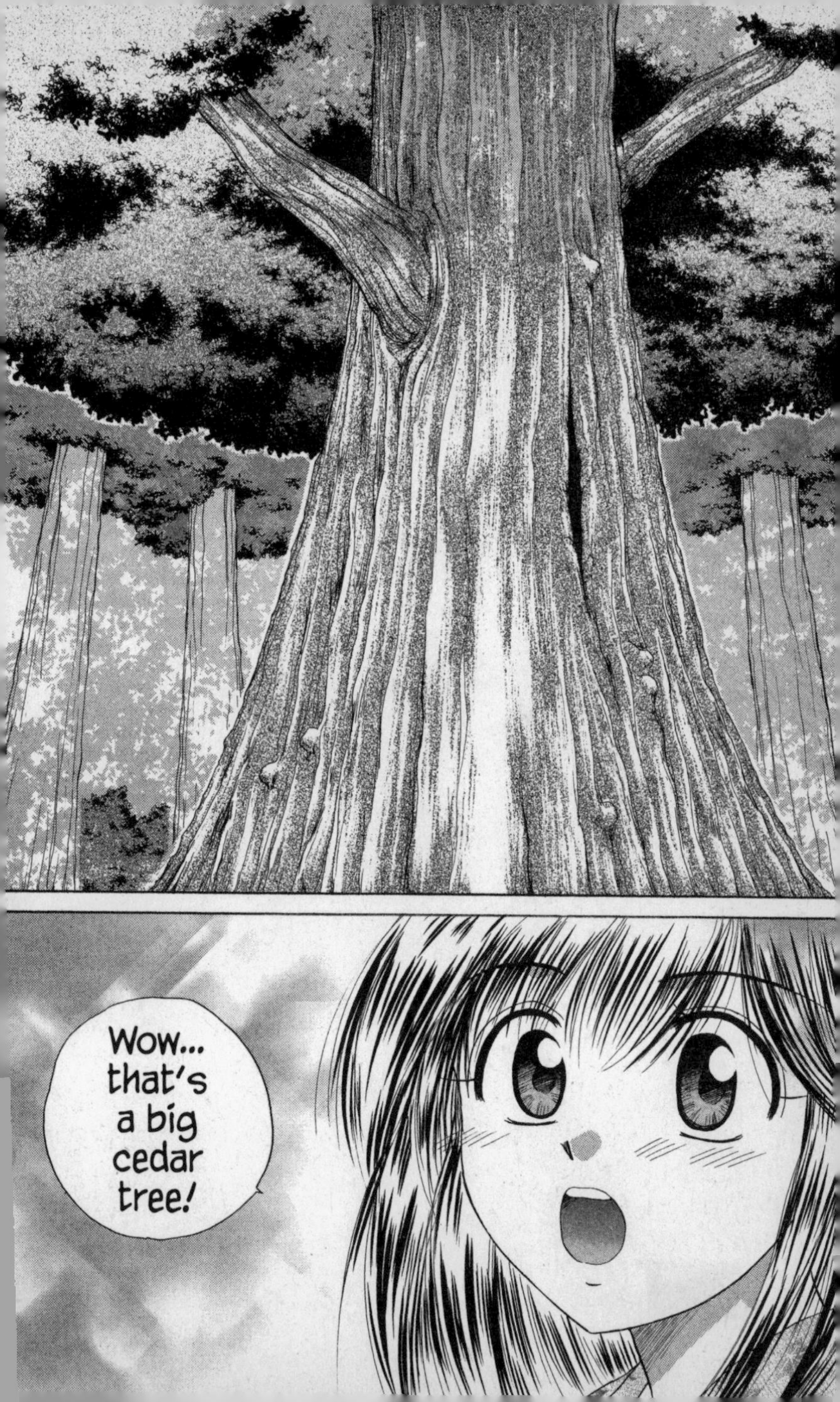
Wow... that's a big cedar tree!

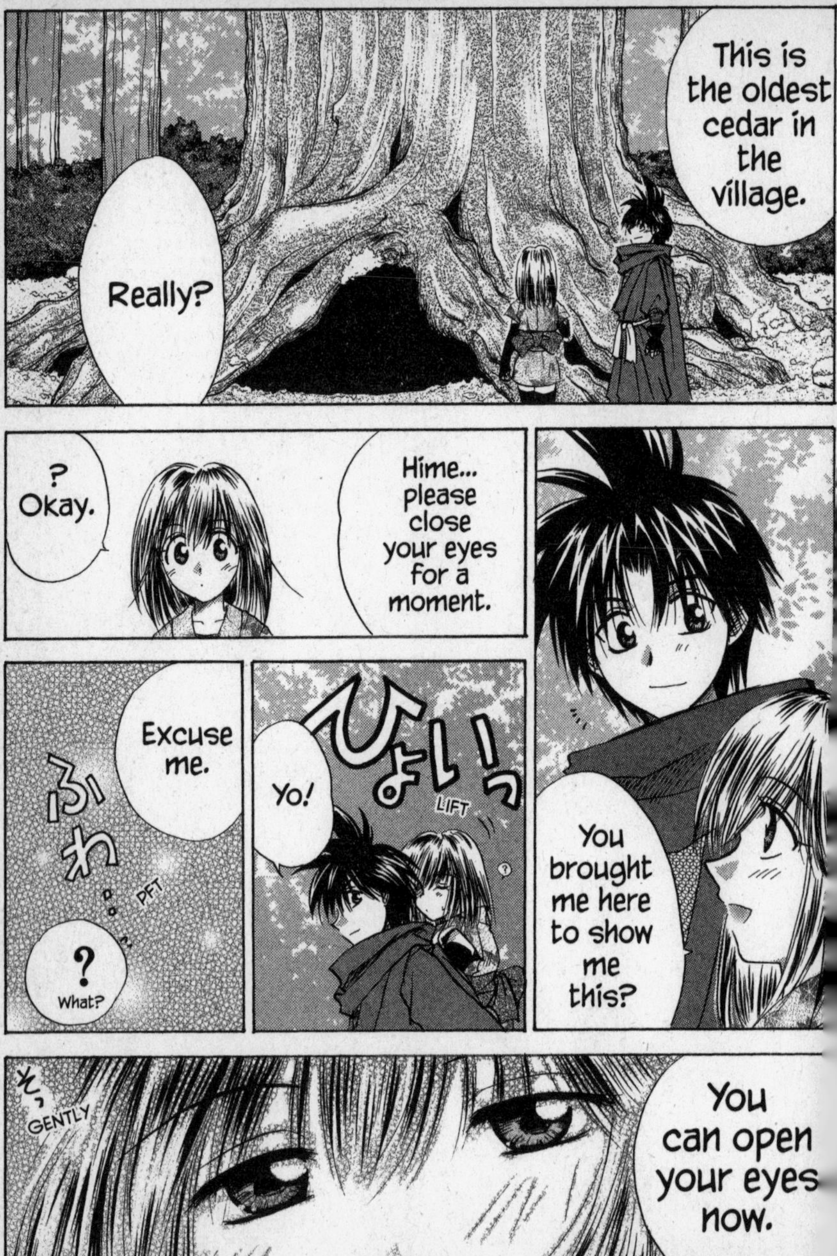
This is the oldest cedar in the village.
Really?
You brought me here to show me this?
Hime... please close your eyes for a moment.
? Okay.
ひょいっ
LIFT
Yo!
Excuse me.
ふわ
PFT
?
What?
You can open your eyes now.
そっ
GENTLY

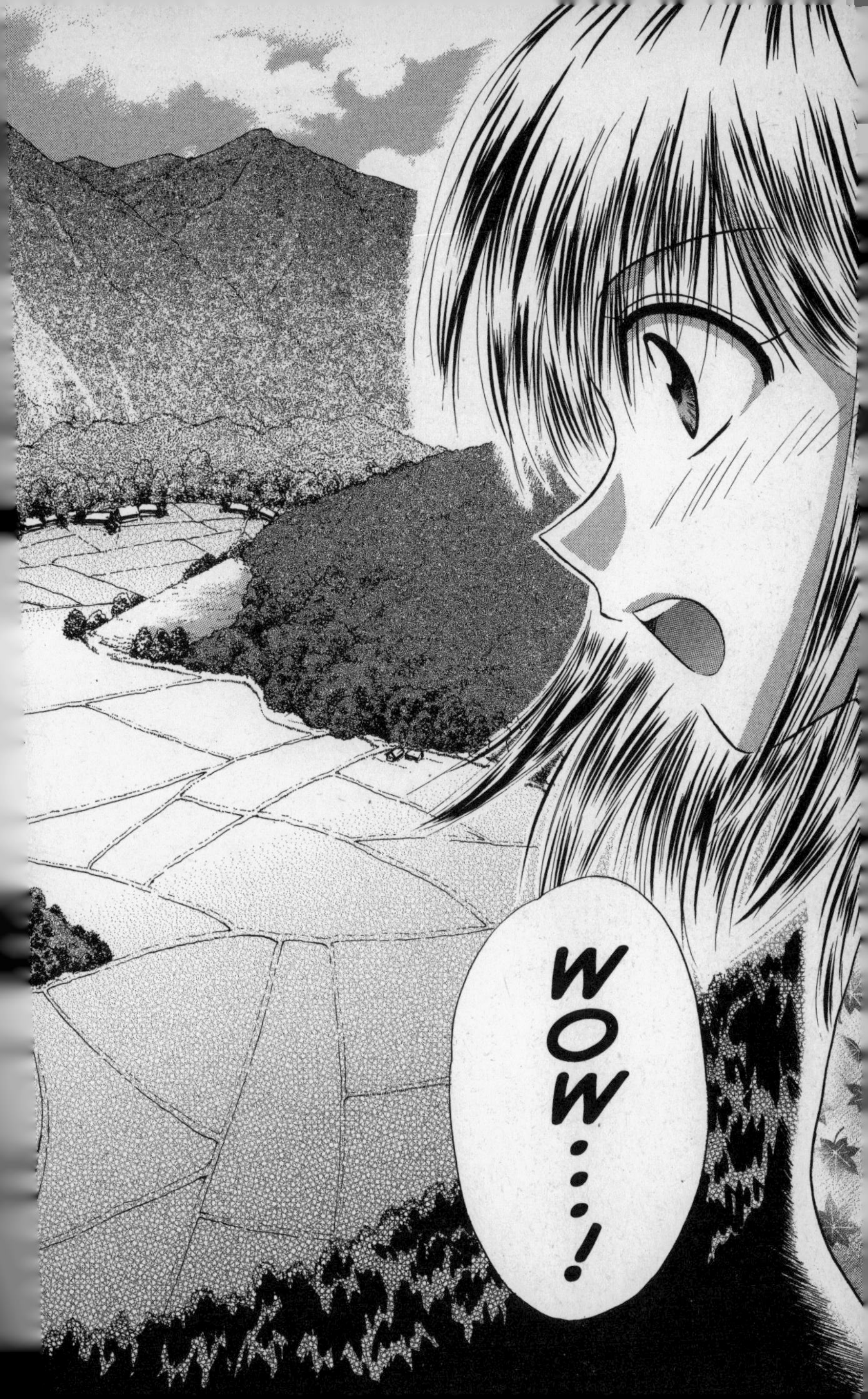
WOW...!

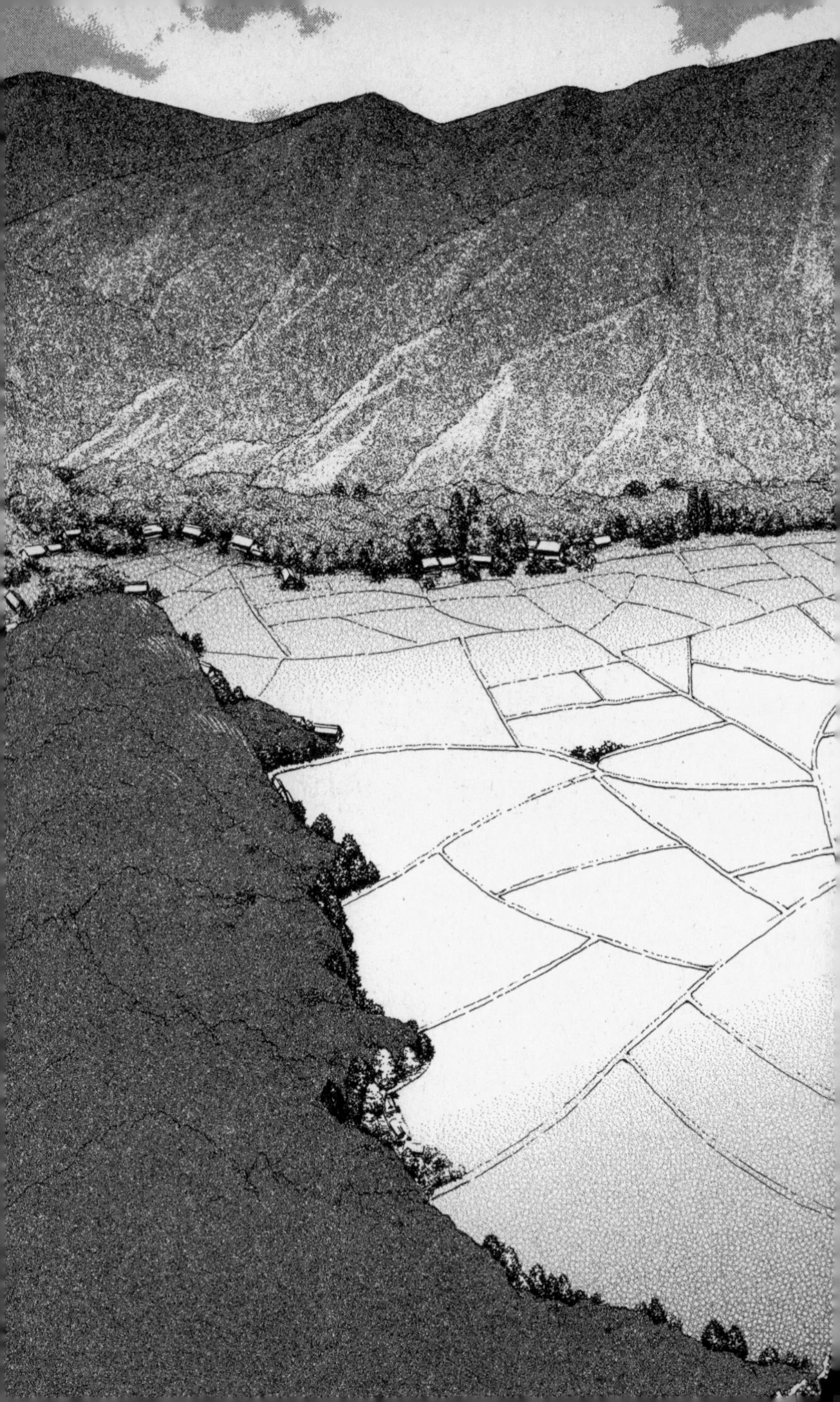

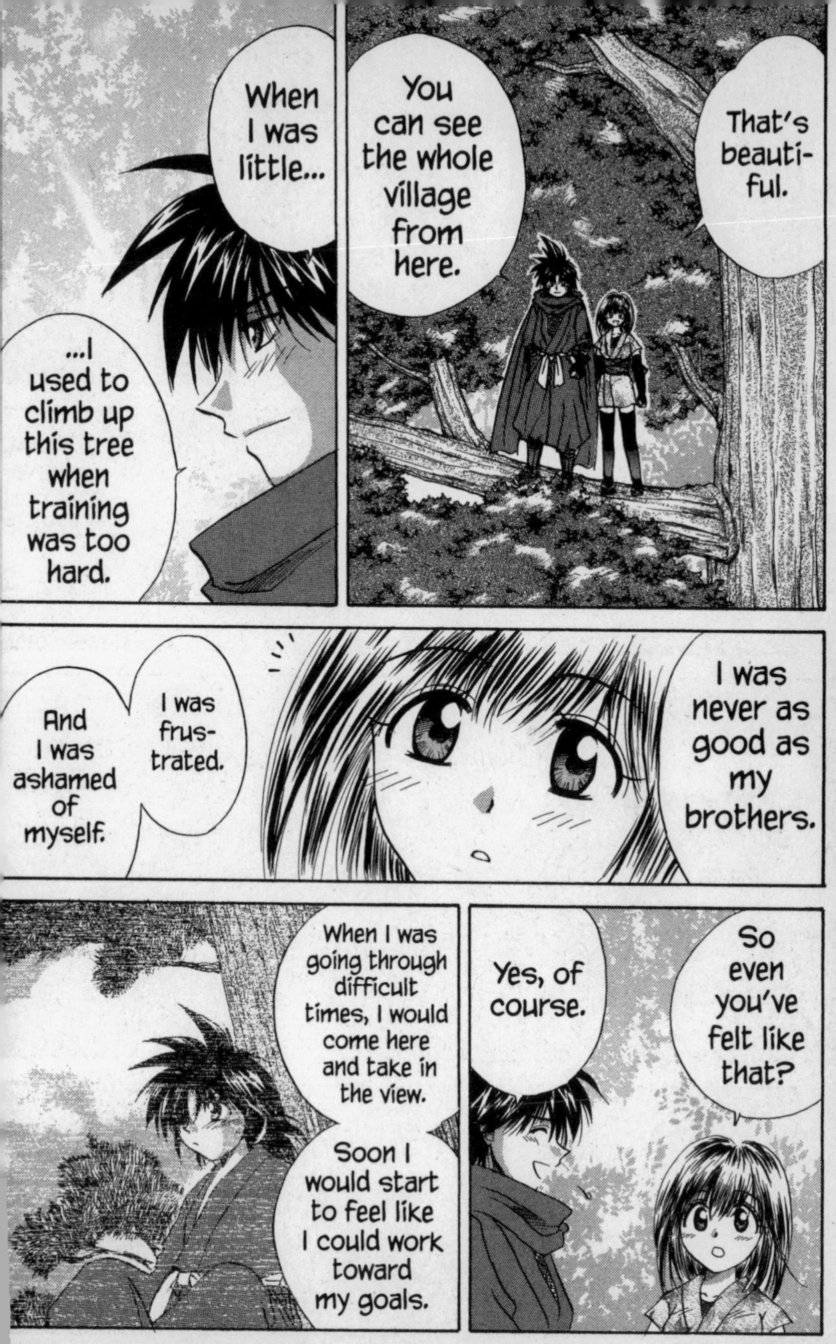
You can see the whole village from here.
That's beauti-ful.
When I was little...
...I used to climb up this tree when training was too hard.
I was never as good as my brothers.
I was frus-trated.
And I was ashamed of myself.
So even you've felt like that?
Yes, of course.
When I was going through difficult times, I would come here and take in the view.
Soon I would start to feel like I could work toward my goals.

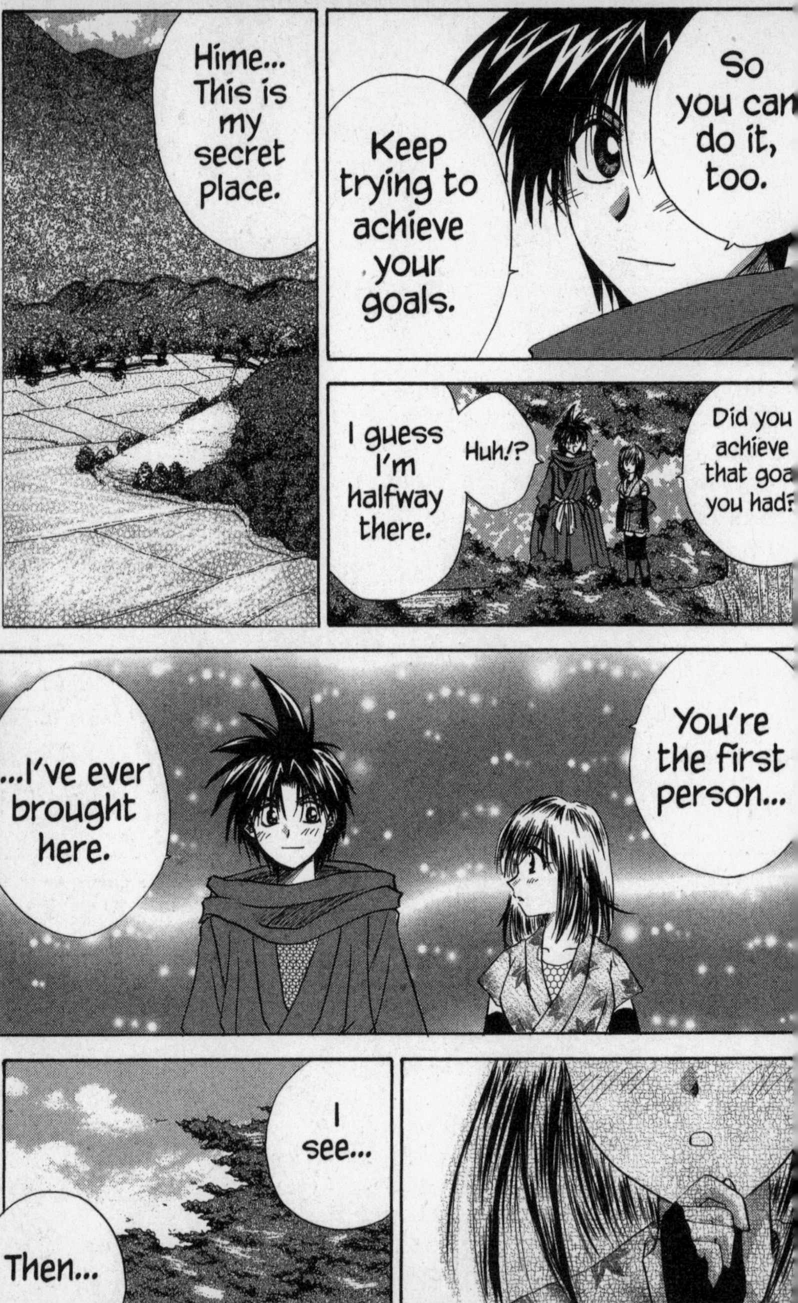

So you can do it, too.
Keep trying to achieve your goals.
Did you achieve that goa you had?
Huh!?
I guess I'm halfway there.
Hime... This is my secret place.
You're the first person...
...I've ever brought here.
I see...
Then...

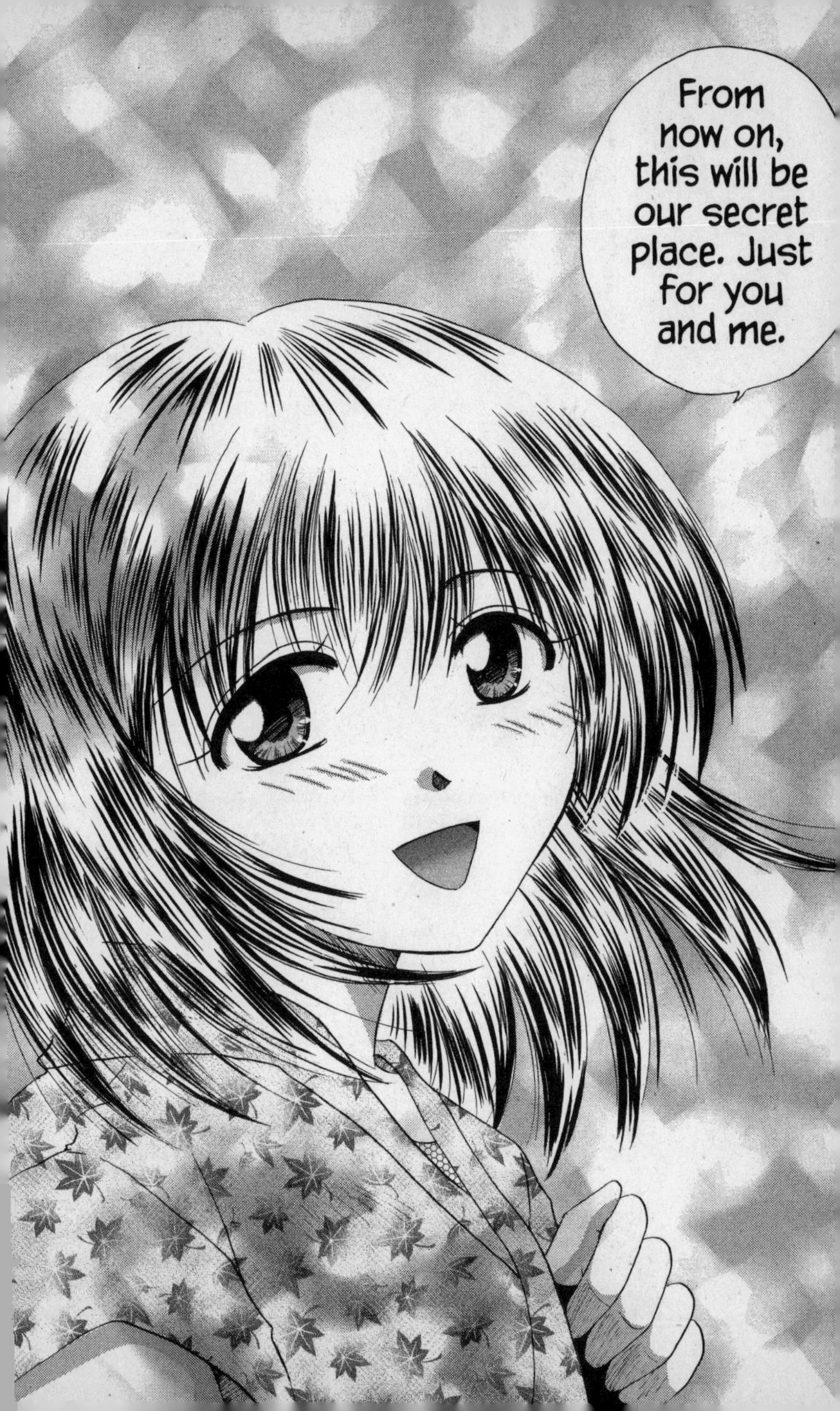
From now on, this will be our secret place. Just for you and me.

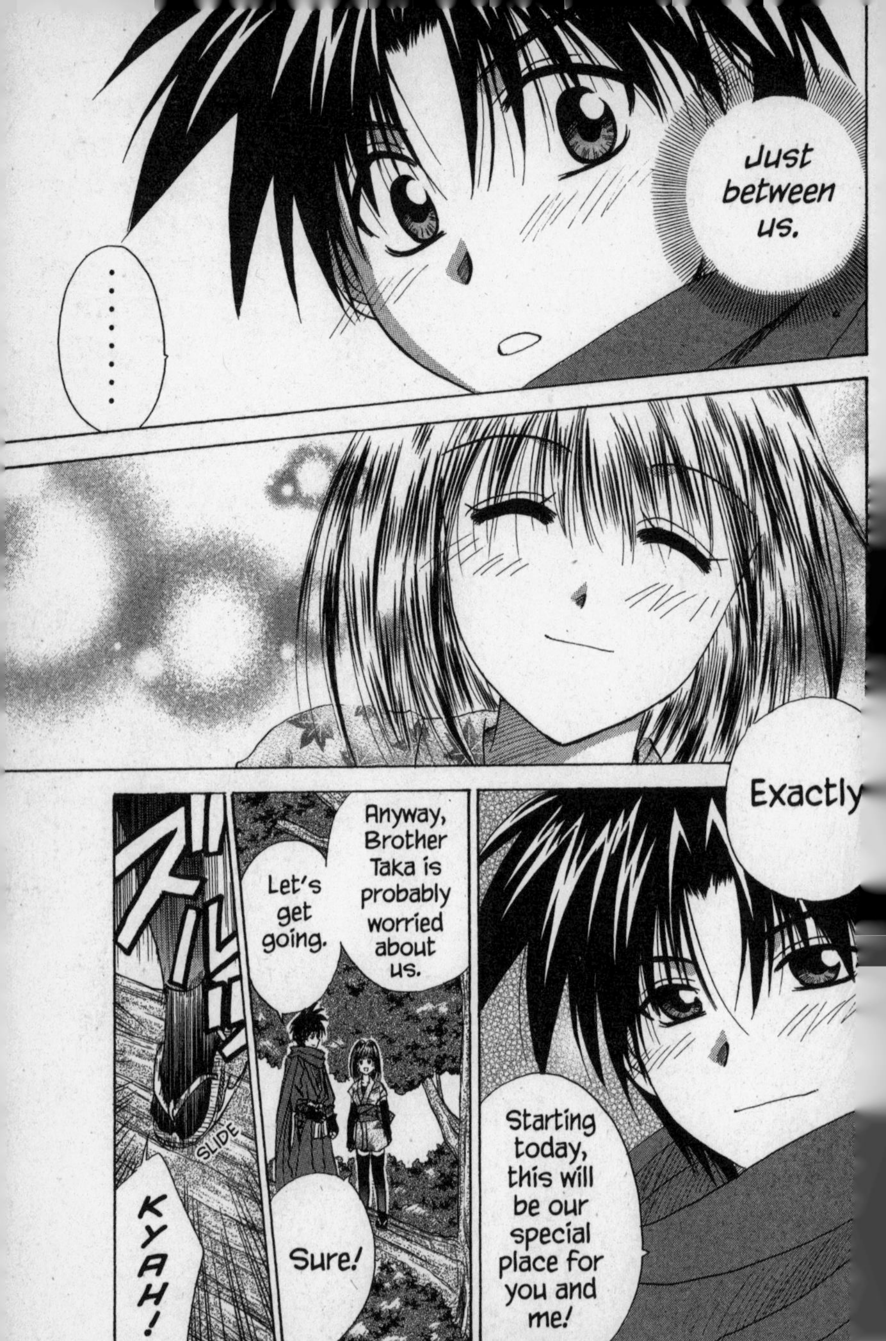
Just between us.
......
Exactly
Starting today, this will be our special place for you and me!
Anyway, Brother Taka is probably worried about us.
Let's get going.
Sure!
SLIDE
KYAH!

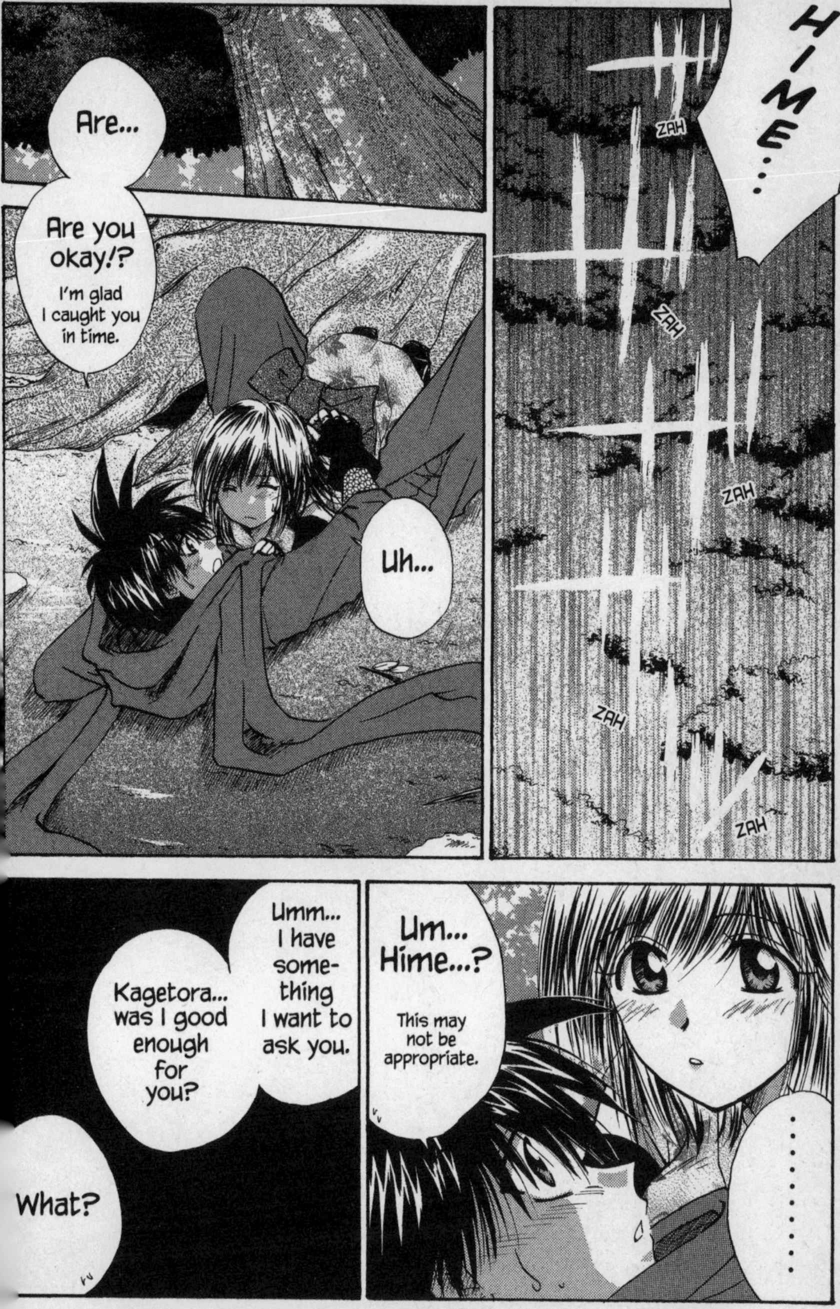
HIME...
ZAH
ZAH
ZAH
ZAH
ZAH
Are...
Are you okay!?
I'm glad I caught you in time.
Uh...
Um... Hime...?
This may not be appropriate.
....
Umm... I have some-thing I want to ask you.
Kagetora... was I good enough for you?
What?

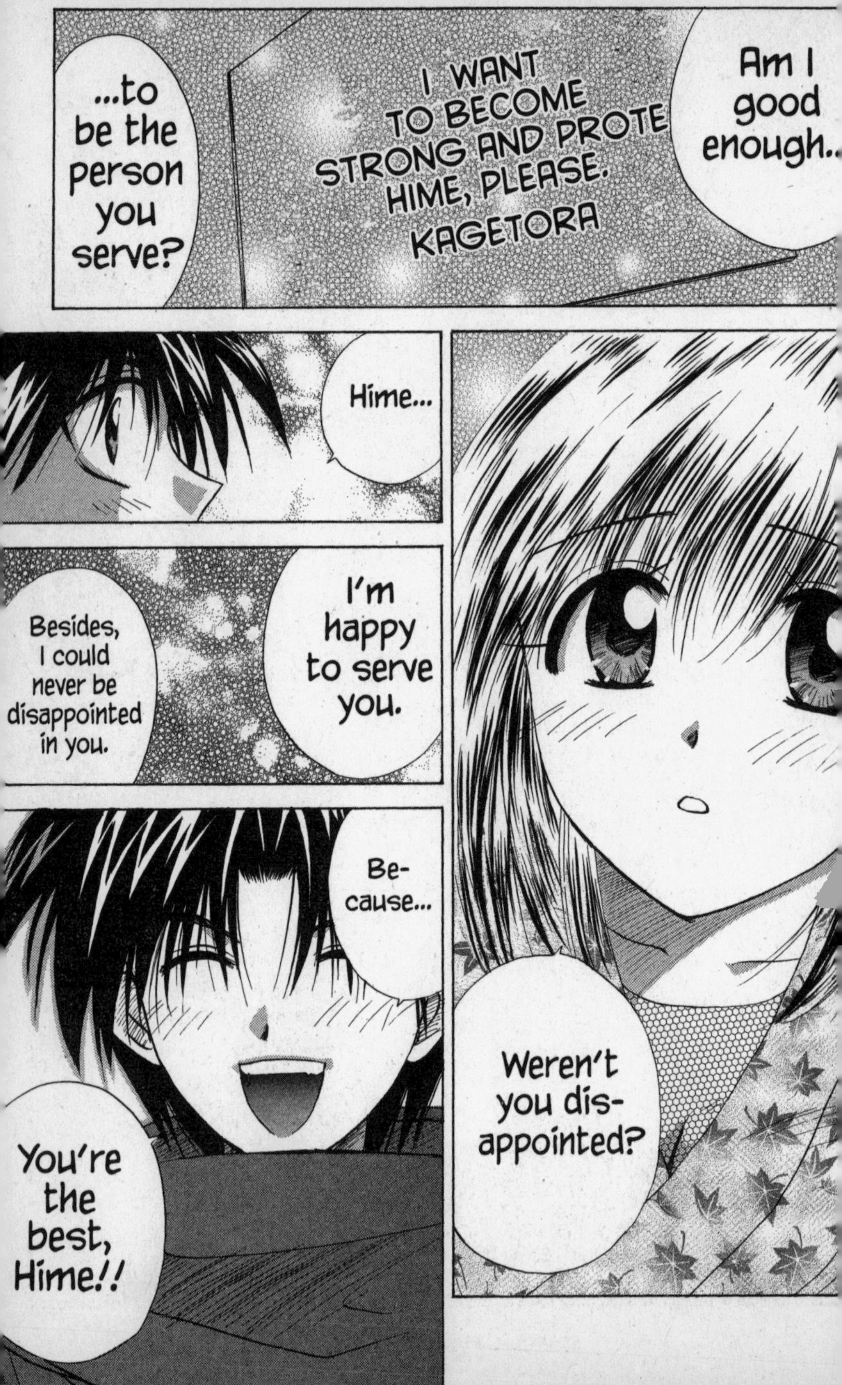
Am I good enough...
I WANT TO BECOME STRONG AND PROTE HIME, PLEASE. KAGETORA
...to be the person you serve?
Weren't you dis-appointed?
Hime...
I'm happy to serve you.
Besides, I could never be disappointed in you.
Be-cause...
You're the best, Hime!!

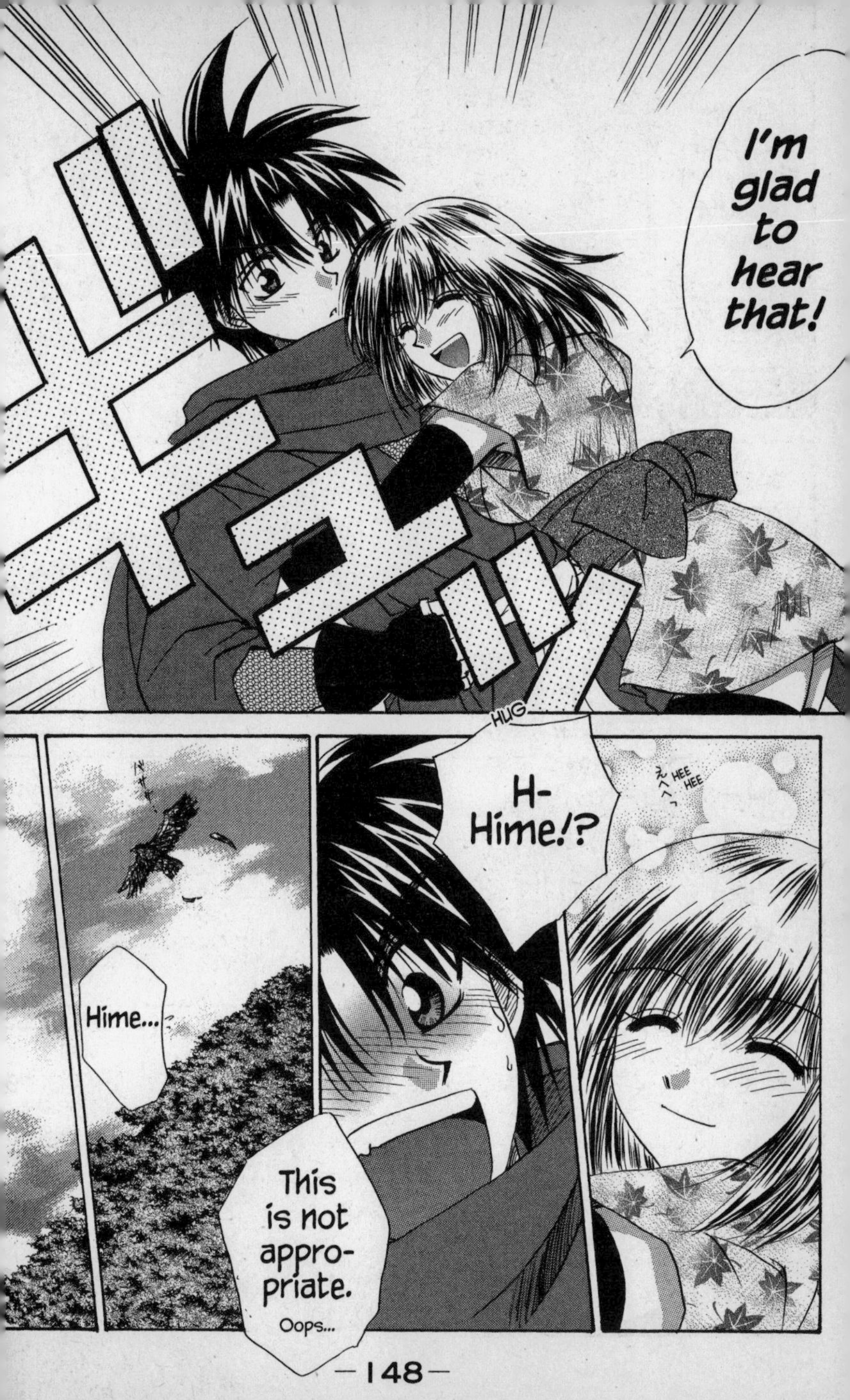
I'm glad to hear that!
HUG
HEE HEE
H-Hime!?
This is not appropriate.
Oops...
Hime...

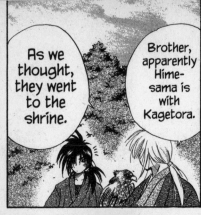

SWOOS
CHIRP
SWOOSH
So what's going on, Kagura?
Brother, apparently Hime-sama is with Kagetora.
As we thought, they went to the shrine.
I wonder if she went to make a wish.
That's very much like her.
Although she doesn't look it, she's very competi-tive.
I bet Kagetora will have a tough time dealing with her.
HEH HEH
That's all part of the duty.
Well, if she's goin to be the next head o Toudou cla she needs to be tough.
Otherwise, she won't be worthy of the Hoorai villagers' protection.
You're pretty harsh.
But it's true.

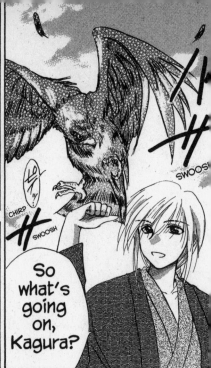

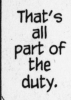

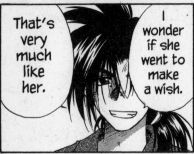

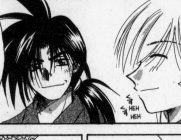

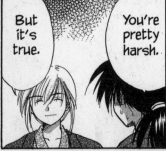

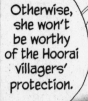

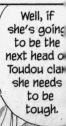

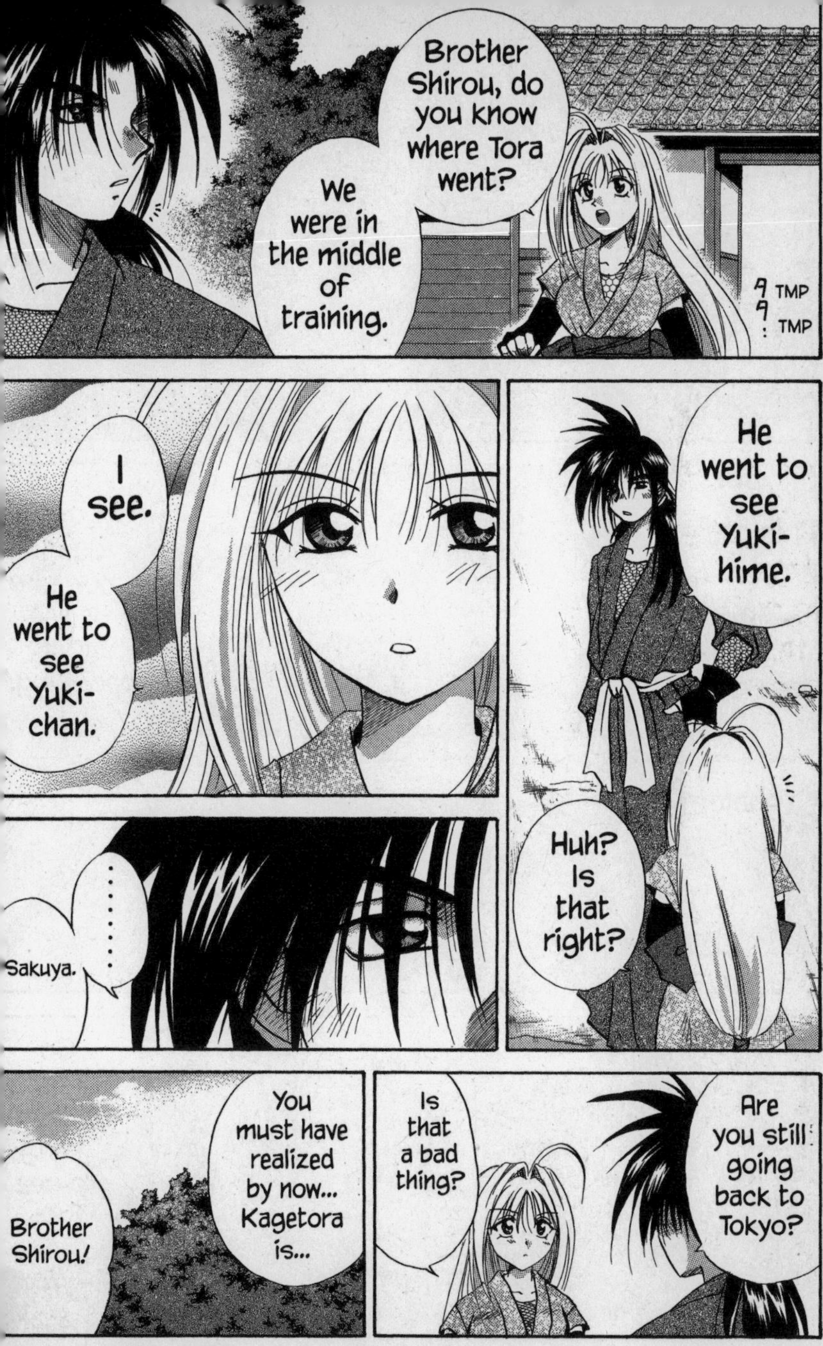
Brother Shirou, do you know where Tora went?
We were in the middle of training.
TMP
TMP
He went to see Yuki-hime.
Huh? Is that right?
I see.
He went to see Yuki-chan.
......
Sakuya.
Are you still going back to Tokyo?
Is that a bad thing?
You must have realized by now... Kagetora is...
Brother Shirou!

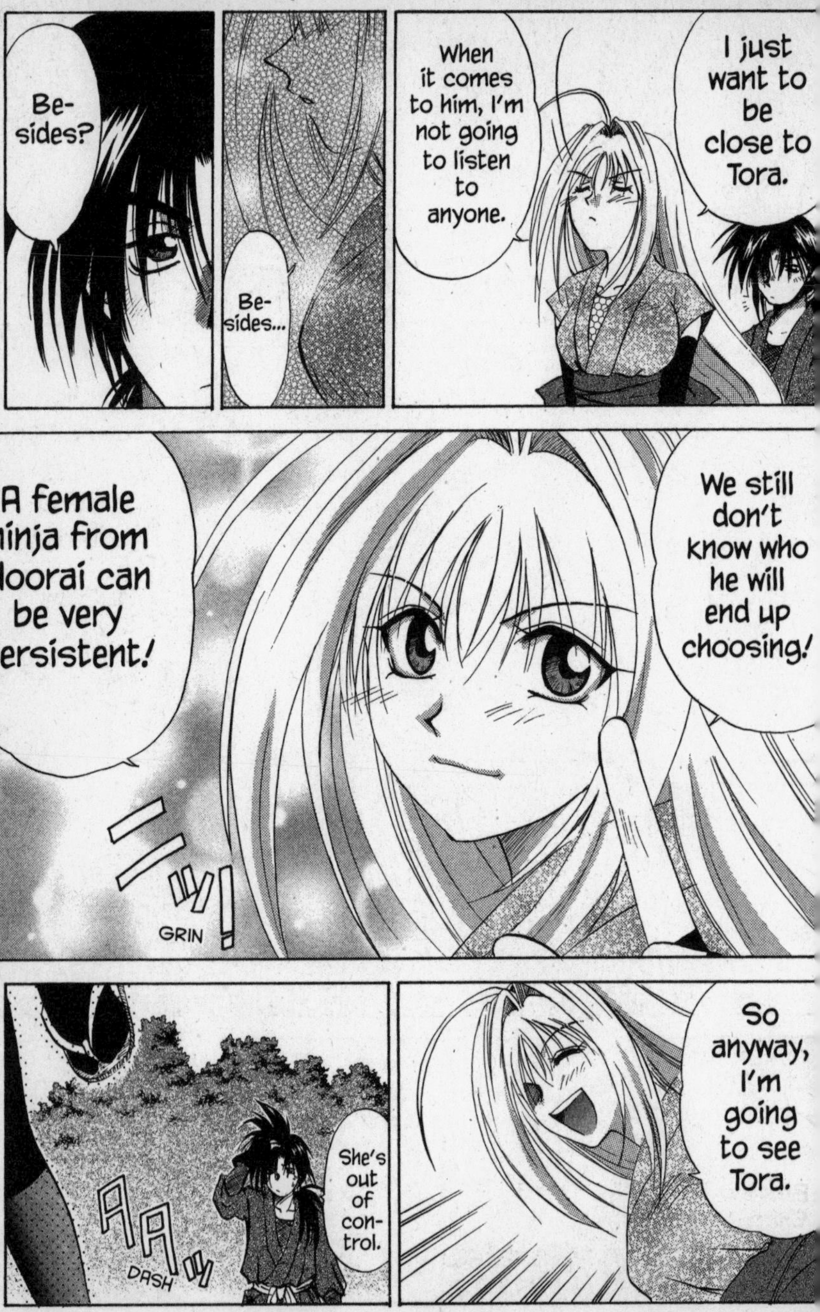
I just want to be close to Tora.
When it comes to him, I'm not going to listen to anyone.
Be-sides...
Be-sides?
We still don't know who he will end up choosing!
A female ninja from Hoorai can be very persistent!
GRIN
So anyway, I'm going to see Tora.
She's out of control.
DASH

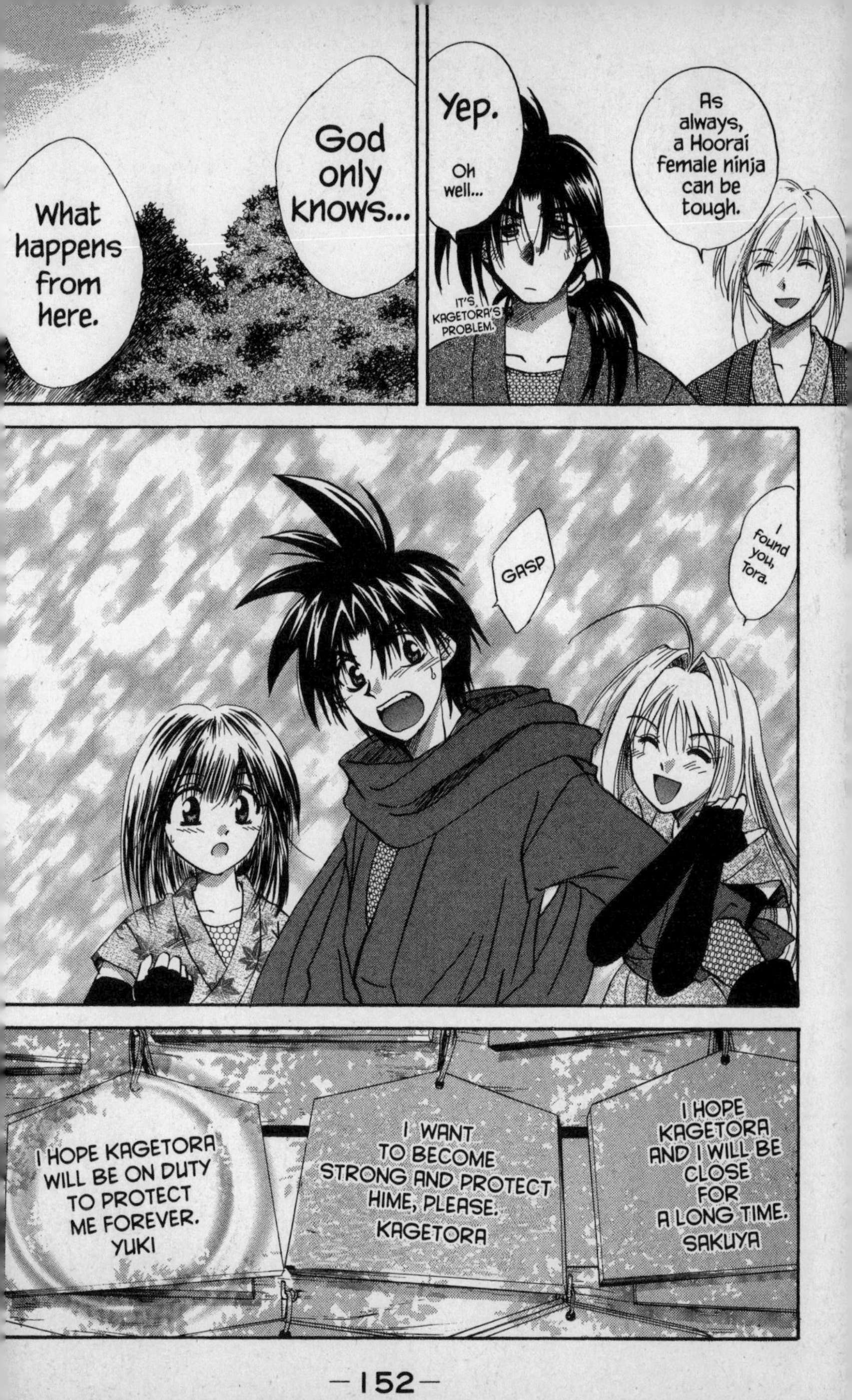
As always, a Hoorai female ninja can be tough.
Yep.
Oh well...
IT'S KAGETORA'S PROBLEM.
God only knows...
What happens from here.
I found you, Tora.
GASP
I HOPE KAGETORA AND I WILL BE CLOSE FOR A LONG TIME. SAKUYA
I WANT TO BECOME STRONG AND PROTECT HIME, PLEASE. KAGETORA
I HOPE KAGETORA WILL BE ON DUTY TO PROTECT ME FOREVER. YUKI

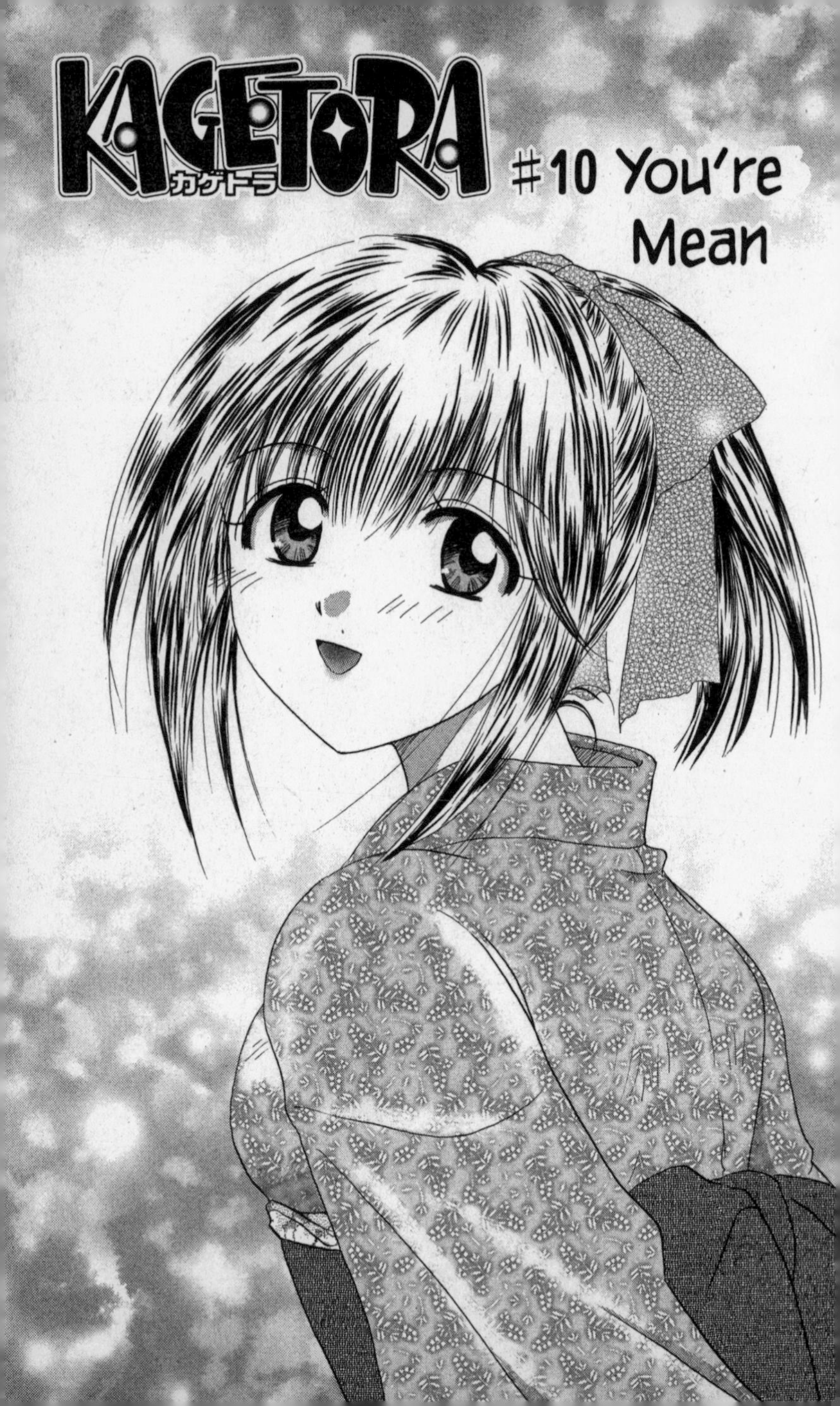
KAGETORA
カゲトラ
#10 You're Mean

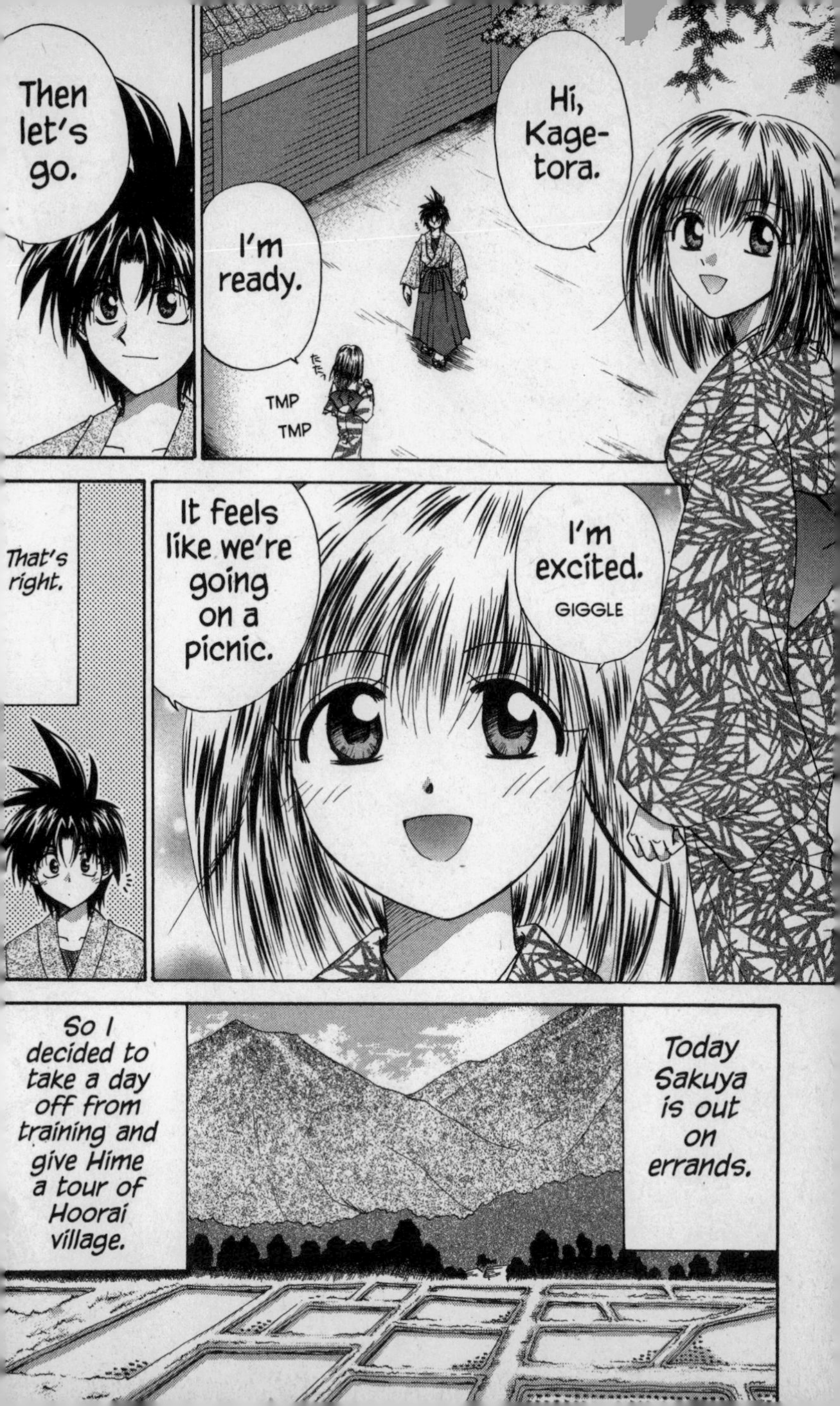
Hi, Kage-tora.
I'm ready.
TMP
TMP
Then let's go.
I'm excited.
GIGGLE
It feels like we're going on a picnic.
That's right.
Today Sakuya is out on errands.
So I decided to take a day off from training and give Hime a tour of Hoorai village.

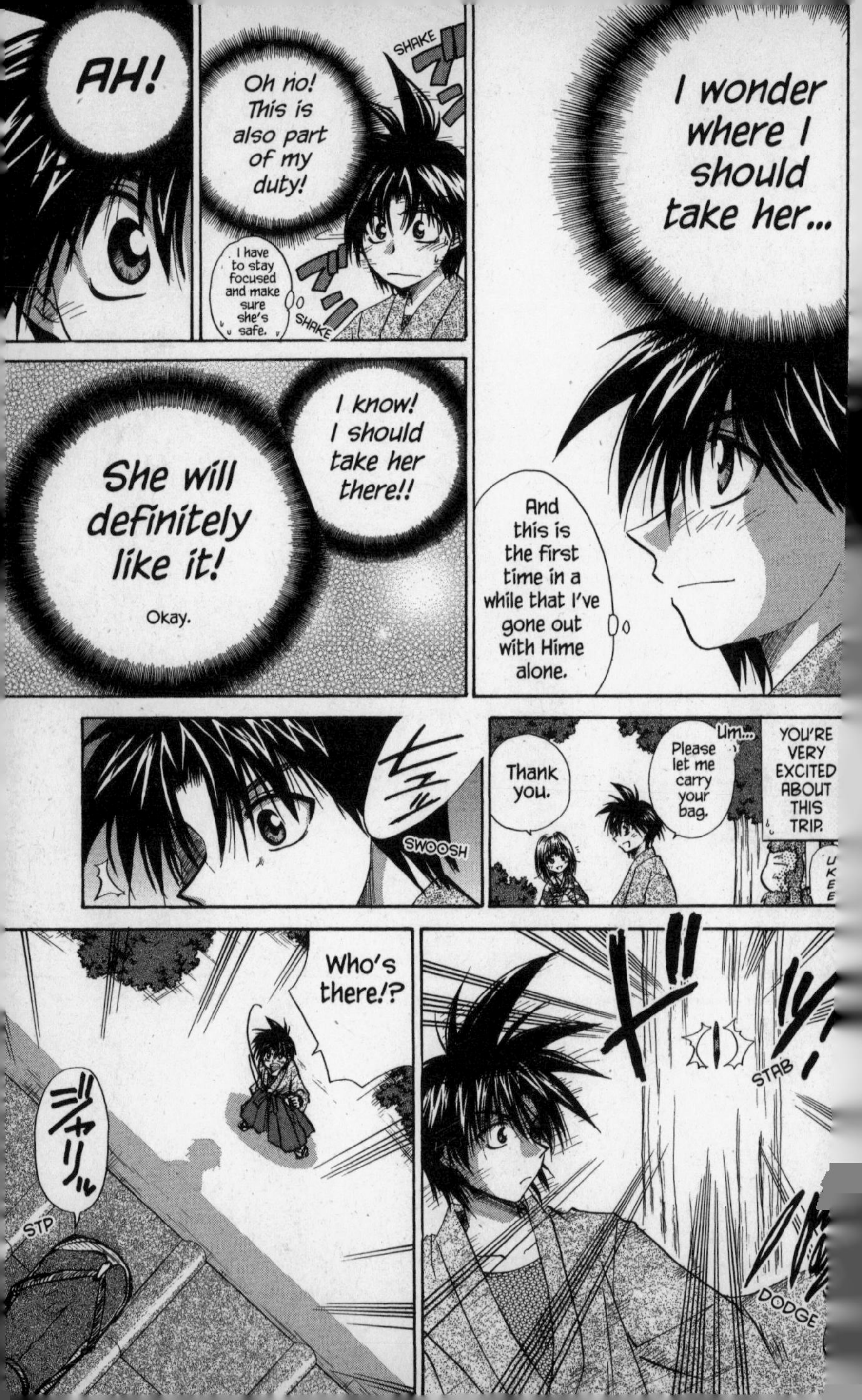
I wonder where I should take her...
And this is the first time in a while that I've gone out with Hime alone.
Oh no! This is also part of my duty!
SHAKE
I have to stay focused and make sure she's safe.
SHAKE
AH!
I know! I should take her there!!
She will definitely like it!
Okay.
YOU'RE VERY EXCITED ABOUT THIS TRIP.
UKEE
Um...
Please let me carry your bag.
Thank you.
SWOOSH
STAB
DODGE
Who's there!?
STP

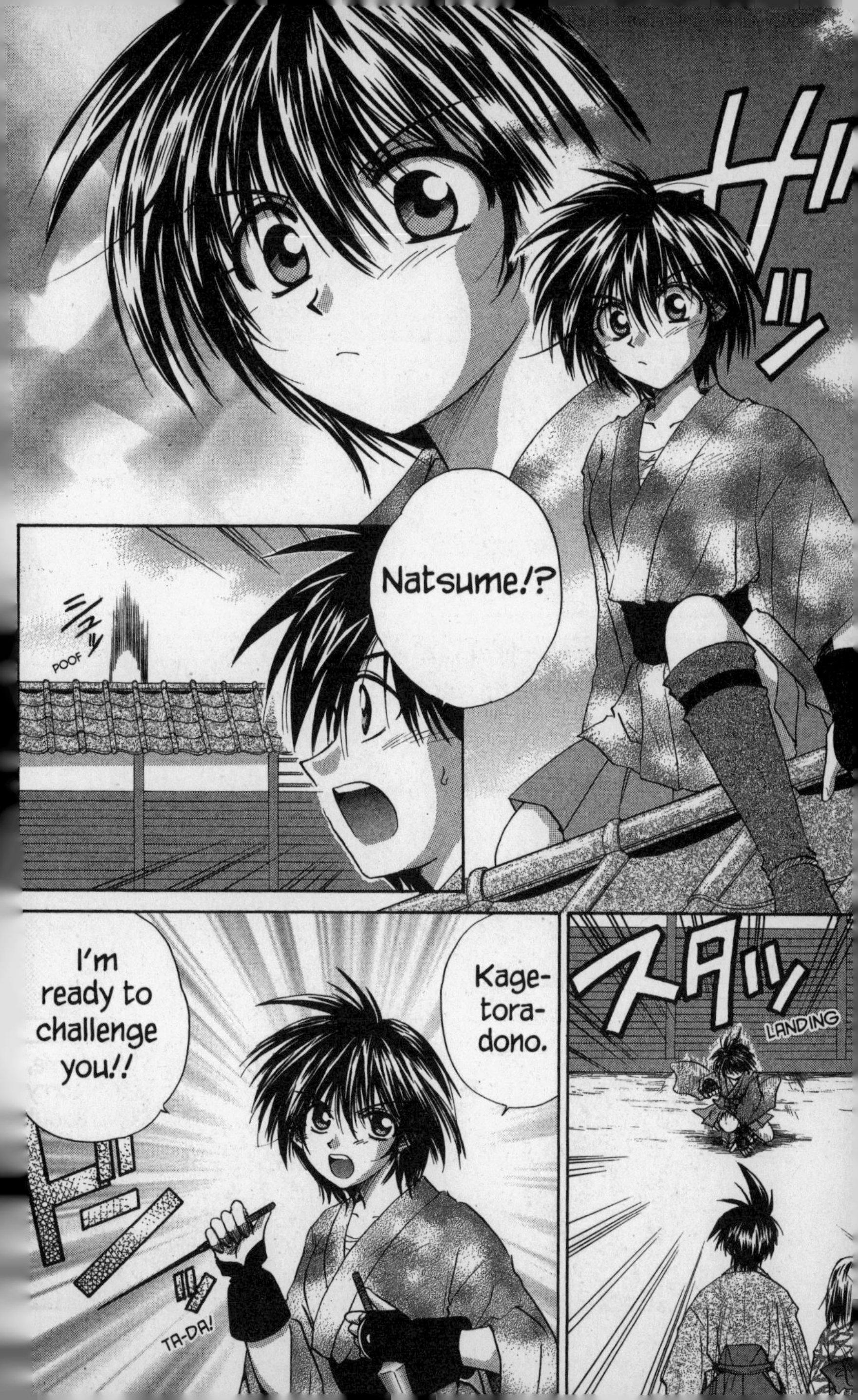
Natsume!?
POOF
LANDING
Kage-tora-dono.
I'm ready to challenge you!!
TA-DA!

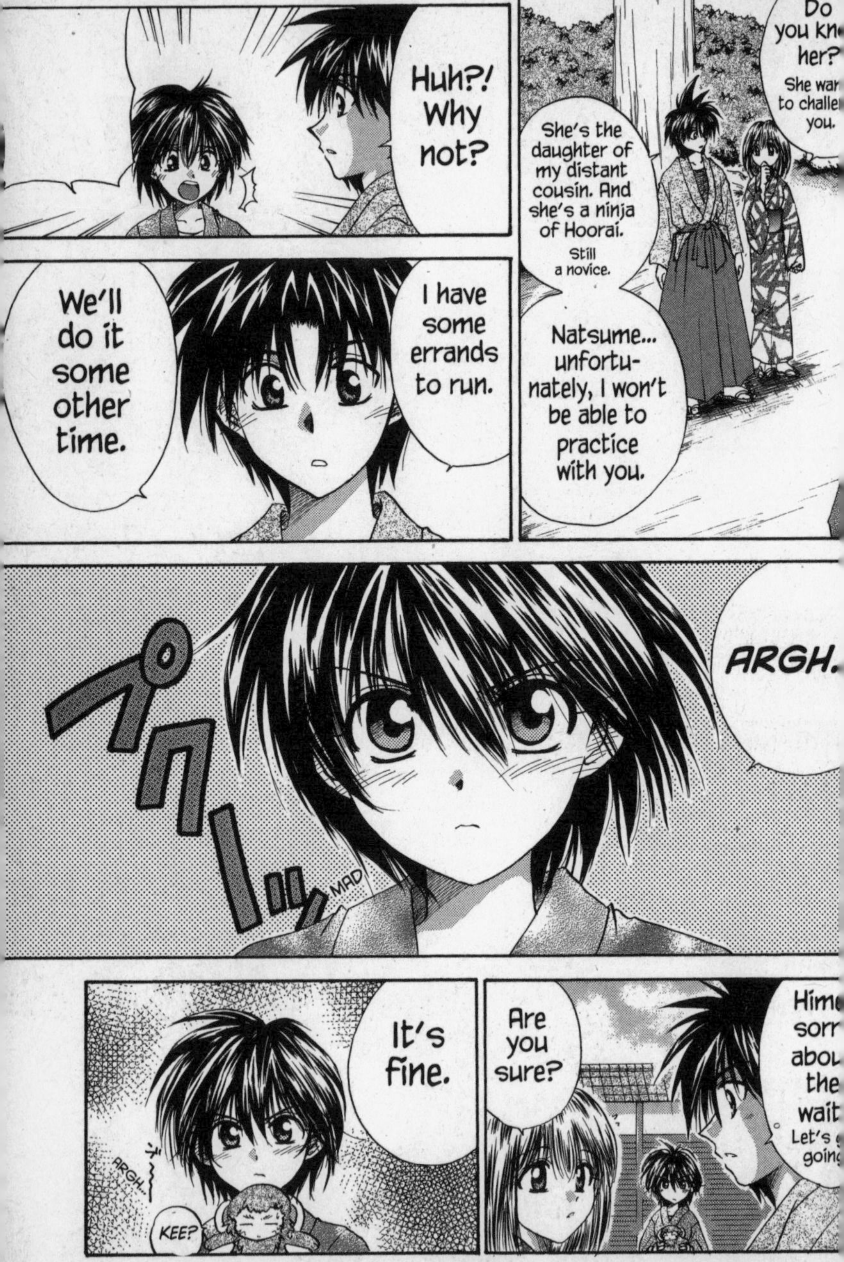
Do you kn her?
She wa to challe you.
She's the daughter of my distant cousin. And she's a ninja of Hoorai.
Still a novice.
Natsume... unfortu-nately, I won't be able to practice with you.
Huh?! Why not?
I have some errands to run.
We'll do it some other time.
ARGH.
MAD
Hime sorr abou the wait
Let's goin
Are you sure?
It's fine.
ARGH.
KEE?

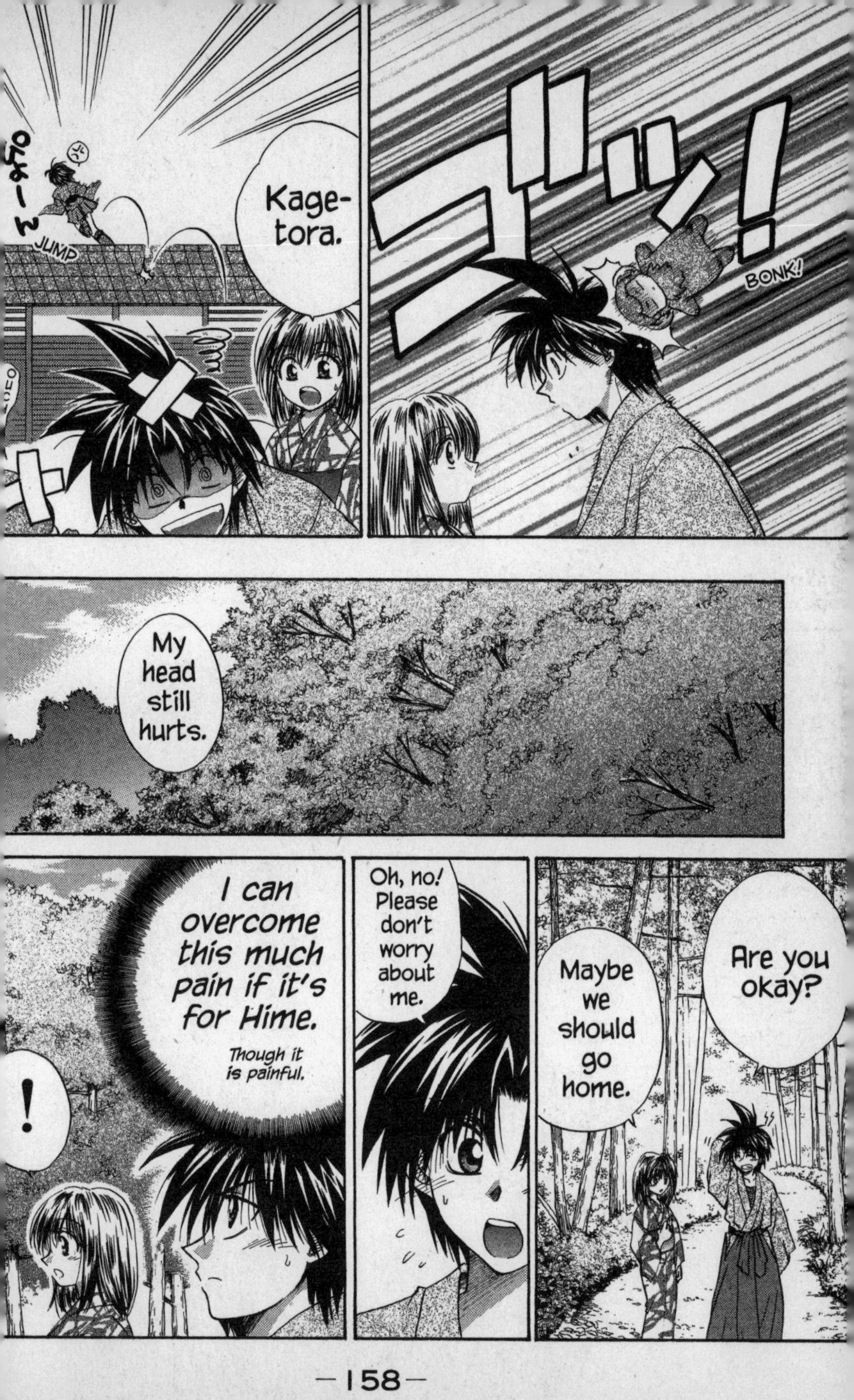
ゴッ!
BONK!
Kage-tora.
JUMP
My head still hurts.
Are you okay?
Maybe we should go home.
Oh, no! Please don't worry about me.
I can overcome this much pain if it's for Hime.
Though it is painful.
!

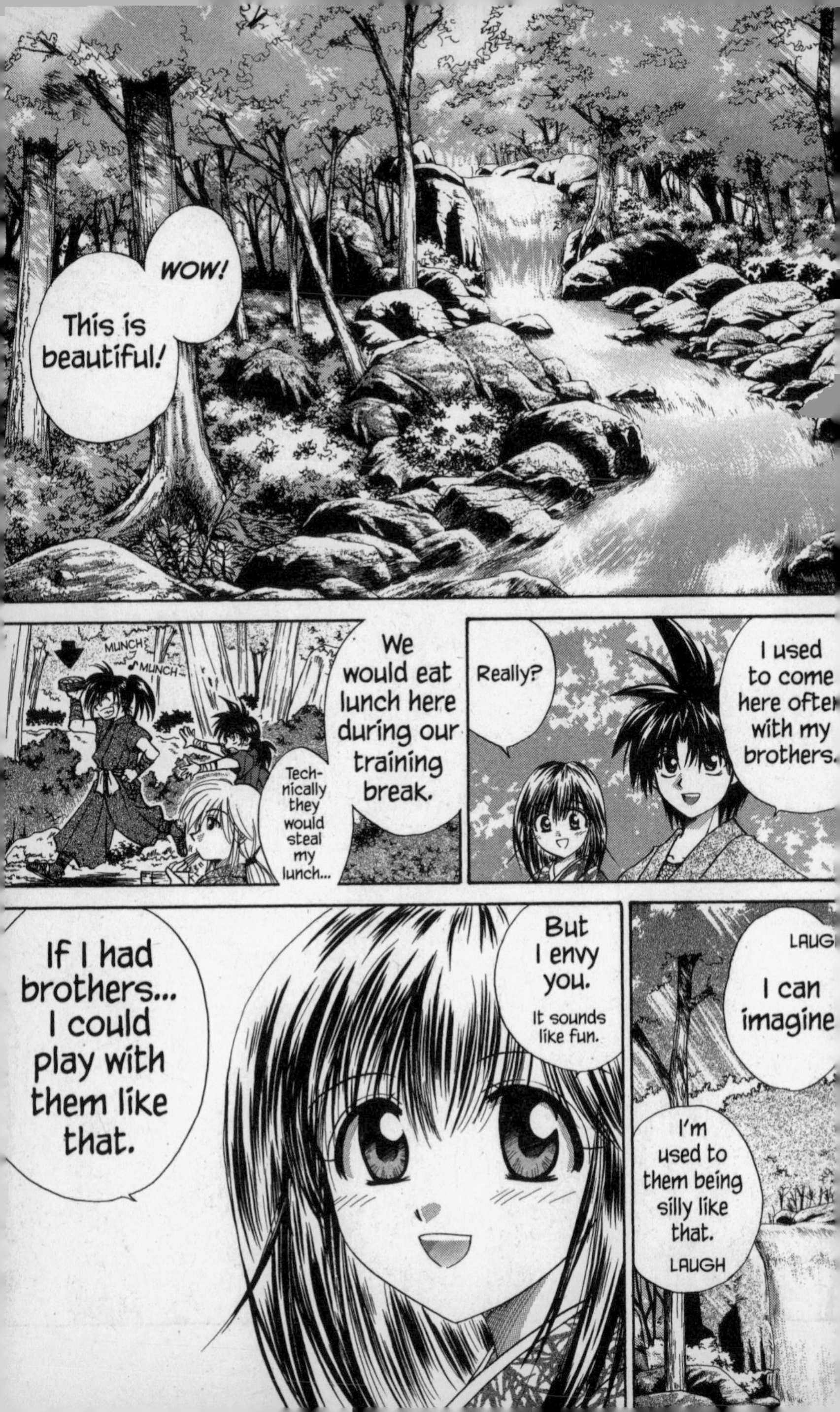
WOW!
This is beautiful!
I used to come here ofte with my brothers.
Really?
We would eat lunch here during our training break.
Technically they would steal my lunch...
MUNCH
MUNCH
LAUG
I can imagine
I'm used to them being silly like that.
LAUGH
But I envy you.
It sounds like fun.
If I had brothers... I could play with them like that.

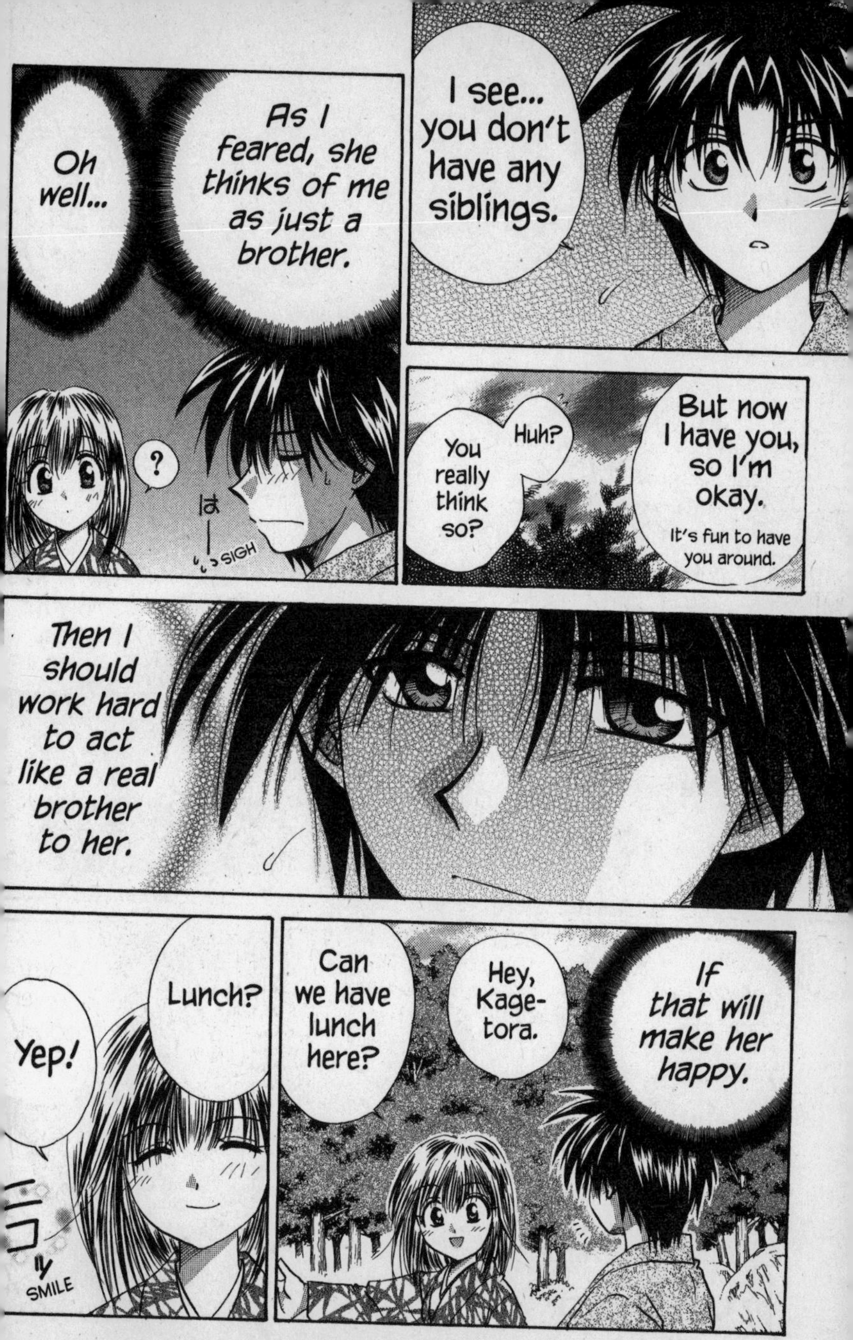
I see... you don't have any siblings.
But now I have you, so I'm okay.
It's fun to have you around.
Huh?
You really think so?
As I feared, she thinks of me as just a brother.
Oh well...
?
SIGH
Then I should work hard to act like a real brother to her.
If that will make her happy.
Hey, Kage-tora.
Can we have lunch here?
Lunch?
Yep!
SMILE

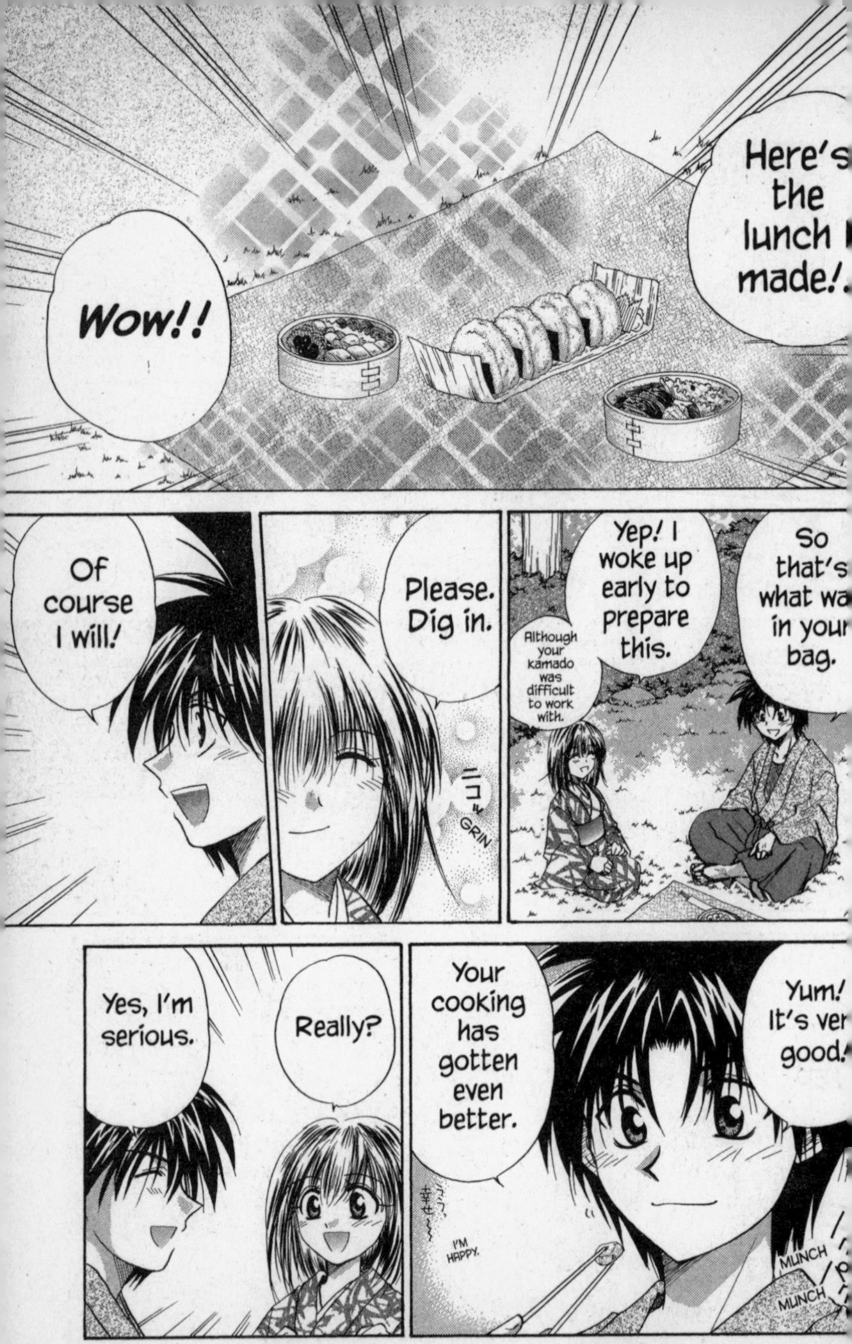

Here's the lunch I made!
Wow!!
So that's what was in your bag.
Yep! I woke up early to prepare this.
Although your kamado was difficult to work with.
Please. Dig in.
ニコッ
GRIN
Of course I will!
Yum! It's very good!
MUNCH MUNCH
Your cooking has gotten even better.
I'M HAPPY.
Really?
Yes, I'm serious.

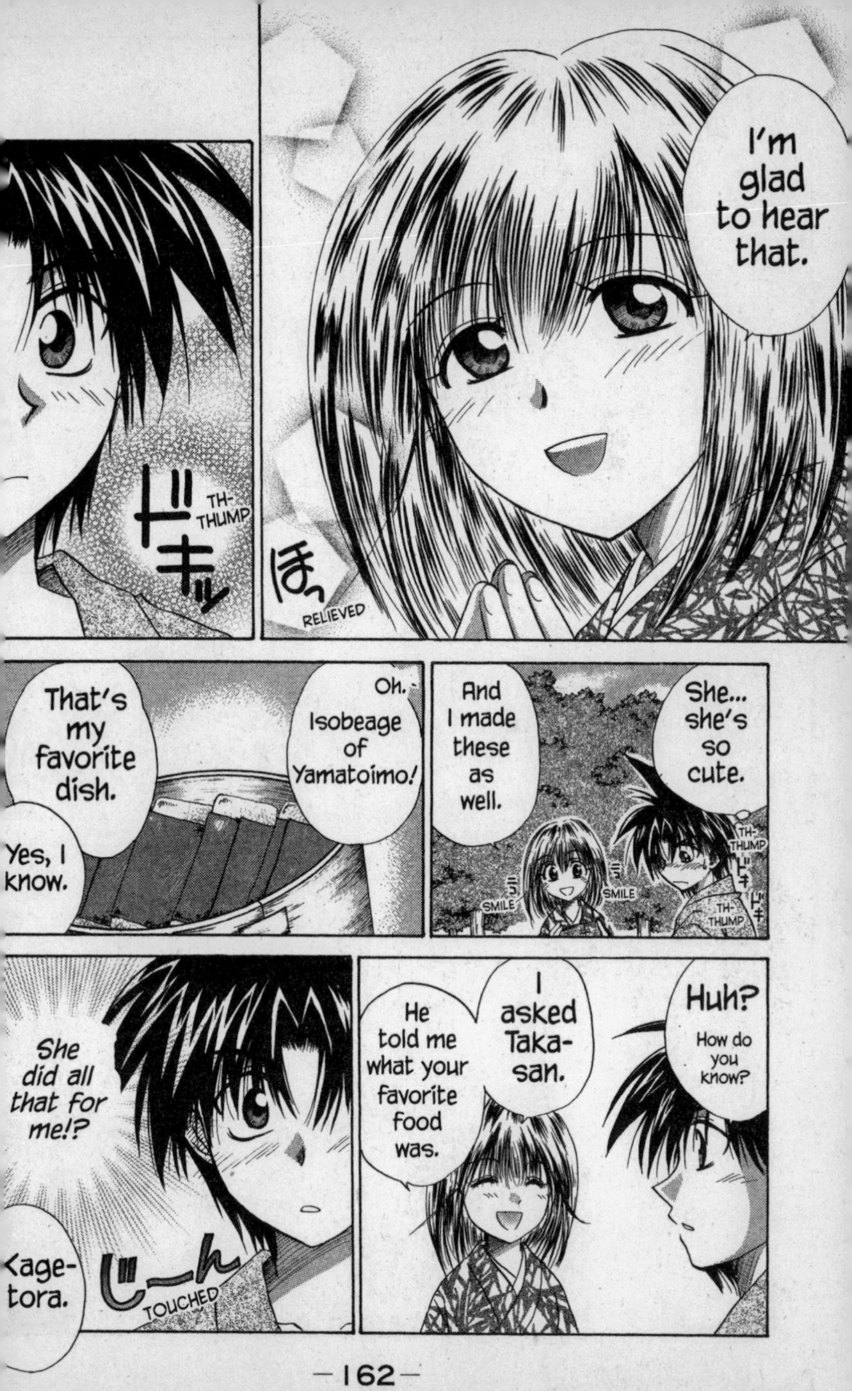
I'm glad to hear that.
ほっ
RELIEVED
ドキッ
TH-THUMP
She... she's so cute.
TH-THUMP
ドキ
TH-THUMP
ドキ
And I made these as well.
SMILE
SMILE
Oh. Isobeage of Yamatoimo!
That's my favorite dish.
Yes, I know.
Huh? How do you know?
I asked Taka-san.
He told me what your favorite food was.
She did all that for me!?
Kage-tora.
じーん
TOUCHED

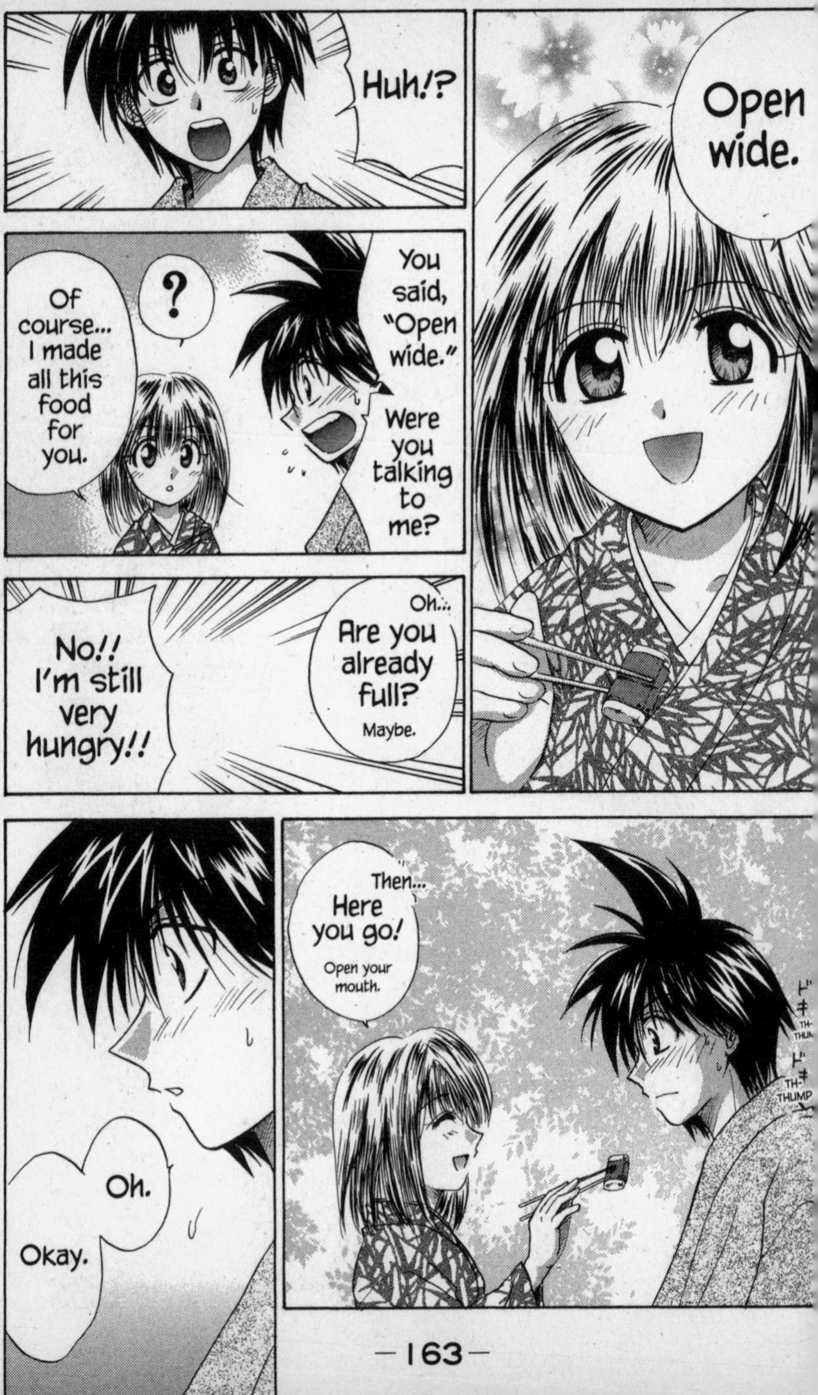
Open wide.
Huh!?
You said, "Open wide."
Were you talking to me?
?
Of course... I made all this food for you.
Oh... Are you already full?
Maybe.
No!! I'm still very hungry!!
Then... Here you go!
Open your mouth.
TH-THUMP
TH-THUMP
Oh.
Okay.

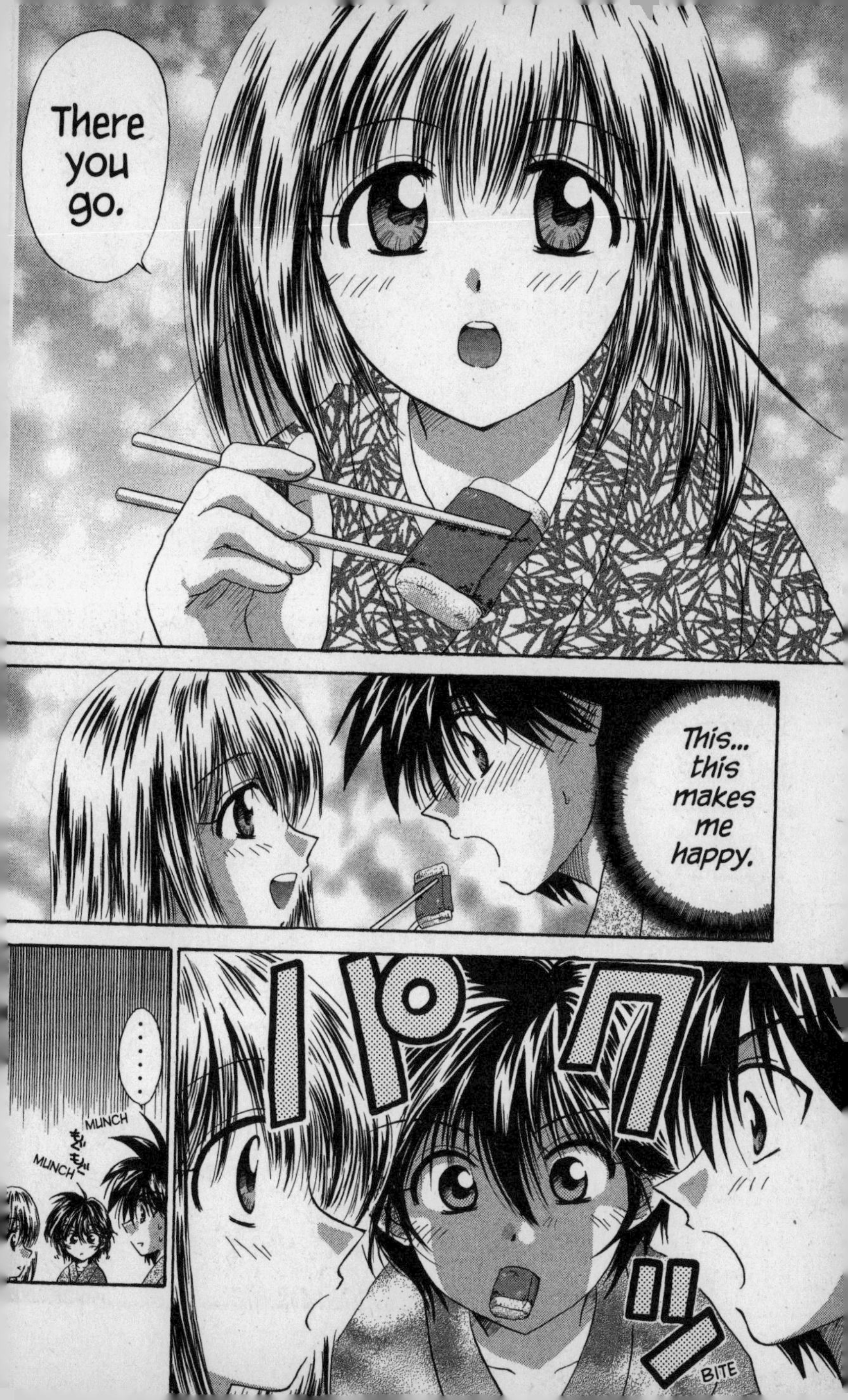
There you go.
This... this makes me happy.
BITE
......
MUNCH
もぐもぐ
MUNCH

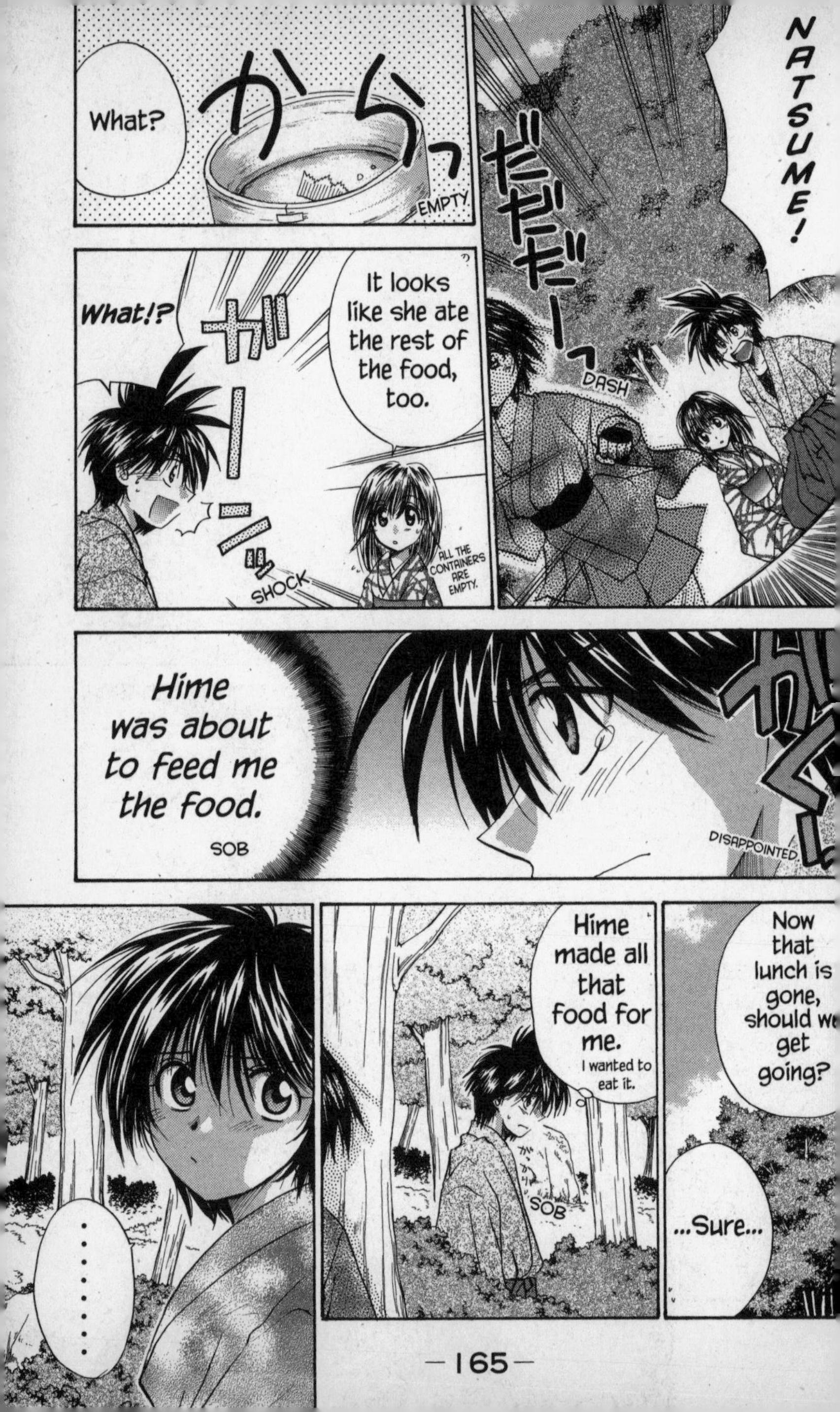

NATSUME!
DASH
What?
EMPTY
It looks like she ate the rest of the food, too.
What!?
SHOCK
ALL THE CONTAINERS ARE EMPTY.
Hime was about to feed me the food.
SOB
DISAPPOINTED
Now that lunch is gone, should we get going?
...Sure...
Hime made all that food for me.
I wanted to eat it.
SOB
......

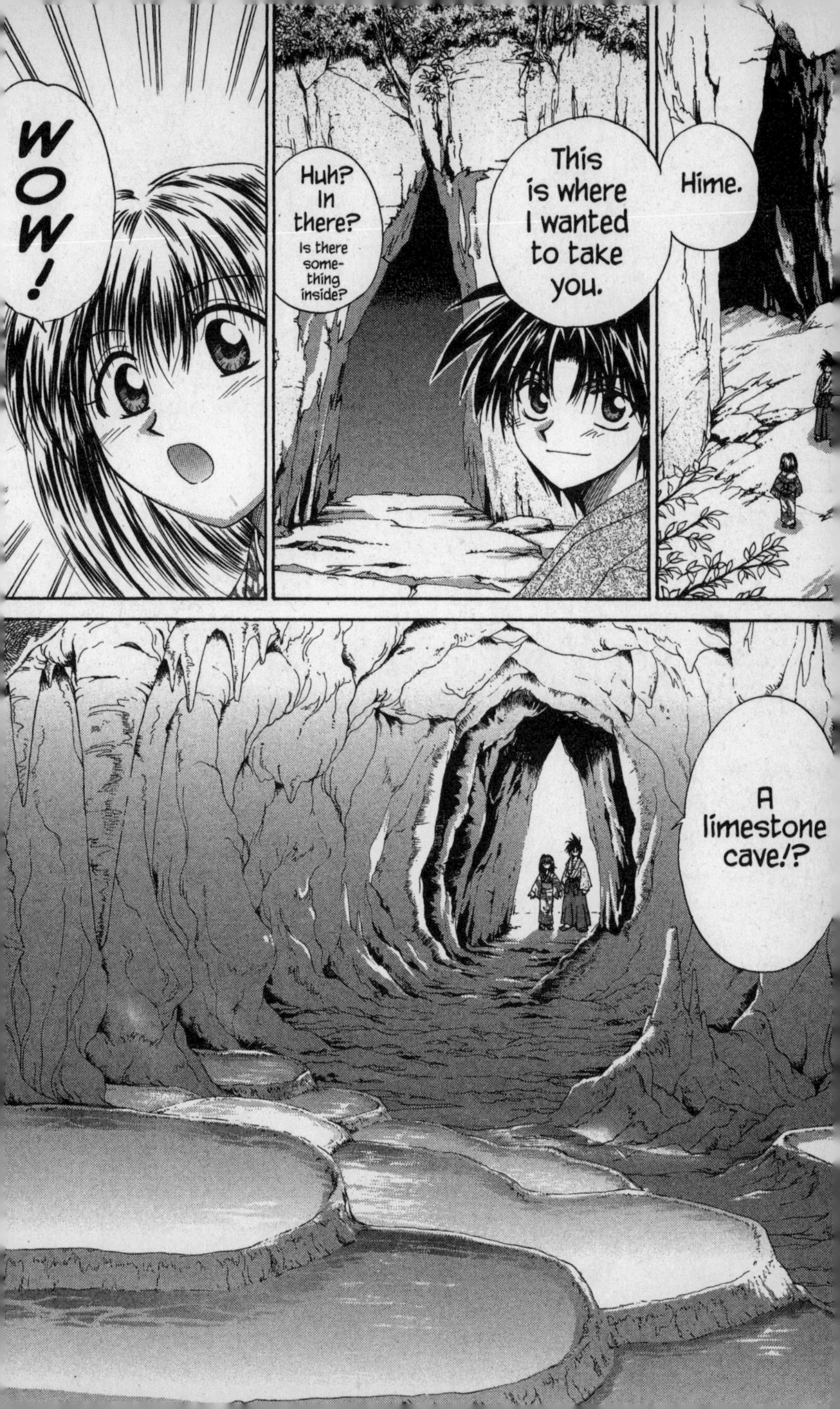
Hime.
This is where I wanted to take you.
Huh? In there?
Is there something inside?
WOW!
A limestone cave!?

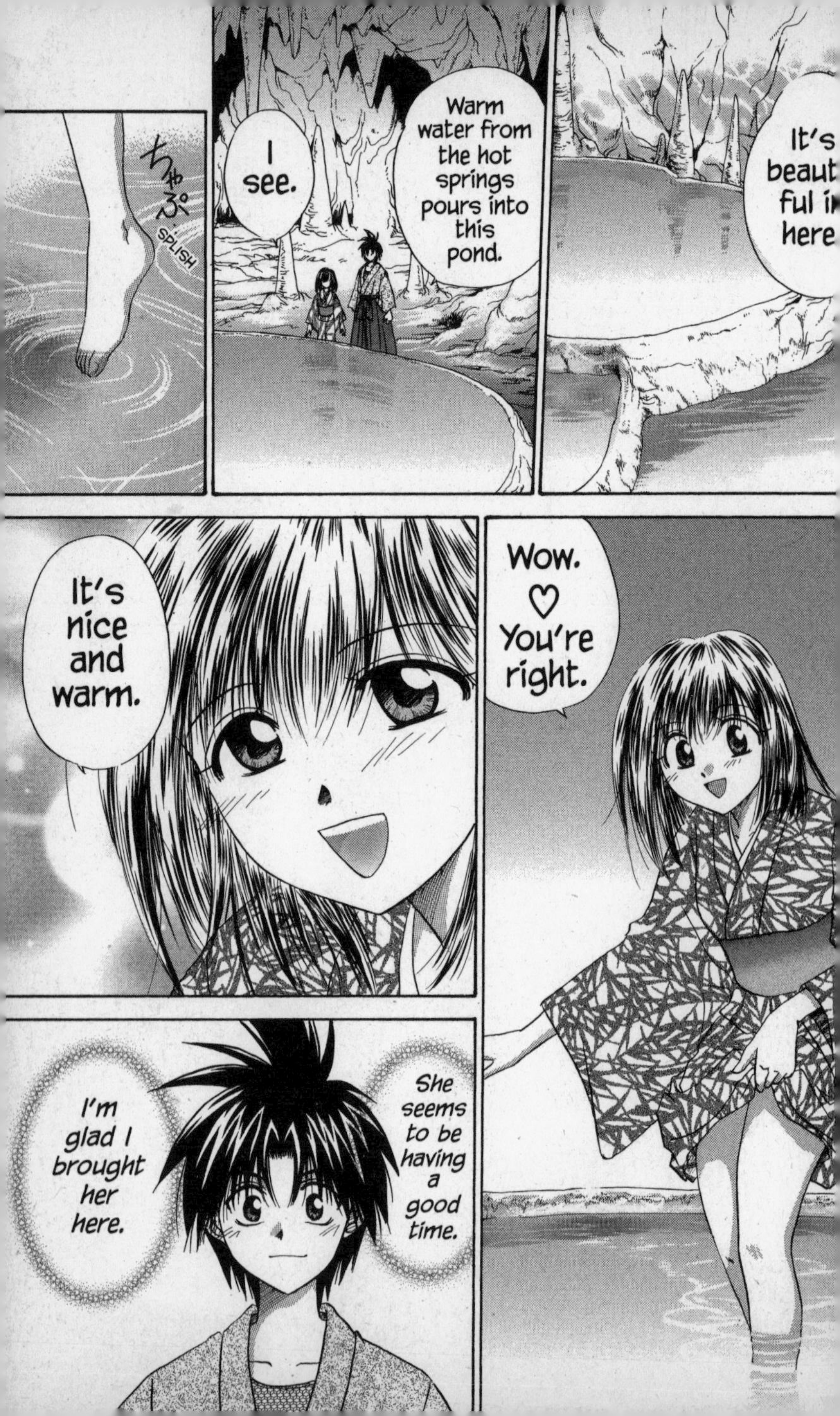
It's beaut ful i here
Warm water from the hot springs pours into this pond.
I see.
ちゃぷ
SPLISH
Wow. ♡ You're right.
It's nice and warm.
She seems to be having a good time.
I'm glad I brought her here.

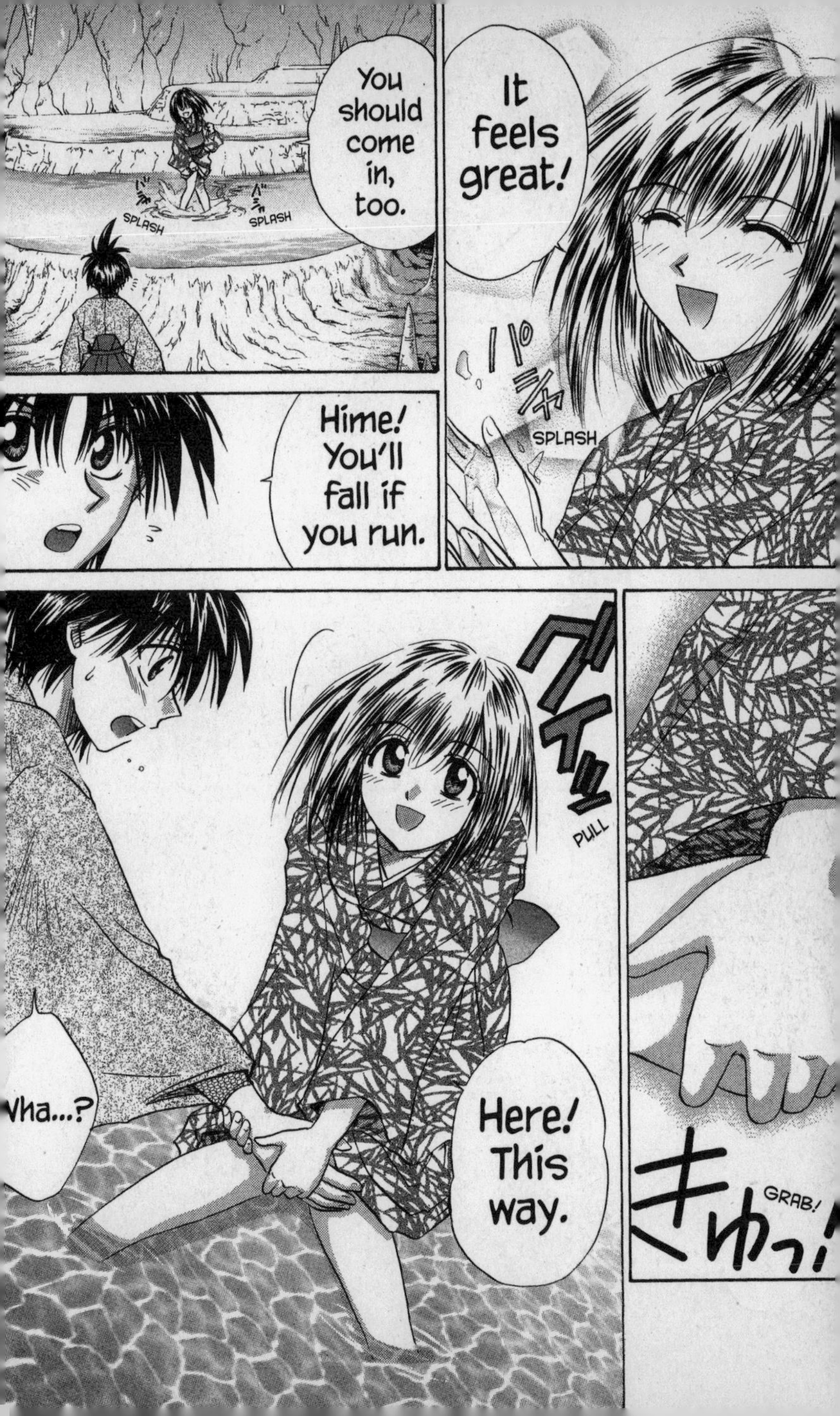
It feels great!
パシャ
SPLASH
You should come in, too.
SPLASH
SPLASH
Hime! You'll fall if you run.
きゅっ
GRAB!
グイッ
PULL
Here! This way.
Wha...?

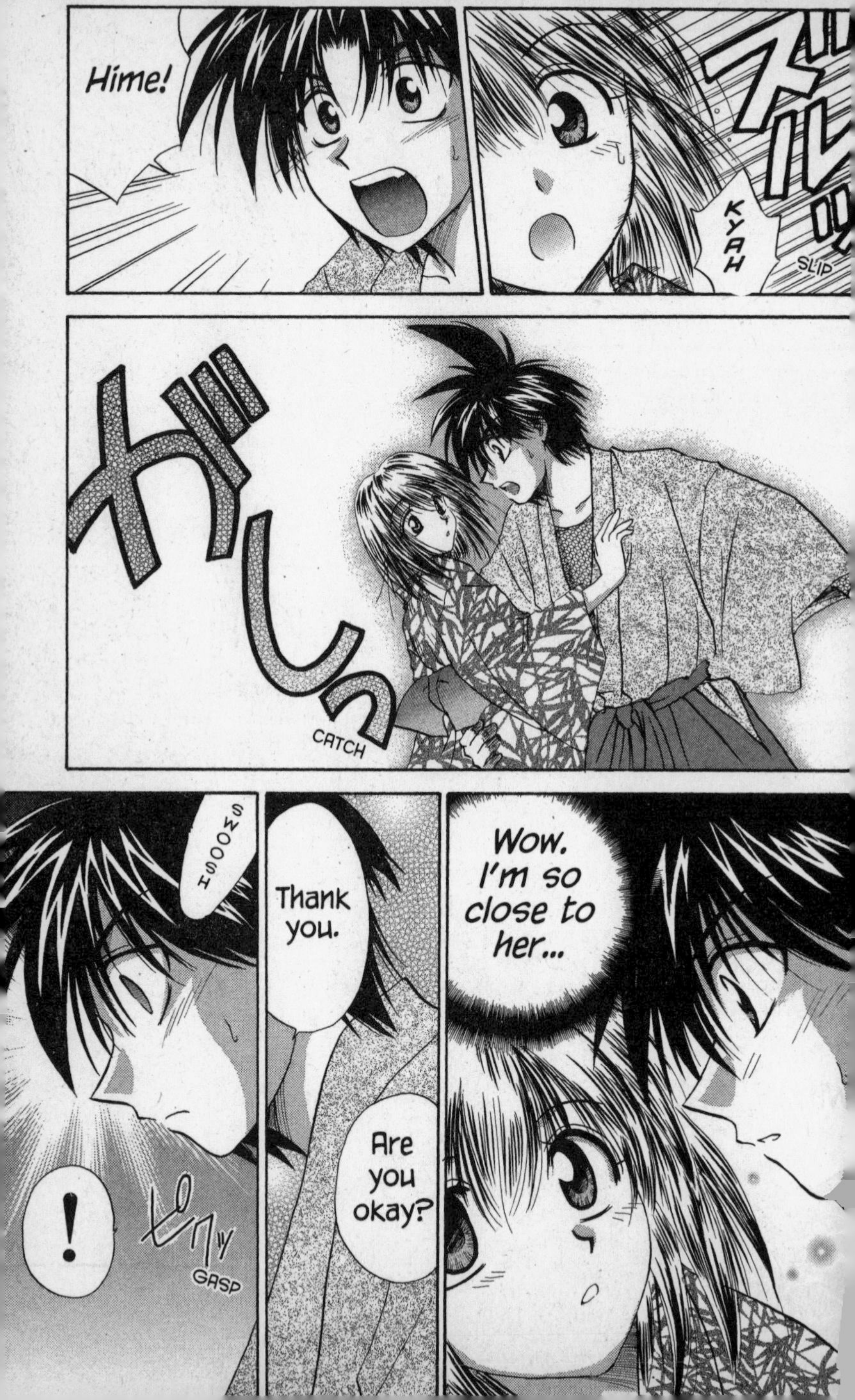
KYAH
SLIP
Hime!
CATCH
Wow. I'm so close to her...
Thank you.
Are you okay?
SWOOSH
!
GASP

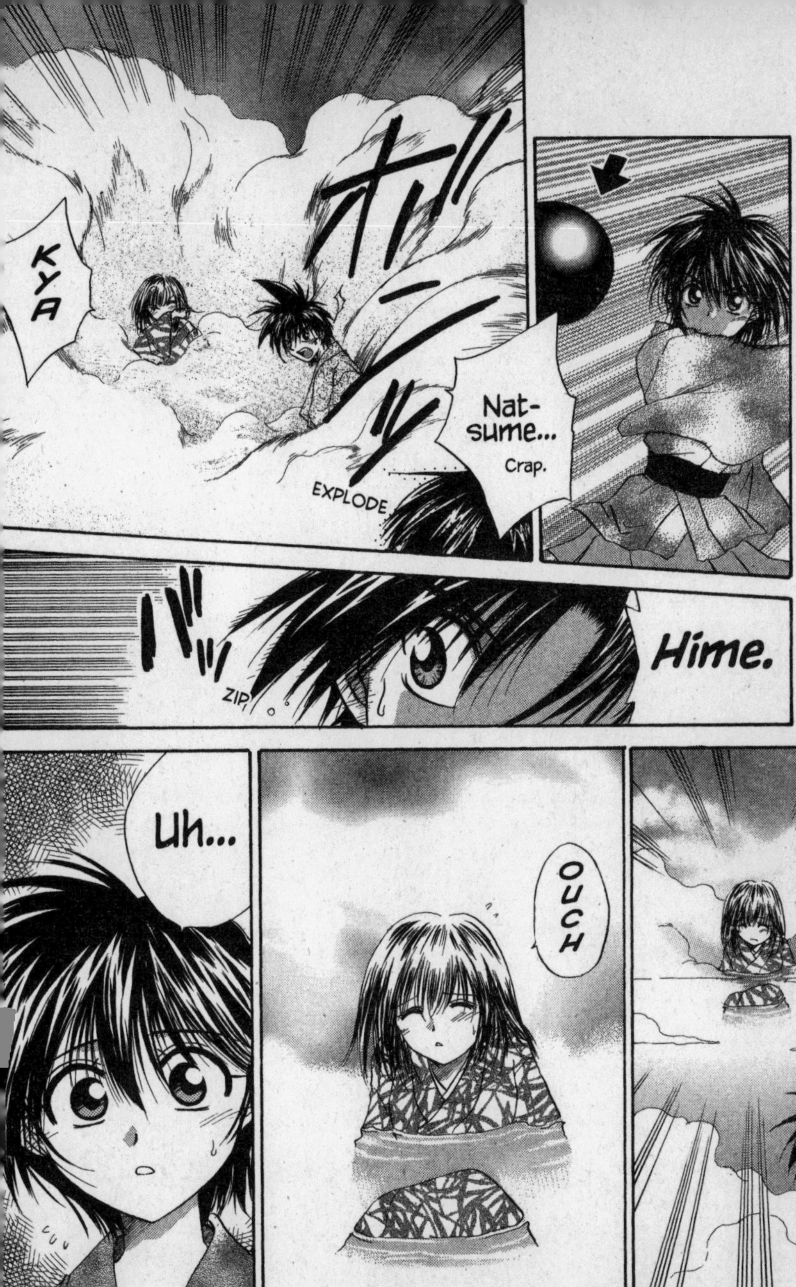
EXPLODE
Nat-sume...
Crap.
KYA
Hime.
ZIP
OUCH
Uh...

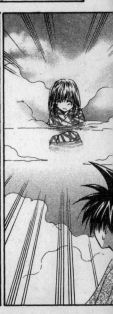

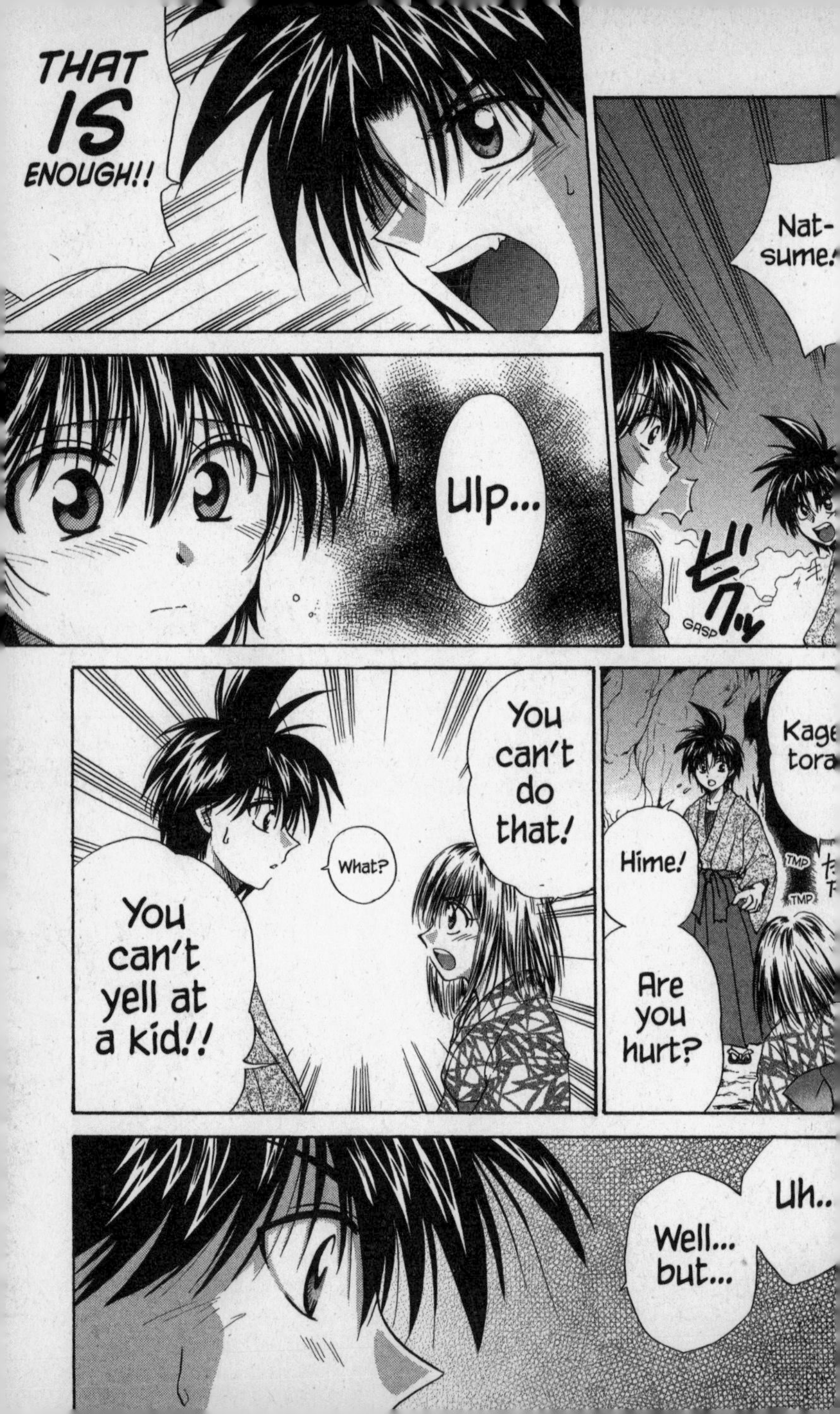
Nat-sume!
GASP
THAT IS ENOUGH!!
Ulp...
Kage tora
Hime!
Are you hurt?
TMP
TMP
You can't do that!
What?
You can't yell at a kid!!
Uh..
Well... but...

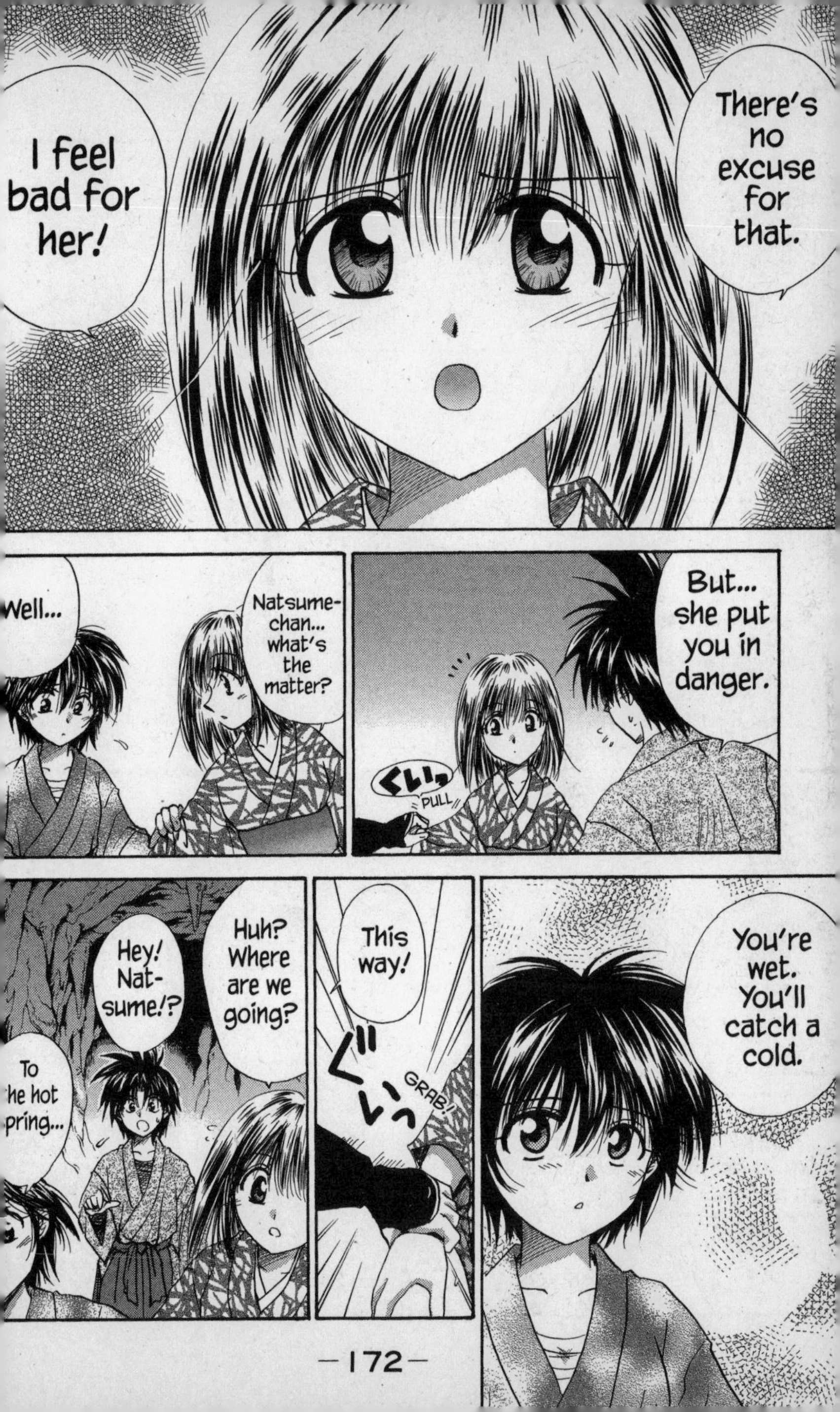
There's no excuse for that.
I feel bad for her!
But... she put you in danger.
くいっ
PULL
Natsume-chan... what's the matter?
Well...
You're wet. You'll catch a cold.
This way!
ぐいっ
GRAB!
Huh? Where are we going?
Hey! Nat-sume!?
To he hot pring...

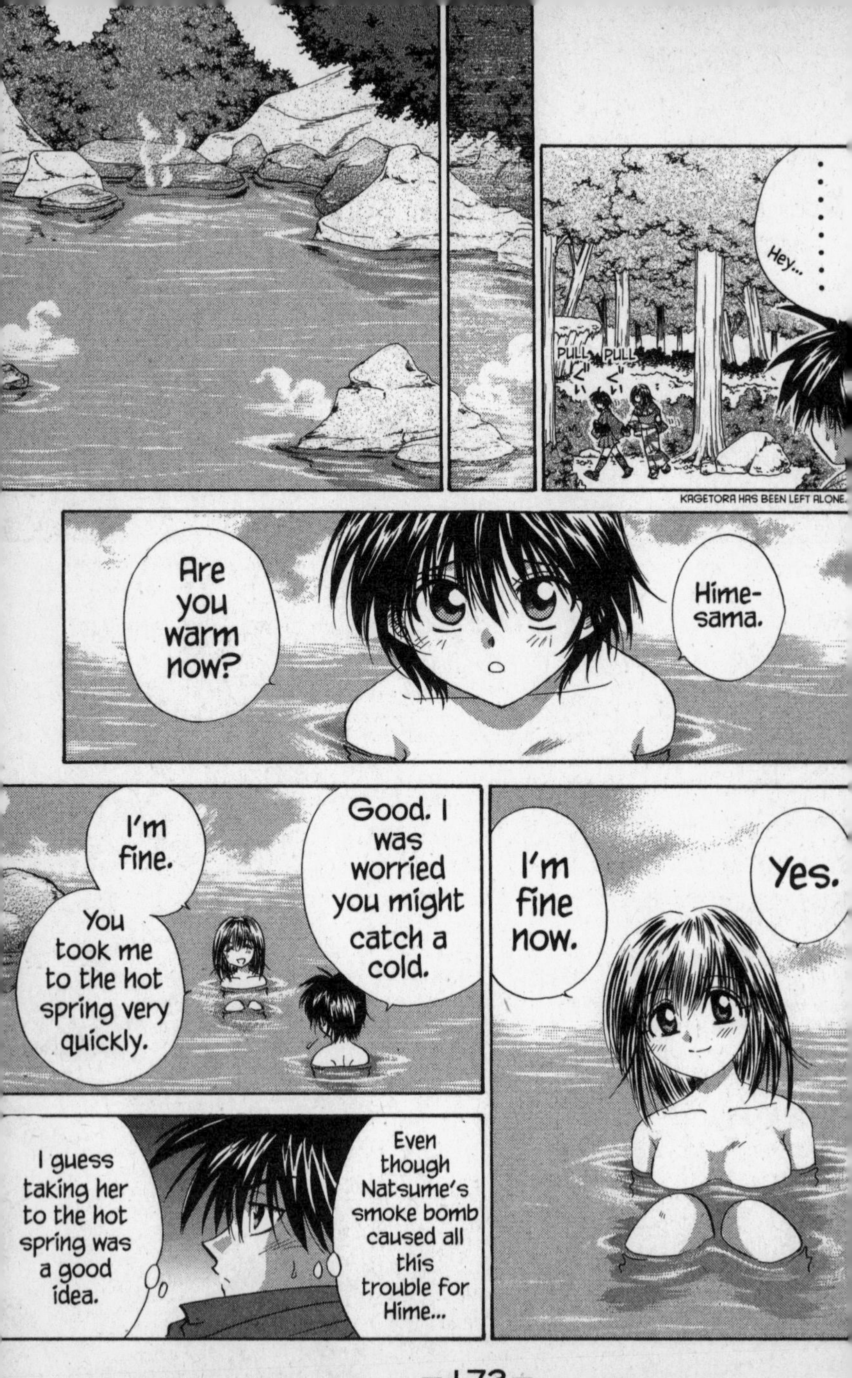

......
Hey...
PULL
PULL
KAGETORA HAS BEEN LEFT ALONE.
Hime-sama.
Are you warm now?
Yes.
I'm fine now.
Good. I was worried you might catch a cold.
I'm fine.
You took me to the hot spring very quickly.
Even though Natsume's smoke bomb caused all this trouble for Hime...
I guess taking her to the hot spring was a good idea.

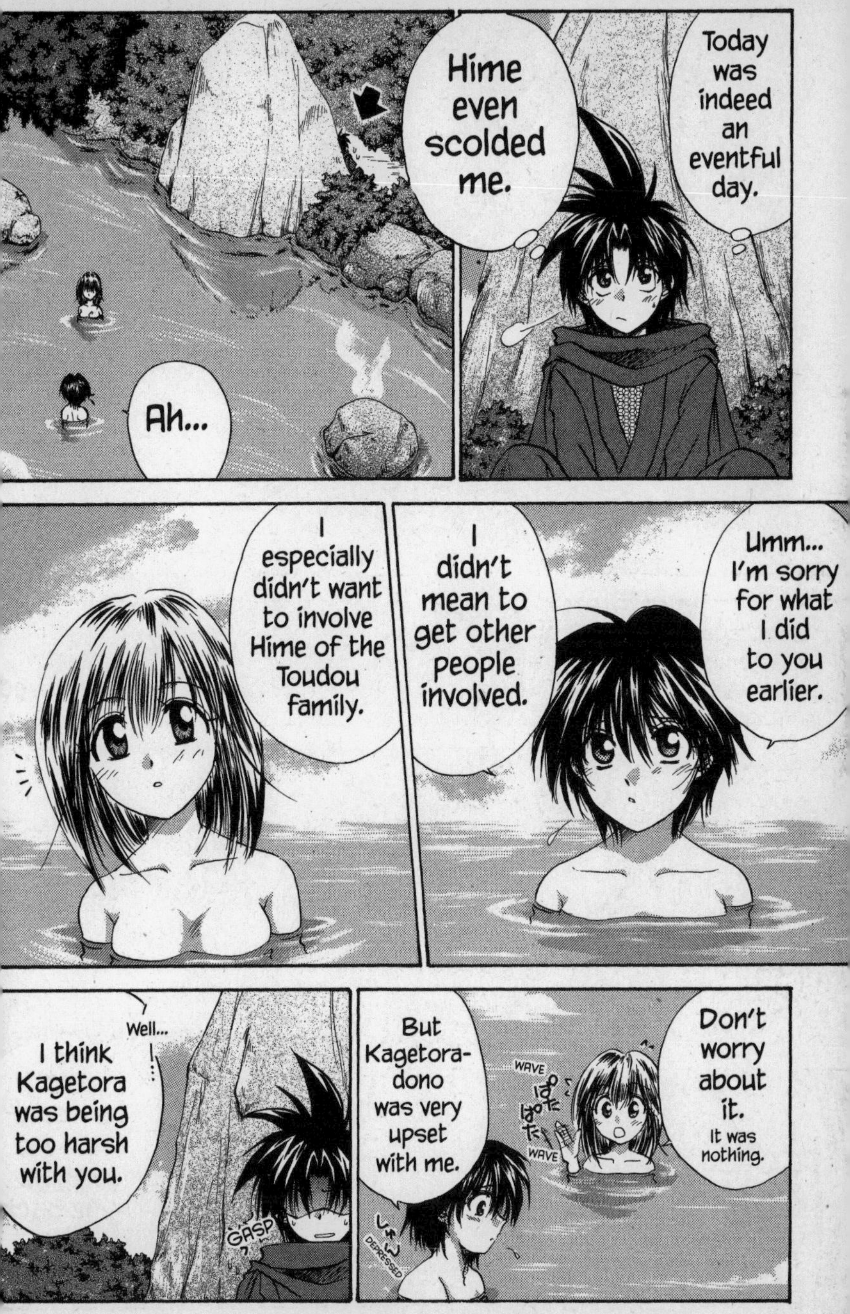
Today was indeed an eventful day.
Hime even scolded me.
Ah...
Umm... I'm sorry for what I did to you earlier.
I didn't mean to get other people involved.
I especially didn't want to involve Hime of the Toudou family.
Don't worry about it.
It was nothing.
WAVE
WAVE
But Kagetora-dono was very upset with me.
DEPRESSED
Well...
I think Kagetora was being too harsh with you.
GASP

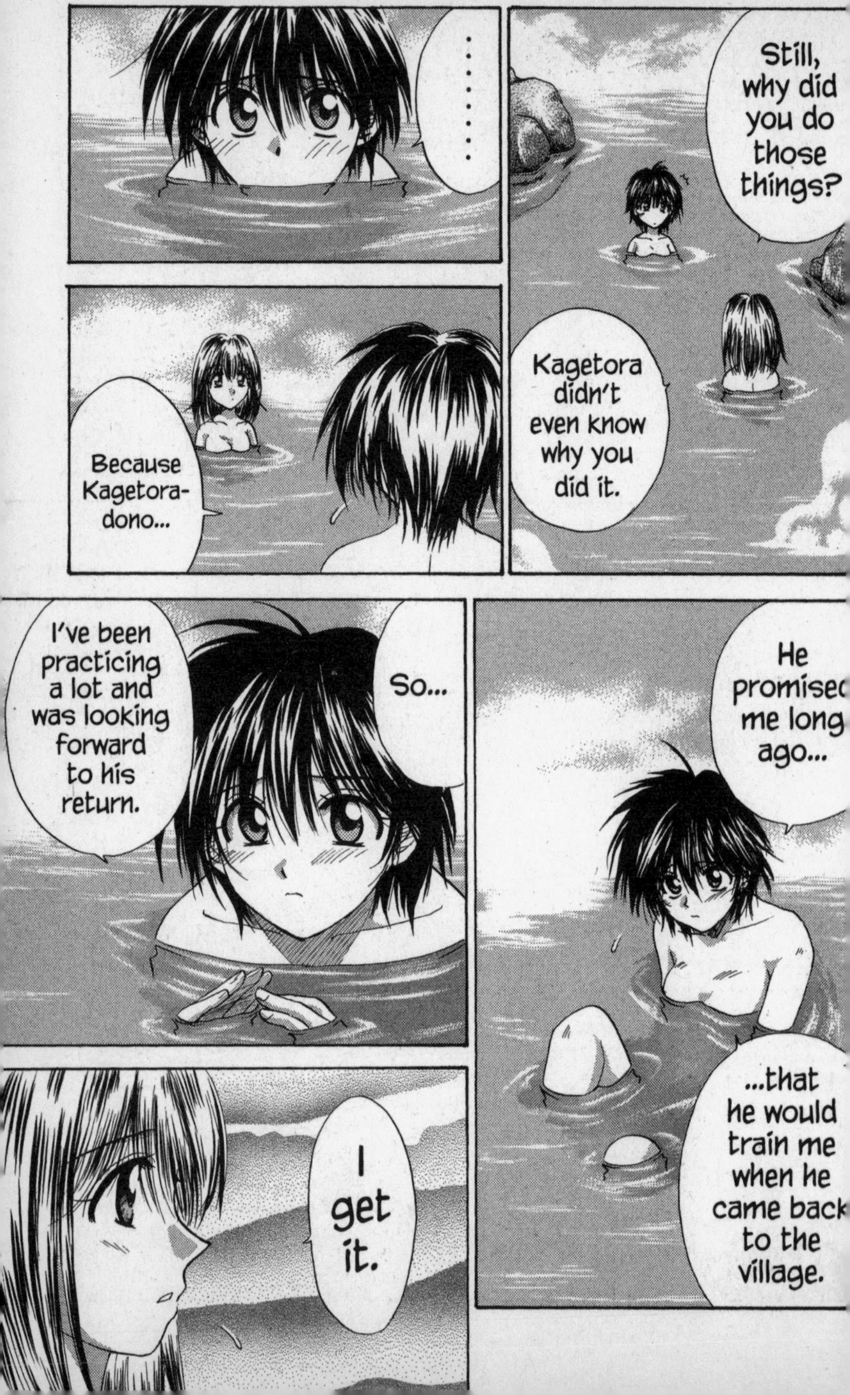

Still, why did you do those things?
Kagetora didn't even know why you did it.
......
Because Kagetora-dono...
He promised me long ago...
...that he would train me when he came back to the village.
So...
I've been practicing a lot and was looking forward to his return.
I get it.

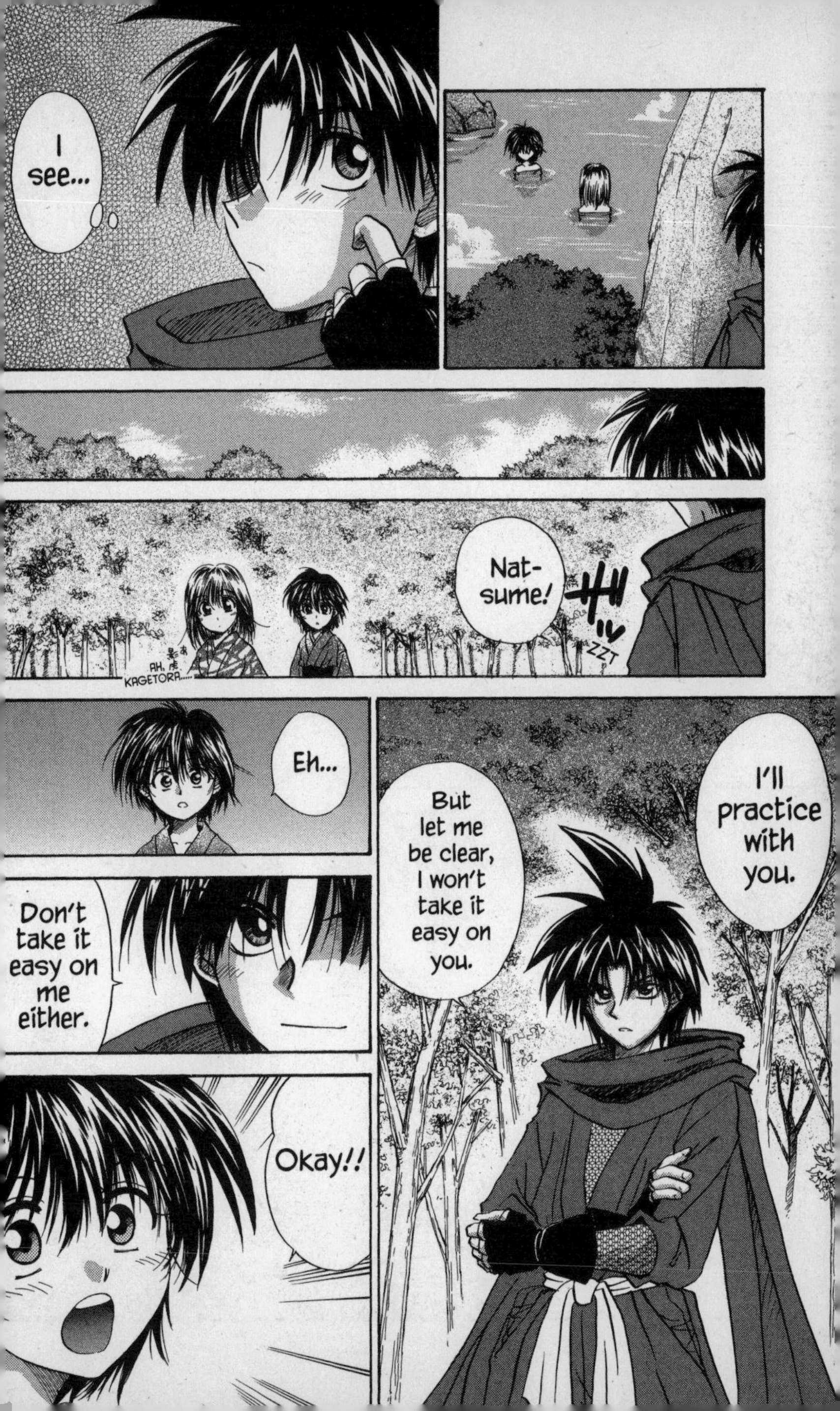
I see...
Nat-sume!
ZZT
AH, KAGETORA...
I'll practice with you.
But let me be clear, I won't take it easy on you.
Eh...
Don't take it easy on me either.
Okay!!

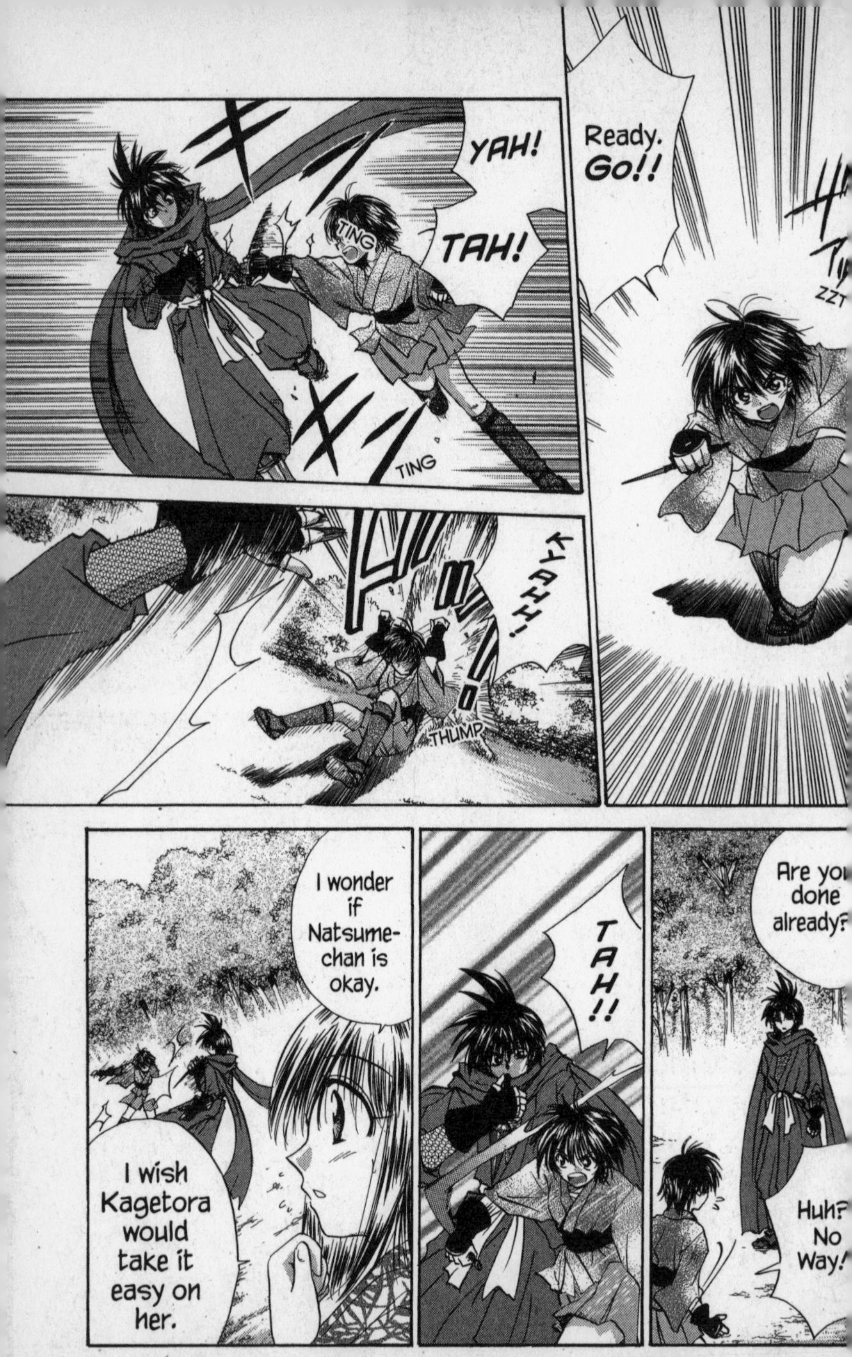
Ready. Go!!
ZZT
YAH!
TAH!
TING
TING
KYAHH!
THUMP
Are you done already?
Huh? No Way!
TAH!!
I wonder if Natsume-chan is okay.
I wish Kagetora would take it easy on her.

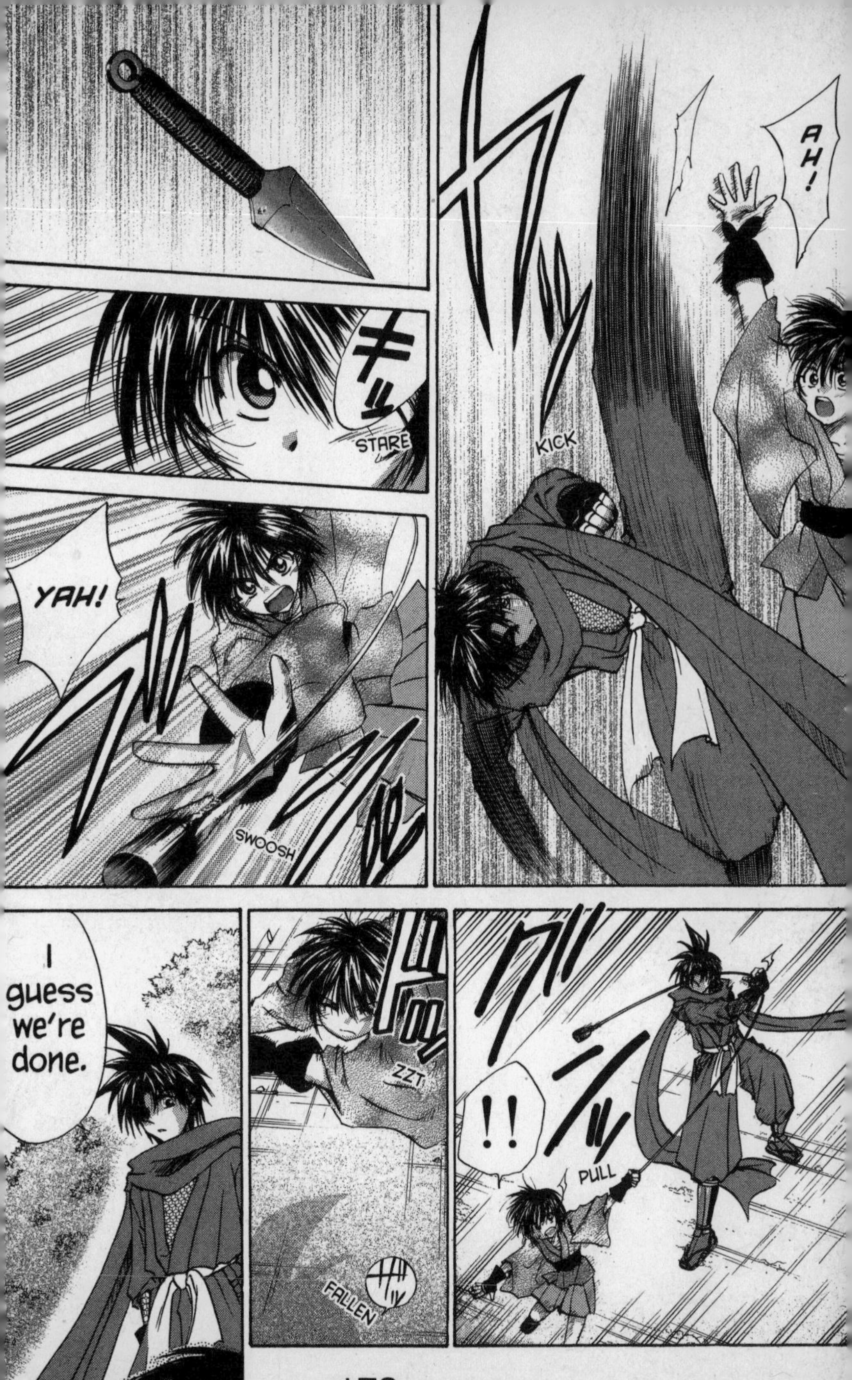
AH!
KICK
キッ
STARE
YAH!
SWOOSH
!!
PULL
ZZT
FALLEN
I guess we're done.

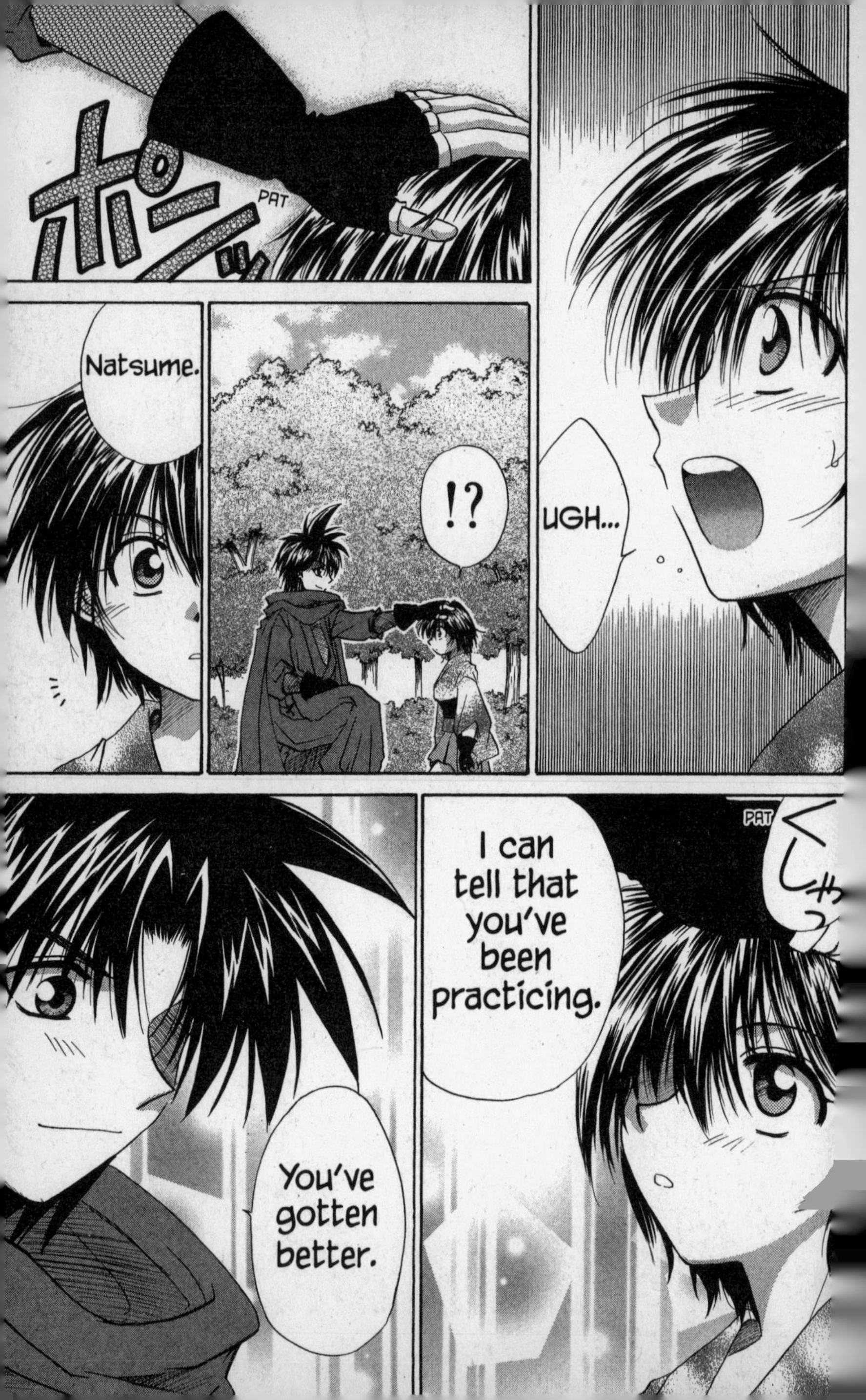
UGH...
ポン
PAT
!?
Natsume.
PAT
I can tell that you've been practicing.
You've gotten better.

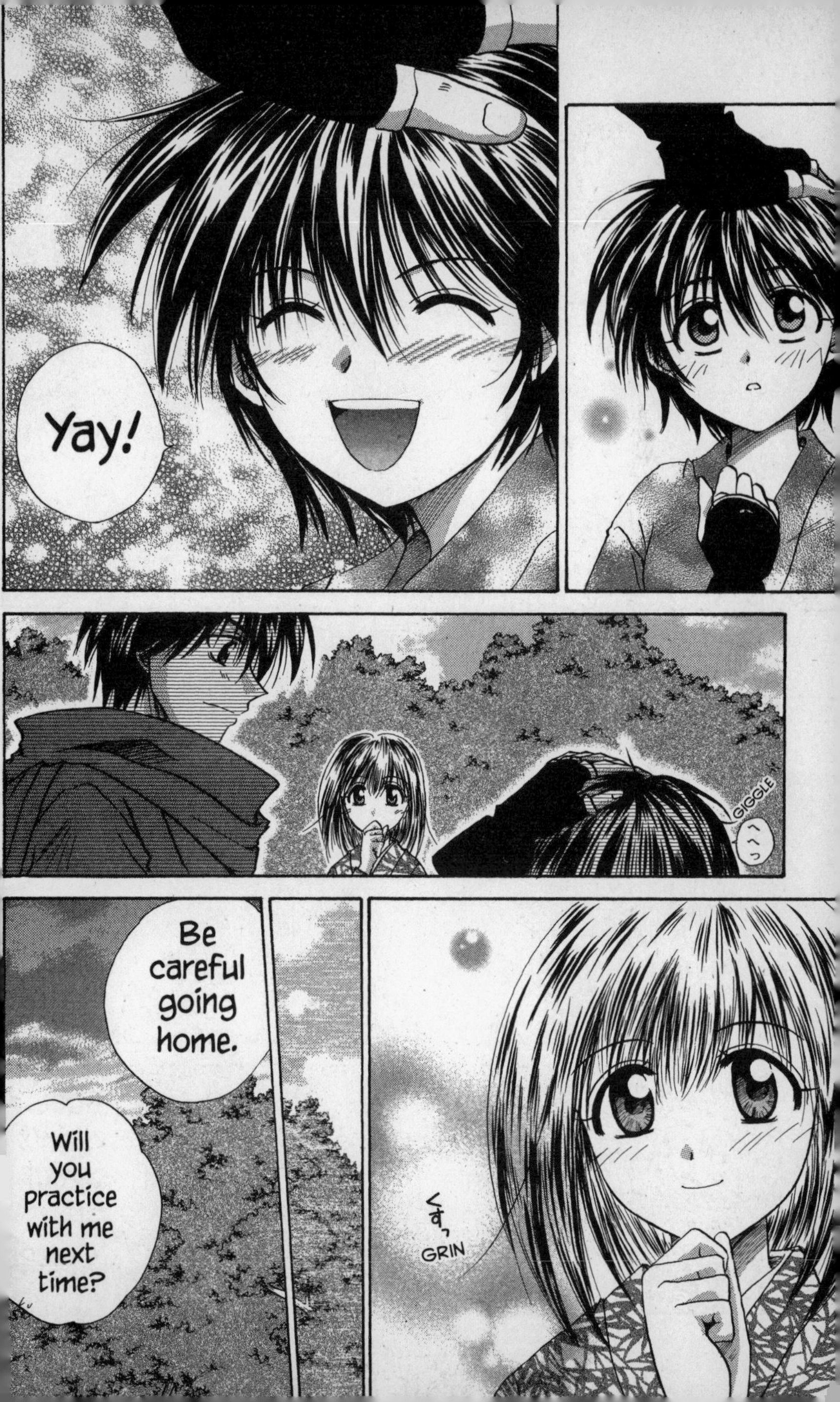
Yay!
GIGGLE
へへっ
くすっ
GRIN
Be careful going home.
Will you practice with me next time?

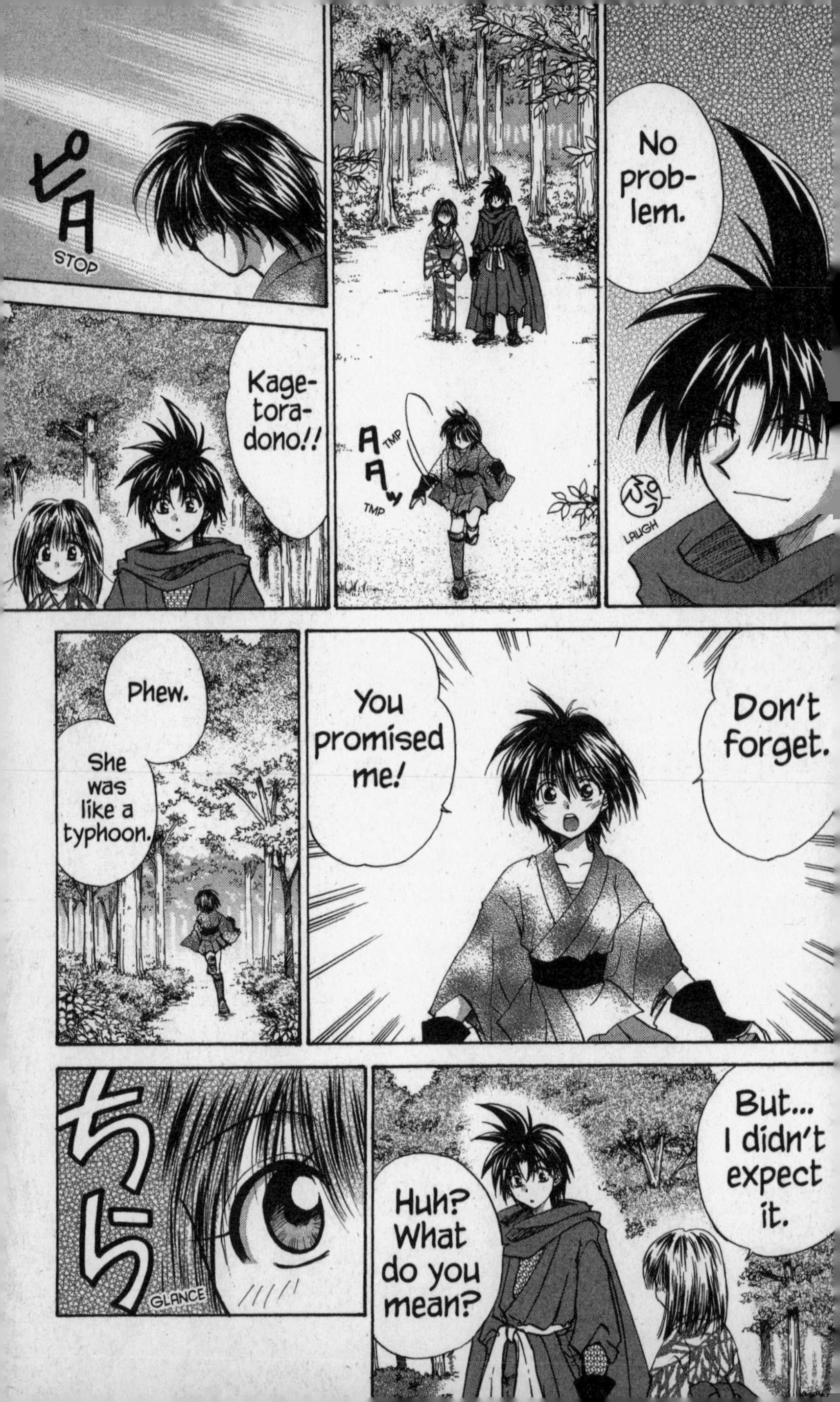
No problem.
LAUGH
TMP
TMP
STOP
Kagetora-dono!!
Don't forget.
You promised me!
Phew.
She was like a typhoon.
But... I didn't expect it.
Huh? What do you mean?
ちら
GLANCE

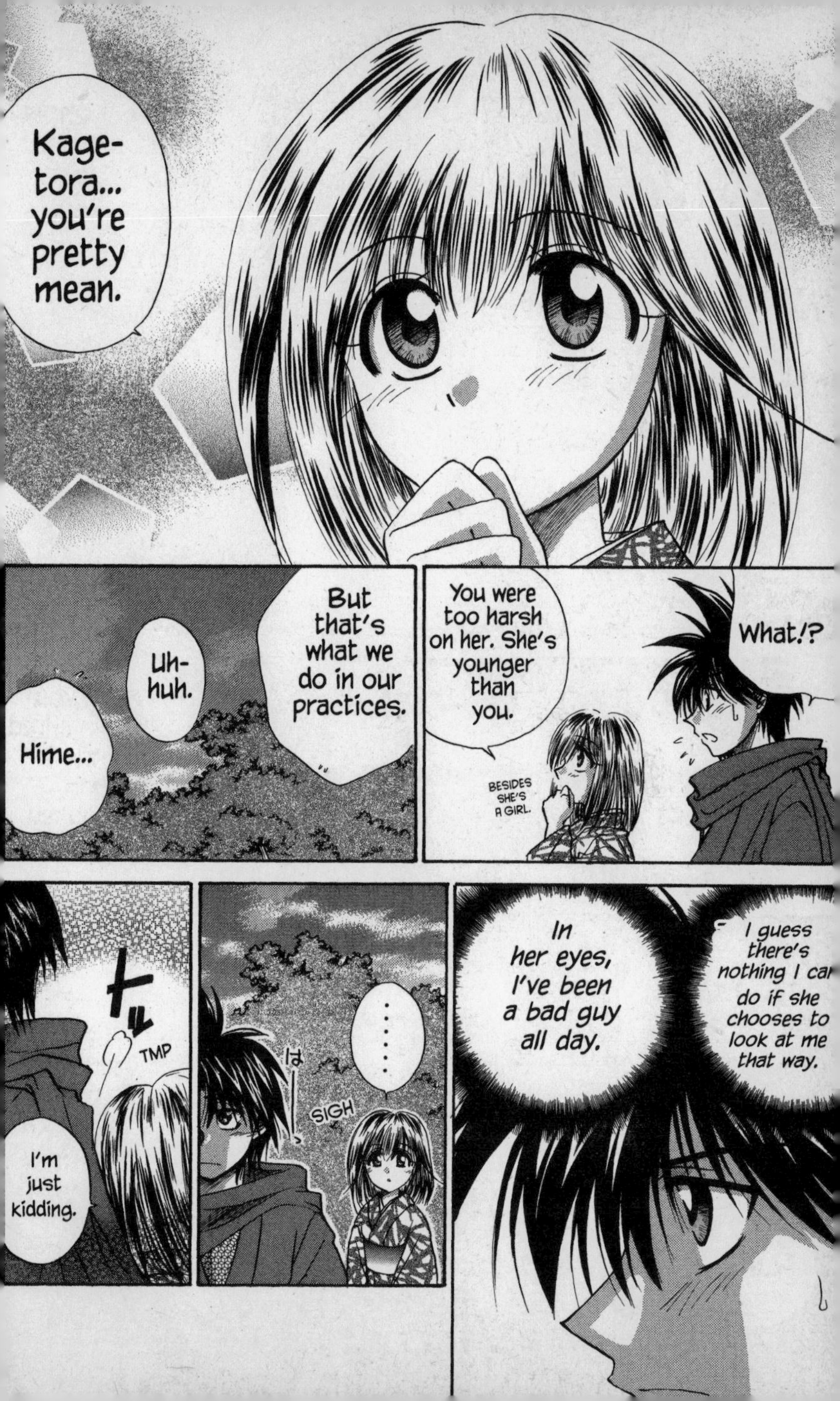

Kage-tora... you're pretty mean.
What!?
You were too harsh on her. She's younger than you.
BESIDES SHE'S A GIRL.
But that's what we do in our practices.
Uh-huh.
Hime...
I guess there's nothing I ca do if she chooses to look at me that way.
In her eyes, I've been a bad guy all day.
......
は
SIGH
TMP
I'm just kidding.

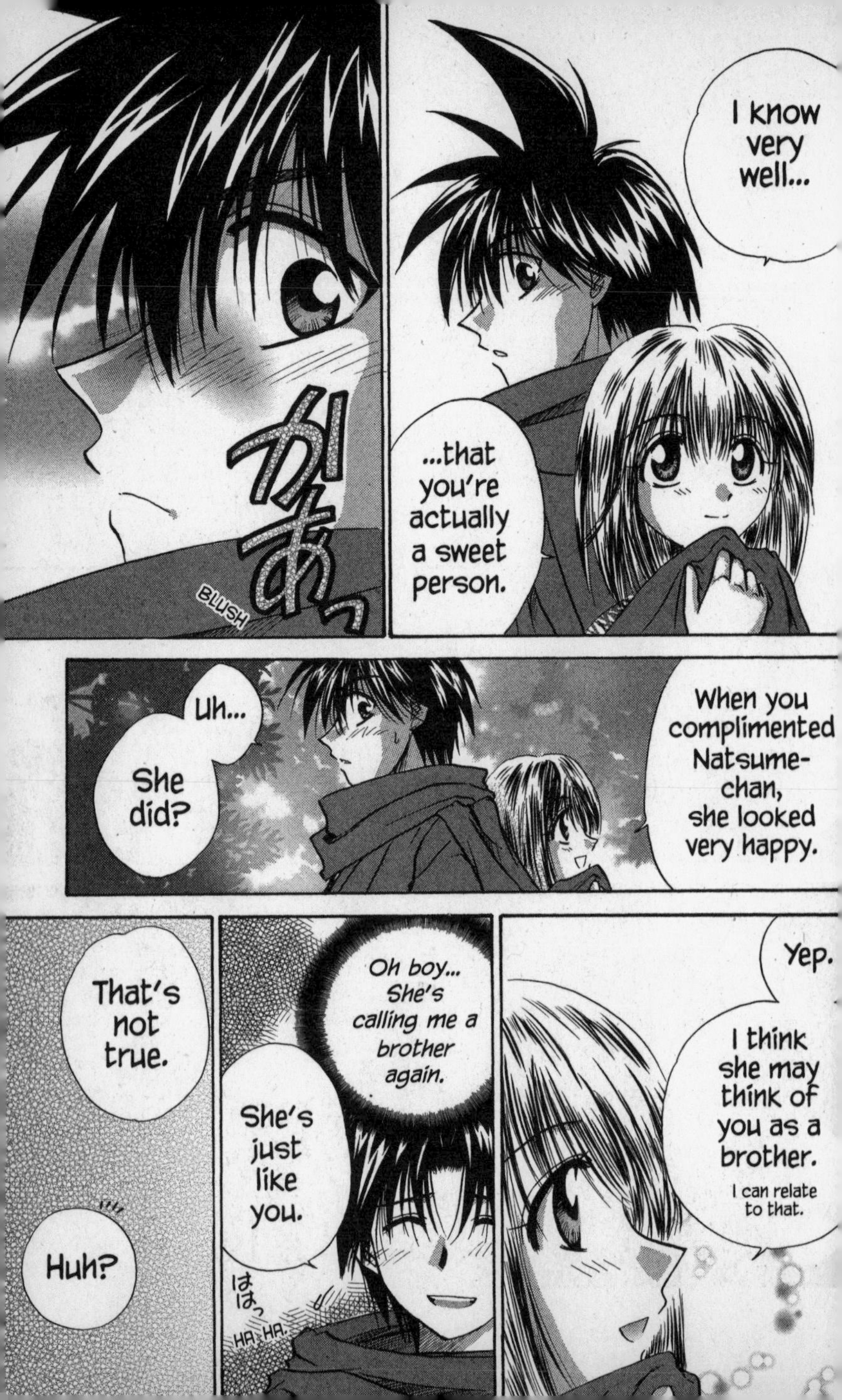
I know very well...
...that you're actually a sweet person.
かあっ
BLUSH
When you complimented Natsume-chan, she looked very happy.
Uh...
She did?
Yep.
I think she may think of you as a brother.
I can relate to that.
Oh boy... She's calling me a brother again.
She's just like you.
ははっ
HA HA
That's not true.
Huh?

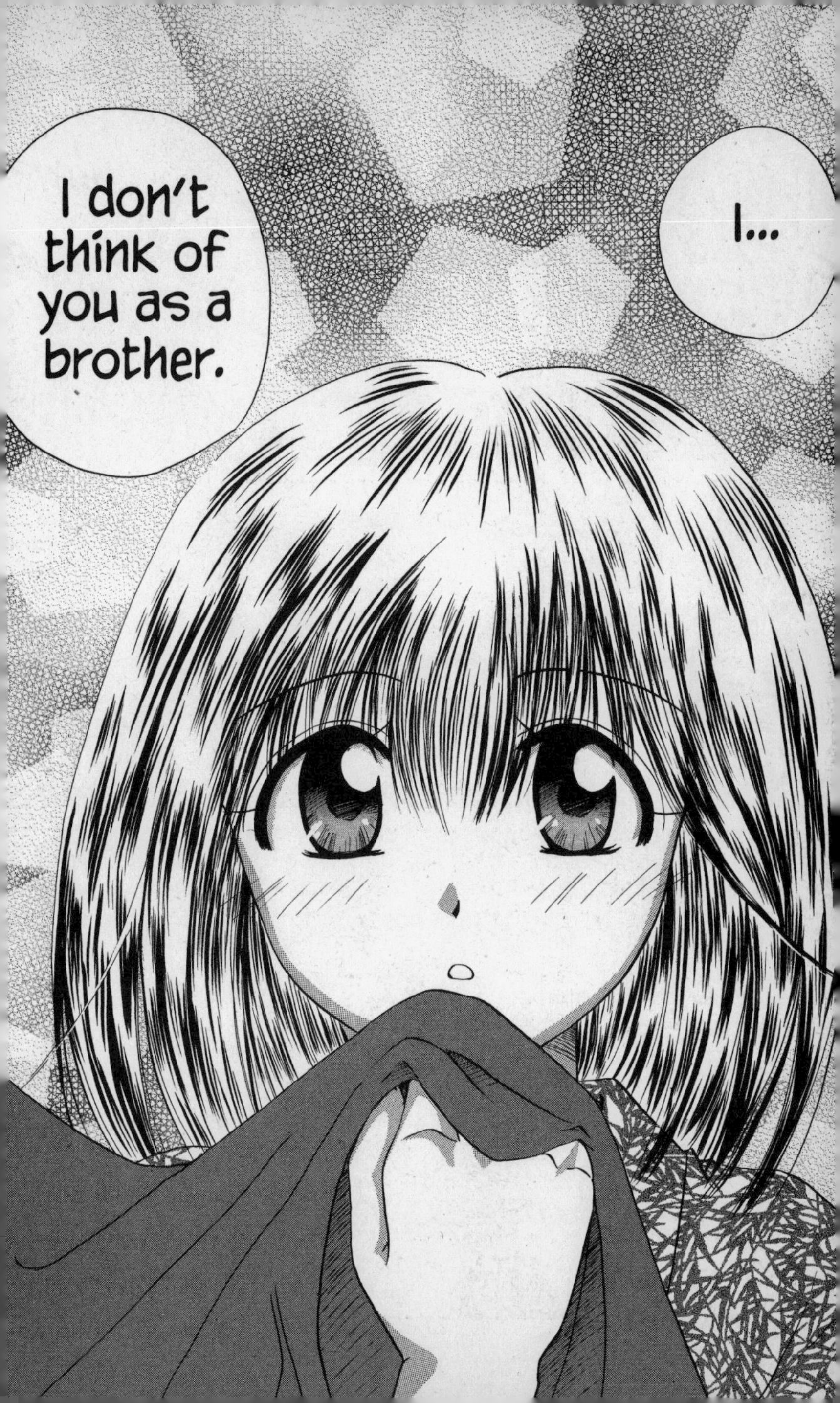
I...
I don't think of you as a brother.

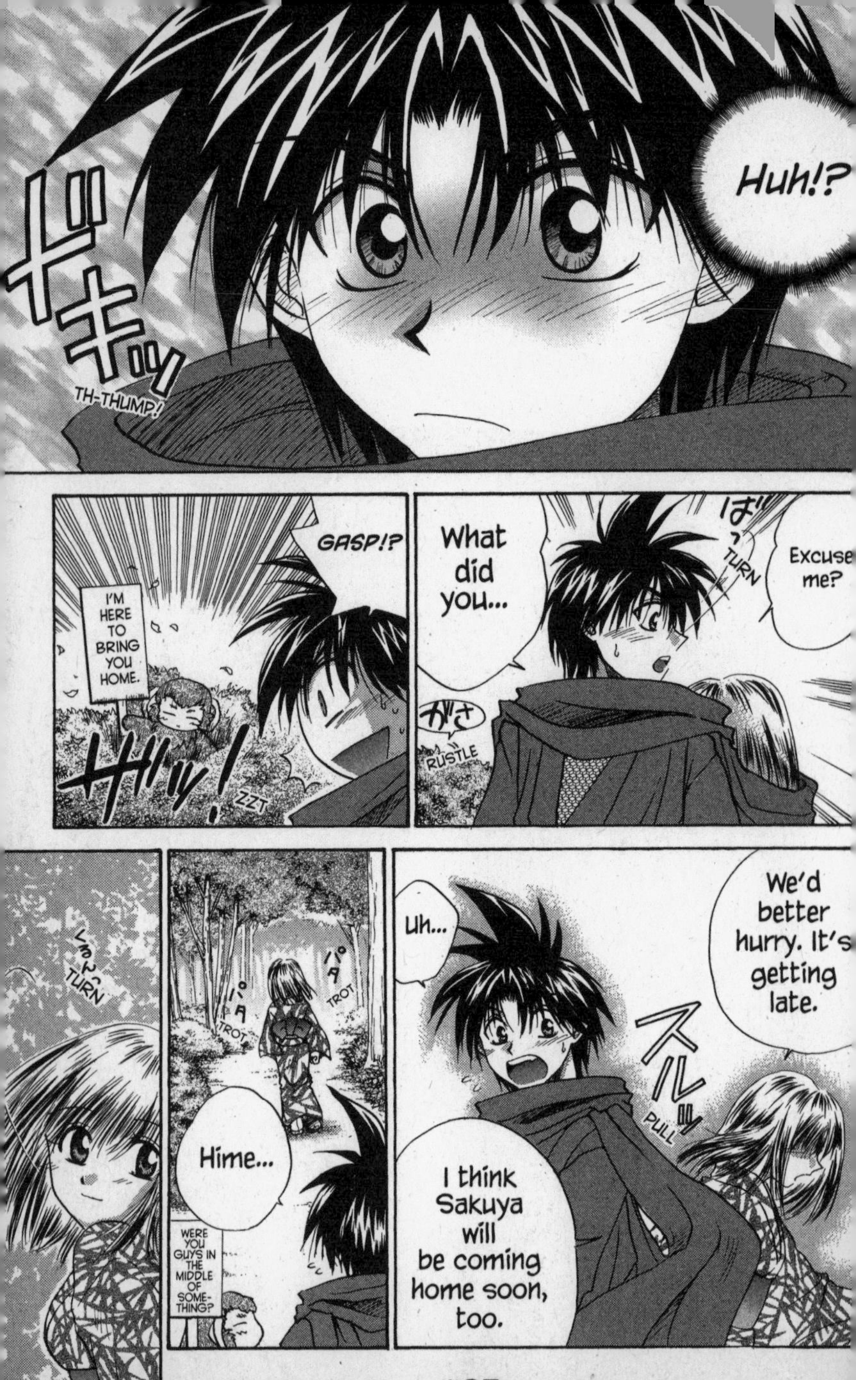
Huh!?
ドキッ
TH-THUMP!
ばっ
TURN
Excuse me?
What did you...
がさ
RUSTLE
GASP!?
I'M HERE TO BRING YOU HOME.
ザッ!
ZZT
We'd better hurry. It's getting late.
Uh...
スルッ
PULL
I think Sakuya will be coming home soon, too.
パタ
TROT
パタ
TROT
Hime...
WERE YOU GUYS IN THE MIDDLE OF SOME-THING?
くるんっ
TURN

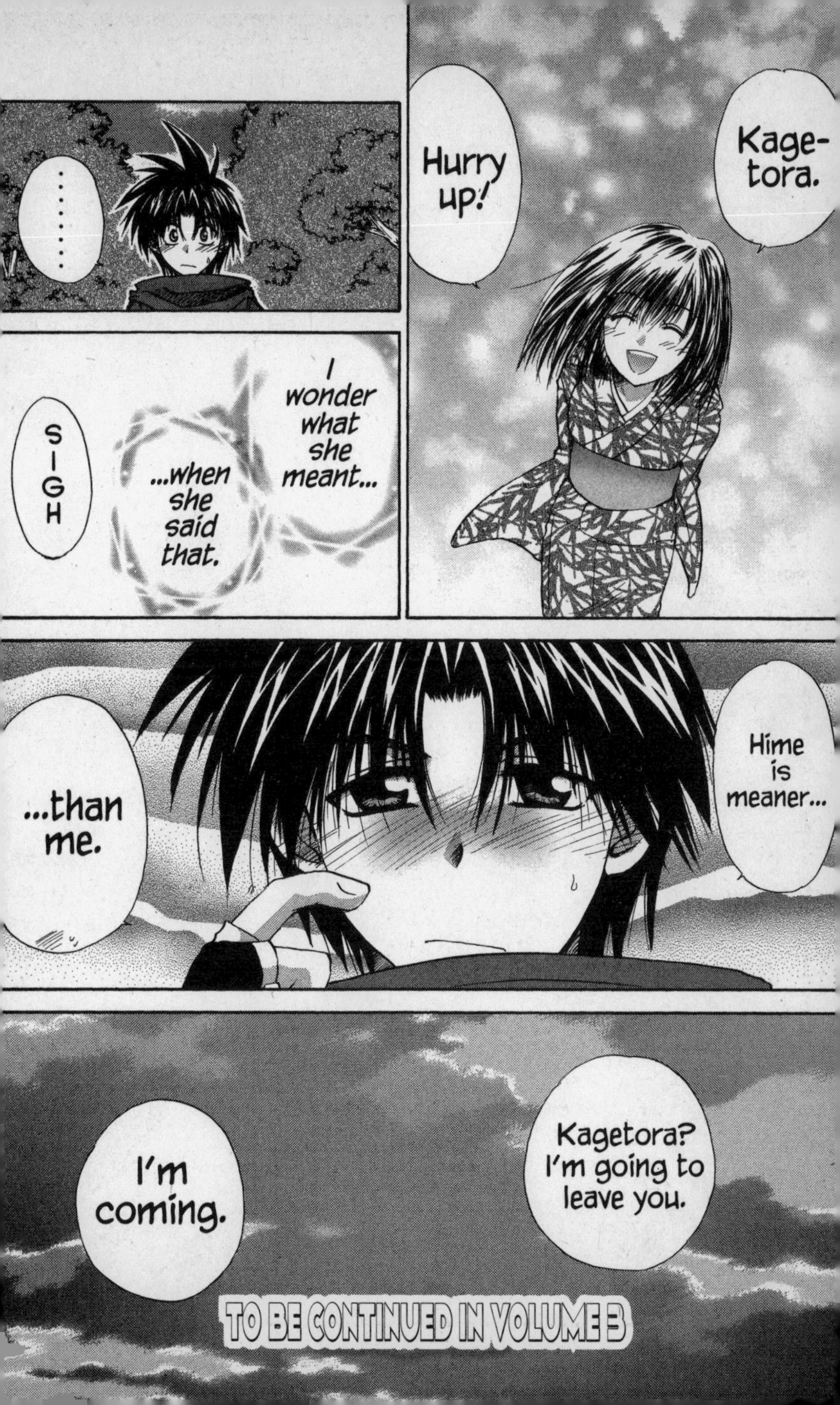
Kage-tora.
Hurry up!
......
I wonder what she meant...
...when she said that.
SIGH
Hime is meaner...
...than me.
Kagetora? I'm going to leave you.
I'm coming.
TO BE CONTINUED IN VOLUME 3

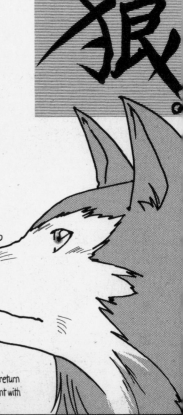

BONUS PAGE

This is **Segami.** How's it going? I'm glad that the KAGETORA Volume 2 is finally out. I'm relieved about that. Also apparently there's extra room for several bonus pages in this volume so I'll try to write about different things. I hope you find them interesting.

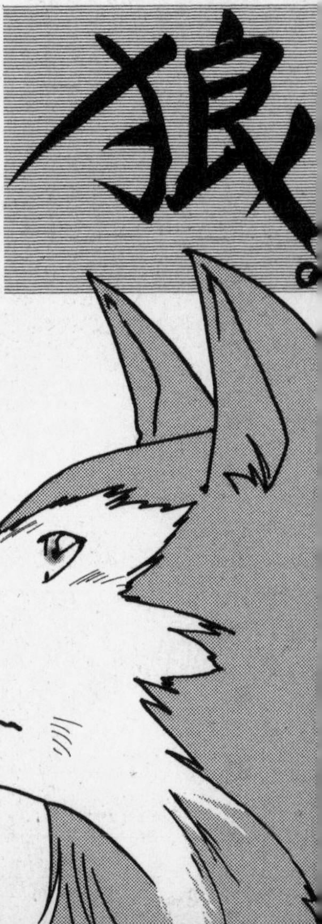
狼

∘ About Ninjas- Part 2

As you might imagine, a ninja doesn't wear regular clothes (when they dress up as a ninja). Therefore I was doing research to get some ideas for a ninja costume. But it's hard to get the details from just looking at the pictures so I actually purchased a ninja costume.

Shinichi Chiba (Ninja) Action Figure

You know, this is a fun figure. *(laugh)* The figure is sitting cross-legged on my TV at home. I also have the Souji Okita (the Masaki Kyomoto version) action figure sitting next to him. These figures make my office look very surreal.

∘ About Sarubobo

Sarubobo is a traditional mascot of the Hida Alpine but it has a peculiar look. I personally think it's cute, though. *It looks like this.*

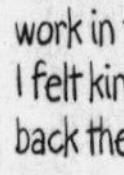

In between my projects, I went to the Hida area just to get sarubobo character goods. A sarubobo noren, a sarubobo towel, a sarubobo cup, and a sarubobo cell phone strap. I purchased many items, since I rarely go there. But when I had to ink my manga artwork in the hotel room all by myself, I felt kind of emotional. I'd love to go back there again.

∘ Thank you.

Thanks to your support, Volume 1 sold well apparently... Thank you. I also read the fan letters. For those who include their return addresses, I try to write back as much as possible. Please be patient with my replies. *(laugh)*

法螺
A Big Joke

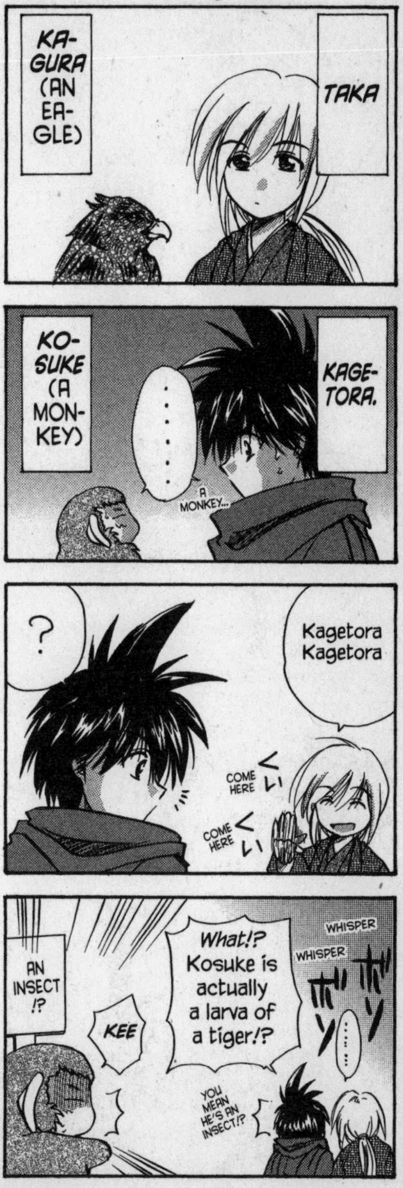
TAKA
KA-GURA (AN EA-GLE)
KAGE-TORA.
......
A MONKEY...
KO-SUKE (A MON-KEY)
Kagetora Kagetora
COME HERE
COME HERE
?
WHISPER
WHISPER
What!? Kosuke is actually a larva of a tiger!?
......
KEE
AN INSECT !?
YOU MEAN HE'S AN INSECT!?

願
A Wish

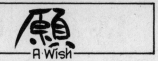

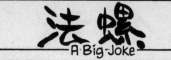

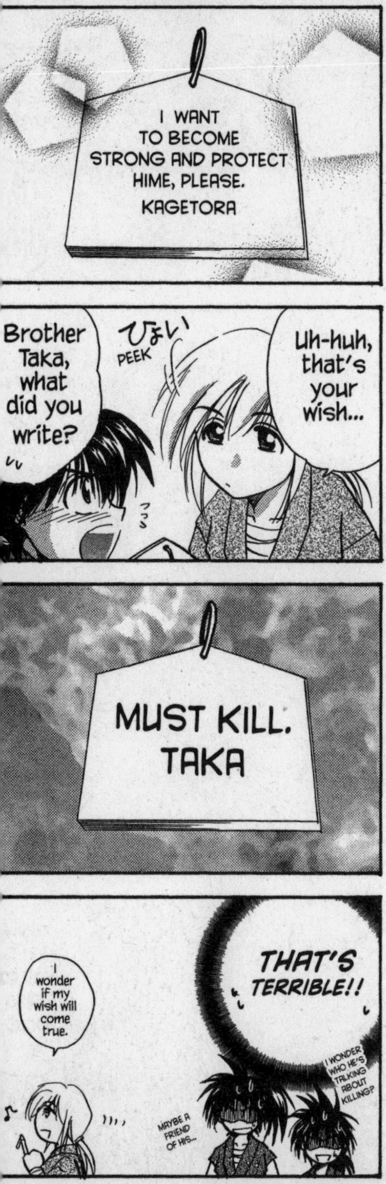
I WANT TO BECOME STRONG AND PROTECT HIME, PLEASE.
KAGETORA
Uh-huh, that's your wish...
ひょい
PEEK
Brother Taka, what did you write?
MUST KILL.
TAKA
THAT'S TERRIBLE!!
I WONDER WHO HE'S TALKING ABOUT KILLING?
MAYBE A FRIEND OF HIS...
I wonder if my wish will come true.

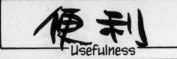

悲憤慷慨
Indignation

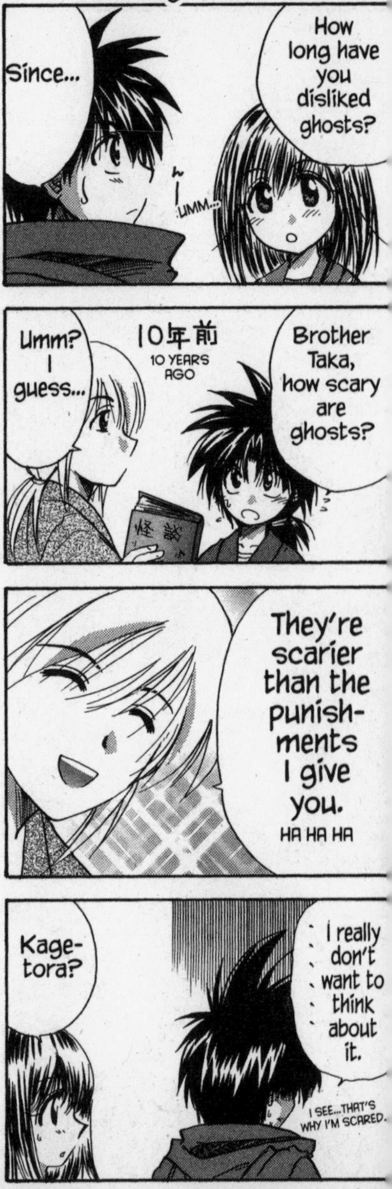
How long have you disliked ghosts?
Since...
UMM...
Brother Taka, how scary are ghosts?
10年前
10 YEARS AGO
Umm? I guess...
怪談
They're scarier than the punishments I give you.
HA HA HA
I really don't want to think about it.
I SEE...THAT'S WHY I'M SCARED.
Kage-tora?

便利
Usefulness

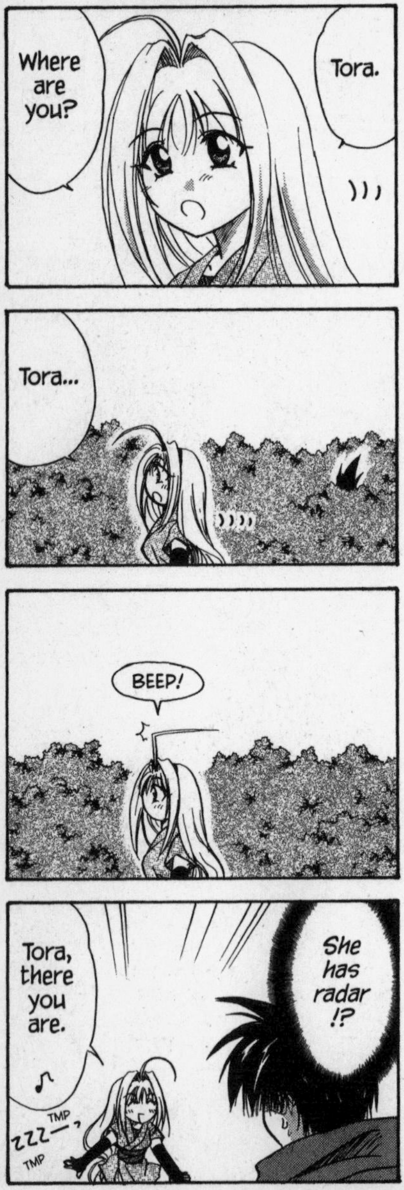
Tora.
Where are you?
Tora...
BEEP!
She has radar !?
Tora, there you are.
TMP
ZZZ—
TMP

●描き下ろし3ショット●

A SPECIAL DRAWING OF THREE CHARACTERS

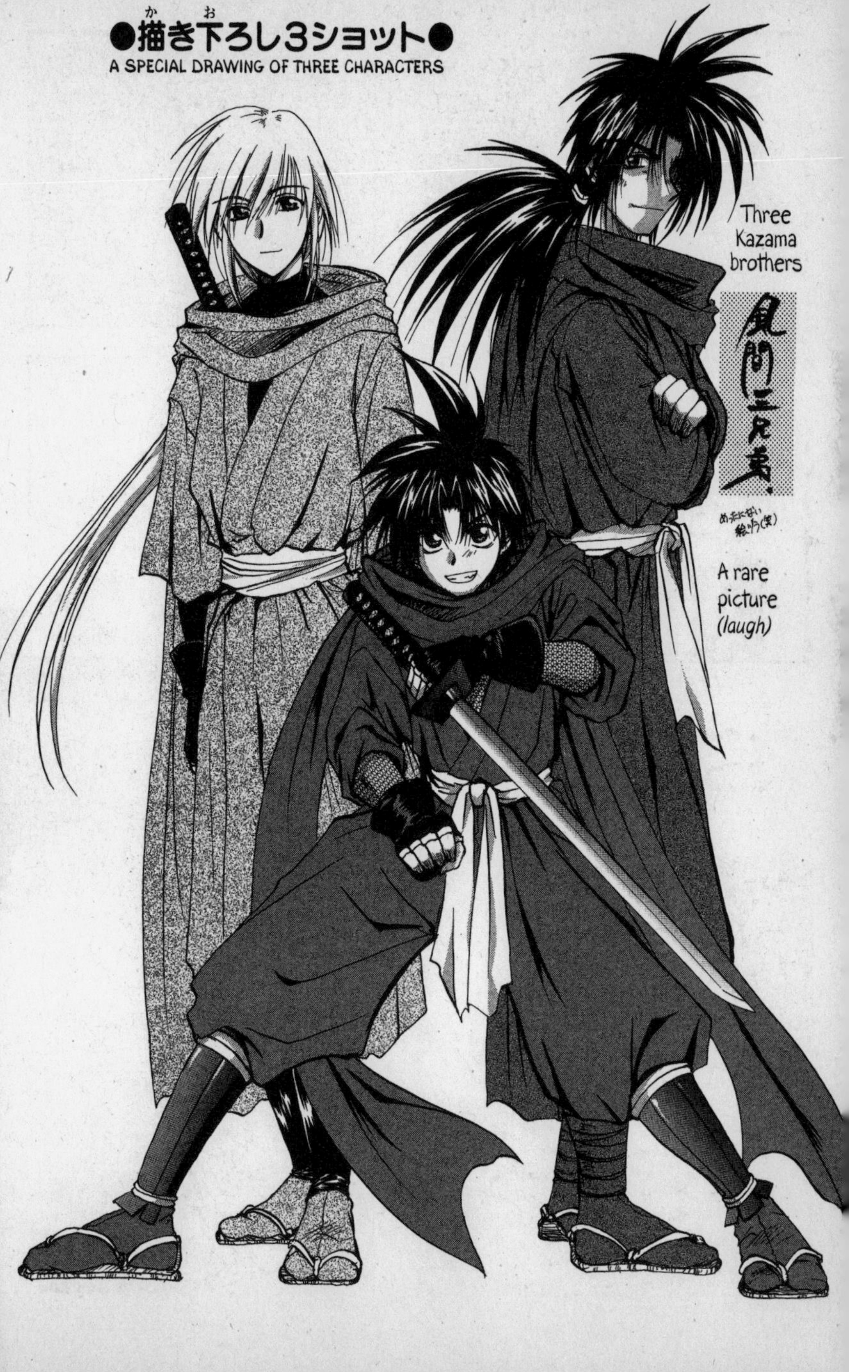
Three Kazama brothers
風間三兄弟
めったにない絵だろ(笑)
A rare picture (laugh)

ウチのアシさん 田中さん・大島ちゃん

DRAWINGS DONE BY MY ASSISTANTS
TANAKA-SAN AND OSHIMA-CHAN

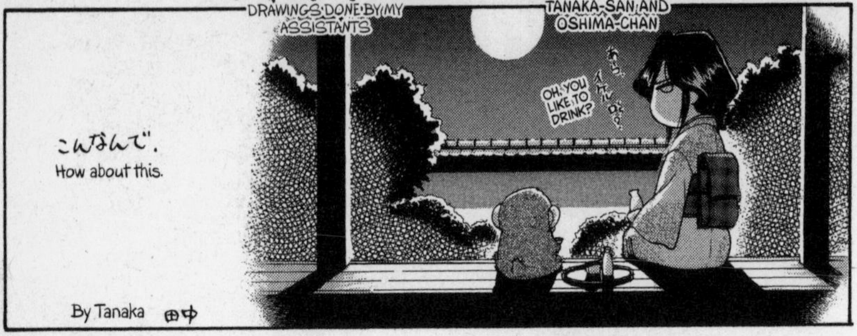
こんなんで。
How about this.
OH, YOU LIKE TO DRINK?
By Tanaka 田中

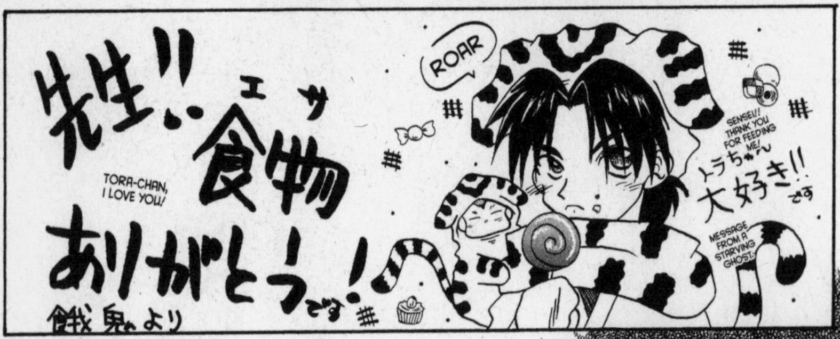
先生!! 食物(エサ) ありがとうです!
餓鬼より
SENSEI!! THANK YOU FOR FEEDING ME!
MESSAGE FROM A STARVING GHOST.
ROAR
トラちゃん大好き!!です
TORA-CHAN, I LOVE YOU!

Special Thanks

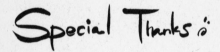

アシスタント
Assistants:
田中亮二くん Ryouji Tanaka
大島真弓ちゃん Mayumi Ooshima
助っ人 Helpers:
もろいとやさん Moroitoya
浅井らぼさん Rabo Asai
担当 Editors:
森田氏 Mr. Morita
松木氏 Mr. Matsuki
コミックス担当
Comic Editor:
法土さん Hatto (Norito)-san

それでは次は3巻で:
See you in Volume 3.
瀬上あきら

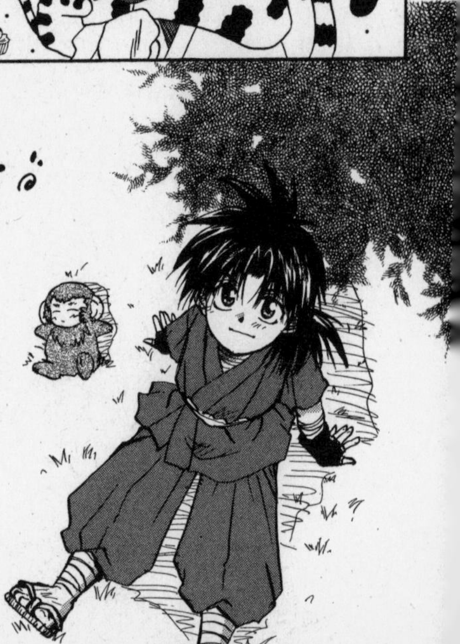
修行中。
KAGETORA IN TRAINING SESSION.

Akira Segami

About the Author

Segami's first manga was published by Shogakukan in 1996. He went on to do a few other small projects, including two short stories entitled "Kagetora" in 2001 and 2002. The character proved to be popular with fans, so Segami began his first ongoing series, *Kagetora*, with Kodansha in 2003. The series continues to run today.

Translation Notes

Japanese is a tricky language for most Westerners, and translation is often more art than science. For your edification and reading pleasure, here are notes on some of the places where we could have gone in a different direction in our translation of the work, or where a Japanese cultural reference is used.

Kimodameshi, page 3

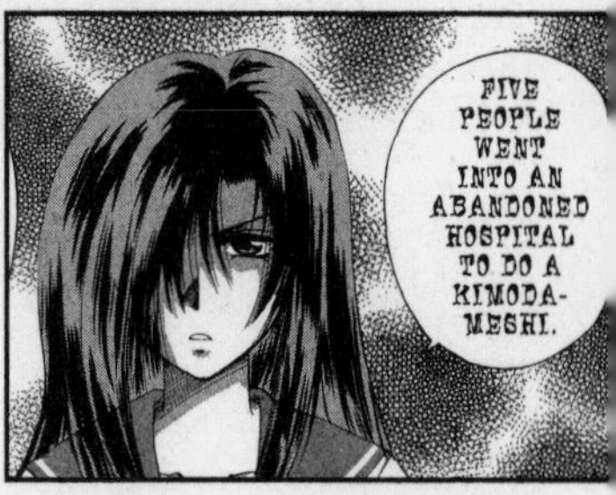
FIVE PEOPLE WENT INTO AN ABANDONED HOSPITAL TO DO A KIMODA-MESHI.

Kimodameshi literally means "a test of a person's courage." A kimodameshi is a game in which one must work toward a goal in a scary setting. It is often played in summer time and the game often takes place in a creepy haunted house, or cemetery-like location. In the process of the game, ghost figures will jump out to scare you, or other scary tricks may be played in an attempt to prevent participants from reaching their goal.

Junji Inagawa, page 7

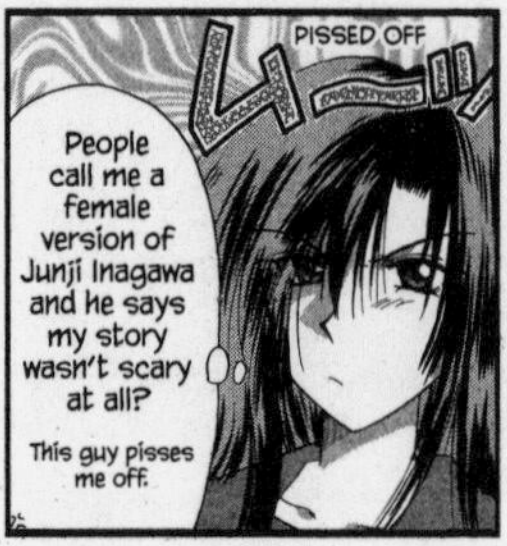
PISSED OFF
People call me a female version of Junji Inagawa and he says my story wasn't scary at all?
This guy pisses me off.

Junji Inagawa is a Japanese entertainer known as a ghost/horror story teller.

Hime, page 8

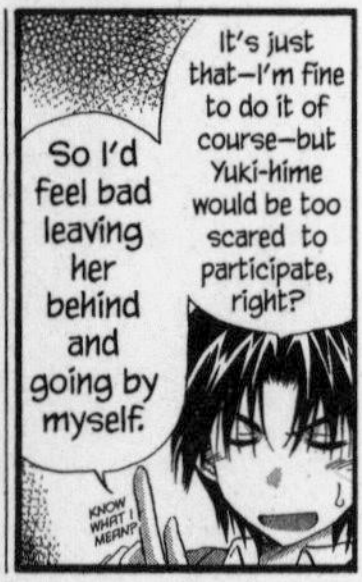
It's just that—I'm fine to do it of course—but Yuki-hime would be too scared to participate, right?
So I'd feel bad leaving her behind and going by myself.
KNOW WHAT I MEAN?

Literal translation of the word *"hime"* is a princess in Japanese. *Hime* can also be used as an honorific for a daughter of a high-class family. In this story, Kagetora refers to Yuki as a *hime,* as she's the daughter of a respected master of the martial arts, and from an honorable family.

Iga and Kouga, page 10

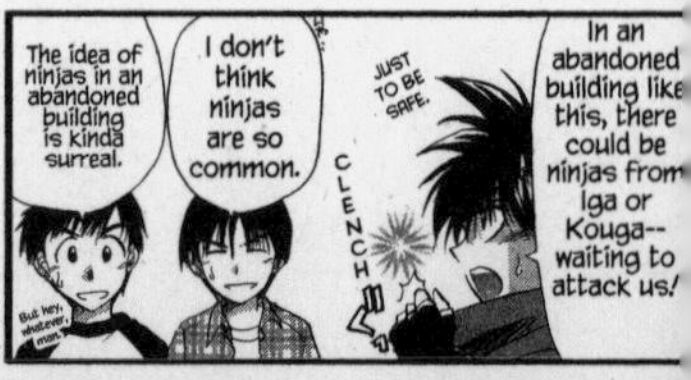
In an abandoned building like this, there could be ninjas from Iga or Kouga-- waiting to attack us!
JUST TO BE SAFE.
CLENCH
I don't think ninjas are so common.
The idea of ninjas in an abandoned building is kinda surreal.
But hey, whatever, man.

Iga is located in the western part of the Mie prefecture and Kouga is located in the Shiga prefecture. Both areas are well known as ninja residential areas. Hanzo Hattori, one of the most powerful and well-known ninjas in Japanese history, lived in Iga.

ɜeckoning gesture, page 16

ɴ Japan, the gesture of beckoning is performed by waving a ıand downward as opposed to the western way of waving a ıand upward.

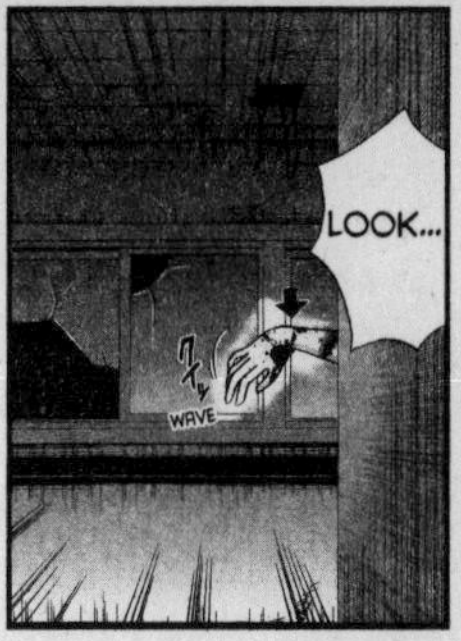

LOOK...
WAVE

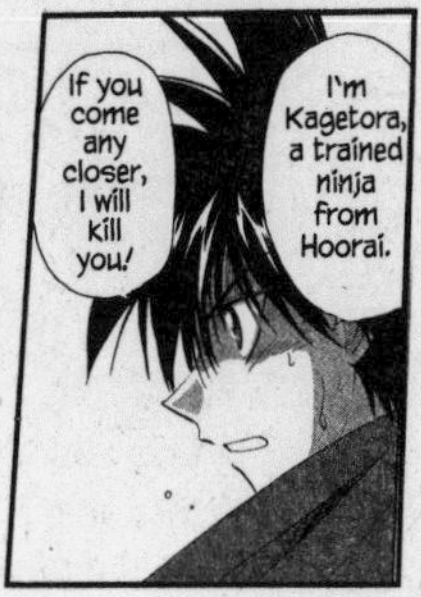

I'm Kagetora, a trained ninja from Hoorai.
If you come any closer, I will kill you!

ɪoorai, page 25

ɪoorai is the name of ʞagetora's ninja village.

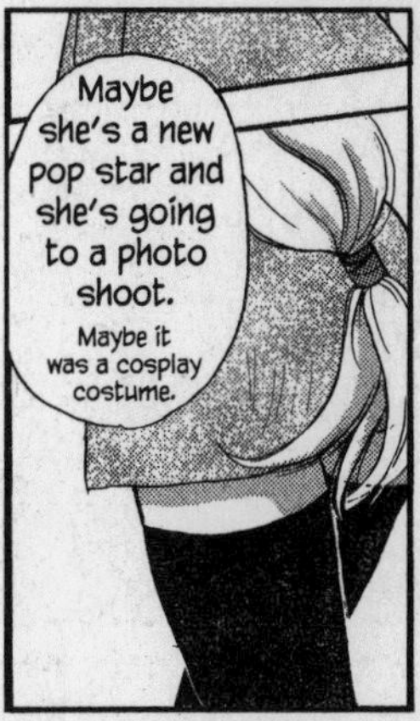

Maybe she's a new pop star and she's going to a photo shoot.
Maybe it was a cosplay costume.

Cosplay, page 35

Cosplay is short for Costume Play. Cosplay means dressing up as a character from manga, anime, and/or video games.

ɜaka wa kase o hikanai, page 37

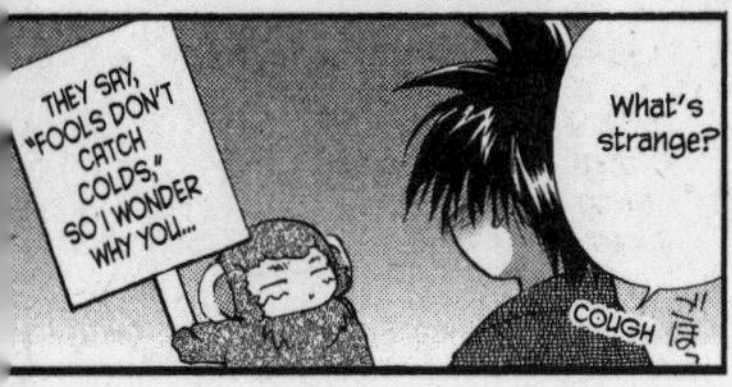

What's strange?
COUGH
THEY SAY, "FOOLS DON'T CATCH COLDS," SO I WONDER WHY YOU...

Baka wa kase o hikanai literally translates to "Fools don't catch colds." This is a Japanese saying which means that fools are so insensitive and/or stupid that they don't even notice when they have a cold.

ƨanta-san, page 79

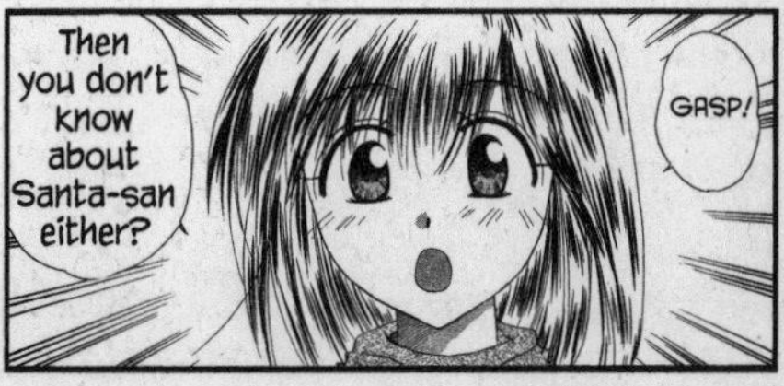

GASP!
Then you don't know about Santa-san either?

ʞagetora doesn't know about Santa Ɔlaus. So when he repeats the name, ıe says "Santa" as in Santa Claus. ʌnd then he says Santa, referring to a Japanese male first name. The characters ıre different in the original text, but ɔronounced the same. Also, it's common ·or people to refer to Santa Claus as *Santa-san*: Santa plus the honorific–san.

Namahage, page 80

Namahage is a tradition in the Akita prefecture area on (or around) New Year's eve (in some areas Namahage is practiced on January 15). Several men in the village wear frightening masks, raincoatlike costumes made of straw, straw sandals, and carry wooden replicas of kitchen knives wrapped in aluminum foil and wooden pails. The men go in pairs from house to house. The head of the house is told in advance that they are to come and gives the okay before they enter the house. The purpose of the Namahage's visit is to ensure the good health and safety of the children of the village for the coming year.

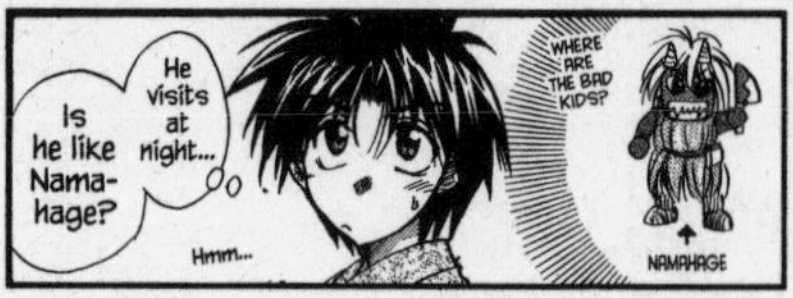
WHERE ARE THE BAD KIDS?
NAMAHAGE
He visits at night...
Is he like Nama-hage?
Hmm...

BOO, page 84

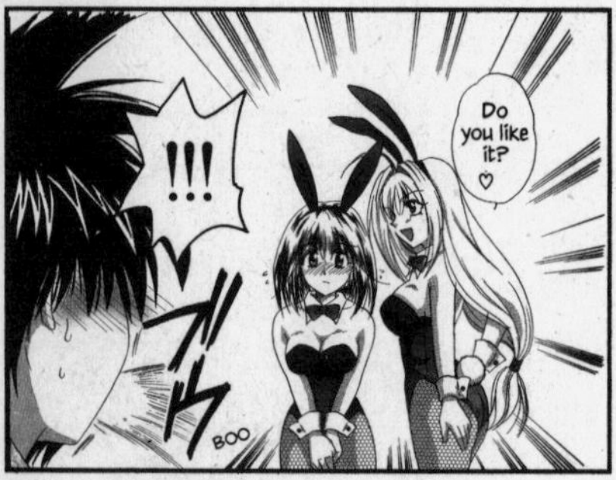
Do you like it? ♡
!!!
BOO

The Boo sound is the sound of Kagetora bursting air out of his mouth—it's an expression of surprise. Here, he didn't expect to see two sexy girls showing up, dressed in their sexy outfits. This gesture of blowing air out of the mouth loudly is commonly used in Japanese manga or comedy. (Similar to the nose bleeding shown in manga when a boy gets excited or sees a naked girl.)

Fuurinkazan, page 113

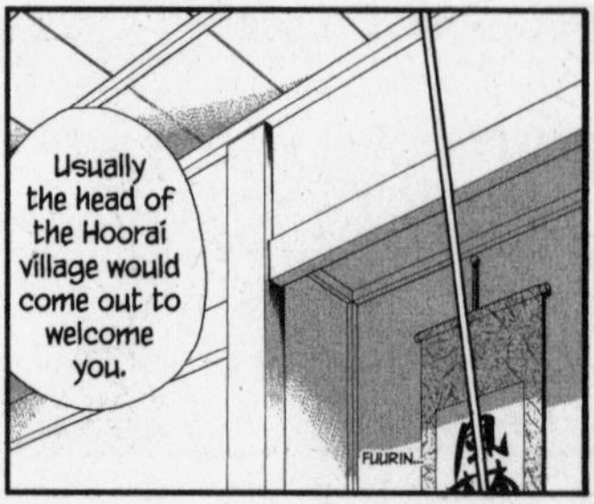
Usually the head of the Hoorai village would come out to welcome you.
FUURIN...

On the scroll in the first panel, the word "Fuurin" is shown. Fuurin is the first two characters of *Fuurinkazan,* which was the motto of Takeda Shingen, a warlord in feudal Japan. *Fuurinkazan* means "Speedy like the wind, gradually like the forest, aggressively like the fire, immovably like the mountain, secretly like the shadow, actively like the thunder." *Fuurinkazan* literally translates to Wind, Forest, Fire, and Mountain. (*Fuu* is wind, *rin* is forest, *ka* is fire, *zan* is mountain.) This saying, *Fuurinkazan,* was taken from Sonshi, a battle strategy text of ancient China.

Hina no surikomi, page 115

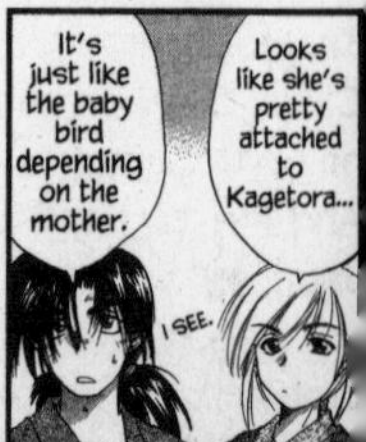
Looks like she's pretty attached to Kagetora...
It's just like the baby bird depending on the mother.
I SEE.

Taka and Shirou are referring to the Japanese saying *"Hina no surikomi"* which literally means the baby bird depending on his or her mother bird who he or she saw at birth. As a saying, *"hina no surikomi"* means that when someone decides that they can depend on someone, they'll follow that person around wherever they go.

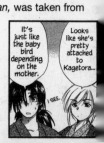

Shuriken, page 118

A *Shuriken* is a throwing blade, often used by ninjas and sometimes by samurais.

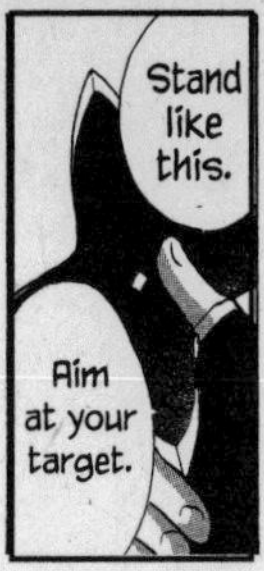
Stand like this.
Aim at your target.

The most common are *hira shuriken,* throwing blades with multiple points, sometimes called Throwing Stars by Americans. Contrary to popular culture representation in comic books and video games, *shuriken* were used as a distraction or tactical weapon, rather than as a primary weapon.

mado, page 131

mado is a small building in a shrine or temple vhere votive picture tablets are offered.

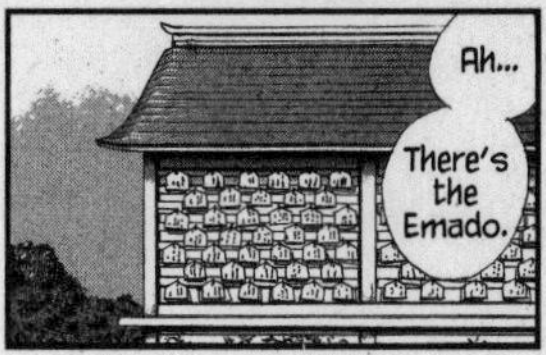
Ah...
There's the Emado.

Kamado, page 161

A *Kamado* is a cooking range, constructed primarly of earth or clay. A *Kamado* was one of the two basic forms of domestic cooking appliances used in pre-modern Japan. Kagetora, being a ninja from the historical village Hoorai, is familiar with the *Kamado,* whereas Yuki, who is from a modern city like Tokyo is not familiar with it and had to learn how to use it for the first time.

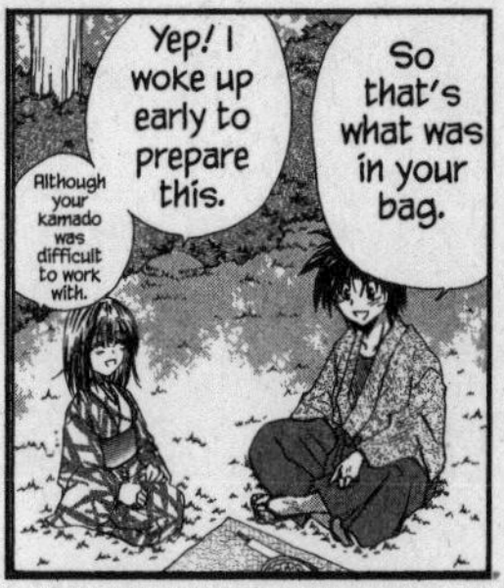
So that's what was in your bag.
Yep! I woke up early to prepare this.
Although your kamado was difficult to work with.

sobeage of Yamatoimo, page 162

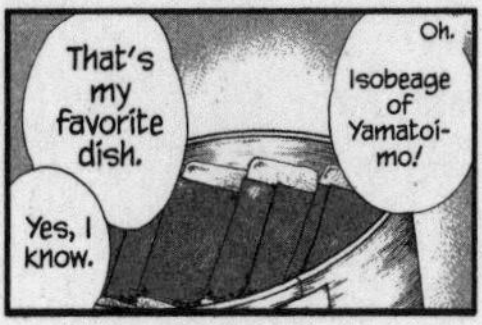
Oh.
Isobeage of Yamatoi-mo!
That's my favorite dish.
Yes, I know.

Isobeage of Yamatoimo is a fried Japanese yam wrapped in seaweed. *Isobeage* means the dish is fried and wrapped in seaweed. *Yamatoimo* is a Japanese yam shaped like a ginkgo leaf.

Shinichi Chiba, Souji Okita, and Masaki Kyomoto, page 187

Shinichi Chiba is also known as Sonny Chiba and is a popular actor in Japan. He played the ninja, Hanzo Hattori, in *Kage no Gundan.* He played the same character in *Kill Bill.*

Souji Okita (1842–1868) was the head of the *Shinsengumi* 1st team.

Shinsengumi (1863–1869) was a squad of soldiers, organized by many of the talented, yet lower class samurai, under Tokugawa Shogunate. They were known for their radical activities and extraordinary strength in fighting.

Masaki Kyomoto is a popular Japanese actor.

Noren, page 187

Noren is a split shop curtain which is hung outside the entrance and has the shop's name on it.

Preview of Volume 3

We are pleased to present you a preview from Volume 3. This volume will be available in English on September 26, 2006, but for now you'll have to make do with the Japanese!

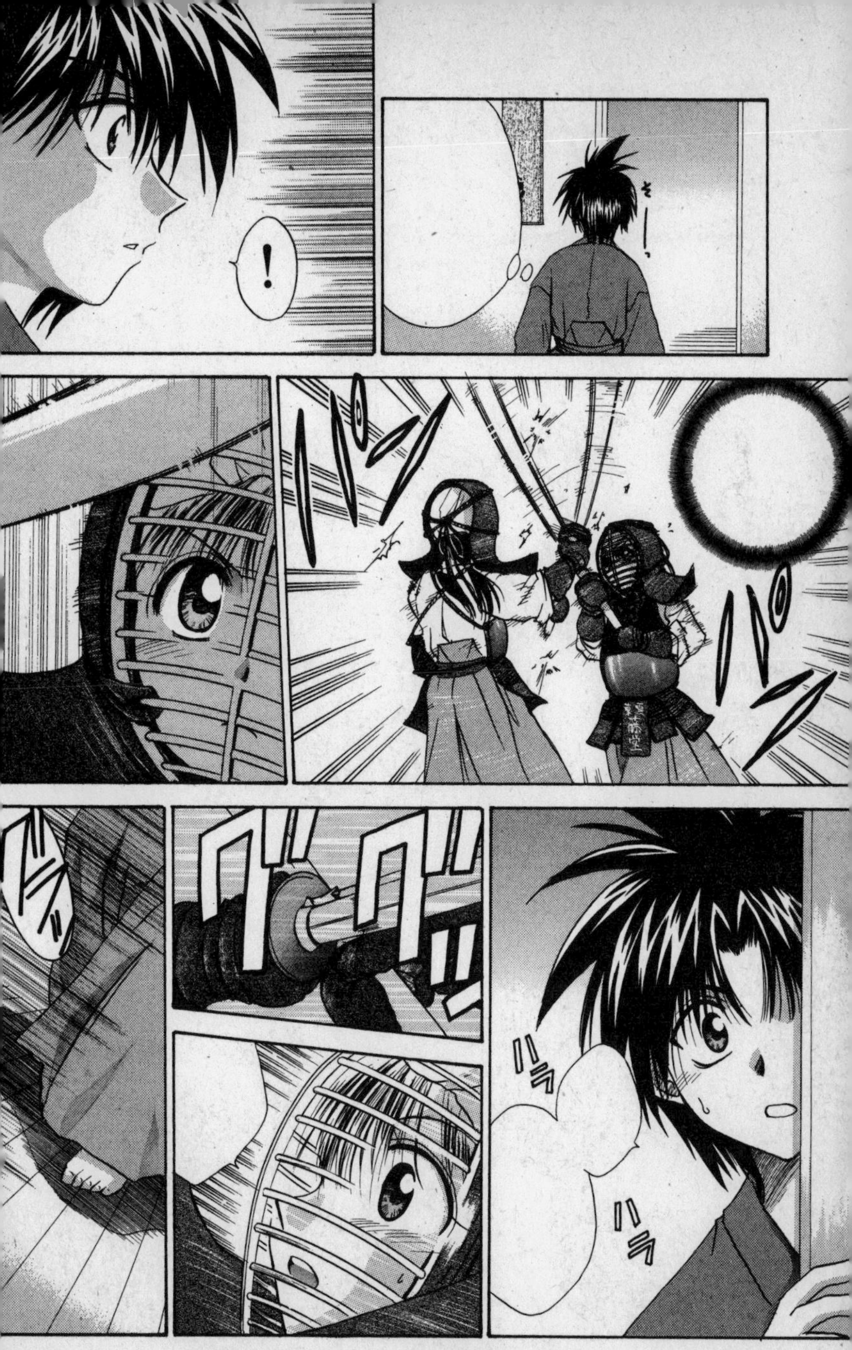

そ～…
!
パン
パン
ハァ
ハァ
ググッ!!
ズズ

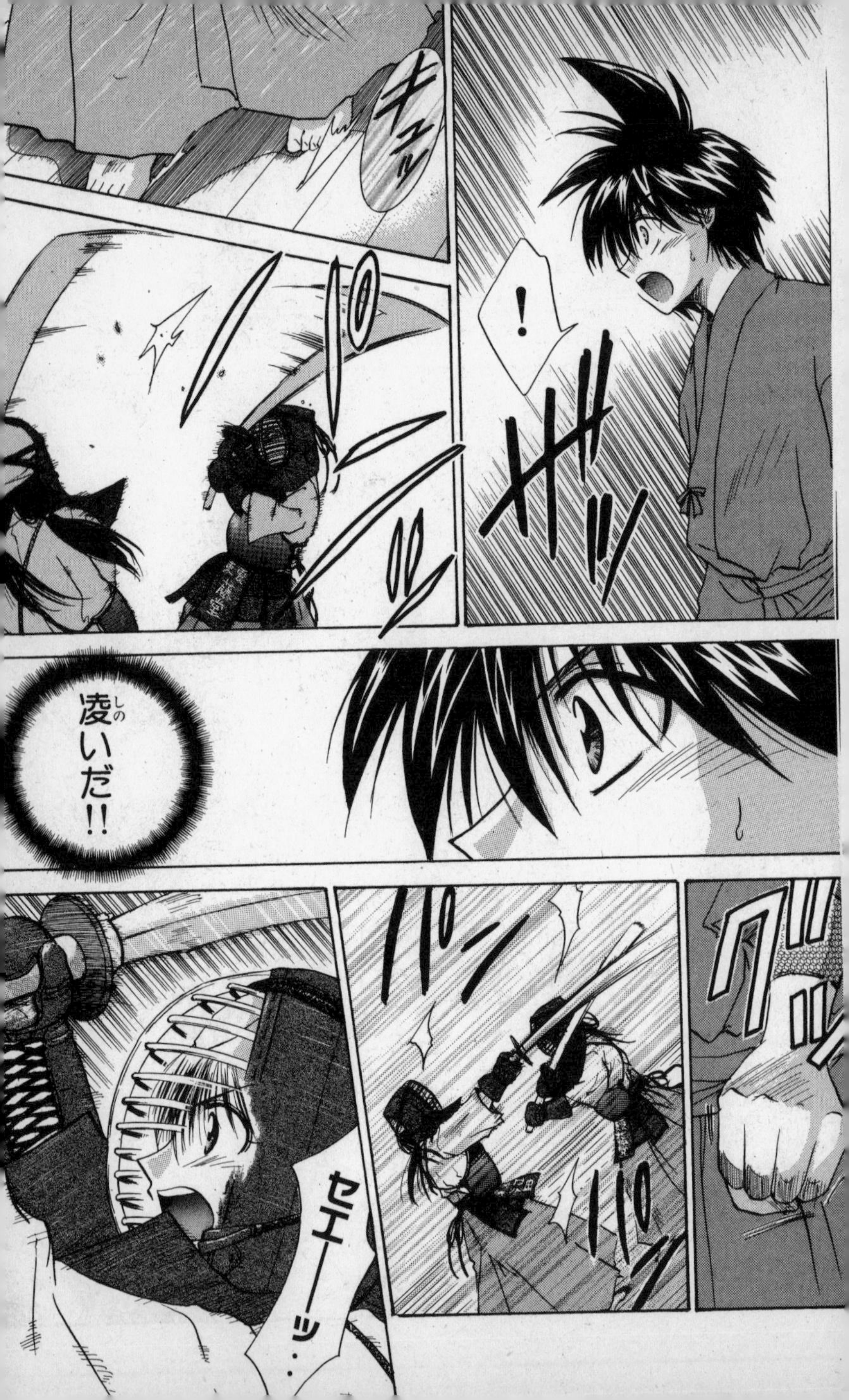
!
ザッ
キュッ
パンッ
凌いだ!!
グッ
パン
パ
セエーーッ・・

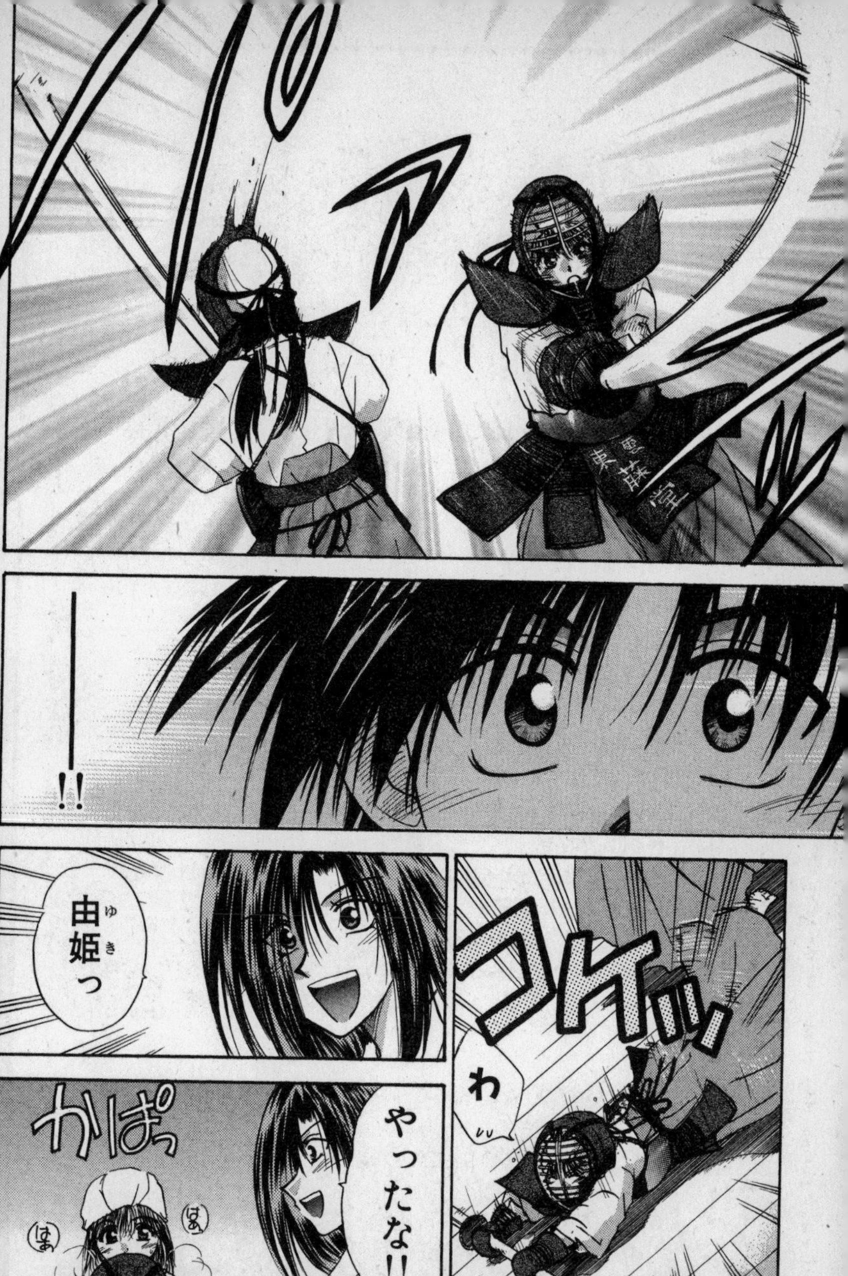
――!!
コケッ
わ
由姫っ
やったな!!
かぱっ
はぁ
はぁ

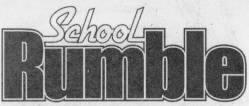

School Rumble

BY JIN KOBAYASHI

SUBTLETY IS FOR WIMPS!

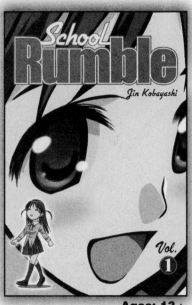

She . . . is a second-year high school student with a single all-consuming question: Will the boy she likes ever really notice her?

He . . . is the school's most notorious juvenile delinquent, and he's suddenly come to a shocking realization: He's got a huge crush, and now he must tell her how he feels.

Life-changing obsessions, colossal foul-ups, grand schemes, deep-seated anxieties, and raging hormones—School Rumble portrays high school as it really is: over-the-top comedy!

School Rumble
Jin Kobayashi
Vol. 1

Ages: 13+

Special extras in each volume! Read them all!

VISIT WWW.DELREYMANGA.COM TO:

- Read sample pages
- View release date calendars for upcoming volumes
- Sign up for Del Rey's free manga e-newsletter
- Find out the latest about new Del Rey Manga series

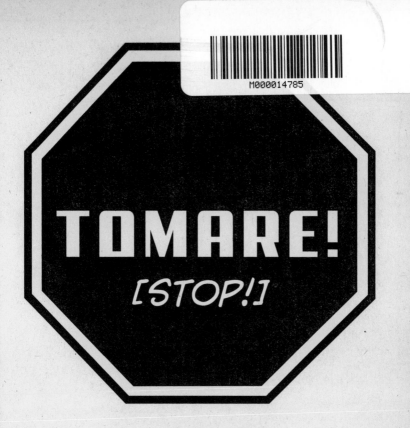

TOMARE!

[STOP!]

You are going the wrong way!

Manga is a completely different
type of reading experience.

To start at the *beginning*, go to the *end!*

That's right! Authentic manga is read the traditional Japanese
way—from right to left. Exactly the *opposite* of how American
books are read. It's easy to follow: Just go to the other end of
the book, and read each page—and each panel—from right side
to left side, starting at the top right. Now you're experiencing
manga as it was meant to be.